THE TRAVELLERS
18 JOY 52

The Story of the
Morayshire Railway

~

By

John Ross

CONTENTS

ACKNOWLEDGEMENTS

My thanks are due to:

*To my wife Linda for her encouragement and assistance.
Keith Fenwick of the GNSRA, Graeme Wilson of The Moray
Council Libraries Department, Scott Tilbury of The Patent Office,
The Scottish Records Office, The Mitchell Library and Williamson
Research Ltd.*

Published by:
John Ross
68 Bailies Drive
Elgin
IV30 6JJ

ISBN 0 902343 114

PRINTED BY ALMAC PRINT LTD., ELGIN.

FOREWORD

On August 10th 1852 a railway service commenced between Elgin and Lossiemouth. The start of the "Railway Age" in Moray was not brought about by a large and well-financed railway company from the southern part of the country. Rather it was through the enterprise and hard work of the local population that this undertaking came into being.

This book not only celebrates this achievement, but also gives the background into the origins of the company, the methods it used to accomplish this notable first and the way it conducted its daily business.

John Ross
August 2001.

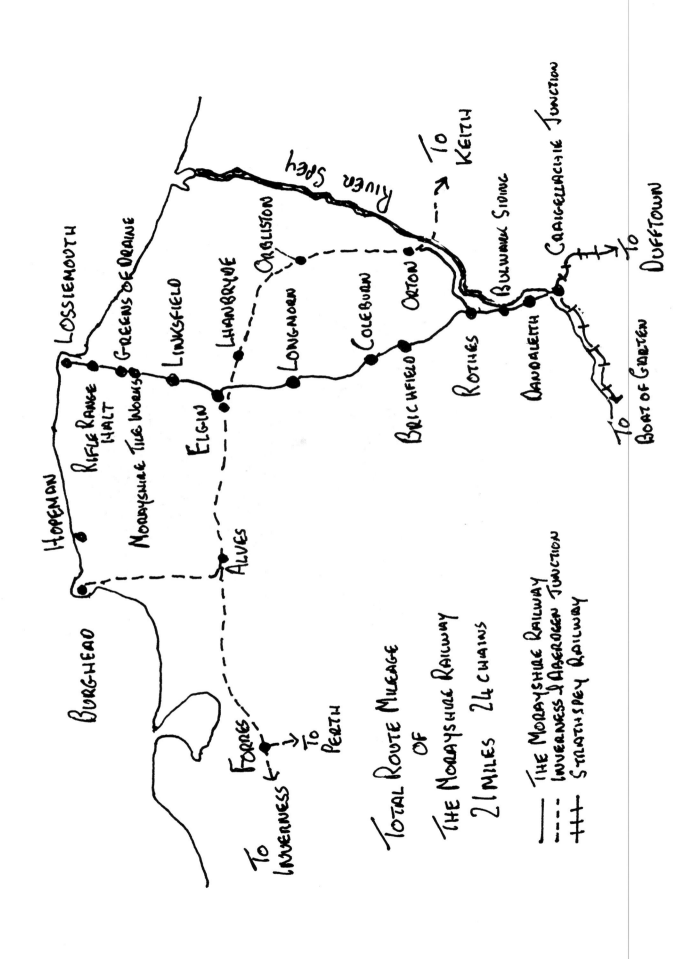

To Inverness

To Forres

To Perth

Burghead

Hopeman

Lossiemouth

Rifle Range Halt

Greens of Drainie

Morayshire The Works

Linksfield

Elgin

Alves

Lhanbryde

Orbliston

Longmorn

Coleburn

Oxton

Birchfield

Rothes

Dandaleith

Bulwark Siding

River Spey

To Keith

Craigellachie Junction

To Boat of Garten

To Dufftown

Total Route Mileage
of
The Morayshire Railway
21 Miles 24 Chains

——— The Morayshire Railway

- - - Inverness & Aberdeen Junction

+++ Strathspey Railway

JAMES GRANT

1 POINT OF DEPARTURE

An Act for making a Railway from Stotfield and Lossiemouth Harbour to Elgin, Rothes, and Craigellachie, to be called "The Morayshire Railway."
(16th July 1846)

WHEREAS the making of a Railway or Railways leading from the Stotfield and Lossiemouth Harbour to Elgin, Rothes, and Craigellachie would be of great public Advantage, by opening an additional, certain, and expeditious Means of Communication between the said places with each other and with the Sea.

These are the opening sentences of the Act for the building of the first railway in this corner of Northern Britain. The person who claims credit for suggesting the construction of the line between Elgin and Lossiemouth is Joseph Mitchell. He had been a pupil of Thomas Telford, the renowned road and canal builder, and as such became very familiar with the area. In 1841 he wrote to a young solicitor named James Grant who had not long set up practice in the City of Elgin. Joseph Mitchell suggested that James Grant form a company to build and run the line and he (Mitchell) would carry out the engineering of the line. The young Mr Grant took up this suggestion with vigour. However, the population of Elgin and area were not in the least bit interested in joining the "Railway Age" and the scheme foundered.

James Grant was a man of strong character and not easily put off by the rebuff of the local population and it was due to his determination that the scheme eventually succeeded. As mentioned above, James Grant was a solicitor by profession, but he was also a man of many talents that will become apparent as this story unfolds. So, please be patient as we rest awhile, before undertaking our Railway journey, to look a little into the background of one of the main players in the Morayshire's tale.

Born on July 25th 1801 at Shenval, a farm at Boat of Avon where his father was tenant, little is known about his early life apart from his place of education which was Inveraven. At the age of 18 years he entered the office at Elgin of Mr Brown Procurator Fiscal, where he served for four years before going on to Edinburgh to study law, qualifying in 1828. A partnership was formed between himself and a Mr Gordon from his own native district. Several years after this he was contacted by Joseph Mitchell for the task of setting up a railway company; the reason he was chosen is not known. By good luck or some other knowledge Joseph Mitchell had picked the right person for the job. Undeterred by the initial setback, young James Grant tried again to interest the folk of the area in railways. On February 3rd 1844 at the Harbour Company AGM, he put forward another proposal for a railway between Elgin and Lossiemouth. That Company still felt that there was no place for a railway north of Dundee.

Undaunted, James Grant, convinced there was great merit in such a scheme, was determined to make it succeed. This determination was on one occasion almost to cost him his life.

Whilst most of the population of Elgin and surroundings were tucked up safe in their beds, in order not to interfere with the conduct of his normal business, James was up with the lark surveying possible routes for the line of the Morayshire Railway. Engaged in the examination of some adjacent ground, he found his horse had strayed with its gig into the loch of Spynie, where it was floundering in the mud. He stripped to the buff and waded in to put shoulder to the wheel. Again the bookish nature of his profession belied the true metal of the man, he was from farming stock and proud of his Clan Grant heritage and was said to cut a dash in the full Highland regalia which he liked to wear. Mr Grant sought to raise the horse and had almost succeeded when the gig swerved. Almost crushed under the wheel, he managed to prevent himself being pinned under the vehicle. Assistance fortunately came in the form of the morning post runner that was passing on its way to Lossiemouth, the driver coming opportunely to the rescue. With our solicitor saved from the loch of Spynie, we return in detail to the matter of the railway.

By 1845 the entire country was in the grip of Railway Mania. The city of Elgin found it was being courted by three alternative schemes to provide a railway to and through its province. Two promoted were from Aberdeen, the first of which was the Aberdeen Banff and Elgin, which would have gone north from Aberdeen to Banff and then along the coast to Elgin, with branches from Banff to Fraserburgh and Peterhead. The second, to be known as the Great North of Scotland Railway, followed the route we now have in the present day between Aberdeen and Inverness. This line was to have branches to either Lossiemouth or Burghead from a junction near Elgin, and to Fort George from a junction at Nairn.

The third scheme, promoted by the inhabitants of the Highland capital, was also initially called the Great North of Scotland Railway. They wanted a more direct connection to the south, so their line left Inverness and followed the same route to Elgin as the Aberdeen version of the Great North of Scotland. It was however at Nairn that things became exciting, as at a junction there the line turned inland, following the old coach road over the mountains to Perth. James Grant's original mentor, Joseph Mitchell, was the civil engineer on this enterprise. Obviously, it was not feasible to have two opposing railways using the same title so the Highland capital scheme was renamed the Inverness and Elgin railway, before becoming the Inverness and Perth Railway.

On Wednesday, February 19th 1845, the promoters of the Inverness and Elgin railway held a public meeting at the Court House in Elgin. A large and impressive array of persons from the Highland Capital were there to give support to their claim to build the first railway in the area. Included in the deputation was the Provost of Inverness and Mr Stewart, a lawyer responsible for the legal affairs of the Inverness company. The civil engineer, Joseph Mitchell, along with senior managers of the Caledonia bank were also in attendance.

The purpose of the meeting was to "talk up" their project. This Mr Stewart did with promises of branch lines to Findhorn and Lossiemouth, and returns on investment of at least 8%, with a much greater dividend when the way to Perth was complete. They had no objection to the Great North coming to Elgin, but made it clear that it should go no further as the people of the North wanted to make their own railway. To underline this point, dark predictions were made, should the Aberdeen company succeed. There would be no branch lines to the coast, with a resultant loss to the investors in the harbour at Lossiemouth, and the prospect of Elgin being bypassed by the Aberdeen line. In closing his address Mr Stewart again appealed to those at the public meeting to co-operate with the Inverness scheme. He held out the prospect of Elgin becoming a busy centre of commerce as goods and travellers interchanged at the two terminal stations, one serving Inverness and one Aberdeen.

At the end of Mr Stewart's propaganda speech, our Mr Grant rose to his feet to deliver his public pronouncement on railways in Morayshire. He told the assembly that he had written a circular the previous evening that he had hoped to have published for this meeting. However, he had found it impossible to have it printed in such a short time and therefore he requested to read it to the meeting. *"Your town and harbour stand at the grand centre point for commerce across the Firth, connecting Caithness, Sutherland, and Orkney with the great leading railways from the South. Never lose sight of this important fact."* This passage sums up well the idea behind what was to finally become the Morayshire Railway. By channelling business through the harbour at Lossiemouth, the city of Elgin would reap the benefit. This point is further strengthened in the rest of his speech by saying that he welcomes any scheme to connect Elgin to the south by rail. *"Who ever succeeds, however be warned that the people of Elgin will do all in their power to stop any company forming a monopoly and interfering with the trade coming from Lossiemouth harbour."* With his note of caution sounded and no deceleration in his intention to try again to build his own railway, Mr Grant resumed his seat.

Mr Mitchell gave a report on how his proposed railway to the south would be built at the least cost and easiest construction of any railway built so far in Great Britain. As good an engineer as he was, I think Mr Joseph Mitchell was being just a tad overoptimistic. Various others from the Inverness party then added to the points, all of course emphasising the benefits to the populace of Elgin. So at the close of the meeting it was not altogether unexpected that an agreement to support the Inverness scheme was unanimously accepted.

James Grant certainly was not the kind of man to hang around. An Inverness-based railway company building a line into the town of Elgin was acceptable to him. What was not, was the prospect of them building a line from Elgin to Lossiemouth. This would mean no interchange of traffic at Elgin, with money and profit ending up in the Highland Capital, not where he thought they rightly belonged, in the City and Royal Burgh of Elgin. It was therefore not surprising that the *Elgin Courant* of Friday, February 21st 1845, at the top of the page carrying the report of the meeting of the Inverness delegation, there was a notice calling for the formation of a General Committee for promoting a railway line to be called the Morayshire Railway. This notice was signed by one James Grant and dated February 19th, the same day that the Inverness delegation had been in town to press their case.

The fever of Railway Mania proved much more fertile ground for James Grant to plant the seed of the Morayshire Railway. A meeting called for 1pm on March 3rd 1845 in the local Court House, produced a provisional committee consisting of 108 Elgin gentlemen, their professions ranging from surgeon to house painter, and all staunch in their support for this project. An additional 56 country members had also come forward most, of these either landed gentry or distillers.

On April 3rd 1845 James Grant, now secretary for the Railway Company, reported that applications for the Morayshire Railway had already been made to an amount far exceeding the required capital. A notice was given for a meeting, again to be held in the local court house on Friday, April 11th, to allot the stock. Encouraged by demands it was proposed that the line should now extend beyond Elgin for 16 miles to Craigellachie and rather optimistically be double track.

For every ray of sunshine a little rain must fall. It is interesting that in the letters page of *The Forres Gazette* on the 18th of April 1845 someone who merely signs himself a "cautious friend" warns the folk of Moray about "speculations" in railway schemes, a fear that, as we will see, was well-founded.

First to lose out was the Aberdeen Banff and Elgin railway. The deputation from Inverness had done a good job. The result was investors at the Elgin end of their proposed line deserted en masse, probably on the prospect of Mr Stewart's 8% return. This loss of finance brought about the complete collapse of the Aberdeen Banff and Elgin Railway.

Being shorter, the Inverness scheme to connect Elgin and Inverness to the south by way of Perth had advantages. This was still in the fairly early days of the railway revolution. Engineers were imbued with the idea that railways working by pure adhesion must be easily graded. To attain this on the route chosen by Joseph Mitchell was going to take huge sums of money. Returns to pay for same would also be difficult because the 120 miles between Nairn and Perth were very sparsely populated. When the Bill for this railway was put before Parliament, it was cut to pieces by opposing Parliamentary counsel. Cruel jibes were made comparing Joseph Mitchell to Hannibal of the Alps. Like many bold thinkers who were ahead of their time, his scheme was rejected by small men with equally small imaginations.

Just one player was left in the game, the Aberdeen based Great North of Scotland Railway. The Bill promoting their line running along the coastal plain from Aberdeen to Inverness was passed on 26th of June 1846. The price of victory in this competition however brought its problems for the Great North of Scotland Railway. The authorised mileage of its scheme exceeded that of any other Scottish railway. Protection for the trustees of the toll bridges on the road between Aberdeen and Inverness, along with a clause to have gatekeepers at every level crossing on the line, were inserted into this Act. This combination left the promoters with legal costs of around £80,000.

Whilst all this was going on in the Granite City, preparations were being made by the Morayshire Railway to seek Parliamentary powers. The canny Mr Grant and his fellow promoters decided to connect their railway with the Great North at Elgin, and construct a line to Craigellachie from Orton, utilising the Great North's Inverness Aberdeen line as the connecting link. The following is an extract from the 1846 Act, page 3213:

> XXII. And be it enacted, That the lines of Railway to be made and maintained under the Authority of this Act shall be following; (that is to say,)
>
> A Railway commencing at Stotfield and Lossiemouth Harbour in the Parish of Drainie to the Town and Royal Burgh of Elgin;
>
> and
>
> A Railway from a point on the proposed Railway, called or intended to be called "The Great North of Scotland Railway" near to Gerbity or Orton, to Rothes, in the united Parishes of Rothes and Dunducras, and to Craigellachie, in the Parish of Rothes.

In this form the Bill was deposited in the 1846 session, and with a little bit of luck and a fair wind, it passed all its stages and received the Royal Assent on the 16th July of that year. Officially the Morayshire Railway had started on its career.

With the Royal Assent being obtained it was required by law that an Ordinary General Meeting should be held within two months. This duly took place on September 9th 1846, and as would be expected there was much self-congratulation. The Directors congratulated the shareholders on having obtained power to construct the Railway that would confer most important advantages on the district and form a valuable investment for the proprietors. The Directors at the same time observed that this result was obtained despite the diligent efforts of "enemies" whose obstruction had increased considerably the expense in passing the Bill. Due to the limit of time between passing of the Act and the Ordinary Meeting, it was not practical to ascertain the liabilities and prepare an exact balance sheet. General receipts and expenditure were stated thus:

	£ s d
To deposit on 3750 shares at £ 2 per share	£7500-00-00
By amount of disbursements	£4908-18-09

The engineer Mr Joseph Mitchell and railway contractor Mr Forbes had been engaged in preparing for the execution of the works as rapidly as circumstances permitted. In the interim our metaphorical rain shower was now falling harder. At the first Ordinary Meeting it was reported that there was to be a delay in the construction of the Great North of Scotland Railway. As it was felt a considerable part of the traffic to and from the upper section of the Morayshire line would be carried over the GNSR, the Directors reluctantly felt that it was their duty to recommend a delay in proceeding with this portion of the undertaking in the meantime. They were however confident that they could continue with the formation of the portion of line from Elgin to Lossiemouth in the spring of 1847.

The Directors named in the Act were proposed for re-election:

Henry Inglis, Edinburgh
Alexander Forteath, Newton
James Wilson, Provost of Elgin
Dr Manson, Spynie
John Walker, Elgin
John Grant, Glen Grant
Alexander Grant, Inverness
George Leslie, Elgin
James Grant, Elgin

Alexander Forteath was duly elected Chairman, George Leslie became Auditor and our old friend James Grant confirmed in the post of Secretary. It is interesting that a man from Edinburgh should become a Director of the Morayshire Railway. Mr Inglis was a solicitor and commissioner for the trustees of the late James Earl of Fife, who had owned land between Craigellachie and Aberlour, land the Morayshire hoped to use in any expansion from Lossie up through Speyside. Shares to the value of £50 were coming from the Trust. In addition, large amounts of capital were at this stage being invested by a number of Edinburgh citizens, most of whom were in the legal profession. Perhaps Mr Inglis was their agent as well, or perhaps they had been student classmates of Mr Grant. Any firm answer to this question seems to have been lost in the passage of time.

Despite the assertion at the start of the meeting that construction of the line between Elgin and Lossiemouth could begin in the spring of the following year, for reasons unknown to the author, by the close of this meeting it had been agreed to defer proceeding with construction for twelve months.

The next meeting of the Morayshire Directors took place on May 30th 1847, with no discussion on a start for the construction of the railway. The talk that day was of the possibility of buying the Stotfield and Lossiemouth Harbour Company. Amalgamation of the two enterprises was seen as having advantages to both parties. There was some concern expressed how this coming together was to be funded. Capital involved would be about £20,000 and half of this amount would have to be paid in cash within a year of obtaining the necessary Act.

No progress on the start of the railway was reported at the next meeting of the Board on 29th of June. The only business discussed was some outstanding bills totalling £842-4s-9d. Loans were secured to pay them.

By the time of the AGM on October 30th 1847, our falling rain had assumed monsoon proportions. The Railway Mania that had been gripping the country had come to the end. Our "cautious friend's" words of 1845 had come true. The opening remarks of the meeting were, *"Due to the deranged state of the money market no steps were to be taken to build the line."* Regarding the inland portion of the network from Orton to Craigellachie, nothing was to be done and this enterprise would be guided by the GNSR. It was proposed that the line from Elgin to Lossiemouth would be built *"as soon as it is prudent to do so."* Possession of the Harbour Company would not occur until the contract to build the line to Lossiemouth had been signed.

At the AGM held on the 31st of October 1848 the terms for the purchase of the harbour had been agreed with the proprietors. The railway still had no date for start of the construction. In all other respect this AGM was very much a holding operation. November however saw our Mr Grant enter the world of politics by becoming a member of Elgin Town Council. Not one to rest on his laurels, within in two days of taking his place on the Council he was Provost, without doubt the quickest promotion in the history of municipal affairs.

By the 1849 AGM it was noted that the GNSR was expected to proceed soon and it was a very *"favourable time for building railways."* The Board therefore wanted to go on with the construction of the Elgin to Lossiemouth line. On December 14th 1849 plans were put forward to reduce construction cost of the railway. Full estimates were to be obtained. It was decided to make a single line, but prepare the works for a double line.

In the spring of 1850, things were starting to gather pace. On April 5th an agreement with the Stotfield and Lossiemouth Harbour Commissioners had been concluded. Consideration was given to advertising for tenders for construction of the line, with estimates of £4000 per mile being looked for. As a possible cost-saving method, it was suggested that contractors could take shares as part payment. Despite the need for prudence, James Grant the Company Secretary complained that he was not being paid enough, at £20 per annum.

The Board were informed on May 7th 1850 that contractors would not take shares unless there was a guaranteed dividend of not less than 4%. Just when the possibility of construction was becoming a reality, the financial affairs of the Morayshire were starting to unravel. The Edinburgh people had seen no return on their investment, with money markets still a little unsettled. Some of them may have lost large amounts of money in the previous year's financial turmoil, feeling the commitments they had made to the Morayshire could leave them further exposed. This may have been the reason that James Grant travelled south to Edinburgh for a meeting with Mr Inglis, who as it turned out was not available. Mr Grant continued on his travels, this time to London to find precise information on new lightweight engines and carriages and a greatly improved permanent way, which was reported to give a saving of 75% in the working of railways.

At a meeting convened on September 4th 1850, Mr Inglis resigned as a director. Dr Manson of Spynie was elected Chairman to fill the vacancy left by the death of the previous incumbent Mr Forteath. There was still no word of a start date for the Great North of Scotland Railway so it was considered to be an advantage to abandon the construction of the railway from Orton to Rothes. This would reduce the capital required from £75,000 to £30,000. Many tenders for the construction of the line had been received. Two in particular had offered to build it for as little as £3000 per mile. These offers had come from John Forbes of Haddo, and Alexander Urquhart of Laurencekirk.

An EGM was called for September 21st 1850. This approved the report for the construction of the line from Elgin to Lossiemouth, along with the calls to be made on shareholders. The abandonment of the line from Orton to Rothes was also agreed.

Six days later on September 27th the Secretary reported to the Directors on correspondence with one James Samuel of London about *"economical construction and working of railways."* It was decided to appoint Mr Samuel engineer for the construction of the line.

James Samuel was a versatile inventor and engineer, aged 27 when he was employed by the Morayshire. Though based in London, he was a native of Glasgow. He had worked in his family's printing and bleaching business as well as the Glasgow Waterworks, before moving south to work on the Eastern Counties Railway, where he first encountered Mr James Grant of the Morayshire. What the *"economical construction and working of railways"* amounted to was a package deal. Mr Samuel would do the civil engineering on the line, engage a contractor, design the engines and rolling stock, the former to be built by Neilson of Glasgow, the latter by Marshall & Co, Birmingham. He would also appoint the general manager, the first engine driver and the first fireman.

The October the 30th AGM was a quiet affair, with only the election of two new directors to report. These were William Topp and William Hemming. In Edinburgh however a storm was brewing.

This first became known on November 8th, when it was reported to the Board that Mr Inglis the former Director, and Mr Burns also of Edinburgh wanted to be relieved of their shares. With the possibility of construction imminent, the need for capital was also imminent. For that reason the Board was strongly against these two gentlemen giving up their obligations as shareholders. They viewed it as the highest order of principle that Messrs Inglis and Burns stood by their commitment. On a conciliatory note the Board would not press for payment of outstanding sums due on the shares, but would allow them to be forfeited in the normal way.

The Morayshire Railway Board on November 22nd 1850 was given notice of another Edinburgh shareholder Mr Allan, who had made objections similar to those of Mr Inglis and Burns. The three gentlemen acting together had gone to the Railway Commissioner with a view to having the Morayshire scheme abandoned. The Minutes of the meeting held that day states *"We cannot help express regret and surprise that any class of men should indulge in making so many unfounded and irrelevant assertions as are contained in the objections."* A rebuttal of all the claims made by the Edinburgh gentlemen was sent to Railway Commissioners.

There was no respite from the attacks in the New Year of 1851 from the Edinburgh shareholders; if anything they became worse. On January 11th the Board met to discuss a request for a meeting with the Edinburgh shareholders to consider their application to the Railway Commissioners to abandon the whole railway. The view from the Directors was that, should such a meeting take place, the prospects of building the line would be severely damaged and should therefore be avoided. Mr Grant was instructed to meet with these shareholders. In the event of them being unable to come to some arrangement he should seek the advice of Counsel.

He reported on the outcome of his meeting with the Edinburgh shareholders to the Board of the Morayshire on January 24th 1851. Things were grim. All but three of the shareholders wanted to be free of any responsibility for the railway. Of these one, wanted payment to be released from his obligations, whilst another two wanted to be released of not only their current obligations, but also have their deposits and any other cash paid, returned to them. On a positive note, Counsel's view favoured the railway company. Mr Grant therefore suggested that they make further application to the Railway Commissioners and await the outcome. In a move to protect the Company, he agreed that if it should become necessary, written legal advice should be sought.

The Forres Gazette of March 12th 1851 reports on an extraordinary general meeting held in Edinburgh on Monday February 24th at which the abandonment of the Morayshire Railway was carried by 1800 shares to 677. Mr Grant, given his full title of Provost Grant in the report, was present at the meeting and protested against the legality of the whole process.

This resulted in a request by the Railway Commissioners on March 21st 1851 to see a list of shareholders, along with the record of attendance at the EGM that had approved the application for abandonment.

After examination of these papers, a meeting was held by the Railway Commissioners at which Mr Grant and the opponents of the railway, along with their Parliamentary agents, were present. The outcome of this was reported back to the Board on April 10th 1851. The Railway Commissioners declared that consents necessary to authorise an application to abandon the railway had not been obtained, so the whole proceedings of the opponents had fallen to the ground. Good news at last!

By May 8th 1851 the shareholder's list was completed, sealed and signed. The advertisement for the abandonment of the section of the railway between Orton and Rothes that was dependant on the completion of the GNSR was published. An EGM was called on May 18th 1851. Despite some question over eligibility of shares, by a vote of 1316 shares to 6 the cancellation of the railway from Orton to Rothes was passed. The obstacles to construction of the railway between Elgin and Lossiemouth were now gone.

Statutory notices to landowners along the Elgin to Lossiemouth line were issued on the 27th of June 1851. At the same time the value of the 2970 issued shares was reduced from £20 to £10 per share. The application to the Railway Commissioners for the abandonment of the Orton Rothes section was also signed on this date.

At an Elgin Town Council Meeting held on August 24th 1851, on the motion of Councillor Alexander Asher, seconded by Councillor John Taylor, the sum of £1000 was voted to enable the Council to become a shareholder in the Morayshire Railway. It was to be fully understood that no part of the money for these 100 shares was to paid over until the contracts were signed and the work begun. I can find no evidence of the hand of Provost Grant in this arrangement, but as long-term champion of the railway, I am certain that he had some influence in this decision.

On September 9th 1851 it was reported that despite objections the Railway Commissioners had approved the Abandonment order for the section of railway from Orton to Rothes of July 7th. It was agreed to obtain a valuation of the land required for the Elgin to Lossiemouth line. The Secretary was told to get a copy of the specifications of work with plans for bridges and sketches of carriages and wagons. The tender of Hutchings & Co for construction of the line was considered.

Authorisation of the contract for construction of the line was given to Hutchings & Co on October 7th 1851. A question was raised by the board whether a 35 foot span bridge would be sufficient for the crossing of the River Lossie.

The contractor required a security payment of £3000 plus 500 shares. This was agreed to by the board on October 21st 1851, on the proviso that the interest was payable from the opening of the line, and not on the delivery of the stock.

At a statutory meeting held at The Royal Hotel * on October 22nd, James Miller and William Fleming resigned from the board. They were replaced by Henry Smale and Alexander Grant. The Chairman Dr Manson of Spynie reported *"This spirited under taking is about to be commenced. The 1st turf is actually expected to be cut before Christmas. Provost Grant is deserved of credit as the head of the municipality for preserving amidst almost insuperable obstacles in securing this great boon for the community over which he so worthily presides."*

By the 31st of October calls of £2 per share were being made. The contract for construction had been signed, the details of which are as follows:

Line to be completed in 7 months.

Line commences near the old Foundry at Rothes Turnpike Road, Elgin.

- Works to be for a single line of 5 miles 27 chains length.
- Sidings 1100 yards in length to be built at Elgin and Lossiemouth.
- Rails to be 24 feet, 60 lb/yd. Two oval holes, 7/8 by ¾ at each end for bolts of patented iron fishing pieces, 18" long.

Two locomotives on Samuel's patented expansion principle with 9" and 12" cylinders.

Five foot driving wheels. The heating surface to be at least 500 feet. Tank to be attached to engine to hold 300 gallons of water.

- Bridges constructed at and of:
- River Lossie, at Elgin, girder with 35 foot span.
- Newmill Road over railway, stone.
- Railway over canal or waterway at Loch Spynie, stone.
- Parish road near Lossiemouth over railway, stone.

Two terminal stations with passenger platforms and covered way, at Elgin and Lossiemouth

- Engine shed and carriage shed at Elgin
- Coke platform and water crane.
- Three gatekeepers cottages.

Carriages as described in the drawings. To consist of 2 first class and 2 second class.

- Eight wagons

Six setts (sic) of points and crossings - to be fixed as directed by the engineer.

* The Royal Hotel was located at 195 High Street Elgin.

The *Forres Gazette* of November 19th 1851 carried the following report on the Morayshire railway:

We are glad to report the valuation of the land in connection with the Morayshire Railway is rapidly proceeding to completion under the management of Mr McWilliam of Sheriffston and Mr Geddes of Orbliston. No date is fixed for the cutting of the first turf, with an extra delay being caused by heavy snow. If all is well with land and the weather clear, a start should be made at the beginning of December.

The actual date for the cutting of the first turf was fixed at a board meeting on November 25th 1851. It had been resolved to commence construction work on Saturday, November the 30th at 1pm and to dine together with a few friends at 4pm.

2 WHEELS OF IMPROVEMENT

No formal arrangements were made to celebrate the cutting of the first turf on the Morayshire line between Elgin and Lossiemouth. When however the Chairman, Directors and friends left the Royal Hotel at 12.20pm, they were met by a large crowd of inhabitants of Elgin and surrounding district. Joined by the Provost, wearing his official insignia, and Magistrates, the Directors and friends walked in a body to Bareflathills, where the ceremony was to take place. Mrs Grant, the Provost's wife, along with Mrs Manson, Mrs Grant of Glengrant, the "Misses Jenkin" of Madia Cottage and several other ladies followed on in carriages. The party assembled at Bareflathills at 1pm. The onlookers had increased in number to around 3000 persons. A loud cheer rang out. Two cannons belonging to Colonel Brander of Pitgaveny, one pointing towards Elgin the other to Lossiemouth, were then fired off. On silence being obtained, Provost Grant gave the opening speech, of which a little now follows:

> I feel called upon for my good Lady, whom you associate with me in this pleasant and important duties of this day, to give expression, in her name as well as in my own, to the feelings we entertain, and the deep sense of the honour you have conferred on us. It might appear somewhat out of place in me to take part in the discharge of those duties, however agreeable to my own feelings, were I not assured by you, that the choice you have made is entirely owing to the honourable position I hold as Chief Magistrate of the Royal Burgh of Elgin; and you deem it fit and proper on that account that I should act the prominent part in the proceedings of the day, which your kindness has assigned to me. I and my partner will most cheerfully perform the ceremony set apart for us.

These opening remarks were met with a loud cheer. Despite his protestations and assertions that he was only being permitted to perform the ground breaking ceremony because he was the Provost, is hardly a true representation of the case. As the man who had done the most to bring this project to reality, it was only right and proper that this honour should be bestowed on him. Of course like all politicians there was a lot more of his speech. He went on to give the background into all the problems that had been overcome to reach this point in the venture, reserving until his closing remarks his venom for those who dared to oppose the Morayshire Railway.

> There are standstill gentlemen who form the drags on the wheels of improvement. They early pronounced that railway communication so far north was preposterous, and at least 40 or 50 years before the age. They prophesied that an Act of Parliament would never be obtained. When an Act was procured - that your line would never be made. Now that it is about to be made, they will no doubt continue the illusion, and say it will never be opened; and should they survive and open their eyes seven months hence, and find it operational. They will still prophesy that it will never pay; and finally, when the dividends will announce that it does pay, they will insinuate, if not say, that it is done by some means other than legitimate means.

This last remark brought forth laughter from the crowd. In closing he went on to say:

> I have adverted to these points, not that I believe you pay the least regard to them, but to tell you that the public are fully aware that there are such things as you. The triumph and victory over such and every obstacle is more valued by the active and intelligent men, who form the bulwark and strength of empires. We shall now proceed with the most pleasing ceremony of the day.

Mr Simmons the engineer then presented Mrs Grant with a neat little spade. With this she raised the first turf of the Morayshire Railway and placed it in a wheelbarrow that was then wheeled to one side by the

Provost. On the contents being tipped out, several rounds of cannon were fired, accompanied by much cheering and hat throwing; a fitting start to the first railway in the north of Scotland.

The Directors and their ladies returned to the Royal Hotel to dine and the crowd dispersed. The return to town took them past the woollen mill of James Johnston & Co of Newmill. The proprietor of this company had been one of the main movers in the Inverness and Perth Railway. Possibly in a rather unexpected show of unity, flags were flying from their buildings as a mark of celebration of the events that had just taken place at Bareflathills. The line of the Morayshire would run to the rear of the mill, so perhaps Provost Grant could take this as another customer for his railway. What is without doubt, is that when the Directors, Magistrates and friends arrived at the Royal Hotel, they enjoyed a good meal and a very happy evening.

The Board of Directors next met in the New Year of 1852 on the 7th of January. This was to discuss the second call of £2 per share. It was also decided to defer for the time being taking any form of legal action against those subscribers who had defaulted on the first call.

By January 28th work on the line itself was progressing at a pace. Squads of navvies of 40 to 50 in a gang were working at four sections on the line. The centre archway for the bridge over Woodside Road was set. Rails had been laid from Bareflathills to the Loch of Spynie. On this section twenty 5 ton trucks were being kept busy moving spoil from the cutting at Bareflathills for use in the embankment being built over the soft ground at the Loch of Spynie. In the opposite direction coming from Lossiemouth a large part of the route was now level towards the loch.

February 16th saw the Morayshire board discussing some minor adjustment to the crossings on the railway. Two bridges, one at Pitgaveny, the other on the road between Drainie and Oakenhead, were to be erected, instead of level crossings. The junction of the road between Linkwood Road and Maisondieu Road was also to be moved, meaning that there would only be one level crossing at this point on the line.

By the beginning of March 1852, the contractor had started round the clock working, the first shift operating from 6am to 6pm, another taking its place from 6pm to 6am. The number of wagons being used to move spoil had also been increased to 40. To cope with this demand the work force had also increased to 300. A report to the Board on March 12th noted the completion of the bridge at Drainie Road. The one over Pitgaveny Road was delayed until consent from the Board of Trade was obtained. A request for an accommodation bridge for a farm at Spynie was approved. By the following week, the site of Lossiemouth station and goods shed had been measured off. There had been thoughts of increasing the size of these facilities, but as this would have added £50 to £80 to costs, this expansion was abandoned.

It may be of interest to note that at this stage in proceedings, Mr Grant was doing all the detailed management of the contractors and then getting the Board's consent.

All this activity was attracting the attention of the local population. The *Forres Gazette*, 24th March 1852, reports that an 80 year old woman who lived at Doocot Park New Elgin, was out at 7am at Spynie with her grandchildren to watch the work in progress. Reports also appeared in the *Banffshire Journal* advising farmers from the surrounding district to go to the cutting at Bareflathills because its depth allowed the observer to view the substructure of the soil. The writer of this article also claimed that the adjoining fields to the cutting were now much better drained than previously, and as a consequence were more productive.

By the Board meeting of April 2nd, it was reported that the work on the railway was half done, with track in place for almost the whole length of the line. However, I do not think at this stage this was the permanent line, some of it I think was just for engineering purposes. Nevertheless, a payment of £900 was made to the contractor's account, resulting in the third call of £2 per share being made.

At that meeting reports appear in the Minute book of a serious disturbance caused by a strike among some of the workforce. Attempts were made to persuade everyone to down tools. This was not successful, and some form of riot ensued. To aid the local police in restoring peace, ten additional constables were appointed, the cost of which was met by the railway company. Four ringleaders were apprehended and sentenced to hard labour for various periods. A fifth, who had assaulted the Sheriff, was awaiting trail in the Court of Justiciary.

What is perhaps most surprising about this incident is that there are no contemporary reports in the local press! There are two versions of the story in local folklore; one states that the problem was caused by an influx of Irish navvies willing to work for a much lower rate than the local labour. The other was that the contractors had initially employed English labour, and it was they who objected to the arrival of the "cut price Irish." I cannot help wondering if the hand of Provost James Grant was involved in keeping a lid on the press. He was not only the Provost, but also a magistrate, lawyer and major shareholder in the railway company. Maybe he paid for a few fine dinners for the gentlemen of the press to protect the reputation of the railway he had so long fought for.

The first two instalments of the contract amounting to £10,000 were due payment in the middle of April. In connection with this, a bill of £2000 was presented by the contractor at the Board meeting of April 19th.

The troubles that had affected the company at the end of 1850 and into the beginning of 1851 by the reluctance of the Edinburgh shareholders to stay with their obligations came to the surface again with a discussion on forfeiture. The following persons were outstanding both the first and second calls:

Address unknown	James Burns Writer, Edinburgh - 250 shares
	John Gordon Distiller, Ballindalloch, now in Australia - 30 shares
	John Gordon Merchant, Elgin, now in America - 2 shares
Address known	
	Henry Inglis, Edinburgh - 250 shares
	Thomas Granger, Edinburgh - 20 shares
	Alexander Hamilton, Edinburgh - 72 shares
	John Blackie, Electric Engineer, Edinburgh - 400 shares
	James Gunn, Edinburgh - 50 shares
	Barbara Robertson, Elgin - 3 shares

The good citizens of Scotland's capital accounted for 1042 of unpaid shares from a total of 1077.

June saw rolling stock matters discussed at the Board meeting of the 3rd. Goods and coal wagons had been inspected at Aberdeen. The coaches were expected daily, but the locomotives were not so advanced. A notice had been prepared for the Board of Trade to inspect the line, as it would be ready for opening on or just after July 5th.

The fourth and final call on £2 shares was made by the board on June 8th 1852. As a result of the reluctance by the Edinburgh shareholders to meet their commitments, an EGM was called on the June 16th. This authorised the Directors to exercise borrowing power, and the forfeiture of shares on which the first and second calls had not been met was approved. The *Forres Gazette* of that day (16th) reported that the permanent track from Lossiemouth to the Loch of Spynie was in place. The station at Elgin was roofed, and two trucks had arrived at Lossiemouth. It was hoped that the railway would be fully operational by the end of July.

With the progress on the line proceeding at a pace, thoughts turned to the employment of staff. In particular it was realised that an experienced and active engine driver would be required. Mr Samuel reported to the Board on June 17th that such a person could be obtained at a cost of £100 per annum. This was a considerable sum, and perhaps demonstrates the regard with which an engine driver was held at that time. The other half of the locomotive crew, the fireman, was also required. He, the board agreed, would have to not only be efficient, but also be able to act in the driver's absence. The price for his labours was not discussed. For the delivery of coal and goods in Elgin, the employment of one Alexander Deeson was approved. I think this gentleman has the honour of being the first official employee of the Morayshire Railway.

The Board meeting of June 17th was certainly busy and varied. Besides the employment of staff there were problems at Lossiemouth with fishermen being able to gain access to their boats that were moored at the old harbour. To avoid having a level crossing at the square, the railway company had proposed to build a footbridge. The fishermen protested, saying that it would be difficult for them to carry their gear over such a bridge. As usual Mr Grant had been sent to investigate and the outcome was an agreement to build an underpass instead of the footbridge. Thoughts turned to the inland portion of the Morayshire, with the agreement to procure ground at Rothes for a coal depot. The remainder of the day's business concerning the construction of coal drops and sidings was held over until the following day.

On the 18th it was decided to defer the building of a coal drop as this would save £800, but to construct a short siding near the goods shed instead. The minutes do not specify which station this refers to but I think it would be Elgin.

After three consecutive meetings, the Board appears to have eased up a bit by waiting until June 24th for their next get together. The business on that day was mundane, dealing with arrangements being made to sell the forfeited stock. The Directors did however agree to walk over and inspect the line.

The press of course are always keen to comment on the changes of the day, and in 1852 things were no different. The town of Lossiemouth was undergoing a boom. Was the press celebrating, sadly no! Their comment on life in the early part of that summer in Lossiemouth: *"There is nothing here but house building, railway making and the din of trade. At present there is no less than 17 vessels in the harbour and the herring season has not started yet."*

More positive news however appeared in the *Courant* of July 2nd 1852, concerning the arrival of the first passenger railway coaches:

> In addition to some of the locomotive* furniture of the line which have been at Lossiemouth. There arrived at the station here on Friday one of the railway carriages.It was conveyed to Aberdeen by rail, whence it was drawn by six powerful horses and being a novelty on the road there was a great turn out everywhere to see it. It was placed on the rails at Pinefield and drawn to the station at the end of Moss Street by 10 or 12 men. It has been visited by large numbers to whom such a carriage is not a familiar object. Its length is about 36 feet. It contains 1st and 2nd class compartments.The former being handsomely filled up and finished. The remaining carriages and engines are shortly expected to be here.

On July 5th 1852, the thoughts of the Board turned to managing the coal trade. It was decided the Railway Company could not do so and it was resolved to set up a separate company to control this business, using the railway as a method of transport. A weighing machine and travelling crane was to be ordered for this traffic. The decision whether the crane was to be 5 tons or 2 tons was to be left to the engineer.

---

* The Morayshire locomotives were still under construction at Neilson's in Glasgow, so I assume the writer is referring to the trucks mentioned in the report of 16th June.

During July one of the workers on the line involved in moving spoil to the Loch of Spynie was injured. His horse had been attached to a loaded 5 ton truck. He then sat astride the animal and started to move off, whereupon it shied. The poor man was thrown back onto the loaded wagon sustaining head injuries. He was attended to by a local doctor, not named in the report, but I wonder if it may have been Dr Manson of Spynie, who was at this time Chairman of the Morayshire Company.

Meeting on July 26th, the Board discussed the employment of staff and the selection and provision of company uniforms. The experienced engine driver recommended by Mr Samuel was appointed as chief engineman. Enter into the Morayshire fold, one William Hewitt at a salary of 6/- per day. Following on was Richard Habergham, described as a stoker, though in railway terms a fireman; he was paid at the rate of £1-1/- per week. Two gatekeepers, James Murray and D Stewart, started work at 1/- per day. John Gordon was engaged as porter and gatekeeper at Lossiemouth on a salary of 12/- per week. Each employee was entitled to one uniform per year. The design for the guard was a green frock coat and vest with scarlet facings buttoned up to the neck. They also wore a cap with a scarlet band onto which was written the words Morayshire Railway in white letters; their trousers were to have a belt with a ticket pouch. They appeared to be the best dressed members of the work force. Next on the list of sartorial elegance were the gatekeepers, who had green jackets and trousers with facings and white gloves. The poor old porters had plain green corduroy uniforms and caps.

In the Forres Gazette of July 28th a report appears suggesting that provided the Morayshire Railway passed inspection by the Board of Trade, and it was hoped to open the line on the 7th of August.

July 31st saw the Secretary reporting to the Board that he had engaged the superintendent recommend to him by Mr Anderson of the Aberdeen Railway, one Thomas Richards. The salary for the post was £80 per annum, a sum considerably less than that of the engine driver. Mr Grant uncharacteristically had failed in a task by being unable to find an efficient guard. The meeting agreed therefore to appoint James Grant, the present driver of the Morayshire road coach, to the railway guard's position.

An opening date was discussed and for some undefined reason it was decided that Saturday, August 7th would not be suitable; it was resolved to open on Tuesday the 10th. At this late stage the locomotives had not arrived from Neilson & Co. The ship on which they were travelling was expected to dock at Lossiemouth on Sunday, August 1st. The Board hoped that an engine would be on the line by Tuesday, August 3rd.

Government Engineer Captain Wynne inspected the line on Wednesday, August 4th, and expressed himself highly satisfied with the efficient manner in which the Morayshire Railway had constructed the line and conducted its affairs. The way was now open for the railway to begin public operations.

A train was started on Thursday, August 5th 1852, which took the Directors, a few friends, and the man from the Government to Lossiemouth and back. This proceeding was intended to be a private affair, but trying to conceal a railway locomotive and its train is not an easy thing to do. Great crowds gathered at both stations and various points along the line, a foretaste of things to come when the line was opened for the masses.

The Board met on August 9th to arrange the festivities for the opening. Wines in the form of one dozen bottles of champagne and another one dozen of sherry were to provided by the Directors. A programme of the use of the pieces of Ordnance was read and approved. It was also decided to hold Highland Games at Lossiemouth, and a list of races and games was confirmed. Debentures were to be signed and sealed.

MORAYSHIRE RAILWAY.

—

THE DIRECTORS of this RAILWAY have pleasure in announcing that the Line will be formally OPENED for the conveyance of PASSENGERS upon *Tuesday the 10th day of August curt.*, and for the conveyance of GOODS in a few days thereafter.

On the OPENING DAY Trains will commence to run from the ELGIN STATION at 10 o'clock, A.M., and every hour thereafter until 8, P.M., and from the LOSSIEMOUTH STATION at 10.30, A.M., and hourly thereafter until 8.30, P.M.

On *Wednesday the 11th August*, and until further notice, Trains will run every lawful day as follow :—

FROM ELGIN. Down Trains.	FROM LOSSIEMOUTH. Up Trains.
7.0 A.M.	8.30 A.M.
10.0 A.M., Express.	11.0 A.M., Express.
0.30 P.M.	1.30 P.M.
2.30 P.M.	3.30 P.M.
4.30 P.M.	6.30 P.M.
7.0 P.M.	8.30 P.M.

FARES—First Class, 9d.; Second Class, 6d.

NOTE.—The Ordinary Trains perform the journey in a quarter of an hour—the Express Trains in ten minutes.

By order of the Board of Directors,

JAMES GRANT, Secretary.

Elgin, 5th August, 1852.

3 Success to the Morayshire Railway

A desire had been expressed by a large body of citizens from Elgin, Lossiemouth and the surrounding district to celebrate the opening of the Morayshire Railway in a manner befitting its spirited undertaking. Tuesday, August 10th 1852 was declared as a holiday, giving the large portion of the community, who had never seen a railway locomotive before, the opportunity to view the beast and possibly travel by rail for the first time.

It had rained all day Monday the 9th, and for a while it looked as though the opening ceremony would be marred by inclement weather. People started to arrive early at the station to glimpse the preliminary proceedings, and in spite of the rain took elevated positions to view the departure of the first service to Lossiemouth. This took place at 8am, when a train containing the workmen who had built the line departed for Lossie. They had been given a free return ticket by the Directors, the return portion of it limited to use on an evening train. The whistle from their departing locomotive was greeted by a loud cheer from the assembled crowd.

At 9am, the skies began to clear and the good people of Elgin were brought to the entrance of their wynds and closes by the martial tones of "two superior" marching bands. One was from Forres and the other was composed entirely of Germans! The local press states that not a shop was open for business, not even the druggists. Only those on *"works of charity and necessity"* were missing from the celebration.

The parade started from the Market Cross, continued eastward round the Little Cross, thence to the west end of the town. On their return eastward they drew up in front of the Trades Hall, where they were joined by the Six Incorporated Trades. The enlarged procession then moved eastward along the High Street, and having once more rounded the Little Cross returned to the High Street, stopping outside the Court House. Here the Magistrates, Town Council, and the Directors of the railway joined the procession. The assembled company was one of the biggest ever seen in Elgin. As a whole it moved west along the High Street, turning into Batchen Street, going eastward onto South Street and then to Moss Street. This particular thoroughfare is about a mile in length, from start to its finish at the railway station. Such was the size of the procession that when its head had arrived at the station, the tail was still some way from entering the farthest end of Moss Street. Marshalling of the parade was carried out by Sergeant Stephen. The following is the order in which it reached the station:

Forres Band

Wrights

Weavers

Tailors

Shoemakers

Watchmakers

Skinners

Hammermen

German Band

Magistrates & Council

Directors of the Railway.

The pavements surrounding the route were also well packed with not only the folk of Elgin, but several large parties from Forres, and almost as large a party from Banff. The latter was brought to the town by the Banff and Macduff omnibus.

The station area itself consisted of four buildings, all built in white sandstone. The nearest was the ticket office, which was of a neat cottage design. The others included a store house, used for handling goods; an elegant arched building for carriage storage; and the last, described as a heating house, was actually the engine shed used for the preparation and servicing of the locomotives. As the major building site, this area had until the last minute been covered by the debris of construction in the form of rubble, broken ground, and fallen trees. By the opening day this had all been cleared away. The ground around the station was enclosed by a white paling fence. Flowerbeds had been created and planted up with a mixture of hollyhocks, fuchsias, and evergreens. Several choice floral decorations were also studded about the entrance, with the actual gate into the station bearing a triumphal arch surmounted by a diadem of roses. The floral arrangements and the grounds themselves had been laid out by Messrs Morrison of the Pinefield Nursery.

With the procession safely arrived at the station, the Trades divided to allow the Magistrates and Council through to obtain their tickets. They, along with the Directors, and some of the members of the Incorporated Trades made up the first official train-load of around 200 passengers. When the number of tickets for each train were sold, the ticket window was closed until the train was loaded and away.

The first train was announced to leave at 10 o'clock but owing to a fault put down to the *"newness and consequence stiffness of the workings of the locomotive,"* departure was almost an hour late. As best as your author can make out, the problem was with a defect in one of the valves of the engine. I am uncertain if both locomotives were in steam that day. If they were it is possible that one engine was failed as it seems certain that the remaining services for the day were worked by one locomotive only. Anyway at 10.30 a locomotive, three carriages and five open wagons were brought alongside the platform. When the assorted dignitaries were safely on board they were off.

"Ride by the Rail"
Report for The Elgin Courant (abridged)

Hundreds are gazing upon us as we shoot along impelled in hot haste by the roaring, rustling monster as it steams and smokes, snorts and shrieks, rattles and rustles on its way. We reach the mail road, which has been raised some seven feet for the railway's convenience. We have crossed the high road, and if we had one we could throw a stone into the "Order, or Ordeal Pot" where tradition tells us in the fifteenth century the superstitious of Morayshire were wont to test the witchery women. Provost Grant bless thy lucky stars that you were born in the nineteenth century and not in the fifteenth for you would have "gone to Pot" for proposing to travel from Elgin to Lossiemouth in ten minutes on an iron horse.

Then comes that old Cathedral of a bygone day, looming down upon this new line of a new age. Well such are the changes that are to be found in the wee bit vapour o' an auld wife's kettle! Now we cross the Lossie. What a quiet harmless stream. Yet twenty-three years ago it swelled to a mighty torrent, overflowed its banks and carried desolation everywhere. Is it not this iron road which now crosses it an example of a lesson taught! We are steaming through Bareflathills, what a shifty, sandy hill you are. You are a poor neighbour for a steady iron road. And yet you are goodly friends with the band's men. Leaving the hill behind us, and the most picturesque part of the line bursts upon our view. To our left lies a wide-extended landscape, beautifully dotted with hill and dale, wood and plain. In the distance, the Hill of Cullen rise richly, nobly green. We rush through a corn field, and come upon the ruins of the Bishop's Palace at Spynie.

Where once the German Ocean roared and nature ruled in all her savagery, the triumph of art now asserts its sway. The loch of Spynie is now behind us and we are driving through a wide breadth of pebbles and sand with which a stout wind shut out the German Ocean centuries ago. This is a strange and wild place, and if thou art is botany, good reader, go and sit down and ponder over the progeny of the vegetable world, and as thou ponderest, the shrieks of an engine shall arouse you to tell you that you have found a place where first the wonder of nature and now the wonder of art run so strangely side by side.

We are in the village of Lossiemouth. What strange old scattered place its unmade streets and low built houses are. The inhabitants! - with wonderment rush out and stare upon us, as though they were so many Rip Van Winkles just awakened from a century's slumber! Now the sea rolls in on us and we are at journeys end, and must scrape a new point to our pencil to take note of the Sports at Lossiemouth.

With his comments on the town and the population of Lossiemouth, I would be surprised if the reporter from the *Elgin Courant* had helped his proprietor to sell many copies of the paper in that town.

The folk of Elgin were not so sophisticated that they took the arrival of the railway in their stride. As stated earlier, it was a holiday in Elgin, and a goodly part of the population was standing at the line side observing the comings and goings. Crowds stood at both sides of the line from the station out to the cutting at Bareflathills. Besides the bands on top of the cutting, there was also a gun which was fired as the train entered the cutting. This signal was acknowledged by another piece of ordnance stationed on the Quarry Hill at Lossie, which continued firing a salute until the train arrived in Lossiemouth.

In the country, crowds gathered to cheer the train at the level crossing at Pitgaveny. Farmhouses and cottages on the way had flags fluttering in the breeze. Similar decorations were also to be found on the houses at Lossiemouth. Rather than greeting the first train in open-mouthed amazement, the folk of Lossie cheered and waved the progress of the train in a manner we would probably describe as a "Mexican Wave".

Besides the crowd at line side, the whole length of the Coulardhill was a mass of people. The vessels and fishing boats in the harbour were dressed with ribbons and pennants carrying such mottoes as *"Success to the Morayshire Railway; Long live Provost Grant"*. A salute was fired off by Captain Burton and his men of the Preventative Service (Coast guards), who were stationed at the northern point of the old harbour. This was replied to by some cannons belonging to Colonel Brander of Pitgaveny. These pieces subsequently marked the arrival and departure of trains from Lossie for a good part of the day.

A magnificent triumphal arch was erected over the railway at the entrance to Lossiemouth station. The station house itself was decorated with flowers, evergreens and topped off with flags, these arrangements carried out by the stationmaster Mr Robert Brander. The time taken for the Director's train to arrive from Elgin had been 11 minutes. A large marquee had been erected on top of the quarry heights opposite the station, for the Directors and their ladies plus assorted dignitaries and friends. They enjoyed a luncheon at noon, which was admirably served up by Mr Urquhart, confectioner of Elgin.

As train after train arrived in Lossiemouth, the passengers scampered off singly or in parties, some to enjoy wandering along the shore to Covesea, others to enjoy the luxury of a cool dip. Quite a few indulged themselves at the numerous inns and tents set up on the sea front; it was after all now a hot sunny day. Later passengers arriving at Lossiemouth had already been indulging in a small libation before setting out. Despite some being a little noisy, there was as much good humour as there was whisky, and no incidents of violence were reported. The railway itself was finding it difficult to cope with the demand for people wishing to travel to Lossiemouth. So as the day wore on, every form of horse and cart was pressed into service to carry people to the coast.

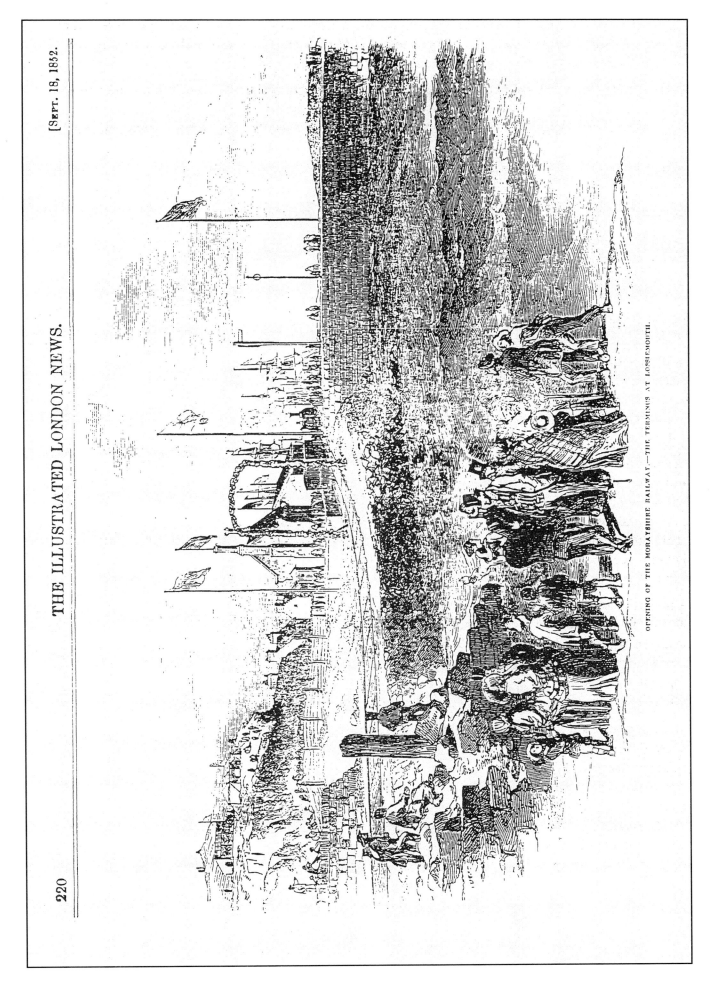

OPENING OF THE MORAYSHIRE RAILWAY.—THE TERMINUS AT LOSSIEMOUTH.

One of the main events at Lossiemouth was a sports competition that was held on the East beach. Unlike the present day there was no bridge linking the beach with the rest of Lossiemouth. To cross to the other side required the use of a boat, to this end the * north of Scotland Steam Packet Company provided passage free of charge. Despite being skilled sailors, such was the rush of sightseers to get across to the beach, that a ducking was a fairly common outcome. Perhaps this explains the comments of one observer that the proceedings at the start of the games were *"more like an English wake, than a Scotch merrymaking"*. Mr Green and Mr Law, two volunteer sports managers took command and things began to perk up with the local population entering into the spirit of things. The prospect of the generous prizes supplied by the railway Directors may have also helped. It certainly encouraged the appearance of a "professional" sports man from England, William Lovell. He won first place in putting the stone, which was a sum of 10/-, first prize of a new hat in the men's running race, and last, but not least a pound of tobacco for coming second in a competition described as a men's race. The winner of the 10/- on this occasion was Frank Henry, who I think was a local man. There were of course races for women and boys. The prizes for these were a gown for the ladies and new hat for the boys.

As a marketing exercise the Morayshire Railway had a running race open only to the fisher women of Lossiemouth and Stotfield. On offer was three uniform fisher women's dresses given by the Directors of the railway company *"to represent the improvement in point of dress which the opening of the railway will enable those individuals to embrace."* For the winner there was also to be a week's free supply of tickets for herself and accompanying fish basket. Seven bonny sunburnt lassies entered into the spirit of the event, and after a hard fought contest, the winners were: 1st Elizabeth Dinnet, 2nd Sibyl Soutor, and 3rd Harriet Stewart.

It had been intended to hold the usual events associated with Highland Games, tossing the caber and throwing the hammer, but due to the fact that no one thought to bring the implements for the activities, these events were abandoned.

The last prize to be put up for competition was a gigot of mutton. To obtain this, the athlete had to climb a greasy pole. Various persons tried and failed, and so a little bit of cheating was employed. Two contestants worked as a team, with one standing on the other's shoulders. More ingenuously another tried coating himself in sand to counteract the effects of the grease, while finally another tried to use a ladder! He was disqualified. Before someone thought of using an axe to chop down the pole, the mutton was hauled down and a foot race amongst the pole climbers decided that Robert Munro should take this prize home. I hope he enjoyed his grease and sand covered dinner.

At 4pm the Provost, Magistrates, their friends and some of the principal inhabitants of Elgin, made their way back to the City by rail. Their ultimate destination was the Assembly Rooms where a gala dinner was to take place. Owing to the large number of people wishing to travel, the number carried in each train load had been increased to 300. Despite this the spaces quickly filled up with some of the guests finding it difficult to obtain tickets. As a result of this the start of the dinner was delayed for an hour.

Seventy gentlemen sat down to table at 6pm, with the post of honour being occupied by Dr Manson as chair of the Morayshire Railway Company. On his right sat our Mr Grant in his official capacity as Provost. Later in the evening the assembly was joined by Mr Samuel, the engineer, and Mr Hutchings, the contractor for the Morayshire Railway. Their entrance was greeted with enthusiastic cheering. With ample justice having been done to an excellent dinner served up by Mr Davie of the Royal Hotel, the cloth was removed from the table and glasses primed. The usual loyal toasts were given. The Chairman then rose to his feet to give the toast of the evening: *"Success to the Morayshire Railway."* He went on to give a history of the line and the difficulties that it had overcome and then added:

---

* They operated the service from Orkney and the far north of Scotland into the Harbour at Lossiemouth; Mr Grant hoped to exploit their incoming cargo to the advantage of his railway.

These difficulties do not end with the completion of the line. The engines were new, the carriages ungreased and in fact nothing was in a proper state to perform its functions. Yet notwithstanding all were satisfied in the way in which everything had been brought to completion and it was with pride they viewed the manner in which the whole community had turned out to do them honour.

An extensive catalogue of toasts took place, and perhaps the feelings of the evening were best summed up by Mr Hutchings the contractor, who was quite sure that, in these days a town was lost without a railway; and he was delighted to find one so far north of Aberdeen, even though it was a small one. The company broke up shortly before 11pm.

As the Directors made their way home, the Morayshire Railway was still working hard. The normal timetable stated that the last train left Lossiemouth at 8.30pm. Such was the demand for travel on the first day, that the service continued well past midnight. On that day the railway carried just over 3000 passengers, which considering the population of Elgin then was just over 7000 citizens, was good business.

To try to cater for the demand for travel to Lossiemouth, it had been attempted at one stage to increase the number of wagons and coaches, to allow 400 people at a time to travel. Sadly the little engine was not up to the task, and the maximum number of passengers carried at any one time was 300. The officials of the company, it must be said, looked more to safety than to speed. In the midst of the excitement and confusion of the opening, day no accidents occurred. All who had traveled to Lossiemouth by rail, returned to Elgin by rail, even if they were several hours late.

Claims have been made that the Morayshire was constructed at a lower cost per mile than any other railway line in Britain, so it may be helpful at this point to have a look at the cost of its construction:

	£	s	d
Contractor's estimates	£ 19793	10	0
Sleepers & fences	£ 1340	0	0
Incidental expenses	£ 1000	0	0
Parliamentary costs	£ 5000	0	0
Land purchase	£ 3500	0	0
Total	£ 30633	10	0

The length of the line was 5 miles 6 furlongs, with an additional 4 furlongs of sidings, giving a total of 6 miles and 2 furlongs. Construction cost worked out at a little over £5000 per mile. The average cost for railways at this time according to the *Times* per mile in England was £38,290, Scotland £30,781, and Ireland £35,443 giving an average of £34,838. The Morayshire was thus constructed for a seventh part of the cost of all lines in Great Britain and Ireland up to this point.

4 SAMUEL'S SPECIFICATION

Construction of Railways, Steam Engines, etc

Any traveller from the South who had attended the opening of the Morayshire Railway would have found an enterprise that differed somewhat from the rest of the 1852 network. Provost Grant had spent a great deal of time looking for someone to construct his line at a low cost. Mr James Samuel provided the ideal candidate for the task. The deal for this project was not all one-sided, as in the Morayshire James Samuel had a test ground for a number of his patents.

Having left his native Glasgow he set himself up as a civil engineer, working out of Willoughby House in the county of Middlesex. It was from here on the 5th of April 1850 that he applied for his first patent, which covered track, locomotive, and a donkey engine for pumping water into a boiler. This specification was stamped for statute on the 5th of October 1850.

The Track

Though some railways in Scotland had adopted a gauge of 4 ft 3 ins, the Morayshire was not that bold and it was built to the British standard of 4 ft 8½" ins. Mr Samuel's patent did however differ from the system to be found elsewhere on the British network. His permanent way was formed of rail weighing 65 lbs per yard of the accompanying section, and spiked by means of barbed spikes to transverse sleepers, 12 inches broad by 6 to 8 inches in depth, placed at central distances of 3 feet apart. The joints were held together by wrought iron fish plates placed on each side of the joint and fixed by means of two bolts on each side of the joint. The Board of Trade Inspector believed that this form of track had some advantages inasmuch as it dispensed with chairs and wooden keys, but he thought it would require extra attention, as the spikes with which the rail was held to the sleepers might possibly become loosened. Mr Samuel was confident in his design, and claimed that it was in use on the Prussian railway system. He moreover claimed that he had adopted it on the Morayshire Railway because of the low cost; in particular the larch sleepers, which had been used, only cost 1/7 apiece.

The track was supported on shingle ballast, which according to the official report, had been taken from the beach. I suspect it may have come from quarry workings at the Oakenhead Wood, close by the railway at the entrance to Lossiemouth.

The Engines

As I mentioned earlier, the engines for the Morayshire Railway were built by Neilson of Glasgow, or to give the builders its correct title at that stage in their history, Neilson & Mitchell. Although this locomotive builder eventually became part of the mighty North British Locomotive Company, supplier of locomotives to the British Empire, the records pertaining to its history before 1864 sadly appear to be lost. This mishap probably occurred when the company moved from Finnieston to Springburn in 1862, so the following is at best the scrapings of fairly empty barrel.

The engines were built to the principles laid out in Mr Samuel's patent of 1850. The works number issued by Neilson's for them was nos 51- 52. They are described in the opening day press reports and Board of Trade Inspection as being six wheel engines with a tender. From this I would take that they were of what is known in Whyte's wheel notation as a 2-2-2. That is, that the front and rear wheels of 3 ft diameter are non-driving. Power was supplied to the centre wheel, which was five feet in diameter. Total heating surface of the boiler was 500 sq feet with a working pressure of 120 lb per sq inch. The steam was delivered to the two cylinders, which were of novel design to economize on steam and fuel, and again patented by Mr Samuel. The most obvious difference that anyone would notice when looking at this engine head on, is that the cylinders on each side were of two sizes. What Mr Samuel had here was a very early example of what was later to be known as a compound locomotive. Steam was let into the smaller of the cylinders first. Then by means of a steam port the partially used steam was passed on to the larger cylinder, from which, after it had done its work, it was released into the blast pipe and up the chimney. Some 300 gallons of water were carried in the tender. The fuel used was coke, which unlike coal gives good heat, whilst not creating smoke. Fixed to the boiler was another of James Samuel's patents, a small "donkey engine," which was used to pump a supply of water into the boiler. It may have been the action of this mechanism that gave these engines their nickname of "Coffeepots". In full working order each of these machines weighed in at 14 tons.

Both locomotives had official names. One was called *"Elgin"* and the other unsurprisingly was named *"Lossiemouth"*. What is perhaps surprising is the choice of numbers. Where it would have probably been expected that they would have been 1 and 2, they entered service as 37 and 38! Was Mr Grant trying to impress the unsuspecting public that his railway was bigger than it really was? Livery for the engines follows that of the staff uniforms in being green, and unlike other railway companies, there appears to be little or no lining out or decoration.

In a very meticulously entry in the Morayshire's accounts, the sum charged to the capital account for these two machines was £2,622-7s-8½d.

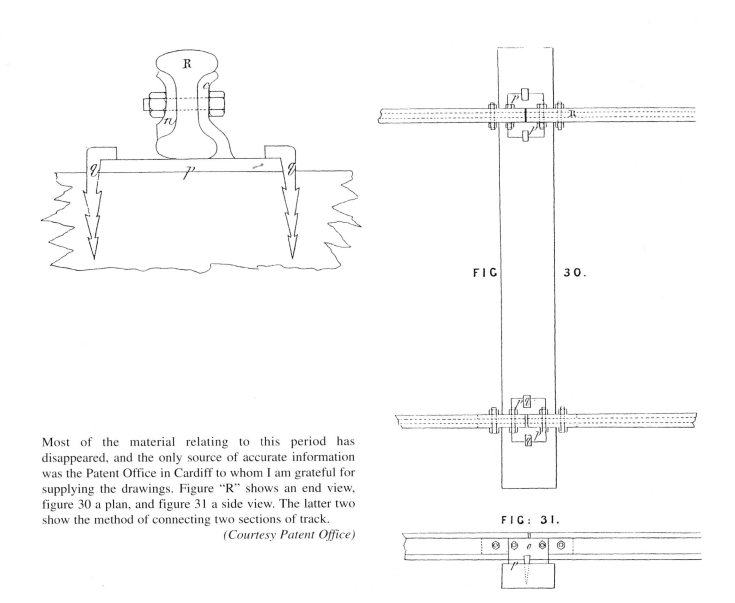

Most of the material relating to this period has disappeared, and the only source of accurate information was the Patent Office in Cardiff to whom I am grateful for supplying the drawings. Figure "R" shows an end view, figure 30 a plan, and figure 31 a side view. The latter two show the method of connecting two sections of track.

(Courtesy Patent Office)

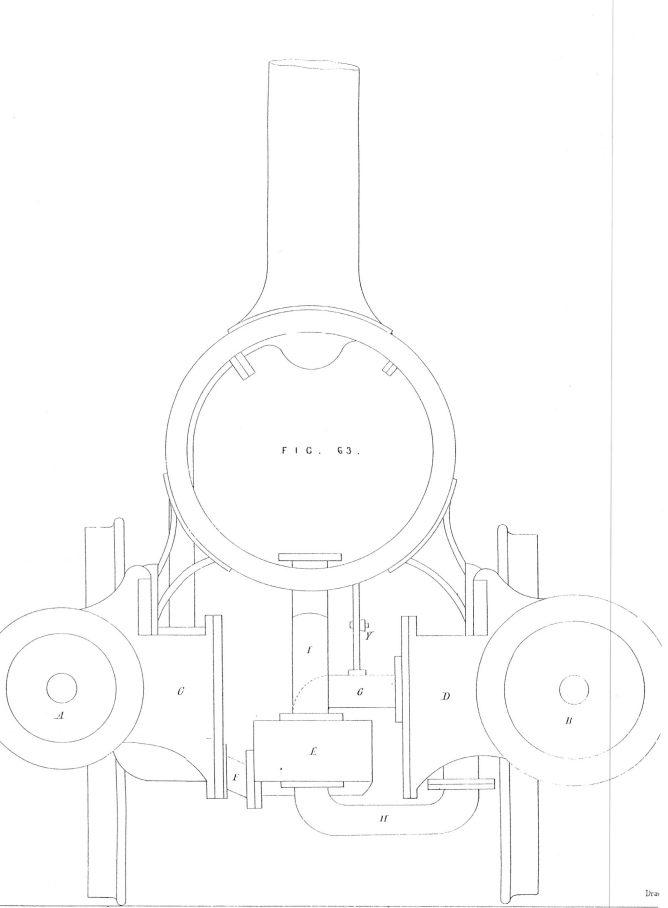

FIG. 63.

Drav

Photography was still in its infancy when the Morayshire came into being, so there is no known photograph of either of the first two Morayshire Railway company locomotives. I have included the drawing figure 63 supplied by the Patent office in support of Mr Samuel's invention of the lightweight locomotive. This is only a front view, and for reasons of his patent, much detail not connected to his new idea for a railway engine is omitted. The other known drawing, which might show what these beasts looked like, is the sketch of Elgin station in 1855, which gives a rather strange angled end view. Finally there is the Morayshire Railway Directors pass. This shows a side view of a 2-2-2 locomotive, but this is probably just a copy of a standard printer's block of the time, used for advertising on railway timetables, etc.

The Coaches

Demonstrating the relaxed state that the Morayshire Railway had in keeping records of its rolling stock, though stock numbers were used, the language of the nursery found favour as a means of identification by the operating staff. The coaches were known as "the small carriages" and "the large carriages."

On the opening day there were three vehicles available, which were all composite: that is they would accommodate first and second class passengers holding in total 40. Captain Wynne of the Board of Trade thought that these vehicles, which were 36 foot in length and became known as the "large carriages," would be ample for the anticipated traffic on the line. They were constructed of teak wood by Brown & Marshall under the "all inclusive deal" for the building and fitting out of the railway. A little after the opening date the passenger rolling stock was supplemented by two other vehicles, both of which were brake carriages of 23ft 6ins length. The smaller coaches would have accommodated the guard, any parcels traffic, and possibly had seating for second class passengers.

Most railways of this period had third class to meet the requirements of the Regulations of Railways Act 1844 for travel at 1d per mile. As the fare for second class was only 6d for the six mile journey, this need was met, so third class was not required.

The only official information given on the goods wagons is that they were all supplied with sprung buffers which was quite unusual for the time. I think they would have been of an open design, with possibly a wooden rail running from one end to the other to support a tarpaulin, if the items being carried required to be protected from the rain.

Signalling

There was some form of signal system on the network, which appears to have been located at each of the stations. How it worked, or what it may have looked like has been lost over the intervening 150 years. A possible clue is the drawing from a 1855 map, which shows a signal with a fine-looking finial on top of the post. A lamp can also be seen fixed to the side of the post. This may have swung round to display that the way was clear for the train to move off. If there was a semaphore arm on the apparatus, this must have folded flat against the post.

The normal method of operation on the line was what is known as "one engine in steam." All the services to and from Lossiemouth were worked by one locomotive, whilst the other was serviced or on standby in the event of a failure. This technique met with the full approval of the Board of Trade, who were of the opinion *"for the purposes of public traffic the system of operation would not attend with danger to the public using same."*

An additional safety measure, moreover a money-saving one on the part of the Morayshire Railway, was the intention of the Company to keep level crossing gates closed across the roads.

5 A MOST USEFUL LINE

The first weeks of traffic on the Morayshire Railway exceeded all expectations, even after making allowances for people wanting to experience the novelty of rail travel. Tickets bought for the first week in Elgin amounted to 1407 and at Lossiemouth 1508, a good beginning.

Reports in the *Elgin Courier* of August 27th 1852 give a fuller picture.

Another record week for passenger traffic on our small railway. This is most surprising as the weather at the end of the week was unfavourable for the seaside. The number of passengers booked at the respective stations from the 19th to the 25th, both inclusive, is as follows:

		From Elgin	From Lossie
Thurs	19	105	113
Fri	20	141	161
Sat	21	236	251
Mon	23	156	149
Tue	24	119	118
Wed	25	327	335
Totals		1084	1127

As the season advances it is expected that numbers will drop, but even so there are good grounds for believing that this is a most useful line instead of a hopeless and ruinous speculation as some would argue it is.

Some of the increase in the number of passengers would have been the result of Lossie fisher women now being permitted to travel with their creels. I assume that the winners of the fisher women's race would have been amongst the first to take their places on the train, no doubt resplendent in the uniforms given by the Railway Company as prizes.

The large number of tickets sold on Wednesday, August 25th 1852 was as a result of the first Railway Excursion. This was organised by the Rothes merchants, tradesmen, and their families. Despite damp weather, all manner of gigs and carts left Rothes at 8am in the morning, the departing travellers cheered on their way by the rest of the village's population. By 9am the group had arrived at the Gordon Arms hotel in Elgin. It states in the report that a short rest was enjoyed by the travelling company. Liquid refreshments were probably appreciated as part of the break. By 10am all had taken their seats for the "Express" service to Lossiemouth. On arrival the company divided into various groups. One went to the Covesea lighthouse, another to the lead mines, the third for a dip in the sea, and the fourth enjoyed the luxury of a cruise. Towards the end of the day the parties met up and inspected the village of Branderburgh and the "substantial" harbour. All apparently were favourably commented on.

At the end of August there was only a very slight drop in the number of passengers carried, every week with 982 tickets being sold at Elgin, and 1040 at Lossiemouth.

The first full week of September saw the commencement of coal traffic on the line. General goods and merchandise service started the following week (Monday 13th September). Arrangements were also being talked about for an omnibus service to take passengers to Elgin station, and it was expected that a van would be put into service for luggage and parcel collection.

The subject of coal was high on the minds of the Directors when they met on the 13th of September, the first time they had met since the opening day. The cost of coal carried by the railway and put into store

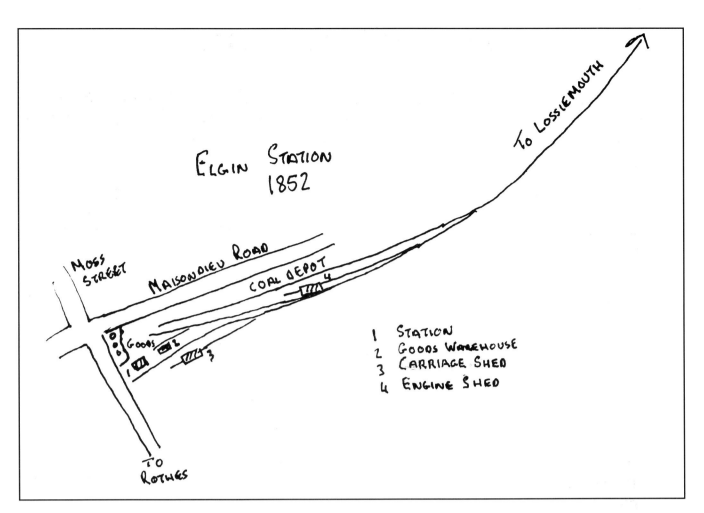

ELGIN STATION
1852

MOSS STREET

MAISONDIEU ROAD

COAL DEPOT

TO LOSSIEMOUTH

1 STATION
2 GOODS WAREHOUSE
3 CARRIAGE SHED
4 ENGINE SHED

GOODS

TO ROTHES

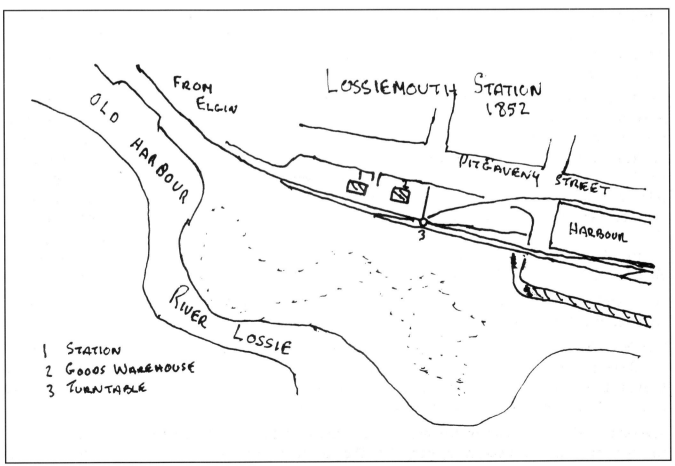

LOSSIEMOUTH STATION
1852

OLD HARBOUR

FROM ELGIN

PITGAVENY STREET

HARBOUR

RIVER LOSSIE

1 STATION
2 GOODS WAREHOUSE
3 TURNTABLE

by the independent coal company was 2/- per ton. There was however competition coming from imports into Garmouth, which were being sold on Speyside for 1/6 per ton. To counter this threat the Directors decided to give a discount of 1/- per ton on all coal sold at or above Orton or upper Banffshire.

An increase in staff occurred with the appointment of John Scott as goods porter at Elgin, and an efficient clerk was to be employed to assist Provost Grant in his role as Company Secretary.

Robert Brander, the Stationmaster at Lossiemouth who lived in that town, was a Director of the Company. It was agreed at the meeting of 13th September that he would continue to look after the running of the station and supply to the Morayshire one of his own clerks to assist him. The permanent appointment of a stationmaster for Lossiemouth would not take place until after the AGM in October. John Gordon, the gatekeeper and porter at Lossiemouth, was to give up his gatekeeping duties and become full-time platform porter. The post of goods porter was given to Alexander Forsythe at 12/- per week.

Independent of the Morayshire Railway, moves were underway to increase the traffic coming through the Harbour at Lossiemouth, with talks being held with interested parties at the opposite side of the Moray Firth. In a forceful letter to the press a correspondent explains:

> It is understood that the proposal to put steamers between Stotfield harbour and the Northern Counties has been well received by the people in that part of the country. If the *Great North Railway is to be made at all. It must come to Elgin, and if so the prosperity of this town, the Morayshire, and the Stotfield harbour depends on securing the traffic to the North via Lossiemouth. Those deeply engaged in the Great North pay no respect to any particular interest. To protect ourselves therefore a Committee is to be formed and a subscription raised to secure a large portion of capital needed to develop the traffic from the North.

Mr Wilson, a bookseller of Elgin was also out to make money from the Morayshire. A report of opening ceremony, along with an illustration appeared in the September issue of the *Illustrated London News*. Elgin citizens who wished a memento of the great day were advised to hurry along and purchase their copy from his shop.

Reports appeared in the *Elgin Courier* of September 17th 1852 advising that *"handsome and commodious luggage vans are now operating between the High Street and the railway station."*

Among other benefits to the community mentioned, is the supply of cheap superior coal, *"a boon to all."* The writer goes on to add. *" To the poorer classes the saving of a few pence on a barrel of coal is a matter of considerable importance and will be much prized as the shillings saved on the tons by the rich."*

The first reported fatal accident occurred on the Morayshire Railway on September 28th 1852. It rather bears attention to a book of bizarre tales than a Board of Trade Report. The 10am express Elgin to Lossiemouth train was passing the Loch of Spynie when a large bird rose from the loch and flew across the line of the railway. Striking the funnel of the locomotive it fell to the ground. When picked up it was found to be a bird not often found on this coast a Northern Diver. It measured, from wing tip to wing tip, 4 feet 4 inches, in length from bill to tail 3 feet. The unfortunate creature was in the act of swallowing a fish measuring 9 inches long by 5 inches broad at the instant it was struck. One half of the fish was embedded in its gullet (which resembles that of a pelican) and the other protruded from its bill.

More important matters concerned the Directors when they met the following day September 29th. Time to pay the contractor and settle other bills. The troubles with the forfeited shares had returned, having been offered for sale at £8 without finding any takers. The Directors agreed to try to arrange private contracts at that price. If shares could be sold under this arrangement, payment would be taken in cash for at least £4 per share with a bill bearing 5% interest for the balance, payable on demand.

*The Great North of Scotland Railway

Other business concerned the erection of buildings. A coke shed and forge were to be constructed at the east end of the engine shed. The old foundry was to be fitted out for use as a stable until the new building was ready.

The AGM held on October 20th 1852 was a quiet affair, with just the election of Mr Alexander Grant to the Board. No mention was made for the provision of a stationmaster at Lossiemouth, as had been promised at the meeting of the 13th of September. By the end of October with the weather becoming colder, the Board provided stoves for the gatekeeper's cabins. On October the 25th it was decided by the Board to have a proper track laying gang. To this end James Thorburn was employed as principal platelayer, at a salary of 25/- per week. A second platelayer was employed at 15/- per week, with a note that up to six other men could be employed on track repair duties at a salary of 11/- each.

Even in November the desire to travel by train was still high. The Directors were displeased to find that some of their patrons were neglecting to buy tickets! In an attempt to prevent this, the Directors arranged for a notice to tell passengers to obtain their tickets before taking their seats. Should the notice fail in preventing people travelling for free, ticket barriers were to be erected at both stations *"where the tickets can be collected previous to the passengers leaving the station."*

The problems of Mr Inglis and Mr Gunn came back to the attention of the Board at their meeting of 13th December. Provost Grant was still hopeful of disposing of their shares. Complaints had also been received from the engine driver William Hewitt about the state of the track. It was up to the standard for the Board of Trade, but did not match the exacting requirements of Mr Hewitt. As the highest paid member of the railway staff, the Board took serious note of his complaint and agreed to the employment of 30 men to rectify the problem.

Among other items discussed at this meeting were additions to the uniform. Greatcoats made of pilot cloth were to be provided for the engine driver, fireman, guard and three gatekeepers.

The Morayshire Railway only operated during daylight hours. Therefore the number of passenger trains were cut back to five round trips per day, with the first train leaving Elgin at 8.30 in the morning, and the last returning from Lossiemouth at 4.30 in the afternoon. Squeezed in between these services were the coal and parcel traffic and now of course additional ballast trains. This kept both locomotives well employed.

The first day of the New Year 1853 was also the first meeting day of the Morayshire Railway in that year. It started badly, as Mr Gunn had issued a summons against the Morayshire to settle his account with the Company. To resolve the problem with Mr Inglis, Mr Grant suggested his forfeited shares should be sold. The Board decided to defer this matter. On a positive note it was reported that the ballasting work had been completed.

Celebration of Christmas and New Year was for the main part still being held according to the old calendar. Excursion traffic for the holidays took place on the 7th and 14th of January 1853 respectively. Christmas was not greatly celebrated in this corner of the world, so the railway did not see a large increase of travellers. New Year however was a different story with all the available rolling stock being pressed into service. *The Morayshire Courier* claimed that the railway could have done with at least two additional carriages per train.

At the Lossiemouth Town Council meeting held on Monday, January 31st, problems with the bridge at the Square in Lossiemouth were discussed. It was found to be too low and narrow for the passage of carts and equipment. Claims were made that Seatown had been cut off for six months, with cartfuls of nets unable to move and loads of dung that could not be carried away. The roadway under the bridge was always submerged in water, on some occasions up to two feet in depth.

The Council road trustee Bailie Cooper contested that the bridge was only seven feet in height, where the plan showed that it should be nine feet high. The Morayshire Board sent Provost Grant to the meeting and he claimed that to alter the bridge would require the permission of the Board of Trade. Bailie Cooper agreed with this statement. Provost Grant went on to suggest that the best course of action would be to stop up the bridge and replace it with a level crossing. If this was acceptable to the Council, the Railway Company would supply one of the porters from the harbour to operate the gates. Some of the members of the Council wanted an enlarged bridge and a level crossing. The Provost countered that there was no requirement for a crossing at the Square in Lossiemouth. He went on to state that it had been placed at that point on the request of the Council, if therefore the Council wished to take over the responsibility for the bridge it could be left in place. Following a heated discussion it was eventually decided to accepted Provost Grant's proposal, to close off the bridge and replace it with a level crossing.

This decision was reported back to the Board meeting on February 9th 1853. The latest situation in the dispute with Mr Inglis and Mr Gunn was then reported. A discharge agreement had been reached with Mr Inglis and a legal defence against Mr Gunn had been approved. The next step in the development of the Morayshire Railway was a proposal that they go into the hotel business with the construction of two hotels, one at Elgin and the other at Lossiemouth.

A large increase in the amount of traffic coming through the port of Lossiemouth was noted in the report by the *Morayshire Courier* of the Harbour Board AGM held on the 11th of February.

By March 26th 1853, the replacement level crossing at Seatown was completed and in operation. The bridge, or more precisely the underpass at the Square in Lossiemouth was not closed off, and remained in place for the next 113 years!

The boom in travel brought about by the arrival of the Morayshire Railway was attracting the attention of Central Government. In a parliamentary paper issued on Scotch Railway Traffic, the number of passengers conveyed by rail in Scotland was showing a marked increase. The Morayshire was singled out for attention because, though it had only been in operation for four months of the twelve month survey, 26,755 passengers had travelled over this small line. A contrast was drawn with the attempt a few years earlier when a few public spirited citizens had started a small road coach to run between Elgin and Lossiemouth. This thrice-weekly service had failed because the number of passengers wanting to travel was so small that the cost of the horse's feed bill could not be met.

Notices that had been placed at each station in November to remind travellers to purchase their tickets before boarding the train, must have had an effect because on April 23rd the decision to erect ticket barriers was abandoned.

Tuesday May 10th 1853 saw the contract signed for the erection of a *"splendid hotel"* at the Lossiemouth railway station. The successful contractors were carpenter Convenor McKenzie, slater and mason F W G Urquhart, plaster work Mr Joseph Stewart, and plumber Mr John Gordon. The tenders for the hotel at the Elgin terminus had been delayed for a few days though the plans had been completed by the architect Messrs A & W Reid of Elgin.

Services on May 20th 1853 were running every half hour that day because of the annual feeing market * at Elgin. Fine weather had also arrived, causing a large increase in the traffic over the Morayshire Railway. Even taking all this into account, Provost Grant and the Board of the railway company still wished to increase the number of passengers on the line. To this end a platform was constructed at the level crossing at Spynie, to be used as a request stop.

The real start of Lossiemouth as a tourist resort can be traced to an Elgin Council meeting at the beginning of June. Provost Grant was of course in the driving seat. The East Beach at Lossiemouth, a beautiful sandy shore, was cut off by the River Lossie. His proposal was to erect a bridge over the river at the village of Lossiemouth to the sea shore, for the convenience of the public. Subscriptions of a

* Employment fair

Lossiemouth, from Canal (The Circus has Come)

The circus at Lossiemouth in the early 1900's, provides a pleasant backdrop to the Morayshire Railway and "that" bridge
(Courtesy The Moray Council)

considerable amount had already been received both in money and material. Chief among the contributors were the Railway and Harbour Companies. Mr Duncan, *"the enterprising"* shipbuilder at Garmouth had supplied good quality foreign timber, sufficient to construct three parts of the structure. This material was said to be to the value of £10. The total expense of this project was reckoned to be £100. Wearing his political hat, Provost Grant claimed that the provision of this bridge would be of great benefit to the community at large and anticipated that the Town Council would have no objection to go to the length of contributing the sum of £5. To cries of *"hear hear"* this proposal was unanimously agreed.

Mr Hewitt was either very confident of his position within the Company or rather foolish. On the 4th of June he demanded that his wife be issued with a free pass to allow her to travel on the line when she wished. His demand was unanimously refused by the Directors.

On June 13th 1853 the Morayshire introduced a bathing train service, along with the first return ticket and the first discount ticket issued by the Company at the cost of 6d. The bathing train service left Elgin at 8pm. A large number of patrons were attracted by the low fare, amongst them a few hardy souls who braved the chilly evening to take a dip in the Moray Firth. Reports of this event in the *Elgin Courier* stated that the folk who took advantage of this outing were of the opinion that this service should be offered between 6 and 8am. *"The morning being universally excepted as a better time for bathing, as the chill of the evening is not only unpleasant but also unsafe. If the Directors agreed with this sentiment the service would be very enthusiastically taken up."* Should however this not be possible the alternate suggestion was that it would be more convenient to start the train at 8.15pm to accommodate the trading and commercial community who shut up shop at 8pm, allowing them to take advantage of the service.

All was not well within the Morayshire Railway Company and matters came to a head at the Board meeting of the 14th of June. William Hewitt the engine driver was efficient, but also autocratic. Not only had he demanded that the track should be above the standard required by the Board of Trade, he had taken it upon himself to interfere in every department of the railway. This caused him to be universally detested by the other staff. Complaints were made to the Board, which were initially ignored. Things however reached such a peak that Provost Grant investigated the man's behaviour. Although the Provost could find no reason to dismiss Hewitt, he was brought before the Board meeting of 14th June, and told clearly to stick to his post and stop interfering with the day-to-day work of the railway. After Hewitt had left the meeting the Board decided that it would be expedient for the fireman who worked alongside Hewitt to take a greater part in the working of the locomotives. The implication being that should Hewitt be dismissed, the company would still have someone capable of driving its trains. Discipline at the stations was also to be properly enforced, with the Morayshire being worked according to Company regulations.

There was better news for all prospective sea bathers, with the completion of the bridge to the East beach expected for the beginning of July. Advantage of this situation was taken by Mr Cook of the new Lossiemouth Railway Hotel who would be providing bathing coaches.

The staff difficulties in the locomotive department rumbled on, with the Directors further protecting their position by employing an additional stoker and occasional driver in the form of one Samuel Bishop. In this case, before Bishop was accepted into the post, he had to supply references from the last railway company he had worked for.

An eventful Board meeting took place of July 12th 1853. Amongst the discussions of loans from the Caledonian Bank, cheap travel on days of play for Elgin cricket club and the review of plans for a coal depot at Elgin, there was a debate over seven days a week service, and major staff changes. Concerning the operation of trains on a Sunday, Provost Grant was asked to find out the costs involved in carrying mail on a Sunday, and what the Government might pay the Morayshire to provide such a service. On the staff front, the resignation letter from Mr Brander the stationmaster at Lossiemouth was on the table. He was as mentioned before a Director of the railway company as well as the stationmaster. This makes his actions resulting in his removal from the post all the more curious.

It had come to the notice of the Board that he was augmenting his earnings by diverting parcel and goods traffic from the Morayshire to local road carriers. A commission for each package was charged by him to the respective carrier, which I assume must have been worth more to him than any dividend that the Morayshire might pay. Mr Thomas McGrigor was appointed Inspector of Company's works, and an advertisement was placed for a General Manager who was also to be stationmaster at Elgin.

Whatever else Provost Grant and his fellow Board members had achieved, it certainly appears that their people management skills were lacking. The advertisement that was placed for a new *station master* was done while Thomas Richards the incumbent was still in post. There also appears to be no reason why Mr Richards was thought to be failing in his duties. Perhaps he was being used as a scapegoat for the personnel ills that were besetting the Morayshire Railway.

On July 29th 1853 the *Elgin Courier* reported that the survey of the Perth to Inverness line had been completed. Under the new proposal a number of significant changes had taken place since the scheme that had been thrown out by the House of Lords in 1845. The main line had been shortened and the gradients made easier. A further saving would benefit the Morayshire Railway and the people of Elgin, as the line would come around by Forres to bring the people of Elgin forty miles nearer Perth than the previous scheme. All of which should increase business over the Morayshire and through the Harbour at Lossiemouth.

Wednesday, August 10th 1853 saw the anniversary of the opening of the Morayshire Railway. This was proclaimed as a general holiday in Elgin and surrounding district. As per last year all business was suspended as the population made for the coast. The day was fine, clear and sunny, with the railway beginning an hourly service from 7am. Even at this early hour all the trains were full, but not uncomfortably overcrowded. By 10am, however, business had reached such a demand that all the passenger coaches were crammed. To try to cope, several trucks fitted out with seats were brought into service. Even with this extra capacity until 2pm, each departing train left a number of disappointed passengers waiting at the station, which was virtually besieged. At 3pm the passenger traffic at the Elgin end of the line had finally become exhausted, as the bustle transferred to Lossiemouth station and continued on until the last departure at 9.30pm.

On arrival at Lossiemouth the traveller was greeted with a display of flags and banners flying from the houses and inns as well as the boats in both the old and new harbours. No arrangements had been made for Highland or other outdoor games. The only sporting activity that took place was a cricket match at Stotfield, between the Union and Mechanics clubs. The fine weather did however tempt hundreds of people onto the Firth for some pleasure sailing. In the late afternoon the various hotels, inns and eating establishments were enjoying a brisk trade looking after the numerous dinner parties.

The exact number of people who travelled to Lossiemouth that day is hard to guess. What is known is that the railway conveyed 2,325 passengers. Somewhere in the region of 400 to 500 people walked to Lossiemouth whilst around 100 were carried in some half dozen carts and gigs. Again as in the previous year, the employees of the Morayshire tended their duties in an attentive and proper manner, and no accidents occurred.

The Directors were of course in attendance and on this occasion left the throng of the day at 3pm and adjourned to the newly built Railway Hotel at Lossiemouth for a celebration dinner. Reports state that wine freely circulated during the dinner, after which the tablecloths were removed, and the tables were replenished with whisky-punch! With all that alcohol sloshing around, each successive toast became more and more self-congratulatory. In his speech Provost Grant revealed that in the first year of operation the Morayshire carried 64,000 passengers and had taken £1566 and some odd shillings in revenue. This he contended, was not only very gratifying to the shareholders, but a benefit to the community, and an example and impetus to other local undertakings.

The remainder of August and most of September passed without anything of note being recorded in the workings of the Railway Company.

Towards the end of September, on the 24th, the Board assembled for a meeting. The minor matter arising was a request from the Chairman Dr Manson, that trains should stop at Spynie Bridge to enable himself and members of his family to join or leave a train. This request was denied, with the Chairman being reminded that it was possible to board the train at the level crossing, which was only a short distance from the bridge.

Provost Grant reported on his meeting with the Post Office, regarding carrying mails on a Sunday, thereby giving the railway an excuse to run a seven day service. It was decided that there was not enough demand at present to have a service on Sunday, so this would be delayed. I think what had happened was the Post Office was unwilling to bank roll this portion of the Morayshire's operation. On a positive note the contract for the construction of the railway hotel in Elgin was signed.

The unusual circumstances surrounding staff appointments at the Morayshire Railway Company bubbled to the surface again. Thomas McGrigor who had been appointed Inspector of Company works, had a change in post. He was now to be Stationmaster at Elgin and Superintendent of Trains at the sum of 25/- per week. The soon-to-be previous Stationmaster, Mr Thomas Richards, on being told about this appointment not surprisingly found alternative employment away from the railway company. The applicant for the post of locomotive superintendent impressed the Board by informing them that he was coming at his own expense to apply in person for the job. Mr Joseph Taylor of the Scottish Central Railway was an experienced man, with as we will see an inventive turn of mind. Why he forsook a large and progressive company like the Scottish Central, which was destined to become the mighty Caledonia Railway, for the quiet backwater of the Morayshire is not explained. It may have been that he just had *"itchy feet."* His career started in Glasgow before moving to Bonnybridge in 1847 and finally to Arbroath, from where he applied for and obtained the Morayshire post, at the sum of 30/- per week.

It was vital to prevent a repeat of the problems that had occurred with William Hewitt. A proper job description was given to Thomas McGrigor on October 4th 1853, detailing exactly what his duties were and his areas of responsibility:

> In addition to the Office of the Elgin Stationmaster, the duties of which you will find in the printed regulations signed by you, you are also appointed to the Office of Superintendent of the Line, the duties of which I will describe:
>
> First- It is expected that you will be at the Station half an hour at the latest before the starting of the first train, and in a Book which will be furnished to you, you will note down the time you arrive, and see that the exact time is noted down when the following make their appearance:
>
> > The Guard.
> >
> > The Platform Porter.
> >
> > The Ticket Clerk.

The name and arrival of one of the Platelayers intimating that the line is clear.

> > The Person in charge of coals.
> >
> > The Carters and Labourers by name.

> As the line is only intended to be worked during daylight, it is expected that the Superintendent will be at his post at six a.m., while it is good daylight, and during the rest of the year at such an hour as good daylight takes place, so as that he may see the day's work fairly commenced by all at the Establishment under his charge.
>
> Before the first train leaves he is to inspect the whole of the Station apartments and see that they are clean and in working order. He is also to inspect the carriages and see that they are clean, and point to the Guard and Porters anything which appears wrong. The Inspector is also to keep regulation at the Station among the Carters and Carriers when necessary, to see that goods or effects are not laid down to form obstructions and in short to ensure that no servant of the Company neglects his duty or remains idle while there is anything to do. The Superintendent should go over the Line once or twice a day if he can spare the time returning by the immediate following train, taking note of anything that he may see wrong on the line or at the other end, co-operating with and advising the Stationmaster there, he is also to note down if the Platelayers are on the line and when working and see if fencing is defective.
>
> At night the Superintendent should see the business of the day closed and the doors of the Houses and Sheds locked. The departure and arrival of all trains must be noted down and the reasons for any delay given, all irregularities on the part of the Officers and servants of the Company or any accidents or damage occurring on the line must be reported to the Secretary without any delay.
>
> All goods arriving by train must be delivered, if for Elgin, without delay; if for the district at or above Rothes they must be forwarded to the Rothes Store. If the goods are for parties in the surrounding country, notice must be sent to the owner to call for them, that the Goods Shed may be kept clear. Charges for goods delivered should, if possible, be collected and squared up every Saturday at the latest that the weekly accounts may be closed up with as little arrears as possible.

The ticket Clerk when not engaged in selling tickets will give all possible assistance. Care must be taken that all goods arriving be properly charged and booked and that no goods be suffered to go over the Line without being charged for.

Even measured by the standards of the Victorian times, it certainly appeared that the Board of the Morayshire Railway wanted good value for their 25/-.

The final day of October 1853 saw the Annual General Meeting of the Morayshire Railway and a dividend of 5%, payable on the 10th of November, was agreed. Generous payments were also made. Provost Grant received £200 as a salary for this year, then fixed at £150 for each successive year. The rest of the Directors were also given a handsome one-off payment of £120 each for their services since the passing of the Morayshire Act in 1846. This was said to be for the number of meetings attended and expenses incurred by the Board members. In actual terms this first full year of operation would be the highlight in the amount of dividend paid, but, dear reader, do not desert the story at this point, as there are plenty of scandals to come.

No other meetings are recorded in the Morayshire's Minute Book for the remainder of 1853. Things however did happen. Mr Hewitt may well have continued to be a thorn in the side of the Morayshire, as towards the end of 1853 he left the employ of the Company under circumstances unknown. In his place came James Ross, who became known as *"Rossie of the Lossie"*, almost as much a legend as Provost Grant.

Like the previous year, the railway only operated in daylight hours with cutbacks to the timetable as winter progressed. As the New Year of 1854 came round, a massive snowstorm hit the whole of the country, causing all forms of traffic to grind or slither to a halt.

That is of course all except for the Morayshire Railway. The new locomotive superintendent Mr Joseph Taylor was keen to show the type of man he was, by designing and bringing into operation what was probably the first ever snowplough used on a railway. The following extract from the *Elgin & Morayshire Courier* explains in detail.

Sometime ago we mentioned that during the late severe snow storm the Morayshire Railway was the only line in the kingdom which was not blocked up with snow. Morayshire, as is well known, suffered as much from the storm as any other part of the county in the kingdom; nor did our local railway escape its share, for on many parts of the line the snow lay to the extent of 5 or 6 feet deep. To avoid the possibility of traffic being stopped, a very ingenious snow plough was constructed, which was found to work admirably. The plough is made in the form of a wedge, about 6 feet long and 2 feet in depth. It is attached, when in use to the front of the engine and is so fitted as to project about 12 inches beyond the rails, so as to throw the snow off the wheels of the engine. It stands about 7 inches above the rails, to avoid coming into contact with anything on the line, but is fitted with two iron plates standing about an inch above the rails, and 10 inches on each side, at the same angle as the plough, to act as scrapers. Immediately behind these plates, fixed to the guard-rails of the engine, are two brushes, which sweep the rails and leave the path of the engine perfectly clear. From the buffer beam of the engine to the point of the plough, the vacant space is covered with canvas, making it resemble the form of a house roof, which prevents any snow from getting in about the machinery of the engine. The plough, consequently, makes a clear passage for the train. On some parts of the line where the snow was lying some 5 to 6 feet deep, the train dashed through it in grand style, leaving the line behind perfectly clear, and without in the least impeding the progress of the train. From the peculiar wedge - like construction of the plough, the resistance of the snow is comparatively trifling. The credit of this excellent and useful invention is due to Mr Joseph Taylor, the locomotive superintendent of the Morayshire Railway; and when we consider the inconvenience arising from the traffic on railways being stopped, such as was the experience lately, it is but justice to the inventor and to the public to bring it under notice, believing, as we do, that its general adoption on railways would greatly lessen, if not altogether remove the inconvenience experienced by the stoppages of this invaluable mode of transit in the winter season.

I think the report was being a bit over generous in claiming that the engines dashed through a six foot snow drift in grand style. Their total weight in full working order was only 14 tons. In day-to-day service, Mr Samuels patented lightweight design engines were giving Mr Taylor plenty of work to keep him busy, as they were proving to be unreliable machines.

The heavy workload on Thomas McGrigor, the combined Elgin Stationmaster and line superintendent was also taking its toll. At a short Board meeting held on February 4th 1854 it was recorded that a new Stationmaster Mr Garron had been appointed at Elgin. Mr McGrigor was to take charge at Lossiemouth. It seems likely that he also ceased to be line superintendent.

The long awaited bus service from Elgin High Street to the railway station began operating on April 7th 1854, with the arrival of a horse drawn omnibus named *"The Union."* In the words of a correspondent for the *Elgin Courier*, *"such a convenience is much wanted and we hope it will be extensively patronised."*

From the same paper on May 17th, it appears that the fisher women of Lossiemouth were taking advantage of the Morayshire Railway. A warning notice was added to the working notices, which stated that all tickets were to be bought at Lossiemouth. These provided for a round trip to Elgin and back for 6d. It was the return portion of the journey that caused the problems, because it was forbidden for any returning fisher women to take any parcel or goods with them. They were not adhering to this rule so a stand was being made by the Company with the words. *"Any infringement of this rule will subject the party offending to the regular fare."*

The problems in keeping the *"Coffeepots"* running were concerning Mr Taylor. He put his thoughts in writing and sent this report to the Board along with some outstanding accounts for work carried out by the foundry.

This letter and the corresponding bills were first for discussion at the Board meeting of June 19th 1854. The meeting disapproved of the terms of the letter and were concerned about the high cost of the foundry bills. Their view was that Taylor's appointment should have avoided such costs. It was decided that the Chairman and the Secretary meet with Mr Taylor and explain to him that on such a small line as the Morayshire, a staff of officers cannot be justified. Flexibility was the keyword on the Morayshire, and it was to be put to Taylor whether he was the right man for the job. In plain language the Board expected Mr Joseph Taylor not only to manage and maintain the engines but to carry out the heavy repairs himself.

Money also figured in the other topic for the meeting of June 19th. It was proposed to introduce return tickets as well as changing the fare structure and goods tariffs from the 1st of July. The fare for first class was to be 1/- single, day return 1/6; second class 9d, single, day return 1/2d. This new fare put the Morayshire above the limits set by Parliament of a 1d per mile for cheap travel, therefore third class had to make an appearance on the Morayshire. These cheap trains known as Parliamentary trains, ran one trip per day. Monday to Saturday. They left Elgin at 7.30am, returning at 9am, and on Saturdays at 4pm, returning at 6.30pm. The timing for the Saturday service was done with an eye to the bathing fraternity, whilst the 7.30am weekday service was deliberately inconvenient to protect loss of income.

Whether the Chairman and the Secretary had had their meeting with Mr Taylor by the 24th of June to explain how they wished him to run the locomotive department is not clear; but on that day disaster struck the Morayshire as this report from the *"Elgin Courant"* explains:

Traffic on the Morayshire was suspended during the greater part of the day causing great disappointment to a large number of parties wishing to travel. One of the valve spindles and gearing of the working engine had given away during shunting operations at Lossiemouth. At first it was supposed that the delay would only be about an hour, but the engineer was unable to have the damage repaired until 8 o'clock in the evening. When the detention first occurred an express rider on horse back was sent off to Elgin station to announce the cause, but before he arrived the Engineer and Secretary had already left for Lossiemouth.

In the middle of June a petition backed by Provost Grant started to circulate in Elgin. This document was to be sent to the Postmaster General with the aim of persuading the Post Office to allow its Sunday letter delivery to be carried by the Morayshire Railway. Initially a large number of persons signed the petition, seeing nothing wrong in using the modern method of railways to carry their letters. However, when it occurred to the local population, the Church in particular, that the railway also intended to carry passengers, a very large backlash occurred. No doubt helped on its way by a hostile press, chief amongst them the *Elgin Courant*.

It maybe argued that to the inhabitants of Elgin, Sunday trains would be a blessing as it would enable them to have a run down to the Firth to perform ablutions for which they have not the time during the week, and admire the beauties of nature. Cleanliness is next to Godliness. To this old claptrap argument we can only say - Fudge! If the Directors really intend opening the line on a Sunday the best argument that can be urged in opposition is that religious feeling of the Community is too strong to admit such a systematic desecration.

Strong stuff, because the Sabbath at this time was strictly observed in most parts of Scotland. Food for Sunday, was prepared the day before, and no work was carried out. The Sabbath was for the serious business of church going. At the Council's meeting on Monday, June 26th, I think for the first time Provost Grant found himself with a large number of his fellow councillors against one of his ventures. The thought of the people of Elgin forsaking their church and going for a dip in the sea was too much to take. The Railway countered that it had never been the intention to offer a service to the public. In all reality the money paid by the Post Office could not have justified running a service only to carry mail. The Morayshire had been caught out by the local population who did not countenance the desecration of the Sabbath.

Still the Morayshire Railway did seem to have some form of social conscience, as from July 1st they supplied Lossiemouth with pure fresh water. This commodity was much wanted not only by the inhabitants, because there was a very limited amount of well water available to this expanding town, but also to shipping interest. This service was intended to be a temporary measure until a regular and abundant supply could be arranged. It in fact took until 1899 before a proper water supply became available to the folk of Lossie.

The only business on July 7th 1854 noted in the Minute Book was for arrangements to be made to hold Games at this year's celebration of the opening of the Morayshire Railway. The serious problems over the attempt to introduce a Sunday service, would I think have been discussed. Suffice to say on the 20th of July, Provost Grant wrote to J. Warren Esq of the General Post Office as follows:

Sir - On the part of the Railway Company, I agree to carry the mail bags between this Post - Office of this town and Lossiemouth, twice every lawful day (and on Sunday by messenger as at present), by such trains as will suit the arrivals and deliveries of the London mails and evening despatch, for the sum of sixty pounds sterling per annum - I have the honour to be, &c

James Grant, Secy

The herring fishing season began on July 13th, but due to the storms the whole of the first week's fishing was lost. In past years this would have caused big problems for the folk of Lossiemouth and Branderburgh. The railway however had helped to establish the tourist trade, and despite the poor weather, lodgings were in great demand, with the overspill being accommodated in the then separate village of Stotfield.

The Morayshire Railway was starting to run into money problems. The good news was that the mail contract was secured under the terms of Provost Grant's letter of 20th July so at least the Company was guaranteed £60 from the Postmaster. It was hoped that the problems of the Sunday trains would soon be forgotten by the public at large. Three first class season tickets at the cost of 13/6 had also been approved. The main cause for concern was a sharp drop in the number of passengers being carried following the fares increase in June. The Chairman had put his concerns about this downturn in business in a letter that was presented to the meeting. After a discussion (July 27th 1854) it was decided to restore the fares to pre - June levels. There would be no return to second class travel. From August 1st, when the new fare structure was to be introduced, the Morayshire would only offer first and third class tickets. It was resolved therefore to establish a third class carriage before the 1st of August. Should this not be possible, two divisions in the small carriage and four in the large carriage were to have the titles on their doors altered to read *"third."* The Board was to look for a permanent third class vehicle capable of holding not less than 40 passengers.

The now annual holiday to celebrate the opening of the Morayshire Railway took place on Thursday, August 10. As in the previous years all business in Elgin and Lossiemouth closed for the day with the notable exception of any that supplied food or drink in Lossiemouth. The weather was again favourable, and a train service capable carrying 600 persons at a time left Elgin every hour. In previous years it had been difficult to obtain a ticket; in this year of 1854, this was not the case. The fare increase of June had damaged the population's appetite for rail travel, coupled with serious competition from the road lobby, a Mr John Murdoch, carrier. This gentlemen had acquired a vehicle, which from its description was not unlike a covered wagon used by settlers out to conquer the wild west of America. Pulled by a team of six horses it was capable of transporting 90 people at a time to Lossiemouth. He started his service at 8am and for the privilege of using his transport he charged no fare. This gentleman, according to reports also supplied 50 carts to transport a body of *"wives and bairns,"* which would have had difficulty in making their way to the port, again gratis. His generosity meant that an additional 900 to 1000 people made their way to the coast.

The members of the Morayshire Railway Board had in the past year been instrumental in forming *"The Morayshire Association for the Encouragement of National Sports."* So it was no coincidence that its first annual meeting accorded with the Railway's celebrations. Holidays in Forres, Findhorn, Burghead, Rothes, Dufftown and Cullen encouraged people to make their way to Lossiemouth in large numbers. The steamer *"Samson"* was used by the folk of Forres, who embarked at Findhorn along with the population of that village to travel by sea to Lossie. This ship also called at Burghead. Many people from the inland portion of Moray did not use the Railway to come to Lossiemouth, preferring to make their way to the seaside on foot!

The games took place at a point to the east of Stotfield. An arena had been roped off and a grandstand capable of holding 500 people was erected at the south side of the sports field. At this temporary stadium, no less than 10,000 people congregated to witness the competitors. It had also been planned to have a series of boat races, but there were not enough participants to hold a race. The numerous tents supplying alcohol did a brisk business all day, though for those who favoured temperance the Forres Coffee Market was also doing a good trade. The day's events concluded at 6pm with the bulk of the spectators making their way home at the close of the event, using all possible means of transport to convey them.

The Directors, as in previous years, had a celebratory dinner on this occasion at Mr Brombelow's Railway Hotel Lossiemouth. Great Britain was at this point engaged in the Crimean War, therefore a large number of the toasts were for the success of Her Majesty's Forces in their enterprise against the Tsar. Prosperity was also voted to the Morayshire Sports Association, and perhaps rather surprisingly to Mr John Murdoch for fitting and supplying carts for the road transport. This gathering broke up at 10.30pm.

6 THE MORAYSHIRE RAILWAY AGAIN!

The fare reduction did not seem to have the desired effect to return the passenger levels to 1853 numbers. Road competition, as demonstrated at the line celebrations on the 10 of August, was also making inroads to the railway's business. Coal imports being brought in from Garmouth were also giving the railway's associated coal operation, which had its headquarters at 139 High Street Elgin, cause for concern. To stem any additional loss to its business, on August 11th the coal company manager Mr Charles Cranstoun announced price cuts. It is worth noting that this is the same Mr Cranstoun who was the assistant to Provost Grant the Secretary of the Morayshire Railway.

The new prices were:

Elgin	For English coal lifted at the Station	19/- per ton delivered bulk 19/6	Delivered bag 20/-
	For Scottish coal lifted at the Station	18/- per ton delivered bulk 18/6	N/A
Rothes	For English coal lifted at Rothes store	17/6 per ton delivered bulk 21/6	
Rothes	For Scottish coal lifted at Rothes store	16/6 per ton delivered bulk 20/6	

A charge of 6d per ton will be charged on all Credit deliveries.

Friday, August 17th saw the first serious accident on the line. The 9am from Lossie was approaching the station at Elgin when the "drag" mechanism used for braking failed. The engine swept past the platform, and only came to a halt by running off the rails and becoming embedded in the soft ground of the turnpike road. Fortunately for the Railway Company there were no serious injuries, though there was some difficulty in sorting out the problem. Train services did not restart until 2pm.

The rest of August, September and October passed without any troubles besetting the Morayshire Railway. That is except for the AGM held on Tuesday, October 31st. Now as we know, the Railway Company had been building hotels, one at Lossiemouth, and the other at Elgin. The newly built Elgin Station Hotel at the foot of Moss Street opposite the Company's station had not found a tenant. So unable to use this building for its AGM, the railway company returned to The Royal Hotel in the High Street.

The meeting was opened by Provost Grant, in his capacity as Company Secretary. He reported that last year the Company had been able to pay a 5% dividend. Due however to circumstances beyond the control of the Morayshire, the dividend for 1854 would be reduced. The reason given for the loss was the decision by the Harbour company to carry out improvements at the port. This resulted in it being closed to traffic from the 15th of April until the beginning of July. He went on to add:

> Irrespective of the loss sustained by the harbour operations, your Directors have reason to be satisfied with the state of revenue. In particular, since the derangement consequent on the shutting up of the harbour ceased, the passenger and goods traffic show a steady increase over the corresponding period of last year.

The dividend to be paid to an ordinary shareholder would be 2½%, payable on or after the 20th of November. The contractors who had built the line had taken £5000 worth of shares as part of their building deal, and these shares had to show a return of 5%. Therefore, there were two rates of dividend, 2½% for the citizens of the area who had invested their money in Provost Grant's scheme, and 5% for the outside contractor who had built it.

As would be expected, the good people of Moray were not pleased that they were receiving less than some outsiders. Their champion was a Mr MacBean, who challenged Provost Grant on this point. The Provost explained the situation concerning the contract, Mr MacBean countered that perhaps the

Company should buy back its shares from the Contractor, so at least all the shareholders would receive the same dividend. Provost Grant seemed a little rattled by this remark, and suggested that perhaps Mr MacBean would form a committee to oversee this transaction. A Mr Leslie came to the aid of the Provost, by suggesting that if it had not been for the contractor taking £5000 worth of shares, the line would not have been built. Ignoring this comment, Mr MacBean went on to ask about the Railway's hotels. The two hotels built in connection with the line seemed to belong to the Railway Company, whereas so far as he knew such was not the case. According to Provost Grant the hotels formed quite a different concern, the money spent upon their erection not being charged against the Company. Mr MacBean countered that if this was the case, the accounts should be kept separate, and not mixed together. The Company balance sheet showed two hotels, and yet the meeting had just been informed that they were an entirely different concern. This he did not understand. At this point Provost Grant interrupted Mr MacBean's questions by saying,

> The Railway Company could build a house and borrow money to do so without interfering with the railway funds. The hotels did not interfere with the railway at all; but if they should happen to be successful and pay a dividend of 7% on the outlay, he had no doubt they would be willingly considered as belonging to the line.

Responding to this, Mr MacBean stated that he considered the Directors were going beyond their borrowing powers. In reply the Provost said that the Directors were still within £200 of that limit. At this point the Chairman Dr Manson intervened by proposing the adoption of the three resolutions placed before the meeting: (1) Accounts along with the 2½% dividend be accepted, (2) Re-appoint the Directors, (3) Re-appoint the auditors. These three resolutions were seconded by John Grant, Esq, of Glengrant, the brother of Provost Grant and fellow shareholder. The meeting was closed.

The Press sensed a good story, in particular Mr MacBean's points which were taken up by Mr Russell the editor of the *Elgin Courant*, who was himself a holder of two shares in the Morayshire Railway. He wrote an article in the November 3rd edition of his paper that carried the report of the AGM. This seemed to stir up a hornet's nest with an extensive and personal attack from the Provost against the Courant's editor appearing in the 10th of November edition, a flavour of which follows.

> In your ignorance real or pretend, you show a wonderful dexterity in trying to make up a case to suit your view. You report that my answer to Mr MacBean's question was, the hotels formed quite a different concern, the money spent upon their erection not being charged against the Company. I made no such statement. What I said was the expenses of the hotels were kept in a separate book, and did not effect the dividend of the line. In conclusion, even your best friends are apt to conclude that you have been wilfully, blindly and deliberately ignorant.

An equally bitter letter from the Assistant Secretary also appears. As for Mr Russell, well he seems unmoved by the attack from the Morayshire.

> We think it is a pity that Mr Cranstoun should have been induced to fire off a pop gun, when the Provost was loading a 68 pounder, which in going off, has recoiled upon himself, without doing any damage to the enemy.

Some feeling of trepidation must have accompanied the Board of the Morayshire when they met on December 1st, as on the agenda was the discussion of additional buildings for the Morayshire. This time no grand hotels, just a proposal to build two gatekeeper's cottages, for the level crossings on the main turnpike at Pinefield and at Linksfield. These along with a pay increase for the staff were approved.

Argument over the hotels rumbled on with the *Elgin Courant* losing no opportunity in adding other points, like the attempt to operate a Sunday service. These exchanges did however point up some large losses in the business of the Morayshire. In 1854 there had been a reduction of 21,000 passenger journeys. Freight had shown a slight increase, but only around 1/3 of the merchants in Elgin were using the railway to carry their products, whilst all the time the number of carts on the road between Lossie and Elgin was increasing at a substantial rate.

Both the arrival of the railway from Inverness and positive suggestions from the *Elgin and Morayshire Courier* concerning the placing of the bridge over the Spey to connect with the Great North of Scotland Railway were being looked at with enthusiasm. The papers were indicating that the proposed line through Lhanbryde, Orbliston and crossing the river at Boat of Bridge should be abandoned in favour of a line along the Glen of Rothes crossing the Spey at Sworden. The reason given for this proposal was that the Glen route would serve a larger population, the land costs were less, and the river crossing would be at a narrower point. They also felt that because a greater number of people would benefit by the railway going along the Glen, it would attract a large number of shareholders.

With £1000 of the citizens of Elgin's money invested in the Morayshire, Mr Russell no doubt felt justified in returning to the attack on Provost Grant and his Board. The editor of the *Courant* had done his homework and was able to show that compared to other local public bodies, the Water, Gas and Market Companies, the salaries of the Board of Morayshire and the number of assistants and officers was way more than any comparable organisation. Perhaps not as personal in their attack as Provost Grant had been in his previous reply, but the readers of the *Courant* were left in no doubt to whom this comment referred. *"The highest paid official receives £150, but whose duties consist of slipping into a useless office in Elgin, or taking a pleasure jaunt on the line. This will not do."* He went on to close the article by assuring the good folk of Elgin that he was carrying out this crusade on their behalf.

December 13th 1854 saw the Secretary enter his *"useless office"* to compose his reply to the latest broadside from Mr Russell. Like the good politician he was, Provost Grant's response was long in length, but said little in substance. It was apparent however that he was tired of these onslaughts. In the closing sentences of his letter, he states that he will not answer to further attacks on the Railway or its management, coupled with a thinly veiled threat of Court action against the paper.

The year did come to a close on a better note for the Good Provost. He was asked to chair the meeting on December 13th, about the proposed railway line from Nairn to the Spey. The Morayshire of course had an interest in this as they hoped to use a part of this line to reach Rothes. The main concern of the prospective investors was whether the line would link the main cities of Aberdeen and Inverness. Of this the Inverness and Aberdeen Junction representatives had no doubt and they were ready to obtain the necessary Act of Parliament to build the line up to the middle section of the River Spey. At this stage in development no one had chosen the actual crossing point. The position and type of the bridge were to be decided by the famous railway engineer Isambard Kingdom Brunel. The necessary maps of the area were in his possession. The local representative of the Great North of Scotland Railway, a Mr Brown of Linkwood, was not so forthcoming about his railway's part in this new venture. Even so with the redoubtable Provost James Grant in the chair, by the close of the meeting it looked as though the missing portion of railway between Aberdeen and Inverness would soon be filled in.

The Morayshire Railway certainly liked its gadgets, and at the beginning of 1855 a new patent for the coupling and uncoupling of railway carriages and wagons was lodged and accepted by the Patent Office. The following information comes from a pamphlet published by an E D Chattaway of the North British Railway in 1855:

> A novel mode of coupling railway carriages and wagons has been recently introduced by Messrs. Taylor and Cranstoun, on the Morayshire Railway. Its general features are described as follows-

> Each carriage or wagon, in addition to draw hooks, has attached to it three parallel - jointed engaging chain - links freely hinged, so as to be capable of being raised or lowered at pleasure. These links are made with a central back stop - joint, in such manner, that whilst

A view of Elgin station in 1855, with both locomotives in evidence. To the front of the picture is the engine heating house, opposite the goods warehouse and in the distance the station. (*Courtesy The Moray Council*)

FIG. 1.

Scale

LONDON: Printed by George Edward Eyre and William Spottiswoode.
Printers to the Queen's most Excellent Majesty. 1855.

they will act with all necessary flexibility when drawing or being shifted in certain directions, yet, when lifted by the elevating lever, they will rise in a rigid condition, as if solid. A transverse coupling or elevating shaft is disposed in bearings beneath each set of links this shaft having upon it a lever frame piece, with stud projections thereon, for the purpose of giving the lift to the links. Each end of the shaft carries a hand lever conveniently disposed for the hand of the attendant, so that when passing along the train he can quickly lift or lower the links, holding pins being provided for setting the levers at the required point. When the wagons are to be coupled the attendant passes along either side of the train and removes the holding pin the links then drop and the necessary engagement is thus instantly effected. When the wagons are to be uncoupled the attendant lifts the links clear off the hooks, by simply pressing down the hand lever, and either allows the links to drop to the vertical position when the wagon is removed, or, by inserting the holding pin, the links are fixed in a position for coupling when the wagons are brought together. Carriages are coupled or uncoupled in the same manner as the wagons, with the exception that the centre or draw link requires to be tightened up, after the carriages are coupled, to bring them closely together, and slackened off sufficiently when they are uncoupled. To effect this a transverse hand wheel shaft is fitted upon the carriage frame; the centre of this shaft having upon it a worm gearing with a worm wheel set in a longitudinal nut link of the draw hook spindle. Hence by turning one or the other of the hand - wheels, the draw - link is tightened or slackened as required.

The *Elgin Courant* was also enthusiastic.

This paper has no doubt that the device designed by Mr Taylor and Mr Cranstoun will be universally adopted thereby repaying the exertions of the two spirited and ingenious patentees who deserve the thanks of Railway Companies and the public at large.

What is of interest to us is that both the pamphlet and the newspaper refer to the two gentlemen as being joint inventors of this device. Mr Taylor, an experienced engineer and the person who had constructed the Morayshire's snowplough, would probably have been the main designer of this device. Mr Cranstoun had worked on other railways, but more on the administration side. It is therefore a surprise that when you check the actual Patent No 2372, there is no mention of Mr Taylor. It appears that when or if another railway company used this device, the only person to benefit would have been Mr Cranstoun. Poor old Mr Taylor. Not only had he lost his staff and been made to carry out all the repairs on the Morayshire himself, but the Secretary's assistant cheated him of any money he could have made from a device he designed.

Trouble never seemed to be far away for the Morayshire at this point in its career. At the Board meeting of February 10th 1855, the outcome of an accident at Lossiemouth caused by a crane not being secured to the track was the only item on the agenda. The Lossiemouth stationmaster Mr McGrigor was deemed to be at fault for the damage valued at £15-12-4d. The Directors decided that Mr McGrigor should pay half the amount of the repair costs, on the distinct understanding that should he not accept this, the Company would hold him liable for the full amount. Ten days later the Board reconvened and the settlement with Mr McGrigor re the accident at Lossiemouth was agreed on the above terms.

Money and loans again returned to the fore in the meeting of February 20th. An office for the Stationmaster at Elgin was required. It was decided to add a building at the east end of the goods shed. To construct the office would require what seems rather a large amount of money - £1000. Despite all the problems caused in the previous year by the cash borrowed to build the hotels, it would seem the Board were now exceeding their own limit of £200 as discussed at the AGM of 1854. The members of the Board approved this expenditure without consulting the shareholders. I wonder if Mr MacBean's ears were burning that day?

The locomotives continued to give Mr Taylor problems, and it had been reported to the Board on March 16th that several springs had broken on the engines. The fault on this occasion was blamed on the track. No respite for Mr Taylor though, as the Board instructed him to oversee the platelayers in bringing the line up to standard. Seven days later the extension of the Morayshire's network was considered. Improvements at the harbour had resulted in an increase in shipping. There was a need therefore for additional siding space to accommodate more rolling stock, and on March 23rd a tender was considered for the laying of rails on the new quays at Lossiemouth.

Staff problems arose again on April 27th. The Stationmaster at Elgin was failing to discharge his duties properly, due in some part to ill health. A successor was to be found for this position. In addition, problems with Mr McGrigor at Lossiemouth were also reported to the meeting, though no decision on his future was made.

The 4th of May 1855 saw notice of the official end of second class service on the Morayshire Railway, as described in the following extract:

> In compliance with the wishes of several parties the Directors established first, second, and third class passenger trains during last year: but now find from experience that the wants of the Community do not require such to continue. Notice is hereby given that on 10th May there will be only two classes. The fares for which will be First Class 9d, 3rd Class 6d. Return First Class 1/6 3rd Class 1/-

> From the above date cheap trains will run on Saturday commencing with afternoon 2pm train from Elgin and 3pm train from Lossiemouth at half price.

> **Note** Fisherwomen 8d return same day.

At the Board meeting on May 26th 1855, Mr Cranstoun was appointed Manager of the Morayshire Railway, the question of salary to be decided at the Company AGM in October. The funds required to build the office for the Stationmaster at Elgin had been secured. The Caledonia Bank would lend the £1000 at 4½%, security for half the amount being offered by Mr Grant of Ballindalloch.

The decision of the Great North of Scotland Railway on its chosen way to reach the town of Elgin was given to The Morayshire Board on July 25th. They were not going through the Glen of Rothes, but sticking to the route they had decided on way back in July 1846, reaching Elgin by way of Orton. Provost Grant therefore had to make an approach to his old adversary Mr Inglis of Edinburgh. Mr Inglis looked after the affairs of the Earl of Fife, and as it was the Morayshire's aim to have a presence on Speyside they would need the support of the Earl's Commissioner to achieve this.

Another member of the aristocracy was spelling possible trouble for the Morayshire and its expansion plans. At the other side of the Moray Firth the Duke of Sutherland had invested money at Littleferry, by Dornoch to provide a cross firth service to the harbour at Burghead. This service had been running for some time. The Morayshire had tapped into this with a horse drawn omnibus from Burghead to Lossiemouth to encourage passengers to use the railway service from Lossiemouth to Elgin. The builders of the proposed railway between Nairn and Keith, which at this stage was the Great North of Scotland Railway, intended to build a branch line from the harbour at Burghead to the main Aberdeen - Inverness line. This action threatened not only the Morayshire Railway, but also the Harbour Company, and the investment made by the Elgin Town Council in both these enterprises. The citizens of Forres however saw that a branch line from Burghead could have a possible advantage to themselves as this following excerpt from the *Forres Gazette* of 1st August explains:

> We understand that the Town Council passed a resolution against the proposed branch of the GNSR to Burghead. The Directors of the Harbour Company at their meeting on Saturday also passed a similar resolution. The Town Council of Elgin has £3000 invested in the

Harbour and £1000 invested in the Railway. It is feared that if this branch is built both the above operations will be swamped. This Paper claims that this is too narrow and selfish a view to take of this most important undertaking. The great objective of having a branch to Burghead is to connect the opposite District of Caithness and Sutherland with the South. That object can never be obtained by the Morayshire Railway and the Harbour Company. The East wind for a considerable part of the winter prevents steamers from approaching or discharging cargoes; whereas at Burghead with the contemplated improvements vessels can enter or leave in all states of wind or tide. The fears of the proprietors of the Morayshire Railway and Harbour Company prospecting the ruin of their property are groundless. The present local traffic will remain and surely that will suffice. Burghead and Burghead alone as the Romans many days ago found out is the only point on this Coast for a universally serviceable harbour. Any resolution to the contrary is as futile as protesting against the East wind!

Before the Board of the Morayshire could defend itself against the criticism from the *Forres Gazette*, they found themselves under fire from an unexpected source. On August 3rd, the Free Synod of Moray launched an attack on the Morayshire Railways Anniversary Highland Games that were due to be held on August 8th. Their argument was that when a large number of people meet together *"moral breakdown in all its disgusting forms occur."* A surprise champion Mr Russell of the *Elgin Courant* appeared in the Morayshire's corner. He wrote a satirical article against the Synod.

Nothing in the scriptures show that out - door sports are sinful. What is it that condemns them? Eating leads to Gluttony, drinking to drunkenness, beneficence to prodigality; religious sorrow to melancholy madness. In plain language all virtues lead to vices and end in misfortune. Out door sports are a detrimental to Moravia.

The Board met on August 4th 1855. The prospectus of the Inverness and Aberdeen Junction Railway had just been published and what it contained gave cause for concern to the Morayshire Railway. A subcommittee from the Morayshire was appointed to meet with the Provisional Committee of the I&AJR to make their views known in respect of the changes in the prospectus.

The Morayshire had given their support to the Inverness and Aberdeen in the previous year of 1854 on the basis that its line was to run by Rothes, and most importantly that the Morayshire was to be the only outlet to the sea. What was now being proposed in 1855 was that their route would now avoid Rothes, and like the plans of the GNSR descried previously, the I&AJR had a branch to the Coast.

Support for the I&AJR would be forthcoming from the Morayshire only if it accepted the proposed Morayshire line from Orton to Craigellachie, along with a proper arrangement for the Morayshire to use the Inverness and Aberdeen Junction's line between Elgin and Orton to access its inland portion to Rothes and Craigellachie. In addition, the proposed branch line to the sea should be postponed until the usefulness of the Lossiemouth line was demonstrated

The Moray Synod appeared to have friends in high places as the day of the Highland Games, Wednesday the 8th of August, dawned foggy and very rainy. At one point it was feared that the Games would not go ahead, as in the words of one reporter. *"Through the thick scotch mist which is well known to wet an Englishman through to the skin not a blow of an artisans hammer was to be heard and the town had all the appearance of a Sabbath."* This was the complete opposite of previous years when Elgin had been a buzz of excitement. The train that left at 9am for Lossiemouth did not require the addition of trucks fitted out with seats. Road traffic was also down on 1854, which had seen up to 80 carts and gigs set off for Lossiemouth. This year however only a few brave pedestrians plodded through the rain to the coast. By 10am the Games site at Lossie looked thinly attended. A German band struck up at 11am in an attempt to raise spirits as the sports events started. However, by midday the weather started to clear and the railway began serious business. The train of three carriages was strengthened by the addition of twelve trucks, as up to 500 people at a time made their way to Lossiemouth. Patrons for the sports also made appearances from as far away as Dufftown, Strathspey, Forres and Cullen. These folk used an assortment of horse drawn transport to get them to Lossiemouth. Total attendance at the field numbered somewhere between 5000 - 6000. The covered stand area took £21-10/-, which was only a little down on the previous year's total of £27-17/-.

The event's organisers were Lt Tod Brown of the Athletics Association and our old friend Mr Cranstoun of the Morayshire Railway Company. The games ran until 5pm, marred a little by the report that the spectators thought that too much time was spent on caber tossing and hammer throwing, and not enough on highland dancing.

What about the Morayshire Railway? Well, it carried 3000 people to Lossiemouth and back without incident. Once again the staff discharged their duties in a professional manner. Possibly this encouraged Mr Russell to have another go at the Moray Synod in his report of the day's proceedings in the *Courant* of 10th August. *"The good and orderly conduct of all present was highly creditable to the morality of the district and was the best answer to those guardians of public morals who would lay an interdict on all assemblies of the populace, from a fear that a flagrant misconduct might ensue."*

Whether the Board's time had been taken up on self congratulations that no major catastrophe or riot had occurred at the Morayshire celebratory Highland Games, is not recorded in the Minute Book. What is apparent was their seeming lack of urgency to meet with the Inverness and Aberdeen Junction Railway to ensure that the Morayshire's line to Lossiemouth was the only route to the coast. The Board met on September 7th and the only point of discussion was that the subcommittee had still to meet the I&AJR Provisional Committee.

By the time of the next Board get together on October 1st, contact with the I&AJR and the problems with sea access had still not been sorted. Problems at Lossiemouth were on the agenda, but this referred to troubles with the various shipping lines using the port. It appears that there were frequent complaints about the handling and transhipment of goods. In an effort to resolve matters, the Morayshire Board proposed to give traffic equally to the Aberdeen, Leith & Clyde Shipping Company and the North of Scotland Steam Packing Company where goods were not specifically assigned to a carrier.

Preparations for the AGM were being made. The Capital Account was nearly closed, so Provost Grant decided to stand down as Company Secretary. The proposal before the Board was that along with being General Manager, Mr Cranstoun should also become the Company Secretary.

There was still no meeting with the Inverness & Aberdeen Junction Provisional Committee by October 15th 1855. However, the Board did resolve at this date to carry out a survey of the line from Orton to Craigellachie.

The AGM was held on Wednesday, October 31st, at the Gordon Arms Hotel. The Chairman was unavailable for the meeting so on the motion of Provost Grant, one of the other Directors a Mr William Topp took the chair for this meeting. The Accounts were given as follows:

> Your Directors express their regret that owing to the harbour being partially closed up for 4 months the traffic for that period was considerably affected.

> Your Directors are glad to say that apart, the circumstances for traffic continue to improve and several arrangements have been made which will lessen expenses.

Accounts from last years balances	£ 133- 8- 9½
Amount to revenue for past year added	£3529-16- 3½
	£3663- 5- 1
Working expenses fue duties, etc.	£2267- 0- 5
Leaving a surplus of	£ 396- 4- 8

Your Directors recommend that a dividend of 2% should be declared on the capital of the Company £29,700 less the portion held by the Contractor £5000, the interest of which is included in the expenditure revenue.

2% on £24,700	£ 494- 0- 0
	£ 396- 4- 8
	£ 98- 4- 8 Balance

The Dividend is payable on or after the 20th of November.

David Davidson and John Grant were re-elected to the Board. A vacancy had arisen due to the death of John Walter, and he was replaced by Provost Grant who had stood down as Secretary. The post as Secretary as mentioned earlier fell to Mr Cranstoun, who was also confirmed as Manager, with the Salary for this combined post fixed at £100 per annum. The Directors awarded themselves £50 each for the services they had provided over the previous two years! Patrick Duff remained as the Company Auditor. Considering the problems that occurred at the 1854 AGM, pertaining to the reduction in dividend payments and the moneys paid to Directors, it passed with no comment this year. This can possibly be explained by the fact that there was a very poor turnout for the 1855 AGM, with Directors far outnumbering ordinary shareholders.

The motion to instruct the Directors to secure support of the proprietors and the public of Moray *"for making the interior section of the Morayshire Railway"* was proposed by Provost Grant. This was unanimously agreed to, spurred on perhaps by promises from the Provost that when complete this portion of the line would double the revenue, whilst the working expenses would be very little affected. An enquiry from Bailie Robert Jeans as to the projected cost and length of the line, was answered by Provost Grant, who informed him that the outlay would be £5000 per mile with the distance being approximately five miles from Orton to Rothes.

Just when the Provost thought that the meeting was going all his way, his protagonist from last year Mr MacBean gave his thoughts to the meeting. He considered that the increase in working expenses would be greater than expected, as a station would have to be provided at Orton. The Provost made no comment on this observation. He did go on however to introduce another motion to the meeting, which concerned the Hotel at Elgin, the very stick that Mr MacBean had used to beat the Provost with at last year's AGM. Provost Grant went on to report.

> It was a matter of great importance to the Directors, in fixing their station at Elgin, that its situation should induce the Directors of the Great North of Scotland Railway to fix their station at the same spot. With this in mind, the Directors of the Morayshire, had built a hotel, and the object in building it had been to some extent accomplished, for the provisional committee of the Inverness and Aberdeen Junction had fixed their station at the same spot, thus realising the object in view. It had however occurred to the Directors that the Hotel would be better in the hands of one or a few individuals, than those of the Company.

The agreed price for sale of the hotel was not to be less than it had cost to build. Also up for sale was the land opposite to the hotel known as the old Foundry. Part of the condition of sale for this was that nothing would be built on that land that would detract from the hotel.

On hearing this proposal, Mr MacBean remarked that he had always thought that it was a mistake to build the hotel, and he was happy to think that it was to be sold. He then went on to propose a vote of thanks to Mr Topp for his conduct in the Chair, thereby ending the meeting.

Oddly there had been no attempt by the Morayshire Board to meet with the Inverness and Aberdeen Junction before the AGM to resolve the matter of the proposed branch line to Burghead. Equally strange, the threat to the traffic on the Morayshire's line by the I&AJ's intention to build a line to Burghead had not been discussed at the AGM. This matter was certainly in the public domain, with exchanges of letters in the press, arguing the relevant merits of the harbours at Lossiemouth and Burghead. It was not until November 6th 1855 that Provost Grant travelled to Inverness to meet with the I&AJR, almost three months to the day after the formation of the Morayshire's subcommittee that was to sort out this matter.

At this meeting Provost Grant was not only representing the Railway, but acting on behalf of the Harbour Company, other interested traders, and the Town Council. Assembled at the other side of the desk were promoters of the Inverness and Aberdeen Junction Railway, who represented a sizeable chunk of the House of Lords, in the form of The Most Noble the Marquis of Bath, the Earl of Seafield and the Duke of Sutherland.

What Provost Grant had to offer was that, if the line to Burghead was omitted from the I&AJ's plans, the interests in Elgin that he represented would provide half the capital required to establish a good and sufficient daily steamer service from Littleferry to Lossiemouth. Pending completion of further improvements to the harbour at Lossie, in the event of poor weather the ferry could call at Burghead. The other half of the sum required would come from the other parties wishing to establish this service.

The Duke of Sutherland was already running a vessel that ran to Burghead three days a week. To take account of this fact, Provost Grant had a second proposal. If preferred the Duke of Sutherland could hire or guarantee a steamer to run a daily service; in this event the interests represented by the Provost would pay half the charge. Any liability to loss that the Duke might have been exposed to would be limited to a fixed amount. The commencement date for this service would be the spring of 1856.

The Inverness and Aberdeen Junction Railway liked what they heard. Before their meeting with Provost Grant, they had read through the prospectus of the Lossiemouth Harbour Company. In view of the improvements to be made to the harbour entrance to make it accessible in all weathers, the Committee of the Inverness and Aberdeen Junction Railway resolved to abandon their line to Burghead. Another factor that aided the decision of the I&AJ was an assurance that they had received from the Town of Nairn that their harbour was to be extended and improved. If there was a disagreement with the Morayshire, the service from Littleferry could be switched at short notice to Nairn.

This agreement was promoted as a triumph by Provost Grant at a meeting of the Elgin Town Council. In reality the Town Council of Elgin, the Lossiemouth Harbour Board and the Morayshire Railway Company would be exposed to potential high costs if the cross-firth ferry operation failed, whilst the Inverness and Aberdeen Junction Railway had little to lose.

All was not quite well with the deal, as Mr Milne of the Great North of Scotland Railway raised an objection to the loss of the line to Burghead. On this occasion this matter was not resolved by Provost Grant, but left to Mr Bruce of the Inverness and Aberdeen Junction Railway to smooth over.

On December 21st 1855 the Board approved the drafting of a Parliamentary Bill for the construction of the inland portion of the Morayshire railway from Orton to Rothes and Craigellachie. The necessary letter to the Commercial Bank to obtain the funds for the parliamentary deposit was also approved.

New Year 1856 opened with a letter of complaint from Mr Cranstoun, now the Secretary and Manager of the Morayshire, which had been sent to the *Times*, with a copy to the *Elgin Courant*. Despite now earning a salary of £100 per year, it appeared that Mr Cranstoun wanted to see his fortune increase by encouraging railway companies to use the coupling device that he had taken out the patent on.

Under the guise of promoting railway safety and cutting the time taken to couple up trains, he claimed adoption of the system under test on the Morayshire would save 50 railway workers lives per year, and 1000 hours daily in making up trains! Information on this device had been sent to various railway companies, in particular the London and North Western Railway, the Board of Trade, and the Railway Clearing House. What appeared to be upsetting Mr Cranstoun was not that all the railway companies had ignored the device, it was the that the Board of Trade did think it was worthy of inspection and would do as it was claimed and save lives. Some 25 railwaymen were killed and 15 injured in 1854, whilst coupling trains.

The Board of Trade confirmed their interest in this device on May 15th 1855, with the promise that Colonel Yolland would travel to the Morayshire Railway to see it in operation. Why therefore, the letter of complaint to the *Times*? Well, at the close of the year the Board of Trade had not kept their word. No, officer had come to look at the coupling mechanism. In concluding his correspondence, he asks that the safety of railway staff should be put before profit, of course in no way being influenced by the profit he would have made from the payments for use of the patent.

This matter off his chest, Mr Cranstoun returned his thoughts to the Morayshire Railway and the way to improve its profits. He set his sights on the potato traffic by charging a price of 2/3d per ton and guaranteed all produce would be entirely secure of damage whilst in transit from Elgin to Lossiemouth. A report in the Courant of February 22nd shows that on that day 22nd the "Jane & Mary" sailed for London with 100 tons of potatoes, 160 tons left on the "Braes O' Moray" for Dublin, and 89 tons were bound for Liverpool on the "Moray."

At the Board meeting on February 27th 1856 it was reported that traffic had increased for the half year by £131-17s-11d over the same period last year. So it appears Mr Cranstoun was making his mark.

The Chairman Provost Grant had been to London to conclude an agreement with the Inverness and Aberdeen Junction Railway Provisional Committee on running powers. The agreement was sealed and forwarded to London for completion.

All was not going smoothly with the plans for the new railways. The I&AJ had refused to give compensation to the Road Trustees along the proposed route, creating opposition to their line and the Morayshire's extension. The Morayshire Board felt confident that they could come to an agreement with the Road Trustees.

There was better news for Mr Cranstoun on the earning potential of "*his*" invention. A decision to fit these couplings to all new stock and any existing stock not already fitted was taken by the Morayshire Board. It appears from the Minute Book that the Board was under the impression that Mr Taylor was the inventor. Extra rolling stock in the form of two 8 ton wagons and a carriage capable of carrying 50 passengers in one, first and four third class, compartments were required. The Morayshire resolved to build the wagons themselves and seek a price from an outside contractor for the coach.

On April 4th 1856 an increase of staff was authorised with an advertisement appearing for an intelligent clerk, and a well-educated youth as an apprentice clerk. For both posts a "liberal" salary "will be given."

Ten days later, on April 14th, the Board sanctioned the addition of a siding at the crossing at Linksfield. The decision to build the two 8 ton wagons was cancelled in favour of a straight purchase from Hendry Brothers in Glasgow.

There were two Board meetings in May, the first on the 12th. At this it was decided to revise the rates for goods handling. It appears a lesson had been learned from the passenger fare increase of 1854. Many of the rates for goods were lowered. Potatoes in particular saw a reduction in price of 3d. The trucks used to handle this traffic was a form of hopper wagon. On arrival at Lossiemouth the cargo was discharged from the underside. Included in the 2/- per ton price was not only the loading, transportation and unloading but also the use of a chute or "conduct" as it was known to load the crop into the hold of the vessel. It was this form of mechanised handling that gave the Morayshire the confidence to claim that potatoes could be transported direct from Elgin to the hold of a ship without damage.

On May 16th 1856, discussion took place on providing a tug at Lossiemouth harbour for assisting the movement of shipping in the harbour and the loading of goods. This seemed a curious matter for the

Railway Company to discuss, as the movement of traffic within the harbour should really be in the realm of the Harbour Board. A decision on this matter was deferred for the time being.

On the Thursday, May 29th a general holiday was declared to allow the population to enjoy a day of boat racing at Lossiemouth. The Railway Company provided a 30 minute service beginning at 8am from Elgin. That day also saw the first official night service on the line, provided for people travelling to Elgin to witness a "Grand" firework display that started at 9pm. To accommodate the expected crowds making their way home after this event, trains ran to Lossiemouth until 11.30pm.

An EGM was held on June 9th 1856 at the Gordon Arms Hotel to approve the Morayshire Extension, and Inverness and Aberdeen Junction Railway Bills. Provost Grant took the Chair. The meeting was required by the standing orders of the House of Lords and was just a formality to approve the two railway bills. He read the notice calling the meeting and went on to read the bills, after which he commented on the principal clauses. Provost Grant moved that both bills be adopted, remarking that when the railways were completed they would be a lasting benefit to the North of Scotland. Mr Topp of Inverlochty seconded the Morayshire bill, with Mr John Grant, Glengrant seconding the I&AJ bill. The seals of the companies were affixed to the Minutes and the meeting closed.

The Morayshire Board met later the same day, with the question of a tug for Lossiemouth harbour again being on the Agenda. This vessel it appears was to be more than just a tug and would be expected to ply to the opposite ports on the Firth. Again as lovers of gadgets the Board suggested that the vessel be fitted with Samuel's patented Expansion Steam Engine, with which it would save an expected 50% in fuel. Decision on this matter was deferred, perhaps helped by the fact that the expected cost for this ship was in the region of £2250.

On Wednesday, June 11th a severe gale hit the area, causing problems for the Edinburgh steamer. The "Queen" called at Lossiemouth where, due to the improvements carried out by the Harbour Board, she had no problem in landing its passengers and cargo. Trouble was met at Burghead however; the "Queen" was not able to enter the harbour and the pilot craft sent out to collect passengers and cargo similarly could not return to Burghead. Both vessels had to make for Hopeman where the passengers, etc, were disembarked, a sign of the poor quality of the deal that the Morayshire Board had made with the I&AJ over the abandoning of their branch to Burghead.

The arrival of the wagons ordered from Hendry Boot was reported to the Board meeting of 14th of July 1856. Mountings had also been bought from this firm to allow the Morayshire to build its own wagons, the first of which was complete. The subject of the Elgin hotel was also discussed. No purchaser had come forward, so the Chairman of the Morayshire Provost Grant offered to buy the hotel and the land opposite at actual cost.

Mr Cranstoun's innovations continued on the Morayshire as on August 1st he introduced "periodical tickets," a form of season ticket that gave unlimited travel over the line for anywhere between one to three months. The cost of was as follows:

Period	1st Class	3rd Class
1 month	19/6	3/-
2 months	32/6	1/8
3 months	39/-	26/-

The price for disposal of the Elgin hotel was agreed by the Board on August 11th for the sum of £2020.

August the month in which the Morayshire celebrated its opening. In 1856 this event took place on the 20th. Now someone once said that a week was a long time in politics. Things do not move that fast in the world of railways; however in the reporting of the line's anniversary, things had turned against the railway. The tentative position of support it had from the press last year, had turned to a full-blooded attack in this year of 1856. *"A shilling for a twelve mile ride in a truck being no great encouragement for any working man to visit the gathering at Stotfield common,"* wrote one reporter. What of the opinion of the general population? Well the first trains of the day were not heavily loaded. By the 10am service, the coaches had to be strengthened by the addition of ten trucks. The traffic on the turnpike road between Elgin and Lossiemouth was also busy with all form of carts and gigs. For those who could not pay for transport *"shanks nagie"* took them to the sports field at Stotfield.

On arrival at the ground it was noticed that there was a lack of adult spectators, one reporter recording a crowd of some two hundred unaccompanied children! He feared that whole affair would be a complete failure. The answer to where all the adults were was to be found in the large number of refreshment tents. Our reporter friend goes on to record: *"Some dirty rags and rotten sticks formed showrooms and on a stage some ladies were dancing and a miserable looking man begrimed in soot, representing a man of colour was intended to be an object of attraction. It is time that such moral nuisances were put down."*

The Highland Games though less well attended, did take account of last year's complaint with more time now being spent on "the Highland Dancing" rather than the heavy events. All went well until the end of the Games, when a minor drunken riot broke out, in which one man was seriously injured and others described in the language of the time, *"had the bark peeled from their faces."*

As ever the arrangements made by the staff on the Morayshire Railway were complete and all the coming and goings of the excursion trains were carried out efficiently. The press of course could not resist making a final dig. *"The number taking advantage of rail travel would have been greater had fares been reduced, which we hope will be the case next season."*

On September 8th Provost Grant gave details of how he intended to pay for the Elgin hotel and the ground opposite. He would take over responsibility for £1200 of the Morayshire's debit and pay the balance of £820 in cash. The Board were to consider this offer.

In his capacity as Chairman of the Morayshire, Provost Grant had a meeting on October 15th with the contractors of the Inverness and Aberdeen Junction Railway. His intention was to secure the delivery of their plant and material through the harbour at Lossiemouth and along the Morayshire Railway to Elgin.

The Annual General Meeting of the Morayshire was held on October 31st 1856 at the Gordon Arms Hotel in Elgin. It was reported that the goods traffic was up on that of the previous year, but as the rates had been reduced there was no major increase in profit. The dividend for 1856 was 2% on the capital of the Company which would be paid on the 20th of December.

Provost Grant then gave a report on the extension of the Morayshire Railway to Craigellachie. He explained that the construction on this new line would not start until the I&AJR had constructed their line up to the point at Orton where the Morayshire intended to have their junction. As it would only take six months to construct the Morayshire's inland portion to Craigellachie, it was proposed to have both lines begin service on the same day. The various arrangements that he had made with the I&AJR's contractor for the landing of iron and masonry were also mentioned. In conclusion, Provost Grant was confident that when the inland portion of the Morayshire was in operation the profits for the company's shareholders *"would be greatly added to."*

Possibly in anticipation of the increase in traffic to be brought about by the construction of the line to Craigellachie, the Board discussed and examined sketches of a third class carriage on November 8th. It was proposed that rather than purchasing it from an outside contractor, it could be built by their own staff a move that I am certain would please Mr Taylor. With goods traffic on the line still increasing, it was also decided to build two additional open-ended goods trucks.

Permission to progress with the construction of the coach, at a cost of £135 was given at the Board meeting of December 8th. The two trucks on the other hand were to be bought from an outside supplier.

On Monday the 15th a slight accident occurred when the 11am train from Lossiemouth came up a few minutes early. The gatekeeper had been assisting with work at the Engine house and had not returned to open the gates at Maisondieu. Consequently they were smashed to pieces by the train. Other than the loss of the gates, no other damage was sustained.

The Contractors for the Inverness and Aberdeen Junction Railway cut their first turf at the cross roads near Linkwood on December 26th 1856. At this point on their line a bridge was being constructed. Work was also about to start at Orton. Reports in the *Elgin Courier* suggest that little progress could be expected to be made during the winter, but with the arrival of spring the contractor would push on with spirit. It was also noted that the Morayshire Railway was being used to land iron and stone for the building of the I&AJR.

7 A MOST MELANCHOLY OCCURRENCE

The New Year of 1857 started badly for Mr Cranstoun he was summoned to appear before the Board of the Morayshire Railway on January 12th. What was giving the Board cause for concern was the behaviour of some of the carters employed to shift goods into the town of Elgin and the Rothes store. It was Mr Cranstoun job as Manager to keep order and ensure that the transhipment of goods went smoothly, but he was failing in this capacity. More damaging to him was that he had used inappropriate language in his dealings with a Mr Allan, a corn merchant and one the railway's largest customers. This resulted in Mr Allan ceasing all his business with the Morayshire. The Board lectured Mr Cranstoun on the powers and responsibility of his position. At the end of the lecture Mr Cranstoun placed his letter of resignation on the table and left the employ of the Morayshire Railway Company. No one seemed concerned with Mr Cranstoun's departure and they went on to discuss a proposal to lay sidings into the quarries at Lossiemouth!

The Morayshire ran without a Secretary and Manager until March 11th 1857, when Mr Topp, one of the Directors, filled the post. This gave him time to sort out matters for the EGM of 9th April for the necessary authorisation required to construct the inland portion of the Morayshire from Orton to Craigellachie. At that meeting, consent was given for the building of this line with 330 individuals applying for shares totalling £12,030. The only minor problem was a concern from the Board of Trade regarding the placing of a level crossing at Orton. That small matter aside, to all intents and purposes, the way was now clear for the Morayshire to fulfil its original ambition of 1846 to connect Rothes and its surrounding district with the sea.

The unreliability of the Morayshire's engines continued to keep Mr Taylor busy. On Thursday 23rd April, he had completed repairs on one of the engines. Along with his nephew William Forsyth, who was also his apprentice engineer, they decided to give the newly-repaired locomotive a test run. A fireman made the crew numbers up to three. With the other engine not due to make its return from Lossiemouth for another hour, they set off at full speed towards Lossiemouth. Mr Taylor stopped the engine just passed the Oakenhead bridge, where for 15 minutes he oiled the motion and checked the valves. Seeing that all was in order he moved off towards Lossiemouth; but had not gone more than 100 yards to where there was a sharp curve in the line. At this point he met the other locomotive that was propelling an empty truck at full speed on its way to collect ballast for one of the ships in the harbour. It appears the driver of this engine had the presence of mind to let off steam from his locomotive. According to press reports Mr Taylor *"seems to have become completely paralysed"* and did nothing to lessen the collision. His engine struck the truck, smashing it to pieces and lifting the wreckage of it onto his locomotive. One of the buffers of the truck struck Mr Taylor, killing him instantly. The other parts of the truck hit the young lad giving him severe bruising to his legs and other injuries. The fireman received cuts to his face and a broken ankle from the debris of the truck, and was also scalded from the escaping steam of his engine. The locomotive that had been driven by Mr Taylor was badly damaged, its tender smashed to pieces. Those on the other engine, five in all, escaped unhurt.

Mr Taylor's body, the injured boy and the fireman were carried to Lossiemouth from where medical assistance was summoned from Elgin. No fewer than three doctors, Dr Paul, Dr Ross and Dr Duff, along with Provost Grant and fellow Morayshire Board member Mr Leslie, arrived shortly after the collision.

Poor old Mr Taylor-he deserved a better fate. By all accounts not only was he a fine engineer, and an inventor of various railway devices, he was also an amiable and well-respected figure in the community. The press reports of the accident again refer to the coupling mechanism, which they credit to him, suggesting that it was about to be adopted by several of the largest railway companies of the time. This did not occur and the coupling device became a mere footnote in British Railway history. At the time of his death, Mr Taylor's wife was expecting their tenth child. Life had also been hard on her, having lost four of these children in infancy.

The collision of both its locomotives and the death of an employee necessitated a full Board meeting on Friday 24th April 1857. The engineering cutback forced on Mr Taylor by the Board on June 19th 1854 now had its consequences. The Morayshire Railway Company had no other qualified engineers in its employment. To repair the damaged locomotive would take the services of Neilson & Co, Glasgow, the machine's original builders. The Morayshire Board could be thankful that the other locomotive was undamaged in the collision, so at least a service could be maintained.

The remains of Mr Taylor were conveyed to Elgin Cathedral for burial on Saturday 25th April. A large number of the citizens of Elgin turned out to show their respects for the deceased. The Railway Company suspended services for a few hours, cancelling the 2pm service to Lossiemouth. The complete work force of the railway company walked in front of the hearse, with the Directors following immediately behind the coffin and chief mourners. He was laid to rest in lair EC1014 within the Cathedral grounds, alongside one of his sons, Henry.

On a favourable note the young apprentice William Forsyth was not as seriously hurt as first feared, and was by the Saturday showing good signs of recovery.

It appears that Mr Cranstoun, who was now working in Perth, which coincidentally was the birthplace of Mr Taylor, travelled to Elgin to make his own investigation of this accident. He reported his findings in a letter to the *Elgin Courant* on May 1st. Leaping to the defence of his old work colleague, he attacked the press reports which claimed that Mr Taylor had frozen with fear and done nothing to prevent the collision. Cranstoun claimed that the exact opposite was true. Mr Taylor had done all in his power to prevent the impact. The blame for the collision was placed by Mr Cranstoun on other officials of the Morayshire Railway who had allowed *"confused and unwarrantable movements to take place."*

I have my own views on this matter, which I will draw a veil over and leave you, dear reader, to decided who should bear responsibility for this accident.

The loss of such a prominent member of its staff seems to have had a sobering effect on the Morayshire Board and the Company maintained a low profile through May and June. Even in July the most exciting thing to happen was the approval by the Board to convert truck number 15 to covered brake van.

Provost Grant was adding to his own empire at this time, with a deal signed on July 14th 1857 for a tenant to take possession and run the Station Hotel in Elgin. Mr James Murray, formerly of the Gordon Arms Hotel in Fochabers, intended to have his new business up and running by August 10th at the latest. To this end he required experienced waiters, hostler, and boots to staff his establishment. Underling the quality of service he expected to give was this note from his advertisement *"none need apply unless they can be well recommended."*

Though only five years old, the Morayshire had become very much a familiar part of the community and in consequence a trip to Lossiemouth was no longer a draw. In view of the poor turnout at last year's Highland games, it was decided to attract the travelling public to Lossiemouth by holding a carthorse race with a first prize of £2. Other events planned for the day included a pig race consisting of a greased pig being let loose into the crowd and the winner being the person who caught it. The pig itself was the prize and finally a wheelbarrow race with a prize of 7/6d on offer for the winner.

The celebrations to mark the opening of the Morayshire Railway were held on the Monday the 10th of August. A number of the population not tempted by the races had travelled inland instead to view the work taking place at Boat O'Brig where the Inverness and Aberdeen Junction Railway were constructing a bridge over the Spey. A few from this party ventured deeper into Speyside, travelling as far as Dufftown and Craigellachie.

All was not lost to the Morayshire as one enterprising band of 200 citizens had decided instead to travel to Inverness. They assembled at 5am on the Plainstones* in Elgin from where they marched, flags flying and band playing to Elgin station to catch a special train to take them to Lossiemouth. Here they boarded the steamer "Streanshalh" under the command of Captain Swallow for the sea journey to Inverness. Their departure at 6am brought forth loud cheering from the crowd who had assembled at the harbour to watch the procession. By all accounts the trip by sea was enjoyed by all, including when trouble struck as the steamer approached Thornbush Pier at Inverness when the vessel became stranded. It took an hour for the tide to free the ship, allowing the passengers to land. Undaunted, the town of Inverness was thoroughly explored before the group set sail at 6pm for Lossiemouth. The "Streanshall" landed its passengers at midnight from whence the Morayshire Railway returned them to Elgin.

The Railway Company had promoted the horse-racing event at Lossiemouth by producing handbills and running advertisements in the local press. The prospect of this event did attract a substantial number of people to the seaside, with the line being well-patronised. I am not certain if it was the railway's intention to cut into the road haulier's business by trying to tempt the owners of cart and gig horses to take part in these races, but if it was, the plan failed miserably: the prospect of winning a mere £2 could not compete with the money to be made from transporting folk to Lossiemouth. Great disappointment and a feeling of being cheated was felt by the public when no races took place. Even as promised, the letting loose of a young pig with a greased tail failed; the animal was caught within a very few minutes. People were indignant with the hoax played on them by the Morayshire Railway Company, with many making the assertion that they would not be *done again."* A second eleven cricket match between Elgin and the Elgin Mechanics teams played at Stotfield helped pass the time for some. Quite a number of people went off to drown sorrows and as a result a large number of quarrels and fights broke out in the late afternoon and evening. The press let their feelings be known.

> Where were the races? They were nowhere to be seen. Who appeared to make an apology for there not being races? Nobody. The whole affair turned out to be a barefaced hoax, utterly unworthy of any Board of Directors - who perhaps sat laughing in a railway hotel at the thousands returning from Lossiemouth.

Something far more serious happened that day concerning the returning crowds. As in previous years, and at other times when the Morayshire was busy, the passenger trains were strengthened by the addition of trucks fitted out with seats. Into one of these (for the 6.30pm departure for Elgin) clambered a Mr William Ross, book-canvasser. Standing talking to a woman beside him, as the train left Lossiemouth station, he leaned against the side of the truck and in doing so the side gave way. Mr Ross fell backwards onto the line, as did a young lad of around eight years of age, the son of Mr Robert McKissock, merchant. Sprawled across the line, the wheels of the train ran over Mr Ross's legs, crushing one above the knee and the other below it. The young lad was more luckless, falling along the length of rail, where the wheels drove over his body, crushing him. The passengers who witnessed the incident raised the alarm, the train was brought to a standstill and the mutilated bodies carried from the track. The boy was taken into a house, but such were his injuries that he died 15 minutes after the accident. Mr Ross was laid down on a green next to the railway line, suffering greatly from his injuries. Dr Taylor of Elgin, fortunately in Lossiemouth, quickly went to the incident, and through the application of his medical skills prevented Mr Ross from haemorrhaging, saving his life.

The train from which the two unfortunates fell then continued on its journey to Elgin. On its return to Lossiemouth, it was stopped short of the station where the body of the child and the badly-injured Mr Ross were loaded into it. The train then went into the station at Lossiemouth where the crowds were waiting to return to Elgin. On seeing the dead child and mutilated Ross, most of the prospective passengers did not board the train, which left almost empty. Conveyed to hospital, Mr Ross had both his

*Town Square.

legs amputated by Dr Paul and Dr Ross, assisted by Dr Taylor, who stayed with the unfortunate man until 3am the next morning.

The serious nature of this event left the Morayshire Railway open to all forms of attack from the newspapers with the *Elgin Courant* chief among them.

> Old thin boards were nailed round trucks in such a way as to be found more a deception than a protection, the rickety frame wiggle - waggling with a push of the hand. We are not surprised that a man and a child fell through this frail fence. Our astonishment is that so few shared the same fate among the hundreds that leaned against the frail railing. We have read of many railway accidents, but never of the likes of this. It stands alone in the black catalogue of railway casualties. Let us never again hear Provost Grant, in the Town Council, proposing a holiday on the anniversary of the line.

What did the Morayshire Board have to say on this matter? Sadly, they attempted to fix blame for the accident on Mr William Ross. Claiming that he was in a drunken state when he boarded the train, witnesses to the event were emphatic that Mr Ross was sober. That avenue of blame closed to them, the Morayshire said no more on this matter. The Press on the other hand was full of letters condemning the Morayshire Board for what was seen as money-grabbing by charging passengers full fare to travel in open trucks. A conspiracy, in the form of the railway promoting events at Lossiemouth, to tempt the citizens of Elgin to travel to the coast was also noted by a number of the writers. It looked doubtful that a celebration of the Morayshire Railway would be held in 1858.

Others of course hoped to make some money out of the adversity as this extract, published in the *Elgin Courier* of August 14th from the Railway Passenger Assurance Company, shows:

> We beg to call attention of such of our readers who are in the habit of travelling by railway. For a mere trifle a person may assure for a single journey or specific period of time. In case of injury a weekly allowance may be secured - and in the case of death a specific sum. In the South such benefits are largely taken advantage of, and judging from what has recently happened at our own door such a precaution is not altogether un-required in the North.

The superstitious among you will probably be aware than it is usual for bad luck and misfortunes to come in threes. April had seen the death of Mr Taylor on the railway. The accident in August had claimed the life of the young lad McKissock, who would be next and where would the awful deed take place? The folk of Elgin did not have long to wait, as the railway claimed another victim on Sunday the 16th of August, to complete the curse.

If there is to be any comfort drawn from the unfortunate event of August 16th 1857, it is that it did not directly affect the Morayshire Railway. This incident occurred on the Sunday afternoon on the Inverness and Aberdeen Junction Railway, at the construction site of a bridge over the River Lossie, at a place known as Palmercross on the western edge of Elgin. It had become the habit of some of the population of Elgin to take a Sunday stroll along the route of the I&AJR to view the work in progress. Amongst the group of walkers were a number of boys who decided to amuse themselves by swinging on ropes attached to pile-driving apparatus, mounted on top of a cofferdam. One of the lads, a John Leslie aged about 16 years, son of William Leslie, carter, climbed one of the ropes attached to the pile driver. For some unknown reason the whole machine shifted and fell upon the lad crushing him. Providentially none of the other lads were close to the machine when it fell, otherwise the disaster could have been a lot worse. The accident was seen by a group of farm servants who were working in the nearby fields of Allarburn farm who were quickly on the scene. On freeing the lad he was taken to Haughland Farm where he had been working on their harvest. Medical assistance was summoned, Doctor Mackay of Elgin. Regrettably, young Leslie's injuries were such that the doctor's medical skills were not enough to save the lad. He lingered for some three hours and in the tradition of Victorian morality his last words were a warning to those gathered round his bed never to break the Sabbath-day.

Elgin Station 1857. Earliest known photograph of Elgin station, taken the year before the I&AJR arrived in town.
(Courtesy The Northern Scot)

Life on the Morayshire Railway seemed little affected by the death of a passenger and the severe injury of another. As per events after the loss of Mr Taylor, it went about its business, though doing its level best to keep out of the public's eye. The Board meeting of September 14th was supplied with a report from the Engineer (name unknown) on repairs required for the portable crane at Lossiemouth. Despite the loss of lives on the line, a full and effective repair of this piece of equipment was not sanctioned. Instead a temporary repair was to be carried out, with estimates to be obtained for a full and proper repair job to be done at a later date. Wagon number 4 was however to be completely overhauled.

Friday, October 20th 1857 was the Annual General Meeting of the Morayshire Railway Company. It was held in at the Station Hotel in Elgin; Provost Grant as Chairman of the Company was in the Chair for this meeting. The report of the year's business was a bit of a *"Curate's egg"*, good in parts, bad in others. The gross revenue for 1857 was £332-18s-9½d, up on last year by £429-14s-0½d.

Passenger numbers however were falling. In an attempt to persuade people to travel on the railway, the Directors had run excursion trains with low-cost fares on two days of the week during the summer months. If it had not been for these services, the passenger figures would have been even lower. The real money being earned by the Morayshire was coming from the transportation of goods. This had increased from 15,517 tons transported in 1856 to 20,477 tons moved in 1857, bringing in £1895-14s-4½d in revenue. Even this increase was tempered with some bad news. The Morayshire was doing what railways do best, moving large cumbersome loads, however the handling of heavy materials at each end of the line required a large work force. Money paid in wages cut into profit margins, and this situation was not helped by a general increase in labour costs. It appears inflation was alive and kicking in Victorian times as well. As a result of the above the dividend payable for 1857 would be the same as in previous years at 2%.

An announcement that the contract for the extension of the railway to Craigellachie had been signed and the contractors had just started work, pleased the Directors. Terms of the contract gave the completion date of this project as the 31st of July 1858. The by-now customary promise of an increase in dividend on completion of the work was again made. The post of Secretary also fell vacant once more, as Mr Topp who had taken over on March 11th 1857, rejoined the Board. No replacement was named at the AGM.

Before the meeting was closed, a petition from Mrs Taylor, widow of the late Joseph Taylor, engineer was read. The lady was asking for the sum of £15 per annum to be paid to her for the loss of her husband. On a motion from Provost Grant, seconded by F.D.Robertson Esq, it was agreed that a sum of £20 per annum be paid to Mrs Taylor. The amount was to be paid quarterly from the date of the accident on April 23rd and would continue at the discretion of the Directors.

As the year drew to an end the Board met on December 22nd to sort out the appointment of a Secretary for the Morayshire. The post went to a Mr James Jenkins at a salary of £100 per year, this appointment to be back-dated to November 1st. Other staff business saw a change of station master at Lossiemouth with the post now being filled by a Mr James Sim at a salary of £50 per annum. Mr Proctor, who had been the gatekeeper at Elgin, was now to become a guard, payment for which was 15/- per week. The locomotive superintendent was asked to give a monthly report on the condition of the line.

The *Elgin Courier* of Christmas Day 1857 gave the following report on progress of the work on the Rothes extension.

> There are no fewer than three parties actively employed on this line - one at Dundurcas, one at Sordens Rock and one at Crofts. The last mentioned are pushing forward an embankment in the direction of Rothes; and should the weather continue to be favourable our railway communication with the South will in a few months be complete - a circumstance which the majority in this quarter will hail with delight. A few it is true are prejudice against this line because of the injury done to their fields. At Sordens ironstone has been discovered, but not in such quantities for a commercial operation. The rock is said in places to be so *"compact"* as to render blasting useless. The excavation is therefore more tedious in this part...

8 ADVANCEMENT OF THE AGE

After the misfortunes of 1857, it was probably with a little relief that the first Morayshire Board meeting of 1858 discussed mediocre matters. January 11th saw the Board approve the plans for the station at Dandaleith at the southern end of the new line and a decision to build a new goods shed at Lossiemouth deferred to a later date.

The advertisement for contractors to build the station at Dandaleith was approved at the next meeting of the Board on January 27th. A demand from the Inverness and Aberdeen Junction Railway for the Morayshire to contribute to half the cost of constructing the embankment to raise the Rothes road over the new railway being built at Orton was also discussed. In this case the Morayshire decided to pay the I&AJR what the Morayshire considered a fair price, this price being arranged by a joint meeting of the two companies.

Saturday, 23rd January brought the arrival of an unusual cargo at Elgin station-a Russian gun a trophy from the Crimean War. A heavy road wagon usually used for moving logs transported the weapon to the foot of Ladyhill. In an operation described in artillery terms as *par buckling*, ropes were attached to the gun and it was rolled to the top of the hill. The progress of this operation was very slow and took until *"glomin"* before the piece was placed in position. Provost Grant was in attendance all day giving directions.

Provost Grant's brother John, more commonly known as Glengrant, was instructed by the Board to inspect and report on the plans for Rothes station at a meeting on February 8th. The appointment of platelayer George Gray to the post of gatekeeper at Elgin was also confirmed at this meeting. His salary was set at 11/- per week.

The *Elgin Courant* gave the following report on progress of the Morayshire's Craigellachie extension.

> The works on the extension line are progressing rapidly. The work is divided into 3 parts, with nearly all the bridges and drains completed. At the places in Rothes where the line crosses part of the village, houses have been taken down to open a passage for it. We believe the line will be complete within the specified time.

Construction on the Orton-Rothes section claimed the life of a worker at the beginning of March. His funeral was held on Sunday, March 7th with the attendance of all the Morayshire construction work force.

Thursday, March 25th 1858 saw the Inverness and Aberdeen Junction Railway open for general traffic. A large crowd assembled to see the arrival of the first train at 1pm which arrived a few minutes past the hour. Disembarking from the five coach train were a number of prominent citizens plus various dignitaries who belonged to the I&AJR Board or were involved with the construction of the line. These were as follows: P & G. Anderson, solicitors, Inverness; Mr Manford, a banker from Forres; Directors of the I&AJR; Eneas McIntosh Esq of Raigmore; Captain Tytler; Mr Dougall, manager and Mr Mitchell engineer of the line; Mr Fanshaw, contractor; and Messrs Dallas & Paterson inspectors of the works.

At 4pm these gentlemen were entertained to a dinner by Provost Grant in the Station Hotel Elgin. A general holiday was not declared by Elgin Town Council for the line from Inverness, despite it being undisputedly more important in the main network of railways of Great Britain. Only the banks and other public offices were closed for business.

For ordinary passengers wishing that day to travel onward to Aberdeen, there were two stagecoaches waiting at the station to transport them on to Keith to join the Great North of Scotland Railway. Horse drawn buses were also in attendance to convey passengers and luggage to the centre of Elgin.

The actual Inverness and Aberdeen Junction Railway station was still under construction at this time and even the completion of temporary refreshment rooms had not been completed by March 25th. Travellers on the new line reported that the journey on the Inverness line was a remarkably easy one, the carriages going along with great smoothness, or as one person expressed it, *"without a single jostle during the whole way."*

An increase in business and trade all along the Moray Firth was looked forward to by the local press. At this time the combined population of this portion of Scotland numbered somewhere around 30,000 people. The coming of the railway sped up communication considerably, coupled with a staggering drop in the cost of travel. The cost of the fare between Inverness and Elgin for the stagecoach was one gold guinea, plus something for guard and driver. Travel by rail on March 27th cost half-a-crown. Granted, this was a cheap day excursion price, but the dawn of affordable railway travel had arrived. The populations of both Elgin and Inverness were quick to take advantage of this cut-price deal. Saturday, March 27th saw some 500 citizens of Inverness arrive in Elgin by the midday train. Going in the other direction were 150 Elgin folk off to visit the Highland capital.

The *Elgin Courant* of April 2nd 1858 could not resist rubbing the nose of the Morayshire in its praise of the Inverness and Aberdeen Junction Railway.

> In looking at the long trains that brought the excursionists on Saturday, we could not but admire what is technically called the rolling stock of the new line. First class carriages on all railways are elegant and comfortably fitted up but the third class carriages on the Inverness Junction are we have no hesitation in saying, the finest we have seen anywhere in Scotland. Everything about the line shows good management and a desire for the public convenience, especially when they show themselves above that grasping and sordid avarice which loses no opportunity of taking every last penny from poor working men. The directors have opened their line so handsomely with a really cheap excursion train we wish them every success.

That short extract from a very extensive article praising the I&AJR must have made good breakfast reading for Provost Grant and his fellow Board of Morayshire Directors.

Spurred on possibly by the arrival of a competitor the Morayshire attempted to improve the dividend paid to its shareholders by the novel means of reducing the wages of the workforce from April 13th as follows:

Fireman	16/-	Down to 15/-
Cleaner	15/-	Down to 13/-
Carpenter	17/-	Down to 16/-
Platelayer	14/-	Down to 12/-
Platform Porter	16/-	Down to 15/-
Coal Porter	14/-	Down to 12/-
Gatekeeper	7/-	Down to 6/-

The engine driving staff and Stationmasters, set aside as professionals rather than mere tradesmen, escaped any cut in their wages.

Accidents never seemed to be far away from the Morayshire, a small child being the victim on Tuesday, April 27th 1858. The youngster, while playing at the harbour, had his foot severely bruised by a goods wagon that ran over it. Dr MacBean was summoned from Elgin to attend. Wounds dressed, the local press hoped that the child would recover.

The Morayshire Railway Company was not alone in feeling competition from the Inverness and

Aberdeen Junction Railway. In amongst reports of yet another excursion, on this occasion bringing parties of school children from Nairn and Inverness to Elgin, there is a comment on the quality and cost of fish now becoming available in the district.

> Much joy as fishwives from Findhorn and Nairn supply good quality fish at reduced prices. Elgin has to date been miserably supplied with fish which makes the price dear - sixpence being asked in the past for just one haddock!

Work on the Morayshire's line to Rothes was nearing completion, but it also brought trouble to the streets of Rothes as the *Elgin Courier* of May 21st reports.

> The railway works in our vicinity are progressing rapidly, not with standing the time taken lately spent by the navvies in making themselves comfortable. The Rothes station is in the course of erection and permanent rails are being laid on a section of the line betwixt this and far famed Craigellachie. We are sad to report that a serious assault was committed in Rothes on Monday last. Three navvies attacked John Falconer, maltman without provocation severely wounding him and fracturing his rib. The assaulting parties have been apprehended and the case is being investigated by the Procurator-Fiscal.

In Elgin on Wednesday, May 26th, an EGM of the shareholders of the Morayshire railway was held in the Station Hotel for the purpose of authorising the Directors to exercise the borrowing powers of the Company. Provost Grant the chairman of the Morayshire presided, and the motion giving the necessary authority was agreed unanimously.

The perceived generosity of the I&AJR may have had an effect on the Board members of the Morayshire who now appeared to be a little more sympathetic in their dealings with the public. At their meeting of the 8th of June, Provost Grant announced that he would pay the sum of two Guineas for a pair of artificial limbs for William Ross who lost his legs in the accident of August 10th 1857. Another Director, Mr Brander, also put his hand in his pocket, to the value of one Guinea to help fund repairs of the wooden bridge from the town of Lossiemouth to the East Beach.

By July 13th the station at Rothes was in the process of being roofed. Work on embankments and track bed had been completed and all that remained to be done was the laying of the track. The Board inspected the work and met at Rothes on that day. Trouble struck-the Inverness and Aberdeen Junction Railway were threatening to renege on their pact to allow the Morayshire to use the portion of line between Elgin and Orton. The original agreement that had been drawn up in 1856 gave right of passage to engines and rolling stock of the Morayshire over the line between Orton and Elgin. In return for this privilege, the Morayshire was to pay the Inverness and Aberdeen Junction Railway rent, tolls and any other charges as may be agreed on. The total amounts of these charges were not to exceed 40% of the gross earnings of the Morayshire for the conveyance of passengers and goods over the line from Orton to Elgin, plus a part percentage of traffic carried over the line from Orton to Rothes. If there was any dispute between either party, the matter would be sent for arbitration under the Railway Consolidation (Scotland) Act 1845. It was decided to deploy Provost Grant to Inverness to try and sort this matter out, with him reporting back to an EGM of the Morayshire to be held on Monday, July 19th, making a very tight time scale.

At that packed EGM in the Station Hotel Elgin, Provost Grant briefed the shareholders. The reason that the I&AJR gave for not committing to the agreement of 1856 was that they felt that the Board of Trade would not sanction running powers of the Morayshire's over the I&AJR. Provost Grant proposed that both Companies write to the Board of Trade to confirm consent. The Inverness and Aberdeen Junction refused to do this. A statement was prepared by Provost Grant and sent along with the 1856 Agreement to the Board of Trade for their authorisation. With a few minor modifications, they were happy with the agreement that had been written up by both companies in 1856. The Provost then returned to the Board of the I&AJR to report his findings. The outcome of this meeting was a reluctant consent on the part of the Inverness and Aberdeen Junction to give the Morayshire running powers over the line between Elgin and Orton. For all his hard work Provost Grant received a sincere vote of thanks from the assembled company at the Morayshire's EGM.

The legal matters between the two companies at last sorted out the way seemed clear for the operation of both to begin. The *Elgin Courier* raised the travelling public's expectations thus.

> Many of our readers will be glad to learn that there is now the prospect of the early opening of the railway between Elgin to Keith, and also Elgin to Rothes. The Board of Trade Inspector is expected to go over the line on Saturday or Monday. If his report is favourable, of which there is little doubt, the line may be open by Wednesday the 28th or Thursday the 29th of July.

The feeling of euphoria was even getting to the usually canny Board of the Morayshire Railway. On Saturday, July 23rd they offered **FREE** rail travel to the members of the Elgin City band to the seaside at Lossiemouth. It was hoped by the Board that good music, combined with the prospect of fine weather for sea bathing, would tempt a large number of the population of Elgin to take the train to Lossiemouth.

Captain Tyler from the Board of Trade inspected the line from Elgin to Keith on the Saturday. He pointed out several major alternations required to be carried out before the line could be opened. The main area of concern was the temporary bridge and associated works over the Spey. The Inverness and Aberdeen Junction Railway assured Captain Tyler that all would be in order in a fortnight. Next for inspection was the Morayshire's extension between Orton and Rothes. Captain Tyler found all to his satisfaction and commented on the quality of the work. This presented a problem for Provost Grant and the Morayshire Board. They could run a train from Orton to Rothes, but could not travel from Elgin to Orton. Resolute to open, Provost Grant set off to London to apply to the Board of Trade to allow the Morayshire to begin operations immediately. He was sadly unsuccessful.

The evening of Wednesday, August 18th saw another serious accident on the Morayshire Railway. A navvy named Andrew McKenzie who had been working on the Rothes line came into Elgin station the worse for drink and wandered onto the track. The engine driver who had been shunting some wagons ordered him off the line and threatened to call the police. MacKenzie took no notice and as the locomotive began to move off, he stepped forward, placing his foot on one of the wheels. He was knocked over and the wheel passed over his leg, smashing it. The luckless McKenzie was taken to Dr Gray's Hospital where his fractured limb was amputated. In reporting the incident, the local press were supportive of the Morayshire Railway and attached no blame to them or their servants. Their only demand was for the police board to supply a constable to the railway station.

The news that Provost Grant had been waiting for appeared in the *Elgin Courant* on Friday, August 20th. Captain Tyler had returned on August 14th and carried out a full inspection of the I&AJR. The work required to bring the Junction Company line up to the standard required, had been completed. The Morayshire intended to start its services on Monday the 23rd of August.

Opening of The Morayshire Extension

Report from the Banffshire Journal 24th August 1858 (abridged)

> The Extension which was opened for traffic yesterday branches off 400 yards west of Orton station. As the travellers by it seat themselves in the comparatively small but tidy and tasteful and comfortable carriages used upon the line, having set their faces towards their destination of Craigellachie take a view of the neat little engine - excellently in keeping with the carriages - which is to wind them up the beautiful picturesque vale. Let them take a glance to the left and close by the bottom of the embankment is the fine house of Garbity,

occupied by Doctor McPherson. The railway crosses the road to Keith on the level past the farm tenanted by Mrs Souter. The view up the east side of the Spey is one of imposing natural grandeur. The line on leaving this haugh by a sweep to the right enters a narrow pass where the rocks on the eastern side of the river jut out and almost touch the western side. The line passes through a cutting in the rock at a depth which permits a road to Dundurcas to cross by a bridge. Emerging from this cutting the burn of Sorden is crossed by a stone bridge.

The first object of interest is just at hand - a steam sawmill with a tall brick chimney owned and worked by Mr Colin McKenzie Elgin. This is soon passed, but we must notice that side rails have been laid by which wagons can be loaded. Whirling along we can view the large and extensively improved and admirably managed farm of Drumbain, tenanted by Messrs J. & J. Grant Glengrant. Close at hand from the right hand window of the carriage appears with fine effect the house of Glengrant a very tasteful edifice and on the opposite side of the burn which is crossed here is the large Distillery of Glengrant, amongst the largest and most celebrated manufacturer of sprits in the North. The train is just at Rothes the line is not yet finished though the works are being rapidly pushed forward. A peep at this lengthy village, what a pity we could not say burgh or even city. Rothes, very aptly was said by our Keith correspondent to be situated in beauty's lap. There are few buildings in it, however of very striking elegance. Strolling up the street (for properly speaking there is but one street, with a number of small lanes, etc.), attention is attracted by a portion of an old wall on the top of an eminence overlooking the town near the southern end. A portion of the wall that once surrounded the castle seat of the one time Earls of Rothes.

If the traveller wants a little comfort he should decidedly call at the *"Grant Arms,"* of Mrs Soutor. The Spey red fish in the locality is excellent. The landlady's skill at preparing for the table the trophies of her angler guests is unequalled.

The population of the town is about 1000. There are no manufactories except the Glengrant Distillery; the inhabitants are chiefly mechanics and agricultural labourers. All the more remarkable therefore that several handsome fortunes have been made here.

To walk the remaining portion of the line is one of the most pleasant rambles imaginable at this present season. The terminus is at the steading of Dandaleith, and half a mile beyond is to be seen the romantic scenery of Craigellachie, with its rugged rock and beautiful iron bridge across the Spey. We cannot leave the traveller in a more agreeable spot. With a hope that the engine from Rothes will soon be whistling at Dandaleith, and a hurrah for Provost Grant, the author of the Morayshire Railway and his fellow Directors, we bow farewell.

Not everyone it seemed welcomed the intrusion of the Morayshire Railway into the Parish of Dundurcas. On Monday, August 25th, a 17 foot length of rail was placed across the track in an attempt to cause a derailment of the train. Fortunately for the Morayshire, this act of sabotage was discovered before a train arrived on the scene. Reports in the *Elgin Courier* of August 27th say that following investigation, a person who lives locally has been apprehended on suspicion of placing the obstruction on the line, and is meanwhile on bail pending further investigation into this *"most extraordinary act."*

Celebration for the opening of the line from Orton to Rothes and the possibly more important completion of the rail network all the way from London to Inverness did not take place on the actual day of opening (August 23rd). It was one week later on the Monday the 30th of August that the Town Council of Elgin decreed a holiday with all merchant trades to shut up shop. James Ross, better known as *Rossi of the Lossie*, temporarily became Rossi of Rothes as he drove the Morayshire's official opening train. On its arrival at Rothes the Directors adjourned to hold a meeting. The general population of Elgin did not have much of an appetite for travel to Rothes on that day, and none at all for a trip

Lossiemouth. Instead some 283 of them had risen at around 5.30am and caught the train to Aberdeen, the opportunity to travel some 140 miles at the bargain price of a crown (25p) too good to miss. Another 480 passengers set off for Inverness at 8.15am, for the price of half a crown. Amongst the passengers on this train was the Elgin City Band who entertained the crowds at Forres, Nairn and Inverness. All the excursionists returned safely some 12 hours later with the Elgin City Band playing to the crowds which followed them up Moss Street before finally dispersing.

September 22nd saw a complaint from the Board of Trade concerning the high rates being charged by the Morayshire for transporting passengers and goods between Orton and Rothes. Adjustments for lower charges were reluctantly made by the Morayshire.

A week later on September 28th at a joint meeting between the Directors of the Inverness and Aberdeen Junction Railway and the Morayshire, it was unanimously resolved that the I&AJR would now convey the Morayshire's stock between Elgin and Orton. It has often been reported that this was due to the unreliability of the Morayshire's engines. This appears not to be the case. Congestion and safety of the travelling public were deciding factors. The number of trains using the stretch of single line between Elgin and Orton was large. The Junction Company had 12 passenger and two freight trains travelling over it. Mixed into this were six Morayshire passenger trains, which also conveyed goods wagons, and there was still the possibility of up to four additional goods trains being run by the Morayshire. Collision was likely, and an accident on the I&AJR just up the line from Orton at Mulben on September 4th was an unwelcome reminder to the Inverness Board. Three employees of the I&AJR were killed and two seriously injured in this incident. A new working agreement was seen by the Junction Company to be urgently required. A safeguard was built into the arrangement of September 28th by which the Morayshire could request that their trains pass over the line between Orton and Rothes should the I&AJR's trains not suit the Morayshire's requirements. It was felt that this measure of control would give a degree of safety to passengers. In return the Inverness and Aberdeen Junction Railway would receive an additional 10%, giving both companies 50% of the income of the Morayshire's traffic travelling between Elgin and Orton.

At around this time the Railway Hotel in Elgin, no longer the property of the Morayshire Railway, but now in the ownership of its Chairman Provost Grant, required another tenant. It appears that Mr James Murray could not meet the exacting standards called for by Provost Grant. In his advert the Provost laid out the type of character he expected to lease this enterprise.

> The Hotel is intended to be maintained in first class style. No, Tenant need apply who cannot satisfy the Proprietor of his ability and fitness for the place. Few such openings occur, and a Tenant of enterprise and possessed of suitable capital will be met with every encouragement.

Perhaps because of the agreement of September 28th the shareholders of the Inverness and Aberdeen Junction Railway were a little uneasy. I think they feared that their company would make a take-over bid for the Morayshire, and in doing so would saddle the I&AJR with a large debt. As a result of this unease following the I&AJR's AGM on October 20th at the Station Hotel in Inverness, a special meeting was held where the Honourable T C Bruce gave the following address on these matters as reported in the *Banffshire Journal* of October 26th:

> When the extension of the Morayshire was contemplated it was questioned whether it should go direct or via Orton and thence to Rothes. Though decidedly adverse to investing the capital of the Company in branch lines, it was felt we ought to offer favourable terms for the conveyance of M.R. traffic along the 10 miles from Elgin to Orton in order to induce the Morayshire to use our line. The Junction Company would obtain none of this traffic. This has been done since the opening but it has been found not to be consistent with public safety to allow the M.R. to run its own independent trains on our line. An agreement has therefore

been entered into to allow the carriages of the Morayshire to be attached to the Junction company trains and conveyed between Elgin and Orton. We will receive 50% of gross receipts of the Morayshire in the portion accruing to the ten miles of the whole line. If however the Morayshire require a special train for any purpose, they would pay for the use of our engines and trains at a fair and reasonable rate.

So ended his report, but before sitting down, Mr Bruce informed the meeting that the directors of the I&AJR were quite determined not embark in any branch lines, a comment that brought forward cheers from the assembled shareholders of the Aberdeen and Inverness Junction Railway.

On Saturday, October 31st 1858 the Morayshire held its own AGM. The business of that meeting was concluded very quickly. Various Directors were re-elected, a dividend of 2% declared and Auditors appointed. The reason for the haste, was like the I&AJR, a special meeting was to be held to discuss the working of traffic between Elgin and Orton. The Morayshire laid out the reason for their wish to run their own trains again between Orton and Elgin. They always expected the passenger traffic to be light but there would be a high demand for goods traffic. This position was the reverse of the Junction company that ran a large number of passenger trains and few goods trains. Problems were being encountered by the Morayshire because it was the habit of the company to attach wagons to the rear of its passenger trains. When the exchange of traffic took place at Orton, the Inverness and Aberdeen Junction Railway only sent the passenger coaches forward to Elgin. Goods wagons were detained at Orton until the I&AJR ran their goods trains at 1pm. There was one other goods train on the I&AJR but it was in the late evening and arrived in Elgin at 9pm, which was after the Morayshire had closed for the day. The Morayshire felt that this was not in the spirit of the agreement reached by the Directors of the two companies. The decision to hold the goods traffic was taken by the I&AJR without any consultation with the Morayshire, instruction to this effect being applied with spirit by the Junction Railway staff at Orton and Elgin. The effect of this dictum was disastrous for the Morayshire. Complaints were being received from their customers, as shipping was being delayed at Lossiemouth, and customers in Rothes who had previously obtained goods in the forenoon now had to wait 24 hours for delivery! The demand from the merchants was for at least three goods trains per day to be run to and from Rothes and the Coast. The decision of the Morayshire's special meeting concluded that the Directors should again meet with the Board of the Inverness and Aberdeen Junction Railway to obtain an improved working agreement. It was noted that the Directors of the I&AJR were always *"desirous and fair"* in carrying out arrangements between them and this company. The blame for the situation at present facing the Morayshire was placed on *"other parties, who are called on to execute and do not."* It was concluded that these parties *"should have their duty clearly pointed out."*

On Monday, November 2nd 1858, it looked as if the new spirit of co-operation between the two Companies would be stillborn. The coaches that should have been attached to the 8.53am service were precluded from joining the main line by the action of the I&AJR staff. The engine from Inverness was positioned over the point work so as to prevent the Morayshire gaining access to the main line. Morayshire staff protested to the I&AJR officials, but the crew of the Inverness train ignored the protests and continued to water their engine. The guard completed his platform duties and the Inverness and Aberdeen Junction Railway train left for Keith and all points east, minus the Morayshire coaches that should have been attached to the train. Things were not much better for services coming from Rothes, with passengers finding themselves stranded in their coaches outside the I&AJR Elgin station, with the Morayshire's locomotive being stopped from shunting them into the Morayshire's station.

Some six weeks later on December 14th 1858 a meeting was finally arranged between the Directors of the respective Companies. It was good news for Provost Grant and his fellow Morayshire Directors; they gained a promise from the Inverness & Aberdeen Junction that these problems, caused by their employees, would now be at an end. This meeting was a little ambiguous on the question of improving the facilities for the transportation of goods between Rothes and Lossiemouth. Nevertheless, the Morayshire Directors seemed to be under the impression all the problems had been resolved and they celebrated by ordering eight new goods wagons at a cost of £530-4s-2d.

An early Christmas present came to Provost Grant and his Board on December 23rd 1858 with the opening of the line from Rothes to Dandaleith. The later was referred to as Craigellachie though it was on the opposite side of the River Spey from that village. Colonel Yolland of the Board of Trade inspected the new line and as before remarked on the high quality of the construction work. Total distance from Rothes to the Morayshire's Craigellachie station was just a little over three miles, giving a complete distance of the Morayshire's extension of almost eight miles. Reports state that the station at Craigellachie was neat and comfortable. Accommodation for refreshment rooms had also been provided, tenanted by Mrs Soutor of the Grant Arms Hotel. The press of the day were certain that the good lady would *supply the best of viands and liquors."*

Mrs Soutor's hotel in Rothes was the chosen venue for the celebration dinner to mark the opening. The great and the good of Rothes and district joined Provost Grant, his Directors and Mr Samuel the line's Engineer, to toast the success of the venture. Always looking to the future in his speech, the good Provost hoped it would not be too long before the Morayshire bridged the Spey. He went on to ask the Earl of Seafield, who was one of the guests, to consider building a railway along the banks of the Spey to the town of Grantown. The toasts and liquor continued to flow, and it is noteworthy that the health of the Honourable T C Bruce, Director of the Inverness and Aberdeen Junction Railway and architect of the September 28th agreement, was proposed by Provost Grant. What the Honourable Gentleman thought of the Provost's expansion plans is not recorded.

Settlement of the dispute between the Morayshire and the Junction Company was brought to the attention of the public by the placing of the following notice in the press.

Special Notice

The public are respectfully informed that the inconvenience and delay experienced by passengers by the 7.30 am & 2.20pm Down Trains for sometime past (which the Directors much regret)

IS NOW OBVIATED

In future Down passengers (from Craigellachie and Rothes to Elgin) by these trains will immediately on arrival land upon the Main Line platform; and their tickets will be collected on passing out of that station. Passengers going farther west can at the same time readily prevail themselves with tickets, and take up their seats in the Main Line Trains.

All Up train Passengers (from Elgin to Rothes and Craigellachie) will have to book and take their seats at the Morayshire station as formally.

By Order
James Jenkins Secy
Elgin 6th Jan 1859

This new mood of co-operation was also mentioned in the Minute of the Directors meeting on January 18th. Provost Grant reported that requests by the Morayshire to run special trains over the line between Elgin and Orton at Christmas and New Year's Day had been readily granted. The train at Christmas ran, but the one at New Year was cancelled due to lack of passengers.

Other points discussed were: the low level of business being conducted at Sorden station. (It was concluded that though sales were small at the moment business was expected to improve.) The cost of constructing the line to Craigellachie was lower than estimated, as a result some £2000 in stock held by the contractor would now be returned to the Morayshire. Good news was also in store for clergymen of the district, who on a suggestion brought before the Board by John Grant Glengrant, could travel first Class on production of a third class ticket.

The first accident on the new section of the Morayshire was reported in the *Elgin Courant* of January 14th.

> On the afternoon of Friday the 7th when the 4.30pm train was entering Craigellachie station, a horse belonging to Mr Cattanach carrier Knockando, took fright and the shaft of the loaded cart struck Mr C. on the side knocking him down. The wheel passed over his body. Fears were at first entertained that his injuries were of a serious nature, and an express was immediately forward for Doctor Gerrard, Aberlour, who was soon on the spot, and found that though Mr Cattanch was much bruised, he had wonderfully escaped without broken bones. He was conveyed back to Rothes by train, and though next day complaining a good deal, he was able to proceed home.

It had now become the habit of the Directors to travel to various points in their railway empire to hold meetings. The first item on the agenda at Rothes, February 8th 1859 was a complaint from the villagers of that town about the inconvenience caused to them by the number of level crossings in the village. Green Street was of particular concern, though the villagers were demanding that there should be a gatekeeper assigned to each crossing place. The Company believed that they had done everything to comply with the wishes of Mr Brown the factor of the Earl Seafield in providing the number of crossings requested by the Estate. The Company could not fund the building of a lodge at each crossing. It was not unsympathetic though and suggested that should the villagers and Mr Brown come up with the money and land, then the Morayshire would construct a lodge at Green Street and undertake the expense of keeping gate.

There was more irritation with the running of train services, which on this occasion were not due to the actions of the Inverness and Aberdeen Junction Railway. On January 26th the service from Elgin to Orton was lost because of the neglect of the Morayshire's locomotive crew. This judgement was reached following inspection of the engine by Mr Blackwood, the line's engineer. He reported no mechanical problems with the machine. It appeared that the crew went home on the previous day without either cleaning the locomotive or lighting the fire in preparation for the next day's service. The Morayshire Directors took a dim view of this action and fined the driver Mr Walker 10/- and his fireman Mr Milne 3/-. Similar circumstance occurred on February 3rd. The offenders this time were driver Ross, fined 10/- and fireman Duncan, fined 5/-. To underline their displeasure at these events, the Secretary was instructed to write to the offending parties, cautioning them that any repeat would result in instant dismissal from the service of the Morayshire Railway Company.

A change of Stationmaster at Elgin took place at this time with the temporary appointment of Mr Hutcheon. Sadly for him the post was not coupled with an increase in his salary.

Mr Blackwood reported defects in the tyres of brake coaches Nos 5 and 6. The tyre from number 6 was taken to the meeting for the Directors to inspect. They decided to have Mr Mills, the assistant to Mr Samuel investigate and report on the possible cause of the tyre failures. General performance of the Morayshire was also felt to be shoddy. The meeting agreed to send letters to all the stationmasters to advise them that any future failings would not be overlooked. Provost Grant himself felt that, as the line was almost complete, the Company required some form of General Manager, efficient in engineering, who could take over the day to day matters, the Board finding it a strain to be involved in these affairs. The Chairman was of the opinion that because of the smallness of the line it would be difficult to find such a person, requesting that if anyone at the meeting knew of such an individual could they advise him with all haste.

Seven days later on February 15th 1859 the Board met in Elgin. The situation in respect of obtaining someone to fill the post of General Manager was getting desperate. Provost Grant had written to Mr Samuel to see if it would be possible for his assistant Mr Mills to join the Morayshire in the post of General Manager.

As demand for the Morayshire's preferential shares was almost nil, the Company was facing financial problems as well as operational ones. An EGM on March 9th hoped to resolve the money problem by offering £10 shares in the Company *"to any such parties as the Directors think fit."* The EGM was followed by a Board meeting that supplied better news on the question of a General Manager. Mr Mills was at that time working in the south, and he had made it be known that he in no way wished to give up his profession as an engineer. He did however expect to remain domiciled in the north of Scotland for some time and therefore was agreeable to becoming resident engineer, General Manager and Secretary of the Morayshire. Mr Samuel, his current employer, was in full agreement with Mr Mill's decision.

Money problems however are never easily resolved. The borrowing powers of the Morayshire were now exhausted, and a trip to Edinburgh to arrange a loan to help pay off debts had been unsuccessful. All the Morayshire's shareholders were to be asked to increase their holding in the Company. These shares would be assigned for a fixed period of time. A circular giving details of this proposal was to be issued to all shareholders with immediate effect.

With both the Inverness and Aberdeen Junction and Morayshire Railway networks complete, the labourers involved in their construction had by March 18th 1859 made ready to move on to new projects. The last act of the navvies was to hand over the remains of their medical assistance fund, which had been raised by the work force, to the Reverend Mr Gray minister of Rothes. The amount given over was 12/-, added to by the remnant of a subscription by the work force to a monument raised to their four colleagues killed during the construction of both lines. This added another £1-13s-11d to the amount in the medical fund. The person who made the presentation on behalf of the work force was a Mr Christison. It was intended that the money was to be distributed among, cases of necessity in the Parish.

On the following day the Board of the Morayshire met at Craigellachie. The appointment of Mr Mills was confirmed, as was his salary; that was to be the same as he was paid by Mr Samuel, £200. The Board agreed to pay a pro rata amount to Mr Samuel to cover the period from January 1st for work done on behalf of the Morayshire by Mr Mills. An allowance of 50 Guineas was also to be paid to Mr Mills as a token of the esteem in which he was held by the Board. The Directors seemed to be in a generous mood as an application for aid was asked for by the Elgin City Band, and a grant of £3-3/- was awarded. In reality, it was noted at this meeting that the Company may have to overdraw its account with the Caledonian Bank, the amount if required to be to the maximum sum of £1500, with each Director being responsible for a portion of any resultant debt. On a slightly upbeat note two preferential shares had been taken up.

Problems between the Junction Company and the Morayshire returned with a vengeance in the middle of April. Small niggles had been occurring since mid January, but a change in timetable by the I&AJR was severely disrupting traffic on the Morayshire. Passengers coming from Craigellachie in the morning were now unable to return home until 5.10pm. To resolve this Provost Grant wanted to run a through-Morayshire service at 2.15pm. Various letters requesting allowance of this train had been sent to the I&AJR Board, all of which had been ignored. If things were bad for passengers, goods traffic was in a turmoil as only one goods train per day was allowed over the line. With 300 tons of goods per week moving between the coast and up country, the Morayshire required a minimum of two goods trains per day. All letters from Mr Mills on this matter were being ignored by the Aberdeen and Junction.

Andrew Dougall the Secretary of the Inverness and Aberdeen Junction Company, eventually replied to Provost Grant. They proposed to supply one of their engines to take the Morayshire's 2.15pm service, at a cost of £2 per trip between Elgin and Orton. Due to a large number of men and horses currently involved in laying double track at Orton, they could not permit an additional goods service. Provost Grant was not best pleased. He informed Mr Dougall that the Morayshire could undertake the journey between Elgin and Orton for 5/10d and he must conclude that the offer from the I&AJR was a refusal to comply.

At the next meeting of the Morayshire Board, there was no mention of the I&AJR. Instead the Morayshire decided to go into the quarry business by renting two quarries at Lossiemouth at £10 and £8 per annum respectively. Track was to be laid into both sites to ease the movement of material. Wooden fences at the Lossie end of the line were in a poor state of repair. It was decided, because of their new quarry business, to replace the fence with a four foot high stone wall. Despite the problems of moving goods on the line, demand for traffic was still increasing and two cattle vans were now required, with quotations being obtained from builders in Edinburgh and Birmingham.

Various accounts were passed by the Board on May 10th 1859, and approval was given for Mr Alexander, watchmaker, to service and repair the company's timepieces. Letters between Hepple and Landill steam tug builders were also discussed re the possibility of building a tug for Lossie harbour. The Directors agreed to hold proper talks with the Harbour Board about hiring a tug to assess if it would be viable to construct one.

The following day the Inverness and Aberdeen Junction held an EGM to discuss the working arrangement with the Morayshire. From the outcome of that meeting, it appeared that the I&AJR were not concerned in any way about the complaints laid before them by the Morayshire Board.

On June 7th the Morayshire met in Elgin. On the table was an account from the Inverness and Aberdeen Junction Railway for £556-8s-10d for the working of the Morayshire's traffic over the Elgin Orton line. The Morayshire Board felt that this account was not fully adjusted and were prepared to only pay £500 to account, pending a proper explanation of the charges. The I&AJR's EGM was also discussed. It seems that the Board of the Junction Company had not written to the Morayshire informing them of the details of their meeting. Rather, they had arranged to have the Minutes published as a leaflet for public release, a copy of which was sent to the Morayshire. This manner of reply to the Morayshire's concerns and the actual content of the leaflet was thought to be highly deficient by the Board of the Morayshire. Legal council was to be engaged and an opinion sought regarding the Morayshire's concerns.

Meanwhile, the Morayshire continued to experience a big increase in demand to move freight traffic. To meet this need an order for 20 new goods trucks of open wagon with side door, open wagon with end door and box wagon were placed.

Mr Jenkins, Secretary, left the employ of the Morayshire for a post in London. A certificate of good merit was given to him along with the best wishes of the Company.

Summer arrived and the population of Elgin took advantage of the two railway companies to expand their horizons as this report in the *Elgin Courant* of June 17th explains.

> We are glad to observe that the public have not been slow in availing themselves of cheap trains afforded by the I&AJR and Morayshire Railway. One can now get from this or any station along the line on Saturday returning that day or Monday, for one fare; in other words half price. Schools are taken even cheaper than these. On Saturday last Mr Morrison of the Academy along with its boarders went for a jaunt to Inverness returning the same evening for a very low rate of 2d. The Morayshire Railway has now begun to give what people all over the kingdom understands as return tickets. The fare on Saturday now being 6d for the drive to Lossiemouth and back. Saturday last showed that this is beneficial both to the railway and the public. For some 400 to 500 people went down to Lossie and enjoyed sea bathing, a sight of a cricket match and the pleasure of our City band.

On July 16th, 1000 people travelled to the seaside on cheap excursion fares. Towards the end of that month a meeting of merchants and tradesmen at Rothes agreed to hold a holiday on August 4th. Both railway companies benefited from this decision, with some of them travelling to Aberdeen and the rest to Lossiemouth.

By August 31st 1859 the Morayshire Railway had had enough of the antics of the Inverness and Aberdeen Junction Railway. The failure to comply with the Agreement of 1856, or come to any sensible accommodation with the Morayshire, led the Directors to instruct Mr Mills to survey a route through the Glen of Rothes, and move to have an Act of Parliament to build the line.

Praise was in the press also for Mr Mills and his design of a new carriage that had just gone into service with the Morayshire. This vehicle, a composite brake, was in some respects a sort of observation coach, which must have made the trip from Orton to Craigellachie most enjoyable.

> Its outward appearance is light and elegant, with the passenger end almost entirely panelled with glass. This first class saloon measured 12 ft x 8 ft with a table in the centre of the compartment. Lighting for the first class was by an oil glass globe lamp with a reflector on top to give maximum lighting output. The inside wood of the compartment was polished teak, varnished to give it a rich appearance. Next comes the third class compartment, which is comfortably fitted up. The guard's end is fitted with lookout duckets, and has an internal measurement of just over 7 ft square and is provided with a powerful brake. Total accommodation is 17 first and 10 third class passengers. External livery is of varnished teak. The builder is Messrs Brown, Marshall & Co. Birmingham.

The cheap excursions run by the Morayshire were doing such excellent business that for September they were run on Monday, Wednesday and Saturday. At the end of September the Directors decided to continue cheap travel on Saturday for the rest of the year.

At the same time the relationship between the I&AJR and the Morayshire had descended to the level of behaviour that would be frowned upon in a primary school playground. In retaliation for the Morayshire's insistence to run its own trains between Elgin and Orton, a threat was made on September 15th by the Inverness Company that they would prevent any Morayshire stock from using the I&AJR's line. Mr Mills reply to the I&AJR lessened the threat little, as the Junction Company accepted that this action would be detrimental to the travelling public. They did however carry out the rest of the threat by stopping goods travelling between Elgin and Orton, with this traffic having to be booked on to the Inverness and Junction. This action meant that the Morayshire lost 50% of the revenue it had previously obtained for goods travelling on the I&AJR's line.

Rather than improving matters this authoritarian arrangement made things worse, culminating in goods being seized on the 15th of September and forcibly removed by the I&AJR staff at Orton. Besides carrying out raids on Morayshire property, it appears the Junction Company had employed *"spies"* at Lossiemouth to watch and report on goods being landed at the port. This paid off for the Inverness and Aberdeen Junction Company when it was discovered that one small cask of whisky had been sent by sea to Lossiemouth from Inverness, rather than by rail! The subsequent letter of complaint was replied too politely by the Morayshire, saying that they had not encouraged the owner of the whisky to send his cask by sea and could not be held responsible if the consignors wished to send items by sea. The madness continued when the I&AJR complained that the Morayshire had sent a parcel from Craigellachie destined for Forres by road from Elgin, rather than hand over the package at Elgin to the I&AJR. On this occasion the I&AJR had shot themselves in the foot. The staff at the Morayshire station had attempted to give the parcel up at Elgin, but the Junction staff had refused to accept it unless they received full payment for the transport of goods between Orton and Elgin. Numerous other allegations were made against the Morayshire for similar transgressions, but being so trivial are not worth recounting.

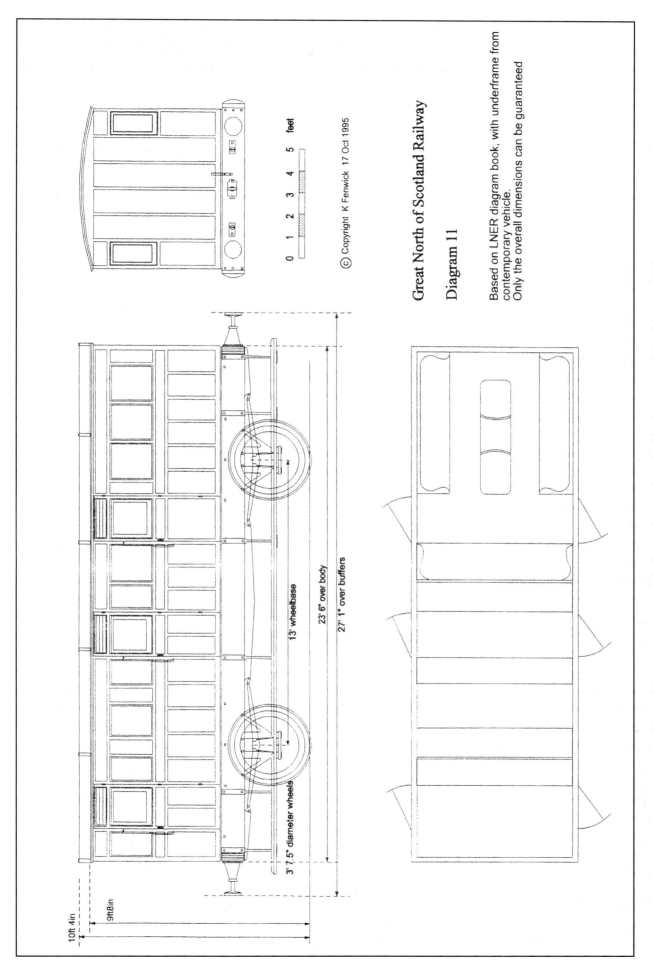

0 1 2 3 4 5 feet

© Copyright K Fenwick 17 Oct 1995

Great North of Scotland Railway

Diagram 11

Based on LNER diagram book, with underframe from contemporary vehicle.
Only the overall dimensions can be guaranteed

23' 6" over body

27' 1" over buffers

13' wheelbase

3' 7.5' diameter wheels

10ft 4in

9ft 8in

Morayshire passenger coach similar to the one described in the press article of August 1859.
(*Courtesy GNSRA*)

The Board meeting of October 13th 1859 saw a more serious demand from the Junction Company-a bill for £900, ostensibly for the Morayshire's share of the construction cost of Orton station. The following day a detailed record of the dealings between the Morayshire Railway and the Aberdeen Junction Railway appeared in the *Elgin Courant* and *Elgin and Morayshire Courier*. Provost Grant's venture into print (copies of the correspondence between the two companies) did nothing to soothe the dispute. Redress was sought by the Inverness and Aberdeen Junction Railway in a printed reply on October 28th, published in the same papers used by the Provost. The author of this piece was one Theodore Martin, who had acted as Parliamentary Agent for both companies, and had drawn up the 1856 Agreement. He started off by stating that he was a long-time friend of Provost Grant, and he found it painful to be at direct variance with him. In a long address he poured vitriol on the Morayshire Railway and its Chairman Provost James Grant, drawing comparisons between the Morayshire Railway in its dealings with the I&AJR, and the Wolf of Badenoch and his dealings with the Elgin Cathedral in centuries past.*
He continued with this theme by suggesting that the Morayshire would not give the Junction Company a sixpence, though it demanded to have its hand continually in the I&AJR's till.

Monday, October 31st saw the AGM of the Morayshire take place at the Station Hotel in Elgin. The main talking point was the opening of the line to Craigellachie, which although taken place in the middle of winter, had added considerably to the revenue of the Company in the ten months of its operation. The tonnage of traffic over the line had increased from 14,808 tons in 1858 to 32,445 tons in 1859. Passenger traffic was also much improved, from 61,069 in 1858 to 102,031 in 1859. An increased dividend was announced, amounting to 4%, the highest it had been since the opening year. Blame was still laid at the door of the Inverness and Aberdeen Junction Railway, stating that if they had remained true to the agreement of 1856, the shareholders of the Morayshire would have had a dividend of 5%. To be fair, there was another burden on the Morayshire the repair, replacement, and increase in their wagon fleet. Questions were raised from the floor by a Mr Forsyth, writer, regarding the accounting methods of the Morayshire. On the whole however the meeting seemed happy with the report from the Board, and following the appointment of Directors and auditors, an Extraordinary Meeting was called to discuss the state of relations between the Inverness and Aberdeen Junction Railway and themselves. All attempts to come to any form of agreement with Inverness and Aberdeen Junction Company amounted to nought. Reference was made to the press statement by Theodore Martin, which the Provost did not wish to reply to in detail at this meeting, preferring to return to the newspaper columns to defend the Morayshire. He went on to make it clear that the intention of this EGM was to seek approval to build a direct line from Elgin to Rothes. As there were no major engineering works, just some small bridges, the Board was confident that the line could be constructed for £4000 per mile. The total cost of the proposed line was to be no more than £38,000.

Mr Cameron, writer of Elgin, in a long and detailed speech seemed to sum up the feeling of not only those present at the meeting, but also most of the population of Elgin. They had grown tired of the antics of the Inverness people, whom they felt were jealous of the success of the Morayshire Company. The motion to build a direct line through the Glen of Rothes was seconded by Mr Walker of Kintrae and unanimously agreed to by the meeting. The Morayshire Railway Company was back in the railway construction business.

Forty miles away in Inverness, on the same day as the Morayshire's AGM, the Inverness and Aberdeen Junction Railway were holding a half yearly meeting. Their Chairman announced a dividend of $3^1/_2\%$ and he stated that *"there was no other matter on which to remark."* They did however publish a lengthy statement, the content of which blamed the Morayshire for all the difficulties. The only conciliatory remark came at the end of the report in which the I&AJR stated that it regretted the differences between the companies and they only wished for friendly co-operation.

*The Wolf of Badenoch burnt Elgin Cathedral in May 1390.

As promised at the Morayshire's AGM, Provost Grant replied to Mr Martin's article in a neat and precise way carried in the local Elgin papers of the 2nd and 4th of November. His only descent into name-calling came towards the end of his writing, when he referred to Mr Martin's Wolf of Badenoch remark. This he counters by stating that the *"wolf most detested by mankind is a wolf in sheep's clothing,"* alluding to the behaviour of Mr Martin, from being a supporter of the Morayshire and its aims, to now being one of its critics.

The local press who since 1857 had not lost an opportunity to censure the Morayshire Railway Company, were now standing solidly behind its direct line to Rothes. The *Elgin and Morayshire Courier* stated:

> The best interests of the community are in having a free and untrammelled line of communication. Money is needed, and it is the duty of the people of this district to give substantial support.

The weather at the start of November seemed as stormy as the relations between Elgin and Inverness. A train on its way to Orton was brought to a standstill by a landslide on the Morayshire line at Millerhill, that is, near the Rothes end of the line. No damage was done to the train, but the turnpike road in the area was also blocked.

A bill of £330 from Brown and Marshall was passed for payment at the Board meeting in Elgin on November 22nd. Provost Grant gave a report on his travels to Edinburgh and London in his quest to secure funding for the direct line. Draft copies of the Bill were available for inspection on December 20th.

9 THE DISPUTE BETWEEN MISS MORAYSHIRE & MR INVERNESS

At Craigellachie on January 10th 1860, the charges from the Inverness and Aberdeen Junction Railway for the use of the Elgin-Orton line were under discussion. The Board of the Morayshire believed that they were totally unreasonable. It was decided the Secretary should write to the I&AJR to inform them what he thought was a fair and equitable price for the use of the Elgin-Orton line.

Notice of the intention of the Morayshire to construct a Direct line to Rothes appeared in the press at the beginning of January. The first hurdle for the bill to pass on its way through Parliament was cleared with the defeat of its opposition before a committee on Monday the 26th of January. This news was met with a large celebration in Rothes on Tuesday the 27th. A crowd of four to five hundred people erected a large bonfire on top of Castlehill. Several cartloads of wood and some barrels of tar assured the surrounding countryside was well lit up. The local population was fuelled on the local *"mountain dew,"* with many toasts being drunk, the loudest being the one for Provost Grant and the promoters of the Direct line. As the fire burned down, the crowd made its way home escorted by the sound of drums, bagpipes and flutes.

The reply from the Junction Company regarding the outstanding charges made to the Morayshire was discussed on February 13th. In short, the Inverness and Aberdeen Junction Railway wanted full settlement of the amount they requested, and did not want to discuss this matter again. Building the direct line would exceed the Morayshire's borrowing limit by £4500. Provost Grant and his brother John proposed to lend this amount to the Morayshire at commercial rates for the period of 18 months.

On March 8th 1869 Mr Hutchison the Stationmaster at Elgin left the employment of the Morayshire to become the manager of the Findhorn Railway; his place was taken by Mr Allan. At this date the £4500 loan from James and John Grant was on deposit in the Commercial Bank.

Saturday, March 17th saw the Station Hotel in Lossiemouth sustain damage as the result of an accident. Sandstone was being blasted at the nearby quarry when a portion of rock weighing in excess of 1 cwt was blown into the air. It came to a temporary rest on the roof of the hotel before smashing through the slates and becoming wedged in the attic. This was fortunate as it prevented further damage by the stone hitting any prospective travellers waiting for the train to Elgin.

To approve the extension of the Morayshire, an EGM was held at the Station Hotel on Monday 16th April 1860. Opposition to the scheme had been gathering, so the meeting was not altogether a foregone conclusion. Chief among the protesters was Mr Forsyth, who had made complaints about the Morayshire's accounting methods at the 1859 AGM. He pursued this theme, suggesting that in its present financial condition, the Morayshire was not capable of constructing the line. Whether his case was a strong one or not, it was swept aside by the Chairman Provost Grant, who ruled that the meeting was to decide whether the line should be built, not whether the Morayshire could afford to build it. The public at the meeting supported the Provost. In the press reports of the meeting, they not only sided with Provost Grant, they went further, suggesting that the Morayshire should waste no time once the Direct line to Rothes was built, by constructing a line up Speyside. Free trade was the thought behind the press's support of the Morayshire's new railway. A rather important observer was at the meeting as a guest of Provost Grant, Walter Montgomery Neilson, the proprietor of Neilson and Co locomotive builder, Glasgow.

Though defeated at the meeting, Mr Forsyth was far from finished in his opposition to the Morayshire's intention. Joining forces with the Lord Seafield, the Inverness and Aberdeen Junction Railway, and a handful of other Morayshire shareholders, a petition against the line's construction was set out. It was expected that this matter would be discussed in Parliament in the next eight to ten days.

Whilst all this was going on, it was still business as usual for the Morayshire as on May 25th the summer excursion season began.

> The first juvenile band of the season were the children of our infant school, who along with Miss Gardiner and her assistants went down to the seaside and enjoyed themselves. We know of nothing more pleasant than to look upon a number of children all in high glee on a pleasure excursion. We hope the example shown by Miss Gardiner will soon be followed by the other teachers. *Elgin Courant.*

The Select Committee to consider the Morayshire's Direct line met for the first time on June 6th 1860. Things went well for the Morayshire on the first day. It was revealed that the backer of the petition against the line was Lord Seafield, who was a major shareholder in the I&AJR. The large number of signatures on the petition fell into two major categories. They were either tenants of Lord Seafield and those who were not, but claimed to be residents of Elgin, when in fact they were actually from Forres and other points west of Elgin. Other shareholders who had concerns about this project- law agents and farmers, who between them held £120 worth of shares of the total Morayshire stock of £70,000. The law agents were employed by Lord Seafield and the farmers were in arrears to the Morayshire and owed that company money. The committee decided that Lord Seafield did have a right to be heard, adding a stipulation that any evidence from him would be confined to his role as a landowner over which the Morayshire's new line would pass.

Mr Hope Scott, QC for the Morayshire, explained why there was a need for an independent line, citing numerous examples of the unreasonable behaviour of the Inverness and Aberdeen Junction Company. The Chairman of the Select Committee agreed that by turning out the Morayshire's passengers from their carriages at Orton, and making them buy tickets from the I&AJR to complete the journey to Elgin, did not make them a balanced partner. Round one to Provost Grant and the Morayshire Railway.

At the start of the following day's proceedings, Provost Grant was asked various questions about the financial position of the Company, in particular about the claim by the Lord of Seafield that where the Morayshire crossed his land rent that should have been paid to him over the last two and a half years was still due. Lord Seafield stated that when this back rent was paid over, the Morayshire's monitory position would be further weakened. Provost Grant answered that the rental money had been paid on time to his Lordship's Tenants. Regarding other financial dealings of the Morayshire, I think Provost Grant did a reasonable job in making his Company look healthier than it really was.

Next on the stand was Mr Mills. The questions asked of him were concerning the working of the line. On the plus side, the Direct line would enable the Morayshire to operate with one locomotive if necessary. The present situation meant that the minimum requirement was two engines. On the minus side the new line had a fierce gradient of 1 in 55 climbing out of Elgin. Mr Mills was nonetheless confident that the Morayshire's tank engines were up to the job. Mr Samuel was next to give evidence. He considered that the line could be constructed within the estimated costs. There then followed various inhabitants of Rothes and Craigellachie all of whom thought that it would be of great benefit to not only their own towns, but the whole district should the Direct line be constructed. At the end of the day's proceedings (round two) I think both sides could claim a draw.

Friday, June 6th opened with Mr Brander, merchant and ship owner of Lossiemouth, giving evidence in favour of the construction of the Direct line. He was followed by Mr Smith, distiller Glenlivet, who also wanted and could see great benefit from the building of the line. A similar report in favour of the line came from a Mr Cumming of London, who owned land in the Glen of Rothes, over which 2½ miles of the proposed railway would run. At the end of his testimony a survey of landowners and occupiers in the Glen was given in evidence. It showed 50 people with interests in the Glen were in favour of the line, nine against.

The next witness to be called was a representative for Lord Seafield. Comment was made about the fact that his Lordship could only give evidence as a landowner in the district and the restrictions this placed upon him. In view of the fact that Lord Seafield held £30,000 worth of shares in the I&AJR and was guarantor for £20,000 more, your writer believes that the Chairman of the examining committee acted correctly.

The main points of Lord Seafield's representative argument were that there would be no saving in time between the Elgin-Orton route and the proposed Direct line. This because an engine could not climb a gradient of 1 in 55 at speed. The doctor in the location was also a farmer, and it was obvious to Lord Seafield's representative, that for him to have time to run a farm the local population were either very healthy, or much more likely very few in number. Industry in the area consisted of a few lime kilns, a granary, and a woollen manufacture. The latter, his Lordship suspected of actually being one sheep, rather than a factory, at most this collection of industry could account for only 12 jobs. The attack continued with a jibe at Mr Mills and his holding of the posts of Secretary, Engineer and General Manager. It was claimed this combining of posts demonstrated that the line was too small to operate as a proper railway. The supply of £4000 by the Provost and his brother was also mentioned, along with other damning evidence of the precarious financial position that the Morayshire was in. It must have been with some relief that an adjournment was called for the weekend. What had started out that Friday as a good day for the Morayshire, had come close to disaster and nearly a knockout.

Monday, June 11th 1860 saw Lord March examined as representative of the Duke of Richmond, owner of Gordon Castle and large tracts of land stretching all the way to Glenlivet. The Duke was against the construction of the Direct line, the main thrust of his argument also being the lack of population in the area. As the Duke owned the shooting rights for the area, he had no intention of giving them up to anyone wishing to farm or set up in some form of business. This being the case there was no likelihood of any increase in traffic for the Morayshire. Next in to give evidence was the Hon T C Bruce, Factor to Lord Seafield and Deputy Chairman of the Inverness and Aberdeen Junction Railway. With that lineage, you've probably surmised, he was in all ways against the Morayshire. Mr Brown of Linkwood (another Factor of Lord Seafield), Director of the Great North of Scotland Railway and Chairman of the Findhorn Railway, tactfully forgot to mention that he also had connections with the I&AJR. Part of his farm was to be crossed by the Direct line, so he too was against the proposal of the Morayshire. The only good points to come from the day's evidence was that Mr Mills had done the estimates for the Findhorn Railway, and that line had been built for the costs he had stated. In addition, the witnesses had tried too hard to ruin the Morayshire's case. If they were to be believed, the total population between Elgin and Rothes amounted too little more than five men and a sheep dog. Even though the complainants were all large landowners in the area, it did seem unlikely that the situation would remain static for all time, so that day, the Morayshire won a narrow victory on points.

Tuesday, June 12th 1860 was the last day of the hearing. The opposition to the line fielded a Mr Blyth, railway engineer. This gentleman in the employ of the Lord Seafield had re-surveyed the Direct line and made unfavourable estimates on the capacity of the Morayshire's engines. Counsel for the Morayshire dismantled Mr Blyth's arguments before summing up with the following points: Light passenger trains worked gradients greater than 1 in 55 at speed every day and goods traffic from which the principal revenue would be derived did not require swiftness of service. Most importantly of all, if the Direct line was such a bad venture, why did the I&AJR oppose it so vigorously. A small and struggling community had promoted and built the first railway in the north of Scotland, and in doing so had pledged to date the sum of £110,000. Viewed as a matter of competition, insurance and protection for the trade in their district, the sum of £40,000 was a wise investment by the communities of Elgin and Lossiemouth, even if there was no chance of remuneration.

The House was then cleared. On readmission of the public, the Chairman announced the following:

"The Committee desire me to state that the preamble to the bill is proved to their satisfaction." The way was now cleared for the lightweight champion to build its Direct line.

It is easy to believe that the Directors of the Inverness and Aberdeen Junction Railway were unimpressed with the Morayshire's victory. Not so easy was the strength of feeling from the periodical the *"Railway Times."* They adversely suggested in their article that the Lord Seafield and Lord March had the best interests of the Morayshire at heart by opposing their plans for the Direct line. Mr Dougall the Hon T C Bruce and Mr Blyth knew the railway business, and if they said a line would not pay, then it would not. Right to the close of the piece the attack on the Morayshire was kept up. *"The wisdom of Parliament has thought fit to punish the applicants by conceding their request. We leave the Morayshire to its fate in the hope that its misfortune may become a warning in time to come."*

The *Elgin and Morayshire Courier* were furious with both the *"Railway Times,"* and the nobility's opposition to the Direct line. Its contemporary the *Elgin Courant* was magnanimous in victory suggesting that being abusive towards the Inverness and Aberdeen Junction Railway would only serve to make them enemies of the Morayshire Railway. The writer went on to say *"in trying to defeat the Direct line the I&AJR spent thousands of pounds, and anyone spending that amount of money must be sincere in their beliefs, however mistaken in their views and general interests of a district of the country."*

At a discussion held by the Morayshire Board at Elgin on July 2nd 1860, Mr Mills stepped down from his day-to-day role of running the railway. This was felt necessary because of the amount of time he was devoting to raising the capital for the construction of the Direct line and dealing with the I&AJR's continuing demands. The person now to attend to these duties was Mr Watt the Stationmaster at Craigellachie. For this to happen, Mr Allan presently on post at Elgin, would go to Craigellachie. To help soften the move, Mr Allan's salary was to be increased by £10 to £40 per annum. The conclusive moves in this reshuffle of personnel was the appointment of Mr Turnbull as Stationmaster Elgin.

The Secretary reported on talks that he had had with Neilson of Glasgow about a new locomotive. The cost for a new engine would be £1775, to be paid half in cash and the rest in bills. The board gave the Secretary the agreement to continue with this transaction. The meeting expressed the hope that Neilson would take one of the Morayshire's present engines in part payment.

Both Provost Grant and Mr Samuel, accompanied by a team of engineers, had been out surveying for another extension to the Morayshire. This time they wanted to continue the railway from Glenavon to Tomintoul, through to the Spital of Glenshee and finally on to Blairgowrie. A look at any map of the north of Scotland will give you some idea of the enormity of the task the Morayshire was setting itself. The *Elgin Courant* reported of its confidence and belief in the abilities of Mr Samuel.

Mrs Taylor's annuity was due to be paid in August, and at a meeting on the 15th of that month in Elgin, the matter was discussed by the Directors. It was agreed to pay her this and the next quarter's payment amounting to £10, but she was to be advised that the sum paid to her in the following year would amount to £10 in total. This reduction was deemed necessary as the Morayshire had to *"practice economy in every possible way."* In addition, an EGM was to be arranged to organise the raising of funds for the building of the Direct line to Rothes. The sum required to carry out the construction was £26,000.

Meanwhile, a quarter of a mile outside Craigellachie station at a place known as the Bulwark siding, the time quarter past eleven Mr William Allan, (recently appointed Stationmaster at Craigellachie) and Thomas Smith, pointsman shunted a truck by hand off the main line into the siding. To carry out this procedure, a key carried by Mr Smith was required to open the points. The wagon safely in the siding, Mr Allan made his way back to Craigellachie to await the arrival of the next passenger train due at ten minutes past one. This service was driven by Thomas Mackenzie who was normally employed as a fireman, but on this occasion was acting as a driver. On the footplate with him was John Mason. The other member of the train crew, James Shiach was in the guards van. The train approached the area of the siding at a speed of 20 mph. Mackenzie observed that the points to the siding had not been reset for the main line. Despite the brake being applied hard, the engine did not have room to come to a halt before striking the wagon in the siding. Both Mackenzie and Masson jumped from the footplate of the locomotive, which carried on down the siding. The wagon left the rails, followed shortly by the locomotive that came to rest in an area of soft ground at the end of the siding. It was fortunate that the engine crew had chosen to jump off the locomotive, as a portion of handrail had become bent and driven into the footplate. This could have had dire consequences for anyone standing there. On the train there were about 12 passengers, one of whom was Superintendent Peter Grant of Elgin Police. These shaken individuals were conveyed to Aberlour. Although the locomotive itself was not severely damaged, it was not one of the better days for the Morayshire Railway.

The purpose of the EGM on September 19th 1860 at the Railway Hotel in Elgin was to empower the Directors to issue £26,000 of preference stock to enable the construction of the Direct line to Rothes. It was proposed that this stock would pay a guaranteed dividend of $4\frac{1}{2}\%$. Provost Grant in his opening address gave a summary of events since the approval by Parliament to the construction of the line. He also gave notice of developments that had occurred, of which chief among them was the proposal to carry the Morayshire line all the way from Craigellachie through to Blairgowrie. The good Provost thought this was a matter of not only local importance, but of national importance. Competition was again facing the Morayshire with a proposal for a line from Forres to Dunkeld and another was to be constructed by the Great North of Scotland Railway from Dufftown up the valley of the River Spey to Abernethy *. As ever Provost Grant was confident that when these two schemes, along with the Morayshire's proposal were placed before Parliament, the logical choice would be the Morayshire's.

Though this declaration was met with loud applause from the floor of the meeting, there were a number of prominent Morayshire shareholders who were against this scheme. Chief amongst the opponents was Dr Paul. This gentleman wanted a delay in the issue of the preference stock. He stated that he had bought shares in the Morayshire Railway not as a means of an investment for himself, but for the good of the town of Elgin. Dr Paul was greatly concerned that the Morayshire had only managed to raise £12,000 of the expected construction cost of £40,000. If the proposal went ahead, £26,000 worth of preference stock required to be issued and this would cause an intolerable burden to the Morayshire Company. Mr Cameron, one of Elgin's legal community, supported Dr Paul's argument. This gentleman was not quite as magnanimous as Dr Paul inasmuch as he invested to receive a return on his money. The prospect of this would have little chance of occurring with so many preference shares. He also thought it would be better to delay construction for two or three years to gather finances. A long and serious debate ensued, through which Provost Grant kept stating the urgency of building the new line to Rothes with all speed, going on to argue that it was now vital to establish the Morayshire's position before any other lines started to tap into the Speyside traffic, which he viewed as the Morayshire's right. Provost Grant however was dogged by the fact that shares sold in the Morayshire for £10 each could, at the time of this meeting, muster only £4, or if you were very lucky £4-10/- on the open market.

Compromise was reached when the major shareholders agreed to double their holding in the Company on the condition that no preference shares would be issued until £20,000 of ordinary stock had been sold. With the matter of funding the new line to Rothes more or less settled, a separate meeting was held by the Directors to discuss the derailment at Bulwark siding. It was decided that both Mr William Allan the Stationmaster and Thomas Smith pointsman were responsible for the accident, and both would be fined a week's wages. It was also to be noted by them that any other occurrences would result in dismissal.

*now known as Nethybridge.

The Morayshire decided to tidy up its property at Lossiemouth by fencing off and levelling up the ground at the Station Hotel. At a Board meeting on October 5th 1860, it was decided to offer the services of the workman engaged to carry out this work to the Harbour Board, with a view to improving their property.

Provost Grant brought to the attention of the meeting that the *"Inverness people"* were now promoting a line from Perth to Inverness. In view of this it was now very important that the Morayshire's Direct line go on with all haste. Mr Mills and Mr Samuel had completed the survey of the line that was laid before the meeting. All the difficult portions of the route were marked. The Great North of Scotland Railway were proposing to build a railway from Dufftown to Grantown. To this end arrangements had been put in hand so the Morayshire and the GNS could work together. Provost Grant and Mr Mills had had several meetings with members of the GNSR board and found them to be very cordial. Interest had also been expressed by the Great North in the Morayshire's route to the South.

A few days after this meeting, a story appeared in the *Nairnshire Telegraph* which suggested that the Morayshire Railway had been bought by the Great North of Scotland. This was not true, and a slightly more accurate report appeared in the *Elgin Courant* of October 12th 1860. They suggested that the Great North had bought £10,000 worth of stock in the Morayshire to aid construction of the Direct line. The Direct line was also to be extended to meet up with the GNS Dufftown line. When this was done the Great North of Scotland Railway would lease the Morayshire and pay the shareholders a fixed percentage.

These press reports seemed to stimulate railway development in the counties of Moray and Banff. The Inverness and Aberdeen Junction viewed any link between the GNSR and Morayshire as an attack upon themselves. Their retaliation was reported on page 5 of the *Elgin Courant* of October 19th 1860. The I&AJR had begun a survey for a line from Alves to Burghead, to take traffic away from Lossiemouth harbour and the Morayshire's Lossie line. On upper Banffshire they were also surveying a route to connect with the Inverness-Perth line.

The true nature of the agreement between the Morayshire and the Great North of Scotland was also revealed on page 8 of the October 19th edition of the *Elgin Courant*. The Great North was to work the Morayshire in perpetuity for 45% of the drawings. When the dividend of the Morayshire reached 5%, the GNSR would receive 50% for working the line; any additional surplus would be divided between the two companies. In the interim the Great North was to give the Morayshire £20,000 to aid construction of the Direct line to Rothes and the extension to meet up with the Keith and Dufftown's Speyside line at Aberlour. When the two lines were linked, the Great North was to take possession of the Morayshire's rolling stock. For this plan to go ahead, it would be necessary for both companies to go to Parliament for a bill.

Towards the end of October, business through the port of Lossiemouth was so good that the Morayshire was proposing to increase the size of the Lossiemouth station to cope with demand. Discussion on this matter did not go very far ahead at the Board meeting of the 25th of October. Enter Mr Inglis and Mr Leslie of Edinburgh, the gentlemen who had caused so many problems for the Morayshire in the early 1850's. They had with them a proposal from the Inverness and Aberdeen Junction Railway to amalgamate with the Morayshire. They also produced a printed leaflet calling for a better working agreement between the aforementioned parties and the Great North of Scotland Railway. The offer affecting the Morayshire was as follows:

> 1. The first party will be prepared to recommend to their shareholders to lease in perpetuity the undertaking and plant of the company of the second party, subject to the conditions after expressed from 1st July, and to pay thereafter an annual dividend of $4^{1}/_{2}\%$ upon ordinary stock so long as the same shall remain unredeemed and of interest on the mortgage debt.

2. The first party to be entitled to redeem the said preference stock on the same terms as the said second party.

3. Application to be made to Parliament in the ensuing session for powers to carry these objects into effect, and to enable the second party to abandon the Rothes Direct line.

4. A formal agreement for carrying out the above proposals, if accepted, to be entered into; and the same to be settled, in the case of difference of opinion by_____ as mutual referee,

Inglis & Leslie.

Edinburgh, 24th Oct., 1860.

This was an interesting offer and with the first choice of a mutual referee being given to the Morayshire, it was worth Provost Grant and the Board of the Morayshire giving it thought. I am certain they would have done, had it come from anyone other than Messrs Inglis and Burns.

The ultimate decision on this matter was held in the hands of those who chose to attend the Special Meeting after the AGM on October 31st.

The AGM held in the Station Hotel Elgin started badly with the news that the Morayshire was not able to pay a dividend for the year of 1860. This failure was put squarely at the door of the Inverness and Aberdeen Junction Railway Company. Their action in the last year had certainly done a great deal of damage. Revenue for traffic coming over the I&AJR's line amounted to nil, with the Junction Company now keeping all the money for traffic passing between Elgin and Orton. The coaches of the Morayshire were no longer attached to the I&AJR's trains so passengers had to rebook their journey at either Elgin or Orton. Goods traffic, which as we know in previous years had been taking up to 24 hours to complete a journey from Lossiemouth to Craigellachie, was in 1860 taking two to three days! Due to the I&AJR's insistence on having goods transferred onto their rolling stock.

The good news, of which there was some, was the sanction to build the Direct line to Rothes. Mention was made of the scheme to construct a railway from the Morayshire's terminus of Craigellachie, down Speyside to Ballindalloch thence over the mountains to Braemar and onward to Blairgowrie. Despite the Director's claims of being able to demonstrate the practicability of this scheme and its moderate cost, it was deemed prudent not to bring this venture before the next session of Parliament, since an undertaking of this magnitude would not attract public support. Additional construction on the Morayshire was to be restricted to a line from Craigellachie to Grantown.

The only change to Board members came with the confirmation of Mr Walker of Kintrae in place of Mr Topp of Ashgrove who had retired early in the year. These matters concluded, the meeting became special for the purposes of considering the amalgamation with the Great North of Scotland Railway.

The proposal document from the GNSR was extensive, containing ten main points. The most important clauses were as briefly explained in the *Elgin Courant*'s article of October 19th. The only other item of note was the method of arbitration to be used if there was a dispute. The appointment of the arbiter was to be done by the Board of Trade. Two small alterations had been made following a meeting between Provost Grant and the GNSR Directors, whom the Provost refers to as *"most friendly people."* The changes to the agreement were the fixing of traffic rates over the Morayshire, which was to be left to the Morayshire's Directors. The Great North of Scotland Railway would receive a maximum 50% for working the line, with any balance over that rate being returned to the Morayshire's Board and divided between its shareholders. In his meetings with the Great North Board, the matter of the Morayshire's intention to build a line down the valley of the Spey had been discussed. The Provost conceded that it would not be prudent for both companies to go to Parliament with the competing schemes. So as *"fair and honest men,"* an agreement was made that the Morayshire would stand aside in its plans to build a line down Speyside. It would though, once a bridge was built by the Morayshire over the River Spey, have a connection with Speyside in one direction and Dufftown through to Aberdeen the other way. Copies of the Inverness and Aberdeen Junction Railway's proposal were then distributed to the meeting. Provost Grant advised that this document had arrived too late to be considered by this meeting and it could only be used as reference in an argument for or against the GNSR's proposal. This did not prevent the good Provost from *"pulling apart"* the Inverness and Aberdeen Junction's statement. He felt to let the line be leased by the *"Inverness people"* would allow them to do as they liked. This would result in traffic being removed from the harbour at Lossiemouth, thereby jeopardising not only that town, but also Elgin and the whole surrounding district. Continuing, he said the promise of a guaranteed $4\frac{1}{2}\%$ per annum return sounded tempting, and indeed it would be if the I&AJR continued to crumple up the Morayshire's traffic. He counter-balanced that point by claiming that, if the direct line had been in place for the year 1858-9, the Morayshire would have paid a dividend of $6\frac{1}{2}\%$. In concluding his attack on the I&AJR he compared the Morayshire to a young woman being called upon by an over-zealous suitor. *"Miss Morayshire has risen considerably in the estimation of her friend from the West, Mr Inverness,"* but he (the Provost) was afraid that their offer is *"not sufficient to buy her."* He then recited the following poem from *"Miss Morayshire to Mr Inverness."*

> *Haud awa, bide awa—-*
> *Haud awa frae me Donald*
> *Wi' a' your 4% per cent,*
> *You're no a match for me, Donald!*

The performance by Provost Grant brought the house down. Amid roars of laughter, Dr Geddes seconded a motion from the Provost to take up the Great North of Scotland Railway's offer of a joint working agreement. There were dissenting voices against the agreement with the GNSR. Mr Allan, corn merchant and Dr Paul were of the opinion that the financial position of the Morayshire was in such poor shape that the claims made by Provost Grant could not be met. Both gentlemen were concerned that the Great North of Scotland Railway would, when connected to the Morayshire, be able to supply coal into the district from Aberdeen at a cheaper rate than having it landed at Lossiemouth harbour. They proposed that the Morayshire Board should go back to the Inverness and Aberdeen Junction Railway, hold talks with them to persuade them to abandon their line from Aviemore to Forres and build instead a route from the south up Speyside to meet with the Morayshire at Craigellachie. This would block the GNSR's expansion plans and protect the Morayshire Railway from the import of goods through Aberdeen Harbour. These two gentlemen were supported in their aims by Mr Cameron, an Elgin lawyer. He suggested that the Inverness and Aberdeen Junction Railway and the Morayshire Railway were natural allies and should stand against the Great North of Scotland Railway. This last remark proved too much for Provost Grant. *"With the exception of Mr Cameron, I think everyone in this room would agree that the Junction Company had been at best an unnatural ally, though in truth a most bitter enemy."* After long and grievous exchanges, Mr Allan decided that because of the overwhelming view of the meeting to join forces with the Great North of Scotland Railway, he would withdraw his amendment. The motion for an agreement with the GNSR was declared unanimously.

The last week of October was a busy time for the Morayshire Railway. Thomas Smith and Stationmaster William Allan were brought before Sheriff Cameron to answer a charge on neglect of duty. Provost Grant as Chairman of the Morayshire Company had, as you may recall, fined both employees a week's wages for their part in this accident. In the court case he was defending both men! The agent for the crown was Mr Groggier Procurator Fiscal. It appears that both Smith and Allan had defined responsibility for the points at Craigellachie station. Regarding Bulwark, no-one had a duty to look to the correct operation of this siding, maintenance not seeming to belong to anyone and as a result, the mechanism for operation was badly rusted with several parts broken.

Rather than incriminating the two accused or the Railway Company, this neglect and lack of clear instruction seemed to assist in clearing blame from anyone, despite having the Superintendent of Elgin City Police as a witness for the prosecution. The jury retired for a short time and upon their return the foreman Mr Kay informed the Court that by a majority the case against Smith and Allan was *"Not Proven."* Your writer cannot help wondering if this meant that the two men had their forfeited wages returned!

The Morayshire Board met at Craigellachie on November 27th 1860. For discussion was the loan of £10,000 from the GNSR to assist in the construction of the Direct line with the plant of the Morayshire Railway being given as security. The terms for this transaction were accepted. One other item agreed to was a request from John Grant of Glengrant to reduce the charges for carrying empty whisky casks from Lossiemouth to Rothes.

Wednesday, November 28th saw disruption caused to the Morayshire by the Elgin Brewery. One of their delivery horses managed to trap one of its hooves between the rails of the Pinefield level crossing. The poor animal fell over and it took its driver some time to free it from the crossing. The 10.10am train to Lossiemouth was delayed for some time, until rescue was affected.

The prospect of a mini-railway boom was causing excitement in the local press. In the *Elgin Courant* of November 30th 1860, praise for this industry was being laid at the feet of Provost James Grant. The writer of the article claimed that the struggle Provost Grant had overcome to build the 10 mile Direct line from Elgin to Rothes was the catalyst. *"A little spark can mak' muckle wark."* Making reference to the prospect of some 130 miles of railway now being constructed from Dunkeld to Forres and Fiddichside to Grantown, as three companies fought to gain a chunk of business, the Elgin writer of this article was biased to obtaining as much of this potential business for his town. To this end he re-encouraged the Harbour Company to deepen and extend the harbour at Lossiemouth to stimulate cross-firth traffic from the far north of Scotland to use Lossie Harbour. This would be a quicker way of moving goods rather than a lengthy rail journey to Inverness, then onward to Forres for a south destination.

Towards the close of the year (December 19th) the Morayshire board met in Elgin. Provost Grant lay before the meeting a copy of the Bill and Petition for the construction of the Direct line through the Glen of Rothes. The Provost's law firm of Grant and Jamieson were acting for the Morayshire, with a new Parliamentary agent of Muggeridge and Bell looking after things in London. Hard times had not fallen on the Morayshire's previous Parliamentary agent, Theodore Martin, rather he was busy with Inglis and Leslie on Inverness and Aberdeen Junction Railway business.

Prospects for the forthcoming year of 1861 looked good, and things started well with over 100 tons of coal destined for the Great North of Scotland Railway being landed at Lossiemouth. A consignment sent by a Mr Priest of Lochside Colliery Fife was unable to enter the River Dee at Aberdeen due to bad weather. The agent dealing with this a Mr Stewart of Craigiebuckler, arranged for the coal to be conveyed by the Morayshire, handed over to the I&AJR and collected by the GNSR at Keith.

Alexander Sime of East Back Street Elgin died suddenly on January 11th 1861. Until the end of 1860, he had been the gatekeeper at the Linksfield crossing. Retired from the post he had held since the line to Lossiemouth had opened, he had been on his way to collect his pension when he collapsed.

That same day Provost Grant reported to the Board of the Morayshire on his recent trip to London. The Bill for the construction of the Direct line to Rothes and the one for building a bridge across the River Spey to connect the Morayshire to the Strathspey had been lodged with Parliament. The Provost had also signed the contracts with the builders, and started the land purchase with the various land owners on the route of the new railway.

The Morayshire Railway (Strathspey Junction) Bill received its first reading on the evening of Friday, February 15th. Even at this late date it was not certain that this Bill would pass through Parliament unopposed. Officers of Parliament had tried to find out if the Inverness and Perth Junction Railway and the Aberdeen and Inverness Junction Railway intended to obstruct the Strathspey and Morayshire Railway's expansion. Despite their best endeavours the Highland parties refused to reveal their intentions. The Elgin Town Council, Harbour Company and the Morayshire, on the other hand, had taken action to oppose the I&AJR's Bill to construct a branch to Burghead. The press in the form of the *Elgin Courant* appealed for all sides to refrain from wasting money in opposing each other in a Parliamentary contest.

The contractor for the Glen of Rothes Railway, a Mr Edward Preston of Caernarfon, had been in the area since February 7th. Reports in the *Elgin Courant* stated that he had been inspecting local quarries and making arrangements for the commencement of works. The first items to be constructed would be some of the bridges.

The Morayshire itself certainly had no intention of delaying the building of the Rothes Line. An announcement appeared in the *Elgin Courant* of February 22nd 1861, advising all and sundry that the turf cutting ceremony would take place on Tuesday, February 26th. The person chosen to do the honour was Provost Grant's eldest daughters, the place the field next to the Morayshire Sawmill * at 1pm. As in past years there was to be a celebratory dinner to mark the occasion, which in this case was to be held at the Elgin Station Hotel. The only difference to past years was that the Morayshire Railway Company was selling tickets to this event. For the sum of 5/6 you would have been able to buy a seat at the meal. It was expected that construction would be completed well within the nine months allowed for the contract.

An indicator of growth in the Morayshire's empire was the arrival of a new locomotive. Described in press reports as a six wheel tank, it was a 2-4-0 tank locomotive. Its weight in working order was twenty-one tons, with a boiler pressure of 120 lbs. The cylinders were 14 x 18 inches, and unlike Mr Samuel's lightweight locomotives, this engine burned coal. To prevent pollution the machine was fitted with A K Clark's patented smoke consuming apparatus, a very effective device. Surprisingly for the time, protection for the locomotive crew was excellent with a fully enclosed cab, something that did not appear on most other railways until the beginning of the 20th century. Design of this machine is credited to W H Mills Esq, the Morayshire's engineer, whilst the builder is given as Wilson & Co. Glasgow. Your writer is not aware of this locomotive builder, and all other sources credit Neilson & Co as builder of all the Morayshire's engines. This locomotive was named *"Lesmurdie,"* after Captain Stewart of Lesmurdie, one of the main supporters of the Morayshire Company. The fleet of locomotives on the Morayshire now stood at four. Along with the newly acquired *"Lesmurdie,"* there was another locomotive of a similar designed named *"Glengrant,"* which had arrived in June 1859. The two original Samuel lightweight patent locomotives *"Elgin"* and *"Lossiemouth"* still made appearances on the network.

Pressure on the Morayshire's coastal operation increased. Reports carried in the local press at the start of March suggest that it was the intention of the I&AJR to extend their proposed branch from Burghead, round to Hopeman. Mr Dougall had been in the area to hold talks with quarry owners and fish merchants.

On the inland portion of the Morayshire, Miss MacPherson Grant of Aberlour had been busy raising yet another petition, this time against the construction of a junction between the Morayshire and the Strathspey line. Despite her best efforts, on March 29th the Morayshire's bill passed through the Committee stage, the third and final reading taking place on Thursday, April 11th. The third reading of the bill for the amalgamation between the Inverness and Aberdeen Junction Railway, and the Inverness and Nairn Railway also took place on April 11th.

* Now the site of the Moray Resource Centre.

The various legal duties connected with the construction of the Direct line, and the shepherding of the Morayshire and Strathspey Junction Bill through Parliament was keeping Provost Grant busy. It did not stop him however in his role as *"the Provost of Scotland,"* attending a major event at Stirling, the laying of the cornerstone of the Wallace Monument.

By May 17th 1861 the Junction Bill had passed through all its Parliamentary stages and was awaiting Royal Assent. The shadow of the I&AJR cast itself over this event, as its amalgamation with the Inverness and Nairn was also ready for Royal signature.

With dreadful timing, accident and injury started making a reappearance on the Morayshire. On Monday, June 9th two workers, Mr Morrison and Mr Sherritt, engaged in blasting operations near Rothes, were hurt in an explosion. They were preparing a rock for shot blasting, but instead of using a wooden rod to pack the black powder into the hole, they used an iron instrument. This must have caused a spark, as the powder ignited causing injury to both men. Mr Morrison was blinded and Sherritt received severe cuts about the face caused by fragments of rock. Despite his lacerations, Mr Sherritt managed to guide Mr Morrison back to Rothes, where both received medical treatment.

There had long been claims, mainly from the Inverness camp, that travel along Speyside to Grantown would not pay. The intrepid writers of the *Courant* were however reporting that it was now usual for up to four fully-laden road coaches to come from Grantown to connect with the Morayshire Railway at Craigellachie. They went on to assure their readership, and prospective shareholders *"Railways have been made and yield moderate returns where one coach could not be supported, and surely in a district where traffic is so abundant as on Speyside, there can be no doubt of good returns."*

On July 18th 1861 on the outskirts of New Elgin, a young lad working on the Direct line had his leg run over by a railway wagon. The section of temporary rail had been laid over a boggy piece of land, allowing the rail to give a little. Therefore, the pressure from the wagon was not as great as it normally would have been, saving his limb.

The gloom of doing business with the I&AJR was given a lift on July 22nd at a Board meeting in the Grant Arms Rothes. Provost Grant was able to announce that the Junction Bill had been given its Royal Seal. This feeling of bonhomie may have extended to three clerks of the Morayshire who were all asking for a rise in salary to £20 per annum on completion of their fourth year of apprenticeship. This rise for Dickson Beaton, Alexander Montach and James Masterson was approved unanimously

The Morayshire Railway was proving to be quite an attraction to the inhabitants of Rothes. Sadly for the Company, this did not result in an increase in business. Rather it appears that the population of Rothes had taken to trespassing on the line on a regular basis, and in particular on Sundays. The Secretary had given instructions that names were to be taken of any person caught on the line. This operation was carried out on July 28th. Most parties when approached left the railway property. One however, a John Christie of Blackhillock, refused to leave the area. Legal proceedings in accordance to the relevant Act of Parliament were to be taken against him with the outcome of the case to be widely publicised as an example to all.

On August 6th 1861 the Board were advised by Mr Mills that he was resigning from the Morayshire Railway. He had been offered the post as joint engineer on the GNSR's Strathspey Railway (Gibbs of Aberdeen were the other party). The Directors wished Mr Mills well in his new post, though he had not completely severed his connection with the Morayshire, remaining as engineer on all the Morayshire's opened lines at a salary of £50 per year until the Morayshire and GNSR lines were joined together. The posts of Secretary and General Manager were to be taken over by Mr Watt at a salary of £150 per annum. Mr Golightly, who was in charge of locomotives and rolling stock, would be responsible for the day to day maintenance of the Elgin and Lossiemouth line under the direction of Mr Mills. This resulted in an increase in his income.

The increases in the borrowing powers of the Company were approved without any objection at the EGM of August 19th.

On August 22nd a small child, the son of Mr Robert Mustard, crawled through the wicket gates at the Lossiemouth level crossing into the path of the 3.15pm train. The child's legs were severed and he died, making it another fatal accident on the Morayshire Railway. A report was sent to both the Procurator Fiscal and the Board of Trade.

Telegraph wires were to be erected along the Morayshire's line and would in turn be connected to the Great North of Scotland's one. This telegraph, although for Railway use, was the first electrical communication system to reach the Elgin area. Mr Mills, overseeing the installation, was also to assist the Morayshire in an inspection of its housing stock to see what repairs were required to keep them up to standard. Progress on the Direct line was good, so it was deemed necessary to put the Morayshire Board meetings onto a two-week cycle rather than as required. The nearing of completion of the major construction work on the Glen of Rothes may explain the Morayshire giving up the leases on the Lossiemouth quarries.

The next Board meeting took place on September 13th. There was little to fill the agenda. A request for information on the condition of the wicket gate at Lossiemouth was asked for by the Procurator Fiscal, Mr McGregor, with this matter to be attended to by the Company Secretary. The only other item was an improvement in the way the Company accounts were written up. For the rest of September no further meetings took place.

10 GLEN OF ROTHES RAILWAY

The *Elgin Courant* was placing its full backing behind the Morayshire Railway and its expansion up the Glen of Rothes and on to its connection with the Strathspey Railway. In order perhaps to whet the public's appetite for travel on the new route, an extensive article was published by them on October 4th covering this subject. A short extract from that piece appears next.

The line starts from the Elgin station of the Morayshire Railway in the same direction as the Lossiemouth line, but has scarcely got clear of the station when it makes a sweeping turn to the right and ascends an embankment which rises higher and higher to cross the Tyock Burn and the Linkwood Road at a height of about 12 feet. We notice the crossing of the Tyock, which flows through a stone arch below the railway. The Linkwood Road is crossed by a bridge made of metal girders. Leaving this bridge we enter a pretty deep, but short cutting through a knoll on Dr Geddes farm of Tyrockside. Continuing along another embankment which raises the line to a sufficient height to cross over the Inverness and Aberdeen Junction line by a bridge.

Here there is a very fine view to be got of Elgin and the country around it. The Cathedral can be seen amongst the trees, near to it are the tall chimneys of the Elgin Brewery and Newmill Foundry and factory. Next appears the fine dome of Anderson Institution, and farther to the west the tower of the parish church in the centre of the High Street. To the extreme west the dome of Gray's hospital appears as if to nestle in the midst of the Oak Wood. Close at hand is the house of Ashgrove, and a little beyond is the elegant Station Hotel.

But if the trains were once running a passenger will scarce have time to notice all these things, when he will be whirled around the corner of a plantation and into a cutting of a considerable depth, where for a short time his vision will be entirely eclipsed. As to the progress of the line we are very happy to see such advancement. There is a small portion of embankment to make up where the line enters Longmorn Farm, and about half a mile further up, some 200 yards of bank are yet to be cut through. With these exceptions however the line is all but finished to where it crosses the Longmorn Burn.

At Longmorn where burn and road are crossed by a bridge of three arches, there is an embankment of some 300 yards in length yet to be made up. This appears to be the heaviest piece of work which remains to be done. There are at present many horses and carts employed in making it up from a hill at some distance. When it is once made up however, wagons will be able to run from the mouth of the Glen of Rothes to Longmorn, and an engine— our old friend *"Elgin"* — has been brought up to work them.

On our left stands Scat Craig, famous in the geology of Moray. Here our late lamented Town Clerk, Mr Duff passed many a day gathering fossils. A rapid stream comes tumbling down alongside the railway at this point, and during the flood of Monday week interfered to some extent with the embankment. From the Scat Crag the line is formed all the way to the farm steading of Coleburn in the Glen of Rothes. Here there are two knolls to be cut through, but in length they are only a few yards each.

The line then enters on the farm of Glen of Rothes, the permanent rails are laid for nearly half a mile, but are stopped short at a crossing of a burn, and neither sleeper or rail are seen again for over a mile. The earthworks are however nearly complete to Birchfield, Mr. Thompson's farm on the west side of the Glen. A little further on there is a portion of permanent rails on the farm of Oldyards. A space next occurs where there is as yet no appearance of a railway, but at about half a mile's distance we come to a deep cutting nearly opposite Pitcragie toll bar.

As we proceed towards Rothes the line comes into contact with the Burn of Rothes and as we cross this stream for the last time we are "switched" on to the rails from Orton to Craigellachie.

The progress made since the works were commenced is very remarkable, especially when you take into account that owing to the wetness of the summer, the men have been able to work on average, only about four days a week.

We bid our readers farewell, wishing them an early and pleasant trip along the line where the other day we packed our way on foot.

The Inverness and Aberdeen Junction Railway stepped up the pressure on the Morayshire by purchasing a half share in Burghead harbour at the beginning of October 1861. Reports in the *Elgin Courant* of October 4th also gave notice of the Junction Company's intention to build a line from Alves to Burghead. Construction was to start immediately and it was hoped to have the service running by May of 1862.

What had become of the fortnightly meetings the Morayshire Board had deemed that were now necessary? They had not taken place! It was not until October 10th that the Directors of the company met. The talk was of sharing costs on a 50 - 50 basis with the Strathspey Company on the construction of a station at Craigellachie. Mr Mills explained various arrangements for co-operation between the respective companies. It was decided that drawings, etc, would be made available for the AGM. Thought was also to be given to holding an EGM for the purpose of authorising construction of Craigellachie Junction and the issue of shares for same.

The two week cycle of meetings started as the Directors next met on October 25th. Authorisation was given by the Board for the fitting of a smoke consumer to *"Glengrant"* of the same design as the one on *"Lesmurdie"*. More pressing was the supply of rails to the Company for construction of the Glen line. Mr Ronald of Aberdeen, supplier of rails, had not been paid in either cash, debentures or preference shares. He was threatening to remove a cargo of rails that was sitting at Lossiemouth harbour. As these were urgently needed, arrangements were made with the Commercial Bank of Scotland for an advance of £3000 to settle with Mr Ronald.

The Annual General Meeting of the Morayshire was held on Wednesday, October 30th 1861 at the Station Hotel in Elgin. In the previous year business had been good for the Morayshire, but after expenses and other payments had been made a sum of only £141-14s-5d remained, too little an amount to make a dividend payment on ordinary shares. Payments amounting to £1382-4s-7d had been paid to the I&AJR in the previous financial year. This figure did not include the loss of revenue for the traffic carried between Orton and Elgin. The Directors blamed the I&AJR for these losses, but they maintained that on completion of the Direct line, a good return on the Company's shares would be expected. In the previous year passengers on the Morayshire's system had increased by 13,253 and tonnage of goods had gone up 10,196 tons, so the Director's optimism was well founded. To give a better picture of the financial state of the company, in future the books were to be closed on September 30th to allow them to be written up for the AGM. The meeting also approved the extension of the Morayshire line to Craigellachie, and authorised the issue of £20,000 worth of shares. The amount of preference shares was to be no greater than £7000 and the dividend payable on them should not exceed 5%.

The Inverness and Aberdeen Junction Railway held its half yearly general meeting on Tuesday the 29th at the Inverness Station Hotel. Things were brighter for the shareholders in this company, with a dividend of $4^{1}/_{2}$% being declared. Possibly with an eye to its easterly neighbour, the Directors of the

I&AJR, *"hoped that this would be the last year that such a low dividend was declared, and next year it would be better and continue to increase year on year."* The I&AJR also bought £50,000 worth of shares in the Inverness and Perth Railway, a move that was probably viewed as a threat to not only the Morayshire, but also the Great North of Scotland Railway.

On November 5th 1861 Mr Grant of Belliheglash resigned as a director of the Morayshire, being replaced by Bailie Alexander Urquhart. A third call on £2 shares was also made.

The Morayshire was in trouble with the Railway Clearing House for retaining wagon sheets from other companies to cover Morayshire wagons. The Directors conceded that the Clearing House was correct in its allegation and on November 15th gave permission to buy eight wagon covers.

Yet another letter had been received from the I&AJR over the charges relative to the Orton station agreement. The Secretary and Mr Mills were to contact the I&AJR about this matter. Permission was given to a Mr Stewart, corn merchant, to use a piece of land at Rothes station as a store, this on the understanding that should the railway company require the land at a later date he would vacate the site. A number of bad debts were also discussed, with the Chairman reminding the meeting that all accounts should be settled by the 5th day of the succeeding month. Letters were to be sent to the offenders telling them that their credit facilities would be withdrawn. A request for a station and a siding at Longmorn had been made by Earl of Fife's factor. To encourage the Morayshire to make this provision, the Estate offered to pay £30 in cash, provide land rent free and allow abatement of £3 per annum in payment due by the railway company as tenant. The Directors agreed to erect a station on these terms.

Action was to be taken to cut costs in the construction of the Craigellachie extension. Among the ideas approved at the Board meeting of November 20th was one to avoid building an embankment at Dandaleith and associated over bridge to the farm. Instead the line at this point was to be crossed on the level for access to the farm.

In respect to the construction of the bridge over the River Spey, it was estimated that this would cost £5400-13/- to build. The Board thought that a considerable reduction in price might be possible, and a meeting with the Contractor was to be arranged. If the Morayshire supplied the rails and sleepers, this left the iron work and the cylinders that were to form the base of the bridge to be supplied by a specialist contractor *"in the habit of making such items."* In the meantime Mr Preston was to be asked for a tender for this work.

Also at this meeting, Mr Grant of Belliheglash was given a free ticket for his long and valuable service to the Directors.

On November 27th the *Elgin Courant* gave the following favourable report on the progress of the Glen of Rothes Railway.

> Crossing the line of the new railway a little above Mr Grant's Wester Whitewreath, we are glad to observe that the large embankment and deep cuttings which are required are now all but finished. The only gap we could see is a little above the farm of Longmorn. If the weather keeps favourable the greater part of the work will soon be finished. The permanent rails are all now laid.

Trouble was reported at a meeting on the 29th, with a number of shareholders who were refusing to pay for their shares in the Direct line. In a similar vein, a number of timber merchants at Lossiemouth were refusing to pay the Morayshire for the carriage of their goods.

A claim against the Morayshire was being pressed by a Mr G H Ramsey of Edinburgh for £6 for the loss of a wagonload of manure. The load had been left out in the rain in an uncovered wagon. The Company had no defence against this allegation and therefore paid Mr Ramsey for his spoiled consignment. The person found to be at fault was the Stationmaster at Elgin. As was usual in such matters, a letter was to be sent from the Company Secretary, asking why the Stationmaster should not pay the Company in full for this loss.

A more serious matter was the damage to the station ground at Lossiemouth caused by ingress from the sea that was washing away the ballast. This damage was being rectified, but the need to supply packing and replacement ballast was now occurring daily. During the recent storms, traffic had been brought to a standstill on the East side of the goods sidings. A full report on this matter was to be prepared by the Company engineer, who was also to report on the work required to bring the Ladies waiting room up to the standard of the recently opened one at Elgin. This work was to be completed before the opening of the Direct line to Rothes.

The Chairman advised the meeting that he had given the Board of Trade a month's notice of the Morayshire's intention to start service on the Direct line.

At the meeting between the Lossie timber merchants and the Railway Company, the relevant Act of Parliament regarding the price per cubic foot of timber charged for movement by rail was read out. The merchants asked for time to think about the arrangement, so it was agreed to reconvene the meeting in eight days time. On December 18th 1861, Act of Parliament or no, the Lossie timber merchants were not prepared to pay the rates required by the Morayshire.

It was announced on December 27th that the Direct line to Rothes would be opened for traffic on Monday, January 1st 1862. Fares for the new line were as follows:

	Single			Return	
	1	3	Par	1	3
Craigellachie to Lossiemouth	3/6	2/3	1/7	5/3	3/6
Craigellachie to Elgin	2/6	1/7	1/1	3/9	2/6
Rothes to Lossiemouth	3/-	1/11	1/4	4/6	3/-
Rothes to Elgin	2/-	1/3	10d	3/-	2/-

There was also to be a change in the rates for goods traffic, coal, stones, slates and other mineral traffic, to be raised from 1/- per ton to 1/3 Lossiemouth to Elgin. Possibly with an eye to the dispute with the timber merchants of Lossiemouth, a rate of 2d per ton per mile for the actual weight of timber carried on the Morayshire was fixed. The actual distance of the Direct line from Elgin to Rothes was two miles shorter than the Inverness and Aberdeen Junction Railway by Orton to Rothes. The Morayshire Board however did not cut the price of transporting goods between Elgin Rothes and Craigellachie by the Direct line, perhaps hoping by doing so they might pay off the debt incurred in building the line a little quicker. Similarly there was no reduction in the price to ship goods from Orton to Elgin until it was seen how much traffic this line would carry.

Just under ten years since the Morayshire Railway had given the north of Scotland its first ever railway, the Direct line to Rothes opened for business on January 1st 1862. On the first day of service there was no grand gathering, celebratory meals, or congratulatory speeches, only an opportunity for the folk of Elgin and District to travel to Rothes and back for the cost of a single fare.

Was the public now taking the railway revolution for granted? It certainly seems that way. Even the Board of the Morayshire seemed unexcited about its new venture. Their first meeting of 1862, which took place on January 10th, did not mention the completion of this project that they had fought so hard for. The whole of this meeting was taken up by mundane financial matters!

The next Board meeting on January 24th returned to a familiar theme, disagreement with the I&AJR over the shunting of wagons at Elgin. They had problems as well with the locomotive *"Glengrant"* which required extensive repairs. Mr Johnston of Newmill Ironworks was present at the meeting and was instructed to go on with the work with all speed. Besides the repairs he was also told to fit sand bottles to both the *"Glengrant"* and *"Lesmurdie"*. Also at this meeting a Rothes corn merchant Mr Stewart asked for and received a yearly ticket, whilst another Mr Stewart of Elgin was issued, at a cost of £6-10/-, with a first class all station yearly ticket. There must have been a loss of stone traffic, as the recent increase in price was cancelled and the previous price of 1/- per ton reinstated. Finally there was good news for J Beaton pointsman at Elgin with an increase in wages to 15/- per week.

Reports of a long meeting with Mr Dougall of the I&AJR were given to the Board on January 31st, indicating an amicable settlement between the two companies.

 The *Elgin Courant* announced the commencement of the construction of the Inverness and Aberdeen Junction's branch line from Alves to Burghead. The cost for the contract to build the 5 mile line was £22,000. There was no heavy engineering on the route, so it was expected to take the contractor McDonald and Grieve a very short time to complete the work.

The Morayshire was reported to be closer to a linkup with the Strathspey Railway. The main item of interest to the Courant, however was the installation of the telegraph system along the length of Morayshire's network. It was described as a two wire system with double-needle indices that gave a speedy transmission. Opened on January 27th 1862, it was as previously stated for railway use only. The posts and system had been installed by Mr Summerfield of the GNSR.

An old protagonist of the Morayshire, Mr Cameron solicitor of Elgin, was refusing to pay his call on shares until the Morayshire Railway paid their subscription to a road-widening scheme for Commerce Street in Elgin. A Board meeting on February 7th agreed to release £10 of Company money to resolve this matter. At the same gathering, complaints about the condition of the Morayshire's tenanted houses were heard, but there was no resolution to that problem. Sales of yearly tickets increased by two with the granting of a yearly ticket between Elgin and Lossiemouth to a Mr & Mrs Branston of Lossie for the sum of £4-14s-6d.

The fascination held by the folk of Rothes for the Morayshire Railway was causing problems again, with reports of people from the town walking on the line and leaving various gates open. John Grant of Glengrant was asked on February 14th, to enlist the assistance of the Company's servants and the local police in identifying and bring to book the offending parties.

This date also saw an attempt by the Morayshire to increase its charges to the Post Office for the conveyance of mail between Elgin and Lossiemouth. The sum being asked for was £65. The Post Office refused to pay the new rate, leaving the Morayshire to settle for the old amount of £41, which they did though cutting the number of trains on which mail would be conveyed from three to two. If the Post Office required a third mail delivery, they would be charged an additional £9. The opening of the Direct line to Rothes did allow the Morayshire to claim an extra £13 per annum for the carriage of mails between Elgin, Orton and Craigellachie.

Company housing in Rothes also appeared to be below standard. A request to repair the Stationmaster's house in Green Street was ignored, with the Morayshire preferring to spend some money on the building of a cattle shed at Craigellachie and on the extension of a shed at Rothes for the use of fisher women.

Mr Cameron was a thorn in the side of the Morayshire Railway. He was representing Mr Morrison of Pinefield Nurseries in an action against the Company for damages amounting to the sum of £150. By the erection of the embankment and bridges as part of the Direct line to Rothes, Mr Morrison contended that the ventilation required to operate his cone kilns had been destroyed. The Morayshire had Provost Grant's firm of Grant and Jamieson acting in their defence. Reports in the *Elgin Courant* state that there was a large number of specialist witnesses from outside the area called in this case, which took three days to hear. At the end of this period judgement was deferred in this action brought under the *"Land Clauses Consolidation (Scotland) Act,"* to allow the arbiter, a Mr Mackie of Woodside, to study the extensive paperwork.

The seesaw of good news bad news that seemed to inflict its self on the Morayshire appeared to be at work again on February 21st 1862. The good news was that the GNSR was to give the Morayshire £1000 as its contribution to the construction of the Craigellachie Junction station. The bad news was that in the previous few days, a great hurricane had completely torn up the goods siding at Lossiemouth and washed away all the ballast on the southern side of the line. The engineer and the Directors were to travel to Lossiemouth to inspect the damage and look into the possibility of enclosing Lossiemouth station behind a sea wall. This would be an expensive and extensive operation, so in the interim temporary repairs were to be undertaken.

Money, money, yet again with a claim from the Elgin Water Company for the sum of £20 for the supply of water to the Morayshire for its locomotives. The Board of Directors and Provost Grant in particular thought this charge was exorbitant. The Secretary of the Morayshire was requested, on March 7th, to write to the Secretary of the Water Company in an effort to have this charge reduced.

The steep incline and possibly some of the curves on the new Direct line were also having an effect on the Company's operation. Alterations were to be made to Brake carriage No5 to cope with the inclines. Perhaps of more concern was the request for a new set of metal tyres for the locomotive Glengrant. These were besides the set already being replaced, as there was a difference of 1 inch in diameter between old and new tyres. If both sets of tyres were not replaced at the same time, it would be necessary to reduce the diameter of the new wheels by 1 inch and thus lose their value. Permission was given to purchase a new set of tyres.

Goods business was fairly promising, requiring the extension of the loading banks at Elgin. This increase excluded the Orton branch, which since the opening of the Direct line had seen a substantial drop in traffic. The Board met on March 14th to discuss the possibility of working the branch with a horse. This, it was decided was not a good thing to do. Instead a decision was made to ask the GNSR how they would operate the branch when they took over the running of the Morayshire. In the interim the spare engine would be used to run the service, with a note being kept of the costs incurred.

Perhaps the Directors of the Morayshire experienced a little *"Schadenfreude,"* with news in the *Elgin Courant* of March 14th that the I&AJR's work force employed to construct the Burghead branch had gone on strike for higher wages. Good progress on the Speyside line was also noted in the same report.

Information on the Morayshire and its extension plans appeared in the *Courant* of March 28th.

> The Morayshire Directors advertised in another column for contractors to construct the link wanted to join the Morayshire Railway and the Strathspey Railway at Craigellachie. The bridge over the Spey is to have one span of 200 ft and another three of 57 ft each. The Dundee Advertiser reports that George McFarlane, Dock Street, Dundee has been successful in obtaining a contract for a malleable iron lattice girder bridge of a span of 195 ft to go over the Spey at Ballindalloch.

On March 31st, a request was received from Mr Priest of the Morayshire Tile Works asking for a reduction in the rate for the carriage of tiles and bricks. This, he informed the Railway Company, would allow him to compete with product coming from the Craigellachie Brick Works. The Directors agreed to this request as the Morayshire Tile Works was on the Lossiemouth branch line, and the prospect of loads moving up country to Rothes, Craigellachie and beyond would give business to the Morayshire.

The first of many complicated exchanges of Preference shares and Debentures took place between the Morayshire and The Great North of Scotland Railway on April 4th 1862. These transactions were to become a feature of dealings between the companies in the months and years to come. They are complex, and I get the feeling that both sides felt that they were gaining some advantage over the other party. In reality this was the start of the end of the Morayshire Railway Company as an independent entity, as with each exchange of Promissory Notes, another piece of the Morayshire disappeared into the

GNSR empire. Amongst minor matters: Mr Proctor, porter at Elgin, had his wages increased to 18/- because his duties now included carriage cleaning. A dispute with Mrs Collier tenant of the Lossiemouth Railway Hotel had also arisen, because *"She was adverse to paying her rent."*

Provost Grant travelled south to London at the beginning of April, though this time not on behalf of the Morayshire Railway. In meetings with the Chancellor of the Exchequer, he headed a deputation of distillers in an attempting to reduce the *"very high duty"* of 10/- per gallon paid on whisky. He inferred that this rate of duty was encouraging smuggling and illicit distilling. It is reported that he met with Mr Gladstone, and was received in a very courteous manner. As a few had done before, and many have done after him, he failed to change the Government's heart and no reduction on the tax was achieved.

Provost Grant returned to Elgin in time for the Morayshire's EGM held on Wednesday 9th April 1862 in the Station Hotel. The purpose of the get-together was to issue preference shares to cover a shortfall in the finances of the Company caused by the recent increase in its size. Despite the money pledged by the Great North of Scotland Railway, the Provost estimated that there was still a requirement to raise £10,000. One of his thoughts on this matter was to persuade the contractor to settle for payment in preference shares, rather than cash. This idea was abandoned because the contractor would have to alter his prices upwards. After a short debate it was agreed to issue 836 shares with a preference dividend of 5%. Some concern was expressed about this tactic by a Colonel Marshall of Newfield. He felt that the GNSR were short-changing the Morayshire in their contribution, because as part of the agreement they became the owners of the Morayshire's plant. Provost Grant assured him that because the GNSR would be responsible for the maintenance and servicing of the Morayshire's rolling stock, this would reduce the Morayshire's capital outlay. The Colonel was also worried that GNSR would bring in coal to the area, thereby damaging the shipping business at Lossiemouth. The promise from the Provost on this point was that the GNSR would carry coal to Dufftown but no further, safeguarding Lossiemouth Harbour traffic. With these positive pronouncements, the motion to issue the shares was passed.

At a Board meeting on April 18th, the Secretary produced a sketch showing a fence for enclosing Lossiemouth station. There was also a request for extra trains and cheaper fares for the workmen engaged in constructing the Strathspey Railway. Mr Barnes, the contractor on this project, also concluded an agreement with the Morayshire to carry stone between Elgin and Craigellachie for use on the Strathspey at 2/- per ton.

The *Elgin Courant* carried the following report on April 25th 1862:

> Messrs Mitchell & Ireland are to do the earthworks and also build the piers of the bridge over the River Spey. The stones are to come from the Middleton Quarries in Arbroath; the Morayshire quarries being unable to supply on time. The piers have to be ready for the iron on which the railway will be carried across, in the course of ten months. The bridge itself will cost about £5800. We may thus hope to see the junction with the Strathspey line ready by the time fixed for the opening of the railway to Grantown in August 1863.

A formal agreement on the construction of the embankment and stone work for the Spey bridge was agreed with Mitchell & Ireland at the Board meeting on May 2nd. Revised costings had also been received for the construction of the iron work of the bridge at a price of £6340. This great deal of money required the Board to employ an inspector to protect this investment by overseeing the bridge building and the construction of the embankment.

Mrs Collier was being reluctant in leaving the Lossie Station Hotel, and had submitted an account for a kitchen grate she had installed. The Board concluded that it was normal for the lessee to take such fittings with them. In a bid to speed Mrs Collier's departure it was agreed to pay for the grate, but only when she had left the Hotel.

A letter from the Inverness and Aberdeen Junction Railway was the first item on the Agenda of May

16th 1862 Board meeting. This time Mr Dougall was not asking for money from the Morayshire. It seems that trade between the two companies had dropped to such a level that the I&AJR were advising that the person employed to oversee traffic passing between the two companies was being dispensed with. Also on the Agenda was a new house, urgently required for the Stationmaster at Lossiemouth. To this end the Secretary was instructed to co-operate with Mr Walker and John Grant of Glengrant in the purchase of suitable accommodation. Later in the meeting the Morayshire Steam Sawmill requested a siding to give rail access to their premises. The engineer of the Morayshire Railway was asked to see if it could be done without the expense of a laying in a new level crossing.

If reports in the *Elgin Courant* of May 23rd are to believed, jealous eyes in the eastern part of Moray were being cast at all the railway building going on at Burghead, Forres and Speyside. It seems that the people of Garmouth felt they were being left out of the railway revolution. At this point in history this village at the mouth of the Spey was an important ship building centre, and so was worthy of a railway. Would Provost Grant come to their rescue?

His mind for the time being was taken up with happenings on the Morayshire. An accident occurred at Rothes on May 29th that resulted in the 4.30pm train from Craigellachie to Orton being derailed. No damage was done to either track, rolling stock, or passengers, only *"a great deal of confusion was caused,"* and a *"conveyance"* had to be procured for the passengers. David Stewart, pointsman at Rothes, was held to blame for the accident. It appears that he had allowed the points to open, when only a portion of the train had passed through. The Stationmaster suspended Stewart and a replacement pointsman was sent out from Elgin.

Mr Stewart did not have long to find out what his fate was. The Board met the following day and decided to dismiss him as an example to the other company officials. Also at this meeting the Morayshire cancelled Mr Barnes' special rate agreement, as he was sending stone to the Strathspey Railway by way of I&AJR. Discussions also included spare leading engine wheels required for *"Glengrant."* These took a long time to procure, so it was decided to buy a spare set for stock and charge this cost to the capital account. Other traffic matters concerned the shortage of wagons. This matter was to be passed to another meeting.

At the beginning of June it looked as if the railway vacuum in the east of the county would be filled by the Banff and Moray Junction Railway Company. This organisation planned to build a line from Buckie, through Portgordon, on to Tynet into Fochabers, thence over the River Spey on a wooden viaduct, costing somewhere in the region of £5000 to build, before finally connecting with the Inverness and Aberdeen Junction Railway at Orbliston station. The I&AJR had also had some thoughts of construction in this part of Moray, with two schemes to build a line from Keith to Buckie, or Buckie by Fochabers to connect with their line at either Orton or Lhanbryde. There was still however no railway link for the people of Garmouth.

Meeting on June 13th 1862, the Board of the Morayshire agreed to the offer from Blaikie's of Aberdeen to build the bridge to carry the Fiddich Road over the line at the entrance to Craigellachie Junction station. An offer was also on the table from the GNSR to hire wagons to the Morayshire. The Board, though interested, wanted to have more details of the costs involved. Goods traffic between Lossiemouth and Keith had brought the Morayshire the sum of £48-18s-3d for the period of 1st January to 30th May. To encourage more traffic, the rate for traffic over this route was not to be increased. Once more on the Agenda was Mrs Collier, who had still not left the Lossiemouth Station Hotel, matters not being helped by the fact that Morayshire Board could not find the original lease document. Plans were also discussed for gatekeeper's cottages at Linkwood and Birchfield with agreement to obtain tenders for their construction. This meeting finished on a low note, as an action had been raised against the Company by a Mr Smith for non-completion of fencing on the Direct line.

The whole of that day, Friday 13th, it had been raining, which continued all weekend through to late on

Monday the 16th. All this water caused problems on the Direct line through the Glen of Rothes, with a number of embankments being washed away. Despite this, services were maintained, though trains were required to pass *"Dead Slow"* on the damaged portions of the line. At Craigellachie three of Mitchell and Ireland's workforce were almost swept to their deaths as they attempted to recover wooden staging that was being washed away by the River Spey. The boat they were using capsized, throwing the men into the torrent. They were saved by the quick action of their workmates who were working on the banks of the river.

A deal with the Great North of Scotland Railway was concluded on June 24th to hire ten wagons. The cost per vehicle was £1-2/- per week, with the understanding that the GNSR would accept back their rolling stock as soon as the Morayshire no longer required it.

Tenders were accepted on June 27th, for the construction of the gatekeeper's crossings at Linkwood and Birchfield. The Company was also willing to put the siding into the Morayshire Steam Sawmill, on the understanding that the proprietors of that business would pay for the cost of the gates. A settlement was also reached with Mr Smith for the fencing on the Direct line, with the Morayshire paying his costs.

By July 2nd the financial position of the Company was starting to give the Board cause for concern. There was an immediate need to find £7500 to meet current obligations, and it was hoped that the GNSR would cover this shortfall. However, they were already committed to £21,000 of preference shares and debentures in the Morayshire. The shareholders of the Great North had already raised concerns at their AGM way back on April 4th to the amount of money that it was putting into the Morayshire. So it seemed unlikely further assistance from this quarter would be forthcoming, but a meeting was arranged.

Provost Grant discussed the outcome of the deliberations between the Morayshire and the Great North on July 11th. The Great North was not prepared to advance any more money until it knew what dividend the Morayshire expected to pay in 1862. Provost Grant and Mr Watt the Secretary went through the books and as a result estimated that a 2% dividend would be possible. This information was quickly telegraphed to the Directors of the Great North of Scotland Railway in Aberdeen. The GNSR at this time were thinking of expanding their empire by building a line from Portsoy to Buckie, tying up their capital and making any more rescue payments to the Morayshire more unlikely.

Nothing had been heard from the Great North Board by the Morayshire's next meeting on July 25th. A payment of £814-8s-6d was made to Mitchell & Ireland for work done at Craigellachie. The heavy rain had returned on July 15th, and subsequent flooding on the 16th stopped the 7.10am Craigellachie service from running. The problem occurred at the first bridge south of Cyers Mill because ballast had been washed away. The interruption to services only lasted for a few hours and the 12.20pm up train passed safely.

It was decided at a meeting on August 1st to prevent further trouble by replacing the 12 ft bridge at Coleburn with an 18 ft girder bridge.

Bridges were again the subject when the Directors next came together on August 6th. The crossing in this case was over the River Spey to make the connection at Craigellachie Junction. Replying to the Morayshire's tender, the firm of McKenzie Clunes and Holland had written on August 4th offering to build the bridge for £5533-17s-4d. The Board thought that this amount was acceptable, subject to the inspection of the design by their engineers. As part of the effort to cut costs, the painting of the completed bridge would be done by the Morayshire Railway. The cash situation within the Company itself was critical at this time, not helped by an instruction from the Great North of Scotland Railway not to ask for any more advances until the Morayshire's accounts were available for inspection.

Nine days later, Samuel & Mills, the engineers to the Morayshire, gave their report on McKenzie, Clunes & Holland's proposed bridge over the Spey. Samuel & Mills were concerned that McKenzie & Co had not built anything as big as the proposed Spey Bridge and therefore they did not wish to place the contract with them. Instead they recommended the firm of De Brugeur & Co, who would build the Bridge for £6228-13/-. The board agreed to this recommendation on the proviso, that the price be reduced by £300-10/-. Mr Mills was to travel to London to give the news in person to De Brugeur, and confirm that they would accept the reduction in price. If they failed to agree to the lower price, Mr Mills was to visit McKenzie, Clunes & Holland to check into the stability of that company, and enquire if they would pay over the sum of £2000 in security to the Morayshire; if they did this then the contract would be theirs.

Finance, or the lack of it was giving the Morayshire Board continued cause for concern and a meeting on August 20th 1862 tried to sort out the problems. The Commercial Bank agreed to give the Morayshire an additional advance of £6000. Good news was reported. The engine *"Lossiemouth"* was now repaired and put to work on the Orton branch. Its sister engine *"Elgin"* was to be fitted with a new set of tyres. A letter had also been received from McKenzie, Clunes & Holland taking a further £150 off their tender to build the Spey bridge. The Directors meeting declined to take up this offer until they had the report from Mr Mills.

On September 2nd following the report from Mr Mills and the lodging of the £2000 security payment, the tender from Messrs McKenzie, Clunes & Holland was accepted. Later that day a joint meeting was held, in the Station Hotel Elgin, of the Morayshire Railway and the Harbour Company. Provost Grant proposed that the two Companies should come together and form a single concern. The object of the meeting was to seek to put a Bill before Parliament to enable this to take place.

The local press were not overenthusiastic of the prospect of the Railway and Harbour Company coming together. Mr Russell of the *Elgin Courant* in particular warned the Directors of both these enterprises, and Provost Grant in particular, to heed the wishes of their shareholders. Other reports in the *Courant* of September 5th give details of yet another scheme to build a railway along the coast from Cullen to Buckie, terminating at Fochabers.

Things took a familiar turn on September 12th, when a letter arrived from the Inverness and Junction Railway, demanding payment for £46-11s-6½d. The Morayshire refused to settle until they had full details from the I&AJR as to what these charges were for.

Provost Grant seems to have taken little notice of Mr Russell's editorial. Details of the proposed amalgamation with the Harbour Company were considered to be urgently required because of the forthcoming completion of the railway connection at Craigellachie that the Provost was certain would usher in steamship communication with the northern counties. As a number of shareholders held shares in both companies, Provost Grant felt confident of the amalgamation going through. It was proposed that the following conditions would apply:

1) The Harbour Company would apply for a loan under Harbour and Passing Falls Act 1861, for the sum of £35,000.

2) When the loan is secured, the Morayshire is to apply for the amalgamation Act. The Harbour Company shareholders will be guaranteed a 4% return, with more in equal parts if the revenues of both companies exceed 4%.

3) Alternatively guarantee 4½% fixed in perpetuity.

4) Or pay off Harbour Company shareholders at par.

The behaviour of Mr Allen, Stationmaster at Craigellachie was discussed. It was disclosed that he was not at his post for the arrival and departure of the first trains and not there to receive the last train at night. Mr Allan had also been seen driving around the country without obtaining leave of absence. The most serious dereliction of duty was considered to be his failure to carry out instructions to forward luggage belonging to a Mr Wilson. Apparently it was only the intervention of the Directors that saved the Morayshire Company from being sued for a large amount of money. Mr Allan was therefore suspended pending further investigation.

In the *Elgin Courant* of September 12th, *"Further reductions on the price of coal. All supplies forwarded by rail from the depot at Elgin and from ship direct to all stations on the Inverness Railway,"* evidence of the Morayshire vying with the I&AJR.

An extensive article appeared on the construction work being carried out at Craigellachie.

> The railway works in this quarter are making rapid progress. Any person who had seen Craigellachie 12 months ago, and not seen it since would not credit their eyes that such a change could have taken place in such a short time. The bridges of both the Strathspey and Morayshire at Boat of Fiddich are open for public traffic and the platform walls are rising fast. The line at this point is nearly all formed. The bridge over the Spey at the same place is also advancing. The two north piers are built. The main pier on the north side has been a serious job, but that is now overcome. Mr Ireland has had a strong force of navvies at work on it day and night for nearly two months, sinking cast iron cylinders for the foundation. At first it appeared almost impossible to get the cylinders down to the required depth; but through the ingenuity of Mr McDonald, the manager of the works, it has now been brought to a near close. Whether the cylinders be an improvement or not, only time will tell.

The outstanding account with the I&AJR was settled on September 26th. A letter from the Directors of the Harbour Company stated that they did not want to continue with the amalgamation at present. This piece of news must have come as a blow to Provost Grant.

The report on Mr Allan was given to the Director's meeting of October 3rd 1862. It was decided not to dismiss him from the Company. As it was claimed that the people of Craigellachie were against Mr Allan, it would not be possible for him to stay in his post there. This left two possible alternatives, either him resigning, or moving him to a post in Elgin. The Directors decided on the latter. They then went on to discuss the locomotive *"Lesmurdie,"* which was getting *"very much out of repair,"* and would require to go into the shop for an extensive repair. Payment was to be increased to the Speyside Coach Company for carrying mail bags on Sundays between Craigellachie and Orton from 2/- to 4/- per Sunday.

Mr Allan seemed to be unhappy at Elgin, as on October 10th he tendered his resignation, which was accepted by the Board.

By the middle of October, preparations were well in hand for the Morayshire's, AGM. In keeping with the decree at last year's meeting the books of the Company had been closed on September 30th, to allow a statement of the Morayshire's financial position to be made. The details appeared in the *Elgin Courant* of October 24th, and showed a healthy increase in receipts, and only a small increase in expenditure. For the first time since 1859, the Morayshire Railway Company was able to pay its ordinary shareholders a dividend. At $2\frac{1}{2}\%$, it was not a great dividend, but it was a return for the shareholders who had stuck with the Company through the past hard years. Provost Grant looked forward to an even better year in 1863, reminding the shareholders that the sums that had allowed the payment of a $2\frac{1}{2}\%$ dividend were not for a full year of transactions.

The AGM itself took place on Friday, October 31st 1862, the shareholders seemed happy with their $2\frac{1}{2}\%$ dividend, and almost everything went well. The sticking point of the meeting was the proposal from Provost Grant to pay the Directors of the Company a sum of £300 each. This sum was to cover for meetings and other expenses incurred for a period covering six years, the last payment being made to the Directors at the 1856 AGM. What seemed to upset the floor of the meeting was not the amount of money, but that a number of people felt that the burden of work fell upon the Directors who lived locally, so they in turn should be paid a higher rate than those based in England. Provost Grant to his credit wanted an even payment to all Directors, and defended the gentlemen from the south, who he said were useful in Parliamentary matters and keeping an eye on the price of iron!

With the matter of the Directors payment out of the way, the meeting became *"Special"* for the purposes of exercising borrowing powers under the 1861 Strathspey Junction Act. The intention was to borrow on mortgage a sum up to £6000. This item proposed by Provost Grant, was seconded by Mr Grant Belliheglash and unanimously agreed to by all at the meeting. A vote of thanks from Mr Walker of Kintrae to Provost Grant concluded the business.

A varied agenda for the Board on November 14th, with the first item being the proposal for a Bill to raise capital to clear obligations, amend tolls for timber, stone and other articles. Part of this intended Bill included the provision to purchase or hire a steam vessel to enable a cross-firth service to begin. The next item dealt with was the approval of the metal work contract with McKenzie & Holland for the Spey viaduct. The last item discussed was the need for another clerk at Craigellachie to assist with duties due to the departure of Mr Allan. James Forbes, clerk from the Morayshire's Elgin office, was to fill this vacancy and an apprentice taken on at Elgin.

The advertisement for the aforementioned Bill appeared in the *Elgin Courant* of November 21st 1862, with Grant & Jamieson acting as solicitors and Muggeridge & Bell Parliamentary Agents. Just below the Morayshire's notices on the front page of the paper was another from the Inverness and Aberdeen Junction Railway, who it seemed were doing their best to keep up the pressure by promoting another line with an outlet to the coast. The good people of Garmouth looked set to join the railway age, as the I&AJR were offering to fund the Fochabers and Garmouth Railway to build a line from the coastal village and shipbuilding centre of Garmouth to connect with the I&AJR's Inverness-Keith main line. One of the main backers in this enterprise was the shipbuilder and owner of land in this area John Duncan. Most of the Fochabers and Garmouth Railway would run on property owned by Mr Duncan, so construction seemed a very real possibility. When completed it would cut into the traffic that Provost Grant was attempting to attract into Lossiemouth.

Money matters occupied the Directors on November 28th. To raise cash, arrangements had been made with an Edinburgh broker to put Morayshire Preference shares on the market. Outgoing items included a claim from Mr Preston for £35,040-5s-9d for the construction of the Direct line to Rothes. The Board were concerned that in this figure was the cost for repairs to the Direct line following the heavy rains in June, before settlement investigations were required. A confirmed agreement between the errant timber merchants and the Railway Company of 2/4 per ton for pit props carried between Craigellachie and Lossiemouth was made.

There had not been much correspondence between the Morayshire Railway and their neighbour, the Inverness and Aberdeen Junction Railway for a few months. Pen however was to be put to paper following the Board meeting of December 12th 1862. The source of irritation on this occasion was goods destined for Rothes and Craigellachie being landed at Burghead. It appears that the handing over of these items was not taking place at Elgin. The I&AJR were squeezing every last drop of revenue that they could out of this traffic by carrying it on their line to Orton for exchange there.

A request from the editors of two of Elgin's newspapers the *Courant* and *Courier* for free travel over the Morayshire's lines did not start 1863 well for the Morayshire Railway. The I&AJR already gave them this privilege. Grudgingly and probably not to be outdone by their Inverness neighbour, the Board agreed to this request but only for use while travelling on reporting duties to public meetings. Another bill, this time from Grigor & Young solicitors for the sum of £12-12/- for a legal action raised by them on behalf of the Company against a Mr Robertson of Auchinroath. The Secretary was instructed to write to Grigor and Young, obtain full details of this charge and if he found them to be correct, to settle the account. Attempt to improve income were also discussed, with an agreement to increase the rate for mineral traffic being approved. Mr Smale, one of the original Directors, tendered his resignation at this meeting, which with regret was accepted. In view of his long and faithful service to the Company, it was agreed that he could keep his free travel pass. Considering he lived in East Anglia, there was little chance that any journeys he made would be a major drain on the Morayshire. Provost Grant suggested that his replacement should be the Right Honourable Earl of Caithness, a move made to strengthen the Morayshire's ties with the northern counties of Scotland. This appointment was unanimously agreed to.

The Contractors building the viaduct over the Spey had objected to the increase in the rates for carriage of stones. The Morayshire Board therefore agreed on January 12th to drop the price charged to McKenzie & Holland from 7/10 per ton, to 4/10 per ton. At the same meeting another letter from Grigor & Young asking for payment of their outstanding bill, was considered. Provost Grant was still reluctant to settle this account, but was more than happy to sanction payment of £55-16s-6d to his own legal firm, Grant & Jamieson, for work they had carried out for the Railway Company.

Apparently it appears that the Earl of Caithness was a bit of a rail fan. Within nine days of his appointment to the Board he had made an extensive tour of inspection (*Elgin Courant*).

> The Earl visited Lossiemouth, for the purpose of inspecting the harbour and seeing the arrangements for conducting traffic there. On returning, he was met at Elgin Station by the Countess, the Elgin Directors of the Morayshire Railway, the Engineer, and a few friends, then all proceeded by train to Craigellachie, where they were met by the upper district Directors. From Craigellachie Station the whole party walked to the Spey viaduct, by which the Morayshire Railway is to cross that river to join the Strathspey line. The Earl, who is well known for his engineering skill connected with locomotives, and otherwise requested a sight of the plans and sections of the bridge, and after having minutely examined them, also the works so far executed, expressed his opinion that the structure would be at once neat elegant, and substantial. The day was wet, and the embankment soft, rendering the journey to the viaduct not the most agreeable walk, but for a noble Countess, and lady companions, who like herself, are more accustomed to the comfortable footing of a Brussels carpet in a drawing room, it was certainly romantic to rough it in such weather, over high earth mounds, rails, sleepers, wagons, buggies, and all the other innumerable implements which navvies employ in their arduous operations. The noble Countess and the ladies accomplished the task with sprit, and the party returned to the Railway station to enjoy a substantial luncheon provided for them by Mrs Soutor. As a Director of the railway, he said he would be happy to do all in his power to develop the capabilities of the line, and to further its interests by assisting in the establishment of steam communication from the south side of the Moray Firth to Caithness. The Earl and Countess and the party from Elgin returned by the four p.m. train, and were loudly cheered at Craigellachie Station as the train departed. Lord Caithness, travelled upon the engine and made searching investigation into the affairs and working of the railway. We hope his connection with it may be for much good, both to the railway and to the district.

It was perhaps advantageous that the Earl of Caithness had left the area before that week's edition of the paper had come out on January 16th. Contained within its pages was a report giving praise to the Burghead branch. *"Since the opening of our new line. The amount of traffic has both in passengers and goods far exceeded expectations. The receipts are steadily progressing and considering the time of year the company is doing a fair stroke of business, which bids fair to further development as the advantage of our harbour and railway become better known."*

Despite the Directors of the Morayshire having a meeting on that day, their thoughts on the Burghead branch were not recorded. Mind you, it must have been some concern to them, as every item landed at Burghead was a potential loss to the Morayshire Railway and a definite threat to their plan to start a steamer service from the Northern counties. The first actual item discussed by them was a letter sent from Mr Mills of the GNSR asking for payment of £419-3s-8d in interest charges; it was agreed to pay over this amount. Mrs Collier, of the Lossiemouth Station Hotel, was still managing to hang on to the tenancy of said establishment. It was therefore duly decided that all outstanding rents must be paid within the next 10 days, or the case would be placed in the hands of the Company's solicitors.

Three days later a joint meeting took place between the Boards of the Harbour Company and Morayshire Railway. To protect themselves against competition from Burghead, it was agreed to look into the possibilities of reducing rates for goods being landed at Lossiemouth and being transported onward by rail. The Harbour Company also felt that it would be useful to have discussion with its Burghead counterparts, with a view to both Companies charging the same landing dues. If the two Harbour Companies could agree, it was the intention of the Morayshire to hold talks with the I&AJR to harmonise rates for goods being transported into Elgin.

A letter on this subject from Mr Dougall arrived in time for the Director's meeting of January 30th 1863. It looked possible that both parties could *"do business,"* on this matter. Further discussion on this item was delayed however as other more pressing money matters required attention. The first of these was the settlement of £406 to Mitchell & Ireland for work carried out on the construction of the embankment and bridge piers to cross the River Spey at Craigellachie. The second was the decision to discontinue the annuity payment to Mrs Taylor. She was to be advised *That with regret that this quarters payment would be the last, as the Company could no longer afford to pay her."* Finally for this meeting, matters military, a request had been received from the local volunteers to put a gate into the fence at the turntable at Lossiemouth to allow them access to the artillery grounds. This would be required three or four times a year for movement of stores of ammunition.

The *Courant* appeared to be attempting to smooth over competition between the two ports of Lossiemouth and Burghead with this report on February 6th.

> Our friends in Lossiemouth gained a triumph in favour of their harbour. The Dundalk steamer from Leith came into the bay when a strong gale was blowing from the South west by west. She had on board a fine new 'bus for the Gordon Arms Hotel Elgin, which was directed to be landed at Burghead. Captain Hodge told Mr Manson, agent at Lossie that he could not land the 'bus at Burghead and would have had to take it to Inverness if it was not sent ashore at Lossie. This is a lucky hit for Lossie harbour, but Burghead will have the advantage some other day. It would be well if there were less jealousy about the two harbours.

The local timber merchants appeared to be causing problems for the Morayshire Railway again at the meeting of February 13th. Consignments of timber being sent by a Mr Ross were to be checked. The declared weight of the loads he sent from Elgin did not match the actual amounts being unloaded for shipment from Lossiemouth. A lot more timber was arriving at Lossie than he was paying the railway Company to transport. The Morayshire Railway Company itself was not beyond trying to get something for nothing, as the Linkwood crossing keeper found to his cost at this meeting. It appears he was prepared to pay the Morayshire £4 per annum for the rental of his cottage, but expected to be paid to open and close the gates. To resolve this, the Board decided that he could have use of the cottage free of charge, in return for opening the gates. However, he would have to pay £4 per annum rental for the ground surrounding the cottage!

On February 18th, arrangements were made for an EGM to raise £25,000 by issuing new shares. Part of this amount was to be for the provision of communication by sea and steam boat in which the railway company had an interest. It was intended that this vessel would sail from the port of Lossiemouth to *"Every port situated northward of the Moray Firth."* If there was any opposition to this Bill in Parliament, Provost Grant would go to London to oversee its defence.

A letter from Mr Dougall was discussed fully, with the outcome that the Morayshire would charge the same rate from Lossie to Elgin, as the Inverness and Aberdeen charged for Burghead to Elgin. The Secretary of the Morayshire was to note that all goods for Orton, Mulben, Keith, etc, landed at

Lossiemouth were to travel by Rothes on the Morayshire system and be exchanged at Orton and under no circumstances to be exchanged at Elgin. This action initially gave a twofold advantage to the Morayshire, firstly by maximising the number of miles that the Morayshire could charge a customer wishing to send goods to the east of Elgin, and secondly by giving the Orton branch some much needed traffic.

A glowing account on the amount of business being conducted at Burghead harbour could be read in the press on February 20th, with additional buildings and a slipway to be constructed. Following this, the Inverness and Aberdeen Junction Railway intended to lay a feeder tramway eastward along the coast to Hopeman. The writer felt confident that such was the demand, the I&AJR would be forced to supply an engine and start a proper railway service. The second and possible most hurtful action to the pride of Lossiemouth was the supply of *"freestone"* from the quarries of Burghead and Hopeman to the Lossiemouth Harbour Company for the building of sea walls at that port. The Morayshire Railway Company was making some money out of this trade because the material was being transported by the I&AJR to Elgin and handed over to the Morayshire to reach its final destination. The hurt in question was that Lossiemouth was famed for its *"Freestone,"* and some of the quarries that could supply it were just a few yards away from the harbour. On this occasion however the Harbour Company had decided that the material from Burghead was of a superior quality for the job in hand. This matter, in the words of the press, was *"something for our Burghead friends to glory over."*

Point work at the Bulwark siding, whose poor condition had been a factor in the derailment of August 1860, was at the beginning of March 1863 lifted and returned to its manufacturer for repair. This work was going to take four months, so would cause a few problems that were discussed on March 6th. It would mean the pointsman assigned to look after them would have nothing to do. The Board decided to redeploy him with the platelayers for the four month period. Timber merchant Mr Sellar had a consignment of wood that was required to be transported to Burghead and he demanded the immediate reinstatement of the point work. The Morayshire Railway Company had had problems with this gentleman in the past and he was among the timber merchants who owed a considerable sum of money to the Railway Company. Employing a few of the tricks he had learned in his dealings with the Inverness and Aberdeen Junction Railway Company, the Provost noted that the siding had not been used by Mr Sellar in the last six months. Further, Mr Sellar had been sending his traffic to Burghead and Findhorn for shipment using the Junction Company at the expense of the Morayshire and Lossie Harbour Company. In consideration of these facts the Morayshire would reinstate the siding but would charge the sum of £2-2s-6d per ton for the use of an engine to move his timber. Mr Sellar informed the meeting that he would consider the Provost's proposal and return in the afternoon with his decision.

Goods rates between Lossiemouth and Elgin, in particular mineral traffic, were to be reduced. The new amounts were 1/1 per ton for minerals and 1/4 for special goods. The Secretary Mr Alex Watt was to write to Mr Dougall of the I&AJR to advise him to adjust the rates accordingly for the Elgin Burghead service.

Mr McBean of the Elgin Coal Company offered a weighing machine to Elgin station for the sum of £12. The Engineer was to inspect this equipment and if he found it to be suitable, the Railway Company would buy it. A person was also to be appointed weight man and chief porter at Elgin.

An action for damage to the value of £12 had been raised against the Company from a Mr Cruickshank for the loss of a field of turnips in the floods of July last year. This was to be defended.

A Special Meeting was called at Elgin on March 16th 1863 to sanction action against shareholders who were in arrears with their accounts. Those defaulting were John Donald shoemaker Elgin, Mr Clark blacksmith Elgin, Mr Stronach bookseller Elgin, James Kellas and Kenneth McKenzie Rothes. The Morayshire Railway Bill and those against it were also discussed at this meeting. Opposition was coming from the I&AJR, Aberdeen Leith & Clyde Shipping Company, and the London Steamship

Owners Association. The last item on the agenda was the recommendation from Messrs Samuel & Mills to settle with Mr Preston. The Board were against settlement as they believed that the charges, in particular the amounts for repairs after the floods of 1862, were too high. They did not want to inform the shareholders at the next AGM that they had paid a large and additional amount of money.

The Morayshire Board was trying hard to obtain support for its bill from surrounding communities and this effort was meeting with some success. Naturally, the peoples of Elgin, Lossiemouth and Wick were all in favour, as was the Harbour Board. Perhaps surprisingly a petition in support of the bill had also come from Forres Town Council. To obtain more backing, Provost Grant had met with Nairn Town Council and succeeded in persuading them not to support the I&AJR in its opposition to the Morayshire's plans. Unfortunately, Nairn Council felt that they could offer better harbour facilities than Lossiemouth and the only thing missing was a good rail link. They therefore intended to approach both the Inverness & Aberdeen Junction and the Great North of Scotland Railway to see which of them would provide the rail connection. The Board of Trade had returned the bill for correction, pointing out section 16 that stated *"Every port situate northwards of the Moray Firth,"* as this would extend as far as Iceland. The BOT believed that this *"Can hardly be intended."* Your writer is not so certain, I would think that the good Provost would welcome any traffic provided it used the Morayshire Railway.

Our new member of the Morayshire Board, the Earl of Caithness, was putting his engine driving skills to practical use on the GWR. He was a guest at the marriage of the Prince and Princess of Wales, but rather than join the happy couple and their other guests on the train from Paddington to Slough, took his place on the footplate and drove. Accompanying him on this journey was the Great Western Railway locomotive superintendent Mr Daniel Gooch. I feel certain the Earl passed on the tips that he learned from the Morayshire and it's pleasing to think that one of the country's smallest railway companies was able to help one of the biggest.

That other *"Great"* railway, the Great North of Scotland held its AGM in Aberdeen on March the 27th. The shareholders were most concerned by the *"terrible burden of the branches,"* which was proving to be a drain on their company funds. Included in the aforementioned burden was the Morayshire Railway. It was not of course part of the GNSR empire, but £20,000 worth of their money was invested in it. After much discussion, the fact that the GNSR would be gaining an independent route to Elgin eventually calmed the shareholders.

The last few days of March were not easy for the Morayshire either. Mr Holland of McKenzie & Holland, the firm building the bridge over the River Spey at Craigellachie, sought an urgent meeting with the Directors of the Morayshire. Work on the Spey viaduct was being delayed by lack of material. The ironwork for the bridge should have been delivered by sea through the firm of Brander & Co, but they were failing badly to comply with the terms of their contract. Seeking the sanction of the Morayshire to have the outstanding material delivered to the site by rail was Mr Holland's solution, otherwise the likelihood of the bridge not being completed on time was very high. This was a delay that the Morayshire could not afford, so it was decided to bypass Brander and go for rail delivery of the iron work.

Provost Grant was setting out on his travels again, this time to Wick. The new Morayshire Bill was due to go before Parliament after the Easter recess, so the trip was to gather evidence and witnesses in favour of the Morayshire's proposal.

On Provost Grant's return from London, Mrs Collier of the Lossiemouth Station Hotel was to be invited to the next meeting of the Morayshire Directors. The Directors of the Company wanted either this troublesome tenant removed from their property, or at the very least their outstanding bills paid. It was hoped that by asking Mrs Collier to attend in person, that this matter could be resolved fairly amicably.

All and all the Morayshire seemed to be doing its best to put its house in order. The Board was determined to sort out their differences between themselves and their contractor over the additional costs for the construction of the Direct line. Mr Mills in his capacity as engineer to the Morayshire, was to put in hand all necessary alterations which might necessary before the GNSR took over the working of the line to accommodate the expected increase in traffic.

The local press seemed to have missed the story of the iron supply problems for the Craigellachie bridge. They were giving lavish praise to the speed that the project was being carried out. According to the *Elgin Courant* of April 10th, the service bridge across the river was completed, and the permanent iron work was being fitted up. The good gentleman of the press assured their readership that within three months they would be able to travel from Lossiemouth to Dufftown.

In the same edition the court case between the Morayshire and Farmer Cruickshank of Coleburn was reported in detail. The farmer, as we know, was suing the Company and Mr Preston for the sum of £12 for the loss of a turnip crop in last year's flood. His solicitor Mr Forsyth claimed that the field was flooded due to the narrowness of a bridge constructed to carry the railway over the burn. Mr Jamieson, acting for the Morayshire, maintained that the burn had broken its bank outwith the railway fence. The Morayshire therefore was in no way responsible for any damage that might have been caused. The chief Morayshire witness had not turned up for the case, as neither had Mr Preston and because of this the dispute could not be settled in one sitting and had to be continued. A week later, Mr Reid architect and chief witness for the Morayshire took his place in the courtroom. He stated that on June 20th of the previous year he had measured the width of the bridge, which he found to be 11 ft 9 ins. It was also his opinion that the burn was in the habit of breaking its banks at Mr Cruickshank's field. Just when things looked to be going the Morayshire's way, Mr Reid admitted under cross examination that on his visit of June 20th he had expressed the opinion that the railway bridge should have been wider. On hearing this comment, Sheriff Smith decided the case against the Morayshire and Mr Preston was proved. Mr Cruickshank was awarded his £12, plus costs.

The Morayshire's Bill in favour of cross-firth traffic was about to come before the House of Lords. This precipitated an exchange of letters between various inhabitants of Lossiemouth and Burghead as to who had the best harbours. The last word on this extensive exchange went to Mr Sim of the Lossiemouth Harbour Company, who claimed without doubt that Lossiemouth had the better facilities, but in the interests of harmony this bickering between the two ports should end.

It appears that the Inverness and Aberdeen Junction Railway had broken its word with the Morayshire. At the Morayshire Board meeting on May 15th, it was reported by a Mr Fleming that the I&AJR were exchanging traffic destined for Rothes at Orton, and charging an additional 6d per ton for the privilege of carrying the goods past Elgin. The Secretary of the Morayshire was again instructed to send a letter of protest to its Inverness neighbour.

The good news to be heard at this meeting was that the House of Lords had passed the Morayshire Railway Bill. Except for the disputed sum with Mr Preston, all other outstanding amounts due by the Company were paid off. A new 45 ft Cowans & Sheldon turntable was on order, and a team of masons were busy preparing the site for its installation at Elgin. It was hoped that this equipment would be operational in time for the opening of the line to Dufftown and Keith. Plans were also discussed for the building of a new station and engine shed at Elgin. The latter was for the use of GNSR engines working through to Elgin, and in view of this it was hoped the GNS would pay half the construction costs. A £1500 portion of the cost of the bridge across the Spey was also cleared for payment at this meeting.

On May 25th 1863, a Special Meeting was called by the Directors at Elgin. The topic of discussion was a letter from Mr Milne, Secretary of the Great North of Scotland Railway. This referred to the appointment of Mr Thomas Elliot Harrison, eminent engineer, to investigate the differences in values placed on equipment by the GNSR and the Morayshire. The Board had no objection to this appointment and Provost Grant was travelling to Aberdeen the following day to meet with Mr Milne to discuss this matter and proposed timetable changes and transfer of Morayshire Railway officials to the GNS. It was also to be ascertained whether the GNS would pay half the cost of the new station at Elgin.

The Provost was to take with him a copy of the estimated cost of the changes at Elgin, which were as follows:

New Engine Shed	£ 950
New Water Tank	£ 160
Provision of 45f Turntable	£ 415
Moving Goods Shed from Dandaleith to Elgin	£ 60
New Station Building with overall roof	£1000
Total	£2585

The main business of the meeting out of the way, a rather shame faced Mr Fleming rose to his feet to apologise to the Directors of the Morayshire Railway. The charges he had claimed the I&AJR were making had come from a letter he had received on March 16th, which was before the two companies had come to an arrangement. Fortunately for all concerned the Secretary of the Morayshire had not at this point sent a letter of protest.

Entertainment for the public in the county of Moray, who had not yet had their fill of stories of new railways opening up their county to the wider world, was provided by The *Elgin Courant* on May 29th. The paper ran to several pages in its description of the new Strathspey Railway and the all-important connection to the Morayshire Railway. A short extract from this work follows below.

The Viaduct at Craigellachie

The viaduct consists of four openings: three of them fifty-seven feet each. These are on the Morayshire side of the river; and over her bed is one span of two hundred feet, beneath which the whole river flows when unflooded. This gives a clear waterway of three hundred and seventy-one feet, sufficient to allow a flood like 1829 to pass through the viaduct, for the girders on which the platform rests are at least twenty feet above the ordinary level of the water. On the Banffshire side, the two piers of the great span, have been founded upon cast iron cylinders, and the land abutments founded upon a great bed of concrete, also at a great depth below the bed of the river. Each pier has a cut water facing up the river, and the tops of all the piers and abutments are surmounted with a bold ornamental copping which adds beauty to the masonry. The stones are of various colours, and are from different quarries, the whole outside of the piers are built of a strong dark coloured freestone from the Middleton quarry near Arbroath, and the interior from Lossiemouth, Spynie, and Bishopmill.

The bridge consists of malleable iron girders securely riveted together at the main pier thus forming one continuous girder from end to end of the viaduct. The girders rest direct upon granite saddle blocks at the main piers, and are bolted down firmly with strong bolts, built ten feet into the solid masonry. This is the only point where the girders are permanently fixed; at the remainder of the piers the girders simply rest upon turned rollers, encased in malleable iron frame. This arrangement is to allow the freedom of expansion and contraction in the ironwork.

The quality of iron in the viaduct has been proved to be good. From a number of tests made upon some of the plates, it was found that the breaking weight varied from 22 to 25 tons per square inch. A train composed entirely of heavy locomotives would not produce a strain upon any one point of more than four tons per square inch, thus showing a large marginal excess of strength.

Considering the magnitude of the work, the time occupied in its construction has been short. The foundation was commenced in April 1862, and all the masonry was completed in November of the same year. The timber service bridge occupied only six weeks in construction. Work commenced to erect the lattice girders on the 6th of April 1863, and are now almost complete. The parties connected with the viaduct are - James Samuel, F.R.A.S., Westminster, and W.H. Mills, M.Inst. C.E.,Craigellachie. Messrs Mitchell & Ireland, Montrose, contractors for the foundations and masonry and Messrs McKenzie, Clunes & Holland, Vulcan Ironworks, Worcester, contractors for the ironwork. Resident engineer on the works, Mr T.H.Smith. We must pause for a week. Before we publish again a locomotive in all probability will have crossed the great viaduct.

Whilst the good folk of Elgin were reading about the new Craigellachie viaduct, the Directors of the Morayshire were hard at work. Provost Grant reported back on his meeting with Mr Mills in Aberdeen. The Great North of Scotland Railway "sort of" agreed to pay half of the costs of the engine shed. The "sort of" was that, yes, cash would be given by the GNS, but this was to be as a loan that was to be paid back to that company. Concerning the station, the GNS would not pay anything towards it, but they would buy an additional £1000 of shares in the Morayshire. Control of the Morayshire Railway Company was slowly slipping away. Never mind, business on the Rothes line was increasing and a request for a station to be built at Coleburn was approved. The platform at this site was to be 100 yards long.

The following day, Saturday, May 30th, two engines and 18 loaded wagons carrying about 140 tons in ballast tested the stability of the Craigellachie viaduct. Reports state that the deflection of the bridge under this weight was imperceptible. On Monday the 1st of June, one engine and two carriages passed along the bridge conveying the Directors of McKenzie, Clunes and Holland. The Directors then walked back along the bridge and went through a ceremony of driving in some rivets, thereby indicating that the work on its construction was finished. Satisfied with this, Provost James Grant christened the bridge "The Craigellachie Viaduct." Several toasts were then drunk, and high praise was given to Mr J F Clunes manager of the works. The actual workmen who had built the viaduct were not forgotten; they too were congratulated for the energy they had brought to bear on the project.

It is noteworthy that the celebratory dinner that took place that evening at Mrs Soutor's hotel was not hosted by the Morayshire Railway. Instead it was left to Mr McKenzie of the bridge company to do the honours. Members of that company, Mr Charles Tilton, chief builder of the bridge at Craigellachie, along with Mr Cameron, superintendent at Worcester, and Mr Philip Pardoe, manager of the riveting, were "presented" at the meal.

After naming the bridge, the Provost returned to Elgin for an EGM at the Station Hotel. The purpose of this meeting was to consider the Bill before Parliament for the raising of additional money for a shipping service from Caithness to Lossiemouth. Steps had been put into place to construct an improved harbour at Wick, but surprisingly the Lossiemouth Harbour Board seemed to be a little reluctant to improve their facilities. Perhaps in view of this, a large portion of the time at this meeting was given over to the congratulations of all concerned in the building of the Craigellachie Viaduct, and the impending completion of the Strathspey Railway. Amongst the questions asked was one from a Mr Smith, who was concerned that the Directors of the Morayshire would lose control of their Company to the GNSR. Provost Grant assured the gentleman that the GNSR could do nothing without the full consent of the Morayshire Directors and the GNS would only be responsible for working the line and nothing else. Time was to tell whether the Provost's assertions were correct.

The question of the construction of a Morayshire Railway station building at Craigellachie Junction was attended to on June 12th 1863, with the awarding of the contract to William North & Co masons. The materials for the building were to be supplied by the Morayshire, with the cost for the construction being £148. This project was "to proceed with all speed." At the same meeting, a tender for the replacement of the fencing on the Lossie line was awarded to Harper & Co Aberdeen. The cost of this work was not noted in the Minute Book.

Thursday, June 25th dawned a glorious day. The Directors of the Strathspey Railway and a large party of their friends departed Aberdeen at 8am to commence inspection of their new line. Reaching Dufftown at 11.40am, their inspection train departed that town along the newly completed line at 12.30pm. In Elgin, Provost Grant and friends left in the Morayshire Company's saloon at 12.20pm. This coach was decorated with a series of floral arcades. The two parties met at the Strathspey Junction station *. The new bridge over the Spey was inspected by all the assembled company. One gentleman in the party was heard to remark that *"this bridge will last forever,"* and the universal feeling of all was that it was the prettiest bridge upon the Spey. Resuming their carriages, the party continued along the Strathspey line towards Abernethy. The train consisted of seven carriages, two vans and five wagons. The goods vehicles contained the Company's stores for the various stations, which were delivered whilst the dignitaries carried out their inspection of each station. A sumptuous luncheon was served in the 55 foot long engine house at Abernethy. The building was liberally decorated with native evergreen tress and at one end five flags, these being the Strathspey Company Seal, the Bon Accord, Elgin and Banff coat of arms, together with that of the Duke of Richmond.

The obligatory speeches followed, with Provost Grant as the guest of honour. He seemed to be genuinely flattered by the attention as after all he was in the land of his forefathers, brought there by a new railway. In his speech he gave an account of the history of the Morayshire Railway to date. Not one to dwell in the past, he gave the assembled company a hint of what his plans for the Morayshire were.

> You know, gentlemen that the county of Moray is separated from the northern counties by an arm of the sea, over which it has not be customary to send railways - but we do know that they are speaking at present of a line from France to England. There is a usefulness of having direct steam communications between the fair land of Moray and the northern counties; and to complete the usefulness of that we must have a railway between Wick and Thurso.

Yes, it appears that our Provost Grant was not going to rest on his laurels. Not being content to be the person who brought railways to the north of Scotland by building the line from Lossiemouth to Elgin, it appears he now wished to be the person to build the first railway in the far north of Scotland, by connecting the towns of Wick and Thurso by rail. From there by a shipping service over the sea to Lossiemouth and on to the rest of the Empire!

The day after the Provost's triumph at Abernethy, the letter arrived from the Board of Trade authorising the opening of the Morayshire's connection to Craigellachie Junction. At this late stage in the proceedings, the Craigellachie viaduct had not yet been painted. A contract was therefore awarded that day, June 26th, to painters E. Dunbar & Co. of Elgin at the cost of £60 to paint the structure. The moving of the goods shed from the original Morayshire Craigellachie station and the slating work on the new locomotive shed at Elgin were also dealt with at the same time. In this case both jobs were given to David Munro, slater of Elgin. Next item for discussion was a long letter from McKenzie, Clunes and Holland informing them that the cost of building the bridge over the River Spey was £450 more than they had budgeted for. The builders were asking the Morayshire to pay this cost, citing the following factors that they claimed were the cause of the increase in the costs. The Morayshire had charged more than it quoted to move materials to the site. The contractor that the Morayshire had engaged to bring in the iron by sea had failed to deliver, so the metal work had to be taken north by rail. Mr Mills had also changed the specification on the gauge of iron used to a heavier one than they had intended and as luck would have it, there had also been a general increase in the price of iron over the period of the contract. Despite the perilous state of its own finances the Morayshire was sympathetic to McKenzie, Clunes & Holland's plight. In their reply they stated that they regretted to learn of the firm's loss and paid over the additional sum of £225 in settlement of the claim.

* now known as Craigellachie.

11 THE NORTHERN SECTION OF THE GREAT NORTH OF SCOTLAND RAILWAY

Wednesday, July 1st 1863 saw the opening of the Strathspey Railway and, what is more important for us, it also saw the GNSR take over the running of services on the Morayshire Railway. Connection of the Morayshire to the GNSR system brought the Aberdeen Company within 40 miles of its ultimate goal of Inverness. Through its running of the services on the Strathspey and Morayshire, its route mileage now stood at 230 miles, which placed it at this time as the fourth largest railway company in Scotland.

What was the effect on the citizens of Elgin at this occasion in the Morayshire's history? Well, the carriages of the GNSR were well-filled that day and a large quantity of goods carried over the line. The business *"Messrs Pickfords & Co,"* appeared in Elgin to deliver goods on behalf of the GNSR and the youngsters of Elgin flocked to the Morayshire station to catch a glimpse of the *"big engines"* of the Great North of Scotland Railway. Only the press was a little grudging in their praise, according to the *Elgin Courant*, of July 3rd 1863. *"The new arrangements seem to suit pretty well in every way except to the mails. A strong effort must be made to have the morning mail delivered from Aberdeen 3 hours earlier than at present."*

The Directors of the Morayshire meanwhile were busy on July 1st, sorting out arrangements for the Morayshire Railway Bill. Two petitions had been lodged against the bill, one coming from the merchant ship owners of Glasgow and Liverpool and the other by the steamship owner's association of London. Discussion of the bill was due to take place in Parliament on Tuesday, July 7th with Provost Grant travelling to London for the meeting. The Secretary of the Morayshire was to supply the sum of £100 to meet the expenses of the witness appearing on behalf of the Company.

On July 3rd they approved payment of extra work at Elgin to improve the facilities for handling trains. For the construction of the turntable and water tower, the masons were paid £53-11s-5d and for laying additional sidings the platelayers received £20-5s-4d. Provision was also to be made by the engineers for cattle pens at Elgin.

Following a letter from Mr Milne secretary of the GNS, it was agreed to exchange passes with the Directors of the Great North of Scotland Railway. This gave the Directors of the Morayshire not only access to travel on the main line from Craigellachie to Aberdeen, but also over the Banff & Portsoy, Strathisla, and the Deeside Railway.

Though the trains were running across the Craigellachie viaduct, the painters were still hard at work painting the structure.

The Morayshire Railway Bill did not come before a Committee of the House of Commons until Thursday, July 17th. Parliamentary business appeared to be crowded, with the Morayshire Bill being heard along with the North British (steam boats) Bill and the Great Eastern Railway Bill because the principles of these were similar to that of the Morayshire. Opposition from the steamship companies related only to the Morayshire Railway Company subsidising to the tune of £600 per year the cost of a ship to travel between Wick and Lossiemouth harbours. Only the Earl of Caithness and Provost Grant's testimony were heard by the Committee. The Chair, a Mr Wood, seemed satisfied by what had been said and the case for the Morayshire's Bill was proved.

Meanwhile, on the same day the remaining members of the Morayshire Board met in Elgin. Letters took up the agenda, one from McKenzie, Clunes and Holland, whom it seems were gratified by the additional payment of £225. Col Yolland of the Board of Trade congratulated them on the quality of the Craigellachie viaduct and Mr Dougall of the I&AJR wrote asking what the intention of the Morayshire was towards the use of Orton station. This last letter was replied to by Mr Milne of the GNSR, who stated that service was at present under review by a Mr Harrison. When he'd completed this, the I&AJR would be informed as to any change in the movement of traffic over the Orton branch. The meeting was concluded following examination of the plans for the new covered station proposed for Elgin.

Provost Grant's success in helping to have the Morayshire Railway Bill passed through Parliament was short-lived. His old adversary the *Elgin Courant* had launched a scathing attack on the proposal to run a steamship service between Wick and Lossiemouth. The main brunt of the assault was the assertion by the newspaper that the harbour at Lossiemouth was not an all weather port. To make the harbour suitable, particularly in an easterly gale would cost huge sums of money, which would swallow any likelihood of a dividend payment by the harbour company. Adding fuel to the fire, the newspaper judged that the figures the Provost had used in the case placed before Parliament were suspect. It appears the Provost had overestimated the population of Caithness and exaggerated the value of the rents and number of farms in the northern district. The Provost as you may suspect did not take kindly to this attack. He attended the Elgin Council meeting of 22nd July armed with copies of the *Courant*, and proceeded to counterattack the newspaper and its assertions. The *Northern Ensign*, the local paper of Caithness, also disagreed strongly with the views of the Elgin press.

James Grant should have known better. Rather than defuse the situation, the attack on the local press provoked more of the same the following week. The *Courant* stepped up its attack on the Provost, suggesting that to improve the facilities at Lossiemouth would require the building of a harbour wall stretching from the lighthouse at Covesea, by the Skerries rock, to connect up with the current harbour at a cost of *"tens of millions of shares at £5 each!"*

From its earliest beginnings The Morayshire had always intended to have a sea connection with the far North of Scotland. By the time the Morayshire's bill had been passed by Parliament, the railway network had reached Invergordon. This made Provost Grant's idea of moving cargo by sea, then on to the Morayshire less likely, an aim further eroded by the state of the harbour at Lossiemouth. Storms and the heavy seas had damaged the harbour wall and parts of the station site, which as yet had not seen full and proper repairs.

On the 24th of July the Morayshire made a payment of £315 to Cowans and Sheldon for the new turntable. Their new partners the GNSR were also looking for a sum of £55-5/- for loan repayments and wagon hire. This demand was accompanied by a request for quick payment as the GNS wanted to close their books for their financial year.

The last Elgin holiday of the year was held on August 10th. Service to Aberdeen and the Strathspey route were fairly lightly loaded, although all the shops and places of business in Elgin were closed. Lossiemouth was the place to be. Some 2500 folk travelled to the seaside in the hope of catching a glimpse of the Channel Fleet that was on its way to the Cromarty Firth. All these holiday makers travelling to the coast must have brought back happy memories to Provost Grant.

On Friday, August 14th the Morayshire Board received notice that the Morayshire Railway Bill had been given the Royal Assent. The Directors also had a letter from Reverend McLinds, asking them to reconsider the position concerning Mrs Taylor's annuity. After a short discussion the Directors agreed to pay her £5 per annum up to April 22nd 1865. McKenzie, Clunes & Holland had also written to the Board asking for their opinion over a claim lodged by Brander & Co for £500. The Morayshire Board advised them to ignore the claim because Brander had failed to comply with the terms of his contract.

Estimate for the new station building at Elgin was given as £1428-1s-3d. This did not include the amount required by the Great North of Scotland Railway to bring the Morayshire up to what it considered an acceptable standard. Mr Harrison had spent a number of weeks travelling over the line and inspecting the plant. His finished report was expected to be with the Morayshire Directors shortly.

More bills arrived on September 18th. Contractors were looking for settlement over the cost of the new engine shed. No payment was to be made until the completion certificate had come from the engineers. The amount outstanding for the cost of the Craigellachie viaduct, less the disputed £500 claimed by Mr Brander, was however paid off. Time was drawing towards the AGM and sadly it seemed that the ordinary shareholders would not see any extra pennies in their pockets.

The statement in the *Elgin Courant*, of October 23rd 1863 saw the directors using all their skills to explain the performance of the Morayshire Railway.

> Your Directors regret that the revenue of the line for the past year has not come up to what was anticipated; and in consequence no dividend can be paid to the Ordinary Shareholders at present. Various causes have combined to bring about this result.
>
> There has not been, during the last twenty years such depression amounting almost to total absence of local goods traffic for export, as has been experienced for the past twelve months. The opening of new and opposing railways, and the consequent derangement of local traffic, has also contributed somewhat to the evil; but those evils are now disappearing, and the traffic is consequently assuming a more steady and improving aspect. The very abundant crops of all kinds in the North this year, as compared with that of last, will of itself secure a very different result as to railway traffic; and your Directors look forward with confidence to an improved state of matters in future.

The actual figures make interesting reading, with the number of passengers using the Morayshire showing an increase of 17,633, resulting in an improvement in revenue to the company of £513-18s-10½d. Goods traffic had decreased, but not dramatically, with only a loss of 3688 tons, amounting to £98-15-11½d less than last year. Where was all the money going? Well, the Directors were making a conscious effort to pay off and close the Capital account. This perhaps, more than the promise of an increase in business through moving *"abundant crops,"* should see some form of dividend paid in future years, if of course, the Great North of Scotland Railway do not try and increase their 45% share for running the services on the Morayshire.

The actual AGM held on October 31st, was not an easy one for the Directors. The question of Mr Harris's valuation of the Company's plant was first. The Board had valued the assets of the Company at £10,000 but following inspection by Mr Harrison it was found that they were worth £10,477, not quite the good deal that it seemed. The Morayshire Board had undertaken work to the value of £700 to bring the Morayshire's plant up to a standard acceptable to the GNSR. Even worse, the amount of money spent on having the Morayshire Railway Bill put through Parliament brought scorn from the shareholders, in particular one Mr Hay. This gentleman was of the opinion that the railway company should not be involved in the shipping business. He contended that if no commercial shipping company would run a service from Wick to Lossiemouth, it was not the place of the Morayshire to spend its shareholders' money to subsidise such a service. He determined that if the Morayshire stuck to the matter of railways, a dividend would be payable to its shareholders. After all railways to either side of the Morayshire were able to pay a dividend and they too were affected by the poor agricultural business of the past year. Mr Hay continued assailing the Morayshire Board, and Provost Grant in particular, for the whole period of the AGM. Uncharacteristically the Provost seemed unable to come up with any suitable answers to Mr Hay's points, having to be rescued from Mr Hay's attack by Mr Morrison, whose call for a vote of thanks closed matters.

Non-payment of £15 due to Mr Forbes of Haddo for survey work carried out for a prospective route from Elgin to Lossiemouth way back in 1846 was brought to the attention of the Board on November 13th 1863. This outstanding amount was paid to the gentleman but with no added interest.

The Morayshire Directors wished to increase the rates for goods carried and passenger fares, but could not do so without the express permission of the Great North of Scotland Railway. This was to be sought urgently.

Mrs Soutor took over the tenancy of the Station Hotel in Elgin on December 30th 1863. She thereby increased her business empire, as she was continuing to look after her original business, the Grant Arms in Rothes. The *Elgin Courant*, wished all success in her new venture.

Close of the year witnessed Provost Grant standing down from political life. The post of Provost fell to Mr Alexander Russell, former owner of the *Elgin Courant* and long time adversary of James Grant.

The Great North of Scotland Railway disapproved of any increase in goods rates and passenger fares. Communication between the Morayshire and the GNS was not as it should be. Despite the refusal of the latter to a fare increase, reports of a rise appeared in the local Elgin press, as per this, which also notes a staff change.

> We are glad to report that Mr Shaw stationmaster at Craigellachie, has been appointed agent at the Banff, Macduff and Turriff Extension Railway. Mr Shaw deserves this promotion. He was very much liked in this part of the country.

> We are authorised to state that a small increase is to be made on the passenger fares over the Morayshire on and after this day. It amounts in some cases to ¼d per mile. On 3rd class fares no alterations have been made, but the return tickets are slightly altered. We would have preferred the old rates, but we have no doubt the Directors feel that a necessity exists for the alteration to be made.

If there was a temporary lack of understanding between the Morayshire and Great North, dealings between the Junction Company and the Morayshire had always been troubled. The Directors of the I&AJR were upset that the Morayshire Directors had sent GNSR passes to them, which they felt would not allow them to travel over the Morayshire Railway! Disputes were certainly in the air, as the Morayshire continue to argue with Mrs Collier of the Lossiemouth Hotel and Mr Preston over yet another request for settlement of his account.

The press, excluding the fare increase however seemed to be fairly impressed with the Morayshire. Compliments were forthcoming on January 22nd 1864 for the extensive work undertaken at Elgin station. By this point, the overall roof had been completed, major alterations to the goods sidings almost finished, and the building of an extensive two road engine shed was almost complete.

On January 27th formal written approval by the Great North of Scotland Railway for the fare increases were received by the Morayshire.

He may have stood down as Provost of Elgin, but James Grant was still working hard for the Morayshire Railway Company, trying to resolve some of the claims made by Mr Preston. In connection with that, on the 5th of February, he had contacted a Mr Millar of Edinburgh to try and find a buyer for the Preference shares held by Mr Preston, sadly so far without success. Other accounts connected with the construction of the Direct Line, held by the Commercial Bank, were successfully settled.

The matter of passenger rates reappeared on March 11th attracting this comment from the *Elgin Courant*.

> We are desired to state that the fares on the Morayshire Railway will be on and after Monday 14th inst.

1st Class single	Journey passenger 2d	per mile
3rd Class single	Journey passenger 1½d	per mile
3rd Parliamentary	Journey passenger 1d	per mile

Daily return tickets 1st and 3rd will be issued for a fare and a half, available to return the same day only; and Saturday return tickets, 1st & 3rd will be issued for an ordinary fare, available to Monday night.

This charge may be so far satisfactory, but three half pennies per mile still makes a charge of 9d for a journey by ordinary train from Elgin to Lossie and the high fare to that place is the cause of very general complaint.

March of 1864 saw a flare-up between the Inverness and Aberdeen Junction Railway and the Morayshire over the exchange of traffic at Orton. The I&AJR station master was refusing to load GNSR wagons with timber destined for Lossiemouth, which the Morayshire wanted to be sent by Rothes. In addition, he was also refusing to accept invoices for goods carried over the Morayshire that had been exchanged at Orton for stations east of Orton on the Junction line. The Morayshire Directors decided to defer taking any action until they had discussed the situation with the GNS Directors in Aberdeen.

The Great North of Scotland Railway had its mind on bigger things. It held its AGM in April at Aberdeen. Afterwards a Special meeting was held to authorise the raising of additional capital, money required to enable the Aberdeen company to contribute further to the Keith and Dufftown Railway, Strathspey Railway and more importantly (for us) the Morayshire. The decision to go to Parliament was proposed by the Chairman of the meeting, one Sir J D H Elphinstone Bart and seconded by a Mr Crombie.

By the end of April, James Grant had travelled to Inverness to meet with Mr Dougall of the I&AJR to settle the problems at Orton. It was agreed that both parties would set up a committee to resolve the dispute and settle any outstanding bills that might be due.

Things were not looking good by May 20th 1864. Overdrafts that the Morayshire had with its bankers were only just being sustained. On top of this the local press added a little spice with a story about the proposed railways to Burghead.

There is now every certainty of a railway from Burghead to Hopeman. The line is at present being surveyed with the intention of commencing work immediately. It is a great pity that the Morayshire Railway have not thought fit to make one from Hopeman joining their line at about Loch Spynie. If the line pays the I&AJR, it would pay the Morayshire, and a union with the Lossie line is more the wish of the Hopeman people than going round by Burghead every time they require to go to Elgin where all business is done in connection with this place.

The pressure at Orton was turned up a little in June. The Inverness and Aberdeen Junction Railway reduced the cost of fares for people travelling from Orton to Mulben and Keith, whilst also doing all in its power to prevent the Morayshire Railway from gaining access to the station at Orton.

The Station Hotel at Lossiemouth reopened under new management on July 1st, with a Mr Fearn taking up the helm.

On July 12th, James Grant secured an agreement with the Commercial Bank to extend its £3000 loan for four months. Consideration was also given to building a station at Orton rather than continue discussions with the I&AJR. It would be located just by the level crossing on the Rothes to Mulben road, on what we now refer to as the B9103.

Actions by the Inverness and Aberdeen Junction Railway, along with the small amount of traffic, saw the GNSR withdraw passenger services from the Orton branch at the end of July. Freight business continued to be run on an as required basis. The loss of this service was balanced a little by the provision of early morning trains on the Lossie branch to cater for those Elgin citizens who wished to have an early dip in the Moray Firth.

The prospect of a new source of revenue came to the fore in August 1864. Mr MacDonald Grant of Arndilly had discovered large quantities of iron manganese and other metals on his property. By the middle of August he was putting the final touches to a contract with a Glasgow firm to start mining operations on the hill of Ben Aigan to extract the ore. The Morayshire's hoped that their line would be used to transport the minerals either to Lossiemouth or Craigellachie Junction for the journey south. It was expected that some form of tramway with a bridge over the Spey would be constructed to connect with the Morayshire network.

12 The Late Captain Grant of Glengrant

The following Battalion Order has been issued in reference to the deceased-

Head - Quarters Elgin

August 30 1864.

It is with the most profound regret that the Lieut. - Colonel Commanding announces to the Battalion the death of Captain Grant of the 4th Elginshire Rifle Volunteers, who expired at Glengrant Rothes on 26th ins. Sir A. P. Gordon Cumming feels assured that he is joined by every officer and volunteer in this Battalion in offering his sincere condolences to Mrs Grant, to ex - Provost Grant of Elgin and his family as also do the members of the Elginshire Rifle Volunteers, as to the great loss they have sustained. The energy, worth and kindness of the late Captain Grant are too well known to need any eulogy. To his family, and to the Corps of which he was so justly proud, his loss will be irreparable.

In token of respect to his memory, the officers of the Battalion will wear crape three and a half inches wide on the left arm when in uniform for four weeks.

The name of Captain Grant will be struck off the roll of the Battalion from 27th inst.

By Order

CHAS. A. THOMPSON
Captain and Adjutant

John Grant of Glengrant had been seriously ill for three months. A regular attendee of all the Morayshire Railway Company meetings, he had last been present at a Directors' meeting on April 29th 1864.

As far as our story is concerned, John Grant is second in importance to the history of the Morayshire Railway after his brother James. To the people of Rothes and surrounding district, at this time, as the public face of J & J Grant Distillers Rothes, founder of the Rothes section of the Rifle Volunteers, * local farmer and landowner he was the most important and not just because the energy with which he conducted his business affairs resulted in a large number of jobs in the town. His charitable nature saw the establishment of a school to give elementary education to the girls of Rothes and district. Even in death he lived up to his motto *"Go Ahead"* by leaving a handsome legacy of £1600 to extend the education of girls to the outlying places of Aberlour, Knockando, Inveravon and Cromdale. A vast number of mourners attended his funeral on Tuesday, August 30th 1864.

The Rothes Volunteers formed up outside Glengrant House to inter him with full military honours. The number including a band was fifty. A party of four was selected to carry the coffin, with the sword of the deceased placed on the lid. For the march through the town of Rothes, the body was place in a hearse, with the members of the carrying party walking by each wheel. The chief mourners, ex-Provost Grant and young Mr James Grant, the son of John Grant, followed on immediately behind the hearse. Next came the clergymen of Rothes, followed by the carriages of the Grant family, then ordinary folk of Rothes and surrounding district. Such was their number that the procession stretched from one end of Rothes to the other. All the shops and places of business were closed whilst the funeral moved slowly and solemnly through the town. The procession continued on through the village of Aberlour and on

* fore runner of the Territorial Army.

arriving at Marypark was joined by a large number of people from the districts of Glenlivet, Inveravon and Strathspey. At the school house of Inveravon, all the mourners left their carriages and continued on foot to the cemetery. As the body was lowered into the ground, the entire Company of Volunteers fired three volleys, breaking the stillness of the quiet glen. For a man with such a wide variety of business and other interests, it was not surprising the funeral of John Grant of Glengrant was the largest ever witnessed in the locality. The band of the Volunteers playing plaintive airs led the procession out the small glen back to Rothes.

Born in 1791, John was the eldest son of the Grant family. This put him at a slight disadvantage to his younger brother James, as he was required to help his father with the work on Shenval Farm, therefore missing out on a full-time education. Thanks also to his mother, he was taught the basics of reading and writing and given a good grounding in the Scriptures. It was also said, when he did attend school (in the winter months), his two favourite subjects were Geography and Arithmetic, both of which were to prove very useful to him in his later life.

As a young Avonside ploughman, he started to look around for an opportunity and began dealing in grain. He soon found this to be much more profitable than farming and it was through this venture that in 1824 he met a Mr Smith, Minmore, Glenlivet. That year he took out a licence as a spirit merchant, becoming Mr Smith's right-hand man, by taking up to a hundred gallons of whisky a week south to Edinburgh. Mr Smith in return gave him the benefit of his advice and a practical insight into the secrets of brewing.

He became well known in the southern markets because, for the most part, the whisky he retailed was the *"real"* Glenlivet. In 1833 he went into partnership with his brother James and two other brothers also called James and John, drapers from Elgin, though Walker was their end name. A lease was obtained for the Aberlour Distillery and they went into production yielding 600 gallons a week. On expiry of the lease at Aberlour in 1840, the brothers Grant feued some ground from the Earl of Seafield at the northeast end of Rothes and the business of J & J Grant Glengrant was born. The distillery was one of the largest in Scotland, contributing some £60,000 per year to the exchequer. Not content to sit back and enjoy this achievement, in 1844 he became tenant of Drumbain Farm, on which he reclaimed and drained some 230 acres of land. He also became tenant of the adjoining Auchinroath Farm that he kept in the highest state of cultivation, with a flock of some 1000 sheep being spread between the two enterprises.

Due to him being an importer of coal and exporter of whisky, he took an interest in Lossiemouth harbour, which of course led to his involvement in the Morayshire Railway, to whose story we now return.

The gloom that descended over the Morayshire Company following the loss of John Grant lifted for the employees a little by a presentation that took place on September 24th at Elgin station. The recipient Mr Florence Turnbull was gifted a Gold Albert Chain as a memento and token of esteem upon leaving the post of Stationmaster at Elgin, to take up a similar position at Struan. A popular figure around the town, members of the local population had also contributed to the cost of the gold chain. A religious man, Mr Turnbull gifted to each of the railway employees a copy of the book *"Peace with God,"* by Rev F Ferguson, Blackfriars Street Independent Chapel, Glasgow.

A further possible glimmer of light may have come from the Fochabers and Garmouth Railway shareholder's meeting of October 20th 1864. It seemed the Directors, who were all I&AJR Directors, had to report their regret in not beginning building the line. They cited the poor state of the money markets for the lack of progress.

Nature made its presence felt as a hurricane accompanied by torrential rain hit the area on this day, causing the Linkwood Burn, which rises in the Marnoch hills on the west side of the Glen of Rothes, to burst its banks. This flooding resulted in some thirty to forty yards of the Morayshire Railway by the woollen mill in the Glen of Rothes being swept away. Mr Hay of the mill made himself a makeshift red flag and stood just ahead of the break in the line to warn the approaching midday goods train. The weather had caused this service to be slightly delayed, leaving Mr Hay to spend longer than he thought in the storm to warn the crew of the impending danger. Thanks to his tenacity the train was halted before it reached the damaged track.

Two large forces of men were sent out from Elgin to make good the damage, ensuring the line was passable for traffic by the afternoon of Saturday 22nd. Flooding had affected some other parts of the line but fortunately all bridges and other embankments remained intact.

The Directors of the Morayshire met for the first time after the death of John Grant on October 24th. Despite the drama of the past few days, the Directors seemed to have little appetite for the running of the Company. The loss of Glengrant had hit them hard. Business had however to continue with the requirement to hold an AGM fixed for October 31st 1864.

Subdued is the best word to describe the AGM, its passing warranting only a paragraph in the *Elgin Courant*. As in previous years, the Directors were unable to declare a dividend to the shareholders.

In the best tradition of *"revenge is a dish best served cold,"* a cartoon originating from Inverness resurrected the *"Miss Morayshire & Mr Inverness"* joke. Four years previously the Morayshire Railway Company had rejected the offer of 4½% dividend from the Inverness & Aberdeen Junction Company. The opening scene on the cartoon was the Assembly Ball in Elgin on October 31st 1860. Pause after the Parliamentary Quadrille.

Mr Inverness - May I have the pleasure of your hand for the Strathspey!
Miss Morayshire - Thank you, I am engaged to Mr Aberdeen for that dance.
Haud awa', bide awa',
Haud awa' frae me Donald;
Wi' a' your 4½ per cent,
Ye'r nae a match for me Donald.

The other picture, placed alongside the above, set the scene as follows:

Miss Morayshire to Mr Inverness October 31st, 1864.

Come awa', come awa',
Come again to me, Donald,
The cauldrife kail o' Aberdeen
Is caulder than yer knee, Donald.
Come awa' wi FOUR per cent,
The half ane I'll forgie, Donald,
Or gin ye'r, doubtfu' o the Four,
I'll maybe gang for THREE, Donald
Oh! man, I've had a waefu dance,
Frae Rothes to the sea, Donald.
The grand STRATHSPEY he promised me,
Was naething but a lee, Donald
Oh! leeze me on the Heilang Fling
But no wi' Aberdeen Donald
The Buchan breeks upon the Spey

Should never ha' been seen Donald.
Oh! wae's me for your four per cent,
Oh! wae's me for your Three, Donald!
My sad lament is NAE per cent,
The deils a bad bawbee, Donald.

The above cartoon did not merit a mention when the Directors of the Morayshire met on November 8th. Ex- Provost Grant had been attempting to lower the interest rates on various loans that the Morayshire had with the Commercial Bank. As for that other monetary matter, Mr Preston's claim, he proposed that in an attempt to come to some arrangement with Mr Preston and his legal representatives, Smith Ellison & Co, he should travel to Chester and Lincoln respectively to meet with both parties. The Board, keen for ex-Provost Grant to attempt a settlement, said due to lack of money they could not afford to send him south, all negotiation had to be done by written correspondence. Later they relented a little on this point agreeing that if he wanted to fund the trip south out of his own pocket then they would be happy for him to do this.

Details of Mr Preston's claim at this point

As the main contractor on the Direct line to Rothes, Mr Preston had charged £35,040-5s-9d. This amount the Morayshire Board had no complaint about. What did concern them was an additional charge made by Mr Preston for £1983-18s-4d. The reasons for this were:

Claim for delay in the delivery of material	£ 992- 2s-11d
Repair of flood damage	£ 196- 7s- 5d
Additional work Elgin Rothes & Longmorn Stn.	£ 279- 8s- 4d
Additional earthworks at Linkwood	£ 25- 1s- 9d
Additional earthworks done on the line	£ 490-17s-11d
Total	£1983-18s- 4d

Evidence of the precarious nature of the Morayshire's finances was witnessed by the need to reduce staff costs. The Board had attempted and failed to locate a new position with either the GNSR or the I&AJR for a time served clerk, by the name of Alexander Fraser who worked at Craigellachie. Soon to find himself in a similar position was another clerk Mr Marrloch. He had almost completed his apprenticeship and was to be informed there was no post for him. This was to be done with all haste, giving him an opportunity to find a new job. New apprentice clerks were then to be sought to fill the two vacancies caused.

Additional traffic from iron mines at Arndilly seemed feasible. According to the *Elgin Courant* of November 18th, a test load of 300 tons of ore was favourably received by the iron master in Yorkshire.

Captain Stewart resigned on November 25th 1864 after seven years of service to the Morayshire. No reason is given for his departure as Deputy Chairman, but the situation of the Company was probably an element. James Grant, perpetually trying to sort out monetary muddles, had obtained a promissory note for £3000 from the Commercial Bank. Security against this amount was as Preference shares in the Morayshire. Besides this sum it was hoped that other cash would be forthcoming with the issue of more debentures.

Difficulty was being experienced in finding someone to replace the late John Grant Glengrant. It had been the wish of the Directors that George Leslie, Sheriff - Clerk would fill the vacancy, but he declined the offer. The position was eventually taken up by George Hay. The quest for money for the Company coffers continued with two substantial claims against the Inverness & Aberdeen Junction Railway, violation over the Orton Branch agreement (£3650), and the resultant loss of business (£2127-11). The

Morayshire Board felt that this claim should be sent direct to the I&AJR to, *"Prevent tedious correspondence!"*

On December 21st a note was sent to Captain Stewart's legal representatives, Grigor & Young, to remind him that although he was no longer a Director of the Company he still had obligations to the Morayshire. One of the debentures for £1000 was due for payment at this time. To meet this call on funds James Grant advanced £1600 of his own money to the Morayshire. Demands for repayment of loans were coming as thick and fast as the December snow. The £3650 due to the Commercial Bank on the last day of 1864, was paid as a temporary advance from the Board of the GNSR. Provost Grant travelled through to Aberdeen to negotiate the transaction, providentially using his Director's pass to pay his fare.

13 THE MAN'S A MARVEL SIR; A MARVEL OF PLUCK AND SPIRIT

With most of the Northeast and Highlands of Scotland engulfed in a thick blanket of snow, the Directors of the Morayshire did not meet during January 1865, and operations on the railway itself were hindered by the weather. It was not until February that things started to stir, and as ever at the centre of it all was James Grant.

The scene for ex-Provost Grant's latest triumph was the first annual festival of servants of the Great North and Deeside Railway Companies, which took place on February 10th at the Music Hall in Aberdeen.

> While Mr John Duncan* as Chairman of the event, made a fitting and forceful address to the large body of railway officials, their wives and families, and sweethearts. Our Elgin friend made himself the observed of all observers, and fairly carried off the belt of popularity. The best fun of all lay in this - that not over half of those who looked at and listened to him in amazement, knew who he was! What a range of subjects he embraced in his speech - he quoted from poets, scared and profane, winding up by singing in his own inimitable style, The Haughs of Cromdale, with its very impressive chorus. The people were in raptures and cheered their spontaneous and impromptu entertainer long and lustily. The man's a marvel, Sir, a marvel of pluck, spirit, and honest outspokenness. Provost Grant is ever the same energetic, shrewd, and fearless Elginite - a chip off the right marble. (*Elgin Courant*'s Aberdeen correspondent)

The Directors of the Morayshire gathered for their first meeting on February 16th. It appears as well as his entertainment prowess, ex-Provost Grant had succeeded in a small way in placing the Morayshire Company on a slightly more secure footing. The Commercial Bank had been repaid, and the promissory notes had been transferred to the National Bank of Scotland, whom it was felt offered lower rates of interest.

Captain Stewart had engaged Grigor & Young to defend himself against any claims made by the Morayshire. James Grant had already met with Mr Grigor to try and resolve this matter without going to court.

A settlement of sorts had been made with the Inverness and Aberdeen Junction Company. Although Mr Dougall denied liability for losses incurred by the Morayshire, a Parliamentary Committee ruled in the Morayshire's favour. The I&AJR very reluctantly offered the sums of £1180-15s-3d and £738-17s-10d in settlement, which considering the state of the Morayshire's finances was accepted.

Mr Preston was not so fortunate. James Grant had not yet travelled to hold talks with the him but he had arranged to meet with Mr Wainwright of the Glasgow & South Western Railway Company. He hoped to gain Mr Wainwright's advice on how to put the Morayshire on a more stable financial footing.

As the Directors made their way home, the light snow fall that had started at the middle of the day had become much heavier. It was now accompanied by a northwest wind, which during the late evening veered round to the northeast. By the morning of Friday, February 17th the snow lay to a depth of sixteen inches, with nothing to break the white plain west or east of Elgin. Even the seaside town of Lossiemouth was badly effected by the snowstorm. The whistle of a railway engine had not been heard in the town; fear was entertained that the snow had blocked the railway line. By 10am groups of people had gathered at the railway station, anxious to know whether a train would be coming from Elgin.

* Vice Chairman of the GNSR.

Efforts to maintain a service were being made and this fact was confirmed by a telegram to the Stationmaster at Lossiemouth. The sound of a whistle was heard at eleven, informing the coastal inhabitants that an engine was nearing the town. Instead of the usual locomotive and train of carriages, two locomotives appeared with our old friend ex-Provost Grant on the footplate. The local press expressed their thanks to the Chairman of the Morayshire for doing his duty on this occasion, an unusual statement, because the operation of train services was the responsibility of the Great North of Scotland Railway Company. Even if it were not, as the Chairman of the Morayshire Railway Company, his place should have been directing operations, not riding on engines. I think he was a real enthusiast who in his 64th year could not resist a trip in the cab of a locomotive.

Train services in the upper portion of Moray were also badly effected. Rothes, like Elgin had snow to the depth of 16 inches in the town, but it lay considerably deeper in the surrounding countryside. Trains from both Keith and Elgin attempted passage along the line, but both failed to travel much beyond the boundaries of their respective starting points. More snow fell on the Saturday and Sunday, accompanied by winds that caused intense drifting; the line through the Glen of Rothes disappeared under some six to eight feet of snow. There was no let-up in the weather on the Sunday and by the time Monday arrived, the line to Lossiemouth was again impassable. On receiving notification of the suspension of services by electric telegraph, the Lossiemouth Stationmaster Mr Sim decided to walk to Elgin along the railway line to ensure delivery of outgoing mails. He returned later in the day bringing the down mails that had lain at Elgin station. The local press summed up the attitude of the local community on Mr Sim's devotion to duty as follows *"the feelings of the community are such that the services of our local station master will not be forgotten."* By the Tuesday a thaw set in which saw the Morayshire network resume business, with trains running to the advertised timetable by Wednesday.

Whilst the weather may have become more acceptable, the Morayshire found itself back in a financial storm. This required an EGM on March 16th 1865 to try and solve the problems engulfing the Company. Apparently the Commercial Bank had not been paid off in full and it was looking for repayment of loans to the value of £3211-15s-10d. The best the Board could do was to obtain a one year repayment delay from the Bank. To speed up the payment of outstanding accounts, Mr Smith Minmore took the place of the late John Grant Glengrant as signatory on Morayshire cheques and paperwork. The Board noted that this change in no way absolved the executors of Glengrant's estate from obligations to the Company.

Seven days later the black hole of debt became a little deeper. The Great North of Scotland Railway planned to take complete control of the Morayshire Railway as a method of reclaiming the money it had lent, James Grant believed that the GNSR would be obtaining *"something for nothing,"* and as he set about raising a petition to contest an amalgamation, squabbles over percentages and traffic receipts broke out between the two companies. The claim from Mr Preston was now sitting at the sum of £5250.

Ex-Provost Grant in May decided to build himself a *"handsome and commodious cottage."* The building was to be constructed on the feu he had bought many years ago at the foot of Moss Street opposite the Station Hotel, which he also owned. Handsome and commodious it certainly was but by no stretch of the imagination was it a cottage. His new home, like the Station Hotel, embraced all modern improvements. Designed by A W Reid architect, the contractors were Messrs Allan, builder; McKenzie, carpenter; Stuart, plasterer; Wilson slater; and Hunter plumber. From his new vantage point, which became known as Dalehaple House *, he could keep an eye on his Hotel business, the Morayshire Railway, and more particularly I&AJR opposition.

In mid-June 1865 a debenture for the sum of £1420 fell due to be repaid. To meet this call a loan was secured, against yet another debenture to the City of Glasgow Bank.

July Monday 3rd, the first Elgin Holiday *"monster trains"* were leaving both railway stations with Moss Street, the thoroughfare to the railway, *"becoming a living mass of excursionists."* The I&AJR carried

* Now The Royal Hotel Elgin.

1000 citizens westward in the direction of Inverness, but it was the GNSR who were the winners with 2410 tickets sold. The bulk of these, 2000, went to Lossiemouth.

On August 14th the City of Glasgow Bank refused to give additional aid to the Company because of the amounts it owed to others

Commercial Bank	£15211-15s-10d.
GNSR	£12620- 0s- 0 d.
Strathspey Railway	£ 2253-12s-5 ½d.
Advances	£ 2837- 8s-6 d.
Contractor	£ 2250- 0s-0 d.
M.R. Directors	£ 3000- 0s- 0d.
Total	£38172-16s- 9 ½d.

In round figures the Morayshire had to find £39,000 not including the sum due to Mr Preston. A report into the ways of doing this was discussed at a Board meeting on August 25th. It was decided the best way to proceed was for the Morayshire to apply to either a bank or group of money lenders to assist in reducing the capital sum. The Directors of the Morayshire would themselves take over the responsibility to pay for the interest on any moneys borrowed and accrued by the capital sum. Mr Wainwright of the Glasgow and South Western Railway Company, who had been asked for his assistance in sorting the problems of the Morayshire, agreed with this course of action. If the Directors were unsuccessful in this scheme, he suggested that the GNSR might be approached for the funds to pay off the capital. The state of relations between the two Companies was such, that Mr Wainwright's latter suggestion would have been a nonstarter.

The Great North of Scotland Railway Directors were at the time of this meeting *"putting their hand in their pocket,"* not to the tune of £39,000, but for a lesser sum. This was to express gratitude to Mr Hay of Coleburn for his actions of October 1864 in averting a possible derailment following the flash flood. He was awarded an inscribed silver snuffbox. The presentation was carried out by Mr Morrison, manager of the northern section of the GNSR. The silver snuffbox was described as a handsome one, on which the following inscription was laid:

Presented by the
Directors of the Great North of Scotland Railway,
to
Mr Alexander Hay
Manufacturer, Coleburn Wool Mill, Morayshire
In testimony of their appreciation of his services and presence
of mind, in signalling the Train on the Morayshire Railway,
On the 20th day October, 1864,
When, in consequence of a flood, the Railway
was rendered impassable

In the report carried in the *Elgin Courant*, Mr Morrison of the GNSR said, *"He hoped and wished that Mr Hay might be long spared to bear about with him this small token of their esteem, and when called upon, in the course of nature, to lay it aside, It might become an heirloom in his family, who would thereby be proudly reminded of their descent from a man whose prompt and humane conduct averted a calamity."*

Good weather in August brought out the folk of Elgin to enjoy the second and concluding holiday of the year. Travels to the seaside seemed to be preferred with 1816 tickets sold at the GNSR station. Going west, 1373 travelled on the newly formed Highland Railway. It had come into being on August 1st by the bringing together of the various companies operating into Inverness. The attraction of the seaside meanwhile may not have been all that innocent. Lossiemouth Town Council had put up notices to keep the sexes to separate sections on the beach. In the best tradition of all prohibition notices, they were completely ignored by the holidaymakers.

Through the whole month of September and a good part of October James Grant worked on. By October 16th, he was able to disclose to a Board meeting that he had reached an agreement with Mr Preston. Under his proposal 600 shares equal in value to £6000 were to be given to Mr Preston in full settlement of the outstanding debit owed by the Morayshire.

Interested shareholders and the Directors gather in the Station Hotel Elgin on Tuesday, October 31st 1865. Business overall had been good in the last year, with an increase in passenger traffic of 13,010 persons and 8342 tons in goods. Prospective sources of business, promised in the New Year, were the iron ore mine at Arndilly and the anticipated completion of the junction between the Strathspey and Highland railways at Nethybridge. This, the shareholders were assured, *"Cannot fail to add a much larger share of through traffic than we have now."*

Now came the bad news: the Elgin and Nairn Roads and Bridges Act of 1863 laid the Morayshire Railway Company liable to a heavy burden of taxes to the sum of £105-10s-2d for the provision of roads, affecting the Company by not only cutting into any profit but also withdrawing traffic from the railway in favour of the roads. It goes without saying, that no dividend was forthcoming to the shareholders. The Directors did hold out the hope of improving on this situation for next year, by going to Parliament to raise new stock in the form of Preference shares, thereby lessening interest now being paid on temporary loans. No mention was made of the quarrels the Morayshire had been having with the Great North of Scotland Railway. On the contrary it was reported that *"The line continues to be satisfactorily worked by the Great North of Scotland Railway."*

After the main meeting was concluded, an ordinary meeting of the Directors was held. At this, it was proposed that Mr Wainwright of the Glasgow & South Western Railway should become Vice-Chairman of the Morayshire Railway. Arrangements were also to be made for talks with the GNSR to try and persuade them to accept promissory notes to clear some of the debt owed to them.

On Saturday, November 11th the Morayshire Directors met and agreed to attempt once more to borrow £1200 from the City of Glasgow Bank.

The following Saturday, the Directors travelled south to Perth to meet with Mr Wainwright at the North British Hotel. They agreed that the Morayshire should apply to Parliament in this session to create first Preference Stock in an attempt to wipe out the debts of the Company. It was further resolved that the GNSR should take up some of these shares and be given the option of shutting the Orton branch. This was to be done on the proviso that the GNSR paid the Morayshire £200 over and above the largest yearly sum that the Morayshire had derived from working the branch, or from the time that the GNSR commenced to work it. The Morayshire retained the power to stipulate expressly that at any time the GNSR would reopen the branch after being given three months notice.

More debentures fell due on December 6th. The Board of the Great North of Scotland Railway invited ex-Provost Grant through to Aberdeen to discuss the possibility of the amalgamation between the Morayshire and the GNSR. The meeting took place on December 19th 1865, but it was curtailed after a short period of time by James Grant, who saw little merit in the proposal. At this time the £1600 that he had lent to the Morayshire in 1864 was due for repayment. This amount was returned to him in full, and he informed the Board that if they required a further loan he would be happy to oblige.

As 1865 ended, every type of bank, insurance company and money lender was approached in an effort to keep the Morayshire Railway Company afloat. All were unsuccessful.

It was not until the end of January 1866 that a Directors' meeting was deemed necessary. A comparatively small sum of £2-2/-, was made available as the Morayshire's contribution to the GNSR & Deeside servant's festival. This was to be held on February 10th in Aberdeen. The half year rent for the Lossiemouth Station Hotel had been secured and the offer of amalgamation with the Great North of Scotland Railway was still on the table. James Grant was to travel to Aberdeen on February 1st to discuss the offer.

On March 13th, the Bill to enable the Company to raise new preference shares ran into trouble. The Parliamentary Committee discussing this bill had made amendments which resulted in it being useless for the purpose that was intended. As ex-Provost Grant set about rewriting the bill for another submission, the *Elgin Courant*, reported the passing of the now useless bill on March 23rd.

In a novel method of attempting to lower the Morayshire's debt burden, letters were written to all the banks to whom the Morayshire owed money complaining about the high rate of interest charges. Subsequent reports on this tactic noted that no influence was exerted and no reduction occurred on the rates charged.

Excursion trains to Lossiemouth to facilitate early morning bathers began running for the 1866 season on May 5th. This service left Elgin at 7.50am. Cheap Saturday fares also commenced at this time

All change at the Station Hotel in Lossiemouth on the 25th of May as the *"famous"* Mrs Soutor of the Seafield Hotel Rothes became tenant. She ceased the business trading as a hotel, intending to operate it as a refreshment room, whilst renting out the rooms on the upper stories as private accommodation for lodgers.

"It is satisfactory to know that the Great North and Highland Companies are now on very good terms," ran a report in the *Elgin Courant* of 1st June 1866 on the subject of the soon-to-be opened link between the two companies on Speyside. The newspaper was looking forward to improved service with the south of the country as well as services between Aberdeen and Inverness. From the comments made by the two railway companies, it was clear that the extensive changes in train services that the *Elgin Courant* wished for were not going to happen. The only betterment was one goods train per day that travelled down the Speyside line to connect with the Highland Railway's service going south, and one express passenger service between Inverness and Aberdeen late in the afternoon, giving little actual opportunity for the Morayshire to accumulate additional revenue.

The prospect of an amalgamation with the Great North of Scotland Railway was brought a little closer, following an extraordinary general meeting held in the Station Hotel Elgin on Saturday, June 23rd 1866. Various railway companies for which the GNSR ran the train services, were now being absorbed into the Aberdeen Company. James Grant, as Chairman for the Elgin meeting, explained the position of the Morayshire in this new arrangement. *The bill takes power to amalgamate several companies with the Great North of Scotland Railway Company the power taken with regard to the Morayshire is merely permissive. We can amalgamate at any time we think it proper and prudent to do so, but there is no provision for immediate amalgamation."* The Morayshire Railway Company lived to fight another day!

There was excellent news on June 29th, if you happened to be a grocer in the City of Elgin. I can only assume that there must have been a considerable number of persons employed in this trade in Elgin, because the GNSR instituted a cut-price fare for participants in this business. On every Wednesday afternoon, which had now been established as half-day closing, the GNSR offered returns at single prices, provided of course you returned that evening to Elgin. The press were impressed by this gesture on the part of the GNSR. *"This is a special privilege to the Grocers of Elgin which they should and we have no doubt will feel obliged."*

July saw the start of the holiday season proper, with the City of Elgin closed for business on Monday, 6th July. Lossiemouth proved the most popular of all the destinations, with most of the 1901 tickets sold by the GNSR for passage to the seaside. The fame of Lossiemouth as a holiday destination was spreading outwith the boundaries of the county. The following week a trainload of visitors arrived from Aberdeen on the 13th and Dufftown on the 16th, all wishing to enjoy the splendour of its beaches.

Mr Preston and his claims against the Morayshire Company returned to the fore on July 24th. The best the Board could do in respect of the gentleman's demands was to pay the interest on the amount he was claiming

Sharp-eyed readers of the local press may have noticed that references to the Orton branch line disappeared from the Great North of Scotland Railway timetable published in the *Elgin Courant* of July 24th. There had not been a regular passenger service on this line for a number of years, and goods traffic was run on an as-required basis. On July 31st, the GNSR withdrew (with a slight protest from the Morayshire) from providing a service on the Orton branch, which made little difference to the population because of the aforementioned cutbacks.

The coming together of railway companies appeared to be the fashion for the summer of 1866. Most spectacular of all, was a proposed merger between the Great North of Scotland Railway and the Caledonian Railway, according to the report in the *Elgin Courant* of August 23rd. Things were at such an advanced state, *"a speedy amalgamation of the two companies, was expected in the near future."* As the heat of the summer made way for the autumn, this story cooled, until it was finally denied on September 14th.

Since the closure of the Orton branch, the Morayshire Board had attempted to obtain their intended payment. The Great North of Scotland Railway advised the Morayshire, on September 25th 1866, that it refuted all its claims in this matter.

On October 10th 1866, the contract to carry mail was rescinded, resulting in the Company books being £443-17/- lighter. The Morayshire Directors laid the blame for this deficit firmly at the door of the Great North of Scotland Railway, who themselves were not having a rosy time. A cattle plague had swept the country, having a dire effect on all railway companies. The Great North, being mainly a rural railway, depended upon the cattle markets in the various county towns for income from farmers and livestock travelling to the weekly markets. At a stroke this source of revenue vanished. Perhaps in order to seize a marketing opportunity, the redoubtable Mrs Soutor sought on the 19th to obtain a liquor licence for her refreshment rooms at Lossiemouth station, offering solace in a wee dram.

Relationships between the Morayshire and Great North of Scotland continued to deteriorate through the rest on October and November, making for an interesting AGM on November 30th. A small band of shareholders joined the Directors at the Station Hotel for the Annual Report on the state of their Company. The revenue for the previous year was sufficient to meet the working expenses and the interest on the Company Debentures. The surplus left, some £2076-6s-4d, was totally consumed meeting the interest required to pay the various temporary advances. Not only had it all been spent, the Morayshire needed to borrow a further £937-18s-7d, to meet all its commitments. All because of exorbitant rates of interest!

Traffic continued to increase on the previous year's figures with an additional 6245 passengers and 3680 tons of goods being carried over the line. This, remember, was against the background of the cattle plague which had closed all livestock markets. If the company could pay off its debt, the core of the Morayshire was financially sound and did offer the prospect of paying their hard-pressed shareholders a dividend.

The neighbouring railway companies of the Highland and the Strathspey also came in for criticism in the way traffic was being routed over the new junction at Boat of Garten. None of this was to the Morayshire's advantage. James Grant had been holding talks with these two parties, and he stated that the situation should be much improved before the end of 1866.

Special mention was made of the deterioration in the relationship with the Great North of Scotland Railway. The meeting was informed that it was the intention of the Board of Directors to go to arbitration to sort out the differences between the respective companies. Chief among the grievances was the closing of the Orton branch, but here I think the Morayshire was being a little dishonest. It was, after all, the Morayshire Directors who had proposed closure on November 18th last year, in exchange for a cash settlement. The lack of payment from the GNSR appeared to hurt more than the loss of the line between Orton and Rothes.

The long-awaited Parliamentary powers to convert £37,120 of disposable capital into preference shares had at last been granted. This would have the effect of preventing earned revenue being lost to interest payments. Indeed, if this measure had been in place for 1866, the revenue account for the year would have been some £600 better off. At the close of business, once again the shareholders went home without a dividend, but they did have the promise of something for the next year.

The hoped-for changes and improvements in the train services serving the customers of the Morayshire Railway came into effect on December 1st. Local press reaction to the new timetable was highly favourable.

14 A HOME IN THE HIGHLANDS

The observant Elgin citizen might have noticed the figure of ex-Provost Grant making his way towards the railway station on the morning of December 12th, nothing unusual in that, most probably on his way to Aberdeen to have talks with the Directors of the Great North of Scotland Railway. Only it was not the Morayshire office he passed nor, the Great North station he entered; he went west into the Highland station and boarded a train for Forres.

Little occurred over the festive period of 1866, and it seemed that business as usual would continue in the new year of 1867, which it did until Saturday, January 12th. There was a strong wind that day, snow fell thickly and the streets of Elgin took on a winter mantle. The quantity of snow was not as great as that of February 1865, but the force of the wind caused serious drifting. The midday train to Lossiemouth stuck fast in the snow at Greens of Draine, which is just over a mile away from the sea. Despite the best efforts of the crew who battled for over an hour to force their way through, they had to abandon the train and walk. The enginemen and guard came back along the line to Elgin, accompanied by the greater bulk of the passengers, the stronger rendering assistance to the weaker. A force of workmen boarded another engine on the Monday morning with the intention of digging the stranded train out. They had to return for reinforcements and it took until the late afternoon to clear the line ready for re-commencement of operations. The snow continued to fall during this time and although the Lossie line remained operational, problems were occurring on the rest of the Morayshire system.

The first train to leave Aberdeen destined for Elgin on the Saturday morning took two whole days to complete the 53½ mile journey to Keith. As the extraordinary weather started shutting down rail communications to the east of Elgin, the first two trains on Saturday morning from Elgin reached Keith safely. The third at 11.10am made it to Craigellachie Junction with considerable difficulty, at which point Mr Morrison superintendent of the line turned it back to Elgin, which it eventually reached at 3.30pm. A curt telegram from the Headquarters of the Great North of Scotland Railway gave the company's intentions. *"All trains cancelled till blowing ceases. Seven engines are snowed up on the system."*

On Tuesday morning with the weather a little more settled, the clearing of the line to Keith started in earnest. A team of men began at 4am to open up the section from Elgin to Craigellachie. This proved no easy task, and it was not until 1pm that their objective was reached. Another company of men had started at the Keith end of this section, and with the aid of an engine reached Craigellachie. Progress was such that the 4.20pm started from Elgin and reached Keith only a little behind time. Troubles, however were not over; some 18 inches of fresh snow fell on the Wednesday night causing the first train from Elgin on that day to become stuck fast at the Wool Mill in the Glen of Rothes. At 11.10am another attempt was made to reach Keith, this time using two engines. It took just under two hours to cover the ten miles to Rothes and another hour and three quarters to cover the two miles and a half between Rothes and Craigellachie. This was only accomplished with the assistance of a third engine and a gang of workmen who had worked through from Keith. Snow had continued to fall and despite the fact there were three engines attached, attempts to reach Keith had to be abandoned half a mile beyond Craigellachie. It was nearly dark, so the decision was made to return to Elgin, but they had great difficulty in getting through the Glen of Rothes. The 12 mile journey took just over two hours and the train had to be backed up, to force its way through the snow drifts some 20 times.

By Friday, January 18th 1867, things had started to improve although the GNSR were criticised for their poor performance in clearing the snow. This judgement was a little unfair, as it does appear that the weather in the north-east corner of Scotland had been considerably worse than in any other part of the country, evidenced by the fact, that during this time mails and papers from Aberdeen were sent to Elgin by way of Perth and the Highland main line.

Our old friend Mrs Soutor received high praise from the *Elgin Courant* for her provision of hot meals to the squads of men struggling to clear the line.

Over the weekend of January 19th and 20th, the snow returned, but the train services managed to run almost to time. On the Monday the temperature dropped dramatically, causing a haze to appear all over the district, as vapour in the air congealed because of the cold. The novelty and romance of snow had now worn off, in particular for the train crews who had to run a service through this inhospitable countryside. Tuesday afternoon the wind strength and direction changed, with a gale now blowing from the south. Fallen snow created new drifts, which reached a depth of eight feet in places between Elgin and Rothes. Train services were cancelled for the whole of Wednesday, but with much hard work and the help of a thaw, things started to return too normal by Thursday the 24th of January.

The nature of the meeting held in Forres on December 12th became evident on January 31st. The parties who met with the ex-Provost on that day were Mr Wainwright of the Glasgow and South Western Railway and Mr Dougall of the Highland Railway. James Grant's proposal was that the Highland Railway should join with the Morayshire. The terms he offered were that the Highland take up the Morayshire's debentures, pay 5% on the preference shares and put the ordinary shares in with the Highland Railway shares to make an equal dividend. The finances of the Morayshire were examined in detail, along with the statistics showing the benefit to be gained from such a venture. Mr Dougall was interested in James Grant's scheme and he agreed to lay the deal before his board.

I suspect the thought of the damage such an arrangement would do to the Great North of Scotland Railway must have played a part in Mr Dougall's decision. It had been the Great North of Scotland Railway's ambition, from its formation in 1846, to connect the two cities of Aberdeen and Inverness. In this desire they had been thwarted, only managing to construct their railway to Keith, 50 miles short of Inverness. By running the services of the Morayshire, the GNSR was nearer the Highland Capital. If the Highland took over the Morayshire not only would they push the Aberdeen people back to Keith, they would also be capable of tapping traffic from both ends of Great North's Strathspey line.

An interesting snippet appeared in the *Elgin Courant* of February 1st, concerning the condition of the bridge at the mouth of the River Lossie.

> The committee appointed at a meeting some two or three months past, for the purposes of raising subscriptions for repairing the bridge across the Lossie, met the other day in Mr Anderson's office and appointed collectors to canvass the place, with a view of raising the money necessary to carry out the object in view. The meeting was but thinly attended.

A letter from the Commercial Bank was received by the Morayshire on February 7th 1867 demanding immediate payment of £3211-13s-5d. Until such payment was made the bank was withholding the Morayshire's overdraft facilities of £12,000. To say the Morayshire Board of Directors were unhappy about this would be an understatement.

The day previous, a letter from Mr Dougall had arrived asking for a full breakdown of traffic returns on the Morayshire. The Directors instructed the Secretary Mr Watt to go to Aberdeen to obtain all this information from the Great North. The intention of ex-Provost Grant, to change the allegiance of the Morayshire from the Great North of Scotland Railway to the Highland Railway, had leaked out into the public domain. Again thoughts of the notion of Miss Morayshire were dusted off. This time, it was not a poem, or a humours cartoon, but a full blown song.

AN AULD SANG IN A NEW SUIT, BY MISS MORAYSHIRE

"Tempus Muntanur."

"Wha gets the skaith while drees the scorn
I've lived to learn; and now, florn
I dream of days when ye began
To woo me first, John Highlandman.

Sing hey! my braw John Highlandman;
Sing ho! my braw John Highlandman;
I trow I've daily rue my plan
Since I forsook John Highlandman

Though nae sae young as I hae been,
An' tired o' Maister Aberdeen,
You'll ablins tak me gin ye can,
An' be my braw John Highlandman.

Sing hey! & etc

Though
"Donald" ance I set at nought,
Time upon me has changes brought;
I've grown mair partial to the clan-
Ye ken yersel'! John Highlandman

Sing hey! & etc

I've lan frae Rothes to the sea,
Frae Orton to Craigellachie;
An' close the Glen if enen maun,
I'll gang wi' you John Highlandman

Sing hey! & etc

Then bless me only wi your smile-
We'll raise the rates a wee per mile
The Elgin folks may curse an' ban-
We'll laugh at them John Highlandman

Sing hey! & etc

I'll never even gay per cent!
Gin ye will only be content
At anroe to tak me by the han,
An' gis your plaid John Highlandman!

Sing hey! my braw John Highlandman;
Sing ho! my braw John Highlandman;
We then might master Moraylan'
For a' that's gane, John Highlandman!

Dundurcas, February, 1867.

Chances of some form of takeover or amalgamation between the Highland Railway and the Morayshire were becoming more credible. A written proposal from the Highland was discussed in Elgin on February 26th. The Highland was prepared to pay the Morayshire Company the sum of £5000 per annum, until an Act of Amalgamation passed through Parliament. Debentures would then be taken over for five years at the rate of 4½% per year. Preference stock would be paid at the same rate as that of the Highland Railway Company, which was 4½%. The Ordinary stock of the Morayshire was to be added in with the Highland stock and pay the same dividend as the Highland Company as from August 31st 1871. For its part the Morayshire Railway Company was to obtain a written undertaking from the Great North of Scotland Railway Company that they would not oppose an amalgamation.

All the Directors from the Morayshire Railway Company, met with the Directors of the Highland Railway Company at Inverness on March 15th and a definitive seven point statement was drawn up.

> *1/ An Act of Amalgamation to be obtained, but the Highland Railway Company will commence operations over the Morayshire lines on the 31st of August 1868.*

> *2/ Highland Railway Company to take over Mortgage Debit of the Morayshire, at present amounting to £37,960 - 8s - 4d, on the 31st of August 1868.*

> *3/ Highland Railway Company to take over the floating debit of Morayshire, amounting to £48,000, on the 31st of August 1868.*

> *4/ Immediate action to be taken by both Companies to provide continuation of loans and preferred payments of liabilities.*

> *5/ Morayshire Preference shareholders to have a dividend of 3% on the 31st of August 1868, with the same amount being payable at the end of August 1870. The amount of 4% to be paid on 31st of August 1871 and then 5% in perpetuity thereafter.*

> *6/ The Ordinary Shareholders to be paid the same dividend as that of the Highland Railway Company from the 1st of September 1868 OR dependent on the statement of accounts at the Amalgamation of the dividend paid to the Highland Railway shareholders at the date of the Amalgamation for the 1st year and thereafter at the full rate.*

> *7/ Two or more of the Directors of the Morayshire Railway Company are to have a seat on the Board of the Amalgamated Company until the obligations of the Morayshire Railway Company are discharged.*

> *(As part of the above the Highland Railway Company would start running trains over the Morayshire Railway on signature of the above agreement.)*

It is not recorded if the Directors of the Morayshire had much say in the items written into the above statement. To the shareholders of the Morayshire Railway Company there was at least an offer of a return on the money they had invested.

The Great North of Scotland Railway appeared to have little idea how far things had progressed between the Highland and the Morayshire. When they did, it was very likely that the GNSR would object to a Parliamentary bill uniting the Morayshire and Highland. This, along with the urgent need of the Morayshire to pay creditors, may explain the contents of a letter sent on March 26th from Mr Watt containing alterations to the conditions set out on March 15th.

Concern was expressed by the Morayshire about the Highland's intention to begin working the Morayshire services on August 31st. It was thought it would be prudent to wait until after the amalgamation before Highland engines and stock appeared on the Morayshire network. However, the auditors of the Morayshire urgently required cash to start paying off the floating debt of the Company. If it was not possible for the Highland to make payments, Mr Watt stated he would try to defer demands from creditors. To make the intention to settle the cash demands credible, he would require a written guarantee from the Highland to pay the interest on any loan and the principal sum within two years from the Act of Amalgamation. A statement to this effect would have to be inserted into the Act of Amalgamation to fulfil the demands of the Morayshire's auditors. This change would have the effect of relieving the Morayshire Directors and the Morayshire Company of the burden that it was facing at this time.

Mr. Watt accepted the Highland Railway's proposal to the amounts to be paid to the ordinary shareholder, feeling that the coming together of the two companies was an advantage to both parties that would see much larger returns than originally concluded. Perhaps he was being a little over-optimistic here. In closing his letter to the Board of the Highland Railway, he informed them that the Morayshire Directors were meeting that day and they were anxious to hear their decision on the amendments. It was not until April 9th that Morayshire's *"anxious wait,"* was over. The Board of Directors assembled at the Company offices to hear the contents of the Highland Railway's reply. *"It was with regret that Mr Dougall must decline the offer of the amalgamation of the Morayshire with the Highland Railway on the terms discussed in Mr Watt's letter."*

The Highland Railway obviously felt that any advantage to them would be swallowed up, however the door to the coming together of the two companies did not appear to be completely closed. They stated that they were prepared to reconsider the matter if the Morayshire Board could show that the monetary value of their company was the same as they claimed at the joint conference. The closing sentence of the letter from the Highland Railway Directors reveals that they had little confidence in the Morayshire's current position. *"In the meantime, it must be understood that the proposal we made, is not now binding on us."*

Ever downward was the direction the Morayshire's fortune was going, so there was little chance of them being able to meet the Highland's demand. Valour being the better part of discretion, the Directors decided in the interim not to reply to Mr Dougall's letter. A home in the Highlands was slipping away. To protect the Morayshire in the case of total failure with the Highland Railway, James Grant and Secretary Mr Watt were instructed to meet with either Mr Milne or Mr Duncan of the Great North of Scotland Railway. They were to ascertain what the GNSR could do to assist in easing the Morayshire's finances.

The Morayshire still had a small amount of cash in its bank account, which had been paid in by the GNSR as its share of traffic receipts. This would be enough to pay off some small overdrafts and charges, but substantial calls on the Company funds were coming in. These it was decided would be acknowledged, but until the Directors knew the outcome of the meeting between senior members of the GNSR and Messrs Grant and Watt, nothing could be done other than acknowledge them.

On April 15th a meeting of the Morayshire Directors was convened for James Grant to report on his progress. Meetings had taken place with Mr Milne of the GNSR and Mr Grigor of the law firm Grigor & Young. Sadly for us there is no written record in the Minute Book recording what was said. I do know, though, that demands made upon Captain Stewart by the Commercial Bank for money due by the Morayshire was the reason for get together with Mr Grigor.

The Morayshire was in such a perilous situation it could no longer afford to pay law agents. They were needed to visit Preferential Shareholders in order to gain their consent to issue more Preference Shares. To work around this problem, it was decided to arrange a meeting at a convenient place at which the shareholders would be advised how much the Company required to clear its debts. Also, to improve the company's cash flow an account to be know as the *"Morayshire Debentures Holders Account,"* was to be set up. The aim of this was to have weekly amounts paid into it which should be sufficient to meet the weekly interest payments of the Railway Company. Various other measures were to be put into place to pay all outstanding accounts, one of which was a letter to Mr Smith of Minmore, a Director, to remind him that he was personally due to pay £1000 as his portion.

Two days later the Chairman James Grant reported back on his meeting with Mr Grigor of Grigor & Young with some good news. Captain Stewart of Lesmurdie would now pay £6000 to the Commercial Bank and £1000 to Mr Preston, taking up Preference Stock for these sums. A list of what was due was drawn up and it was agreed that James Grant would hold meetings with the Bank, Mr Preston, Grigor & Young, and the Debenture Holders to come to some arrangement over settlement of debts owed by the Morayshire. James Grant also undertook to meet with Mr Duncan of the GNSR to arrange formally that traffic receipts be paid weekly to help meet the demands of the Morayshire Debentures Holders Account.

The first of Elgin's trade holidays this year was on Monday, May 1st, with 3897 citizens of the town using the railway as a means of travelling to their destination. Some 1538 travelled west on the Highland system, whilst the other 2359 went by the Great North. The bulk of these, 1792 to Lossiemouth and another 90 to Rothes, thereby contributed 55% of their fare to the coffers of the Morayshire Company. A lesser percentage would also have come from the bolder holiday makers who travelled to Banff and Aberdeen. Despite the weather being chilly, the numbers at Lossiemouth were swelled by others travelling on foot and dog carts to the seaside. It was suggested in the local press that just over half the population of Elgin enjoyed a day at the sea. Particularly note was made of the behaviour of the revellers, *"What is specially worthy of remark among all this multitude not a case of drunkenness was to be seen."*

Back to business with a bump, for the Morayshire Board on May 2nd 1867. James Grant had been unsuccessful in his talks with the Commercial Bank. In view of this he did not think it wise to meet with the GNSR and the Debenture holders. The Secretary Mr Watt and another Director Mr Urquhart had had some success in obtaining money from the Preference Shareholders. This raised spirits a little, and brought about a discussion of the Highland Railway's offer of amalgamation. The floating debt of the Company had been reduced to such an extent that the union between the Highland and the Morayshire was once again possible.

On May 20th a further source of income for the Morayshire was located. Mr Watson, coal merchant at Rothes had been given permission a number of years ago to use land adjacent to Rothes station for a store. The Board of Directors now proposed to sell him this land at its current valuation.

These improvements were noticed. Mr Grigor of Grigor & Young advised the Company that Captain Stewart would continue to keep his shares in the Morayshire Railway for another two years. This is because, he (Mr Grigor) was confident that the Morayshire Railway Company would have paid off all its debts at the end of that time.

James Grant sent a copy of this letter on May 22nd to the Commercial Bank enclosing a letter of his own asking them to look favourably on the Morayshire Railway. After all it was doing a great deal to pay its creditors. A twist of the truth was also woven into his letter. Interestingly he claimed that the Morayshire had not amalgamated with the Highland Railway because the Highland Railway thought, due to its money problems the Morayshire could be obtained by them for little or no cost. James Grant claimed he was acting in the best interests of the Morayshire shareholders, chief among them the Directors of the Morayshire, plus all others who were owed money. By refusing the Highland's offer he had made certain all creditors of the Company would be paid in full. In conclusion to his appeal he told them that traffic was increasing on the railway and that is why Captain Stewart had chosen to remain an investor. The closing passage certainly shows not only the confidence of James Grant but his salesmanship. *"When the Directors gave their guarantee to pay any debts personally, they did not expect to have to pay. They now know that the securities of the Company would cover any problem. The reason these securities have not been cashed in, is this would induce a degree of inconsistency which I am certain the Bank would not want and that is why it has not been done. If the Bank looks favourably on us all will come right in time."*

Mr Preston served a summons on the Company on May 28th. A demand from the Commercial Bank for immediate payment also arrived. Possibly in a state of shock, the Directors adjourned their meeting.

It was agreed on May 31st to pay the interest and capital to Mr Preston and the money due to the bank. The only flaw in this admirable plan was the Morayshire did not have the funds to make the payments. The Directors' proposal therefore was to ask Captain Stewart for the money he had pledged to the company. The sum of £6000 would then be given to the bank to pay part of the £12,000 they were owed. Mr Preston would be given an interim payment of £1000. The Morayshire Board would then attempt to obtain a loan from a bank or other source to pay off the remainder of the debts to Mr Preston and the Commercial Bank. Again there was a small flaw in this plan, as any lender of money to pay the current outstanding debits would receive a bond from the Morayshire that would not be repaid for two years.

Not surprisingly the Directors had great difficult in finding any lender to give them money. Almost a month from the day they had received the Summons from Mr Preston they had managed to scrape together the grand total of £21-1s-9d. A cheque for this amount was sent onto the gentleman. The incoming post brought more demands from creditors!

A formal meeting to discuss payments to their creditors, in particular the Commercial Bank and Mr Preston, were held on June 28th 1867. It was either a brief meeting, or the Directors were stumped for an answer to their problems, as there is only a four word entry in the Minute Book. *"Nothing definite was arranged."*

On July 9th the Directors gathered in the offices of Grant Jamieson (James Grant's law firm) at noon to discuss a circular they had published to try and defend the claim made by Mr Preston. Things did not go to plan. Mr Urquhart, the most recent member to join the Morayshire Board, took great exception to the fact that he would be liable for a share of the money owed to Mr Preston and the Commercial Bank. After a lengthy and heated discussion Mr Urquhart left stating that he intended to seek a legal opinion from his Edinburgh Agents on this matter.

With things this bad, it was once more up to James Grant to try and rescue the situation. This he did by travelling to Edinburgh to hold talks with the Commercial Bank. It is not recorded in the Minute Book, but with no money in the Morayshire's account James Grant probably paid his own train fare to Edinburgh. He reported back to his board on July 28th. After several meetings with the Bank it was agreed that the demands for repayment would be cut back provided the Morayshire Railway repaid £9211-15s-10d of capital. To meet this demand meant that the Morayshire would have to turn to the Great North of Scotland Railway for assistance. In fact James Grant had already had some preliminary talks with Mr Ferguson of that Company. The hope of salvation and amalgamation with the Highland Railway Company was to all intents dead.

15 This Bridge Will Last Forever!

The condition imposed by the Great North of Scotland Railway before it would rescue the Morayshire was that the Board of the Morayshire accept amalgamation with the Great North of Scotland Railway. A start had been made toward this end; however the Morayshire Railway required the GNSR to pay the £33,000 floating debt of the Company before it would approve the amalgamation. Mr Ferguson had no intention of exposing the Great North to such a large liability. The most he was prepared to do was send them letters of advice, the first of which was to sort out the connecting train services at Craigellachie. There was no connection to Elgin for the Strathspey Morning Mails or the later 12.50pm service. Mr Ferguson suggested that by providing this service a substantial revenue would come to the Morayshire. In the interim the Board of the Morayshire prepared to sell off the Company's stable block. Cash to the value of £1000 had been paid over to the Commercial Bank by Mr Smith of Minmore and he wished this fact to be recorded in the Minute Book.

On August 14th, James Grant put his hand in his own pocket to the tune of £2000. This was used to pay off a loan from the City of Glasgow Bank, and some of the interest due to Mr Preston.

The second Elgin holiday of 1867 was held on Monday, August 18th. Due to a sports competition taking place on the local market green, the demand for rail travel was down, with only 3272 taking the train to various destinations. Fortunately, and unfortunately for the Morayshire, Lossiemouth was still the most popular destination with 1071 Elgin folk choosing the seaside town for their day out. This was 721 fewer tickets sold, more than a third down in takings.

Through the rest of August, September and October, low level talks went on between the GNSR and the Morayshire. On November 11th the Banks started turning the screw. That day a Summons was served by the Commercial Bank, demanding payment of £3211-15s- 10d. It was left to Grant and Jamieson to deal with this along with some other smaller financial matters.

Things seemed to be moving. Meetings had taken place between James Grant, Mr Watt, and Mr Urquhart for the Morayshire, and Mr Duncan and Mr Milne of the GNSR at various locations in November, on the 13th at Aberdeen, 16th at Portsoy, and Aberdeen again on the 18th. One suggestion from the GNSR was to close Dandaleith station and transfer traffic to Craigellachie. After checking the returns, it was found that 4198½ passengers used that station and 1670 tons of goods had been shipped. This therefore ruled it out as a candidate for closure

Part of the problem was the general turmoil in the money markets and in particular the railway sector of the stock market at this time. Even the Highland Railway was having a few problems, which had caused them on November 22nd to announce the abandonment of their plans to build a railway from Fochabers to Garmouth. They stated in their withdrawal notice that the line must yield an adequate return before they would lay out the money for construction of the route. Once again the people of Garmouth were denied the chance of joining the rail network

Seven days later on November 29th 1867, the Morayshire held its AGM. After paying working expenses, feu-duties and other general outlays a surplus of £1980-7s-9¾d was left. Regrettably this sum was insufficient to meet the interest charges and the company was in debt to the tune of £270-17s-9½d. However, this was better than last year. The blame for the shortfall was put down to the shutting down of the railway due to the snow storms in February. The Board of the Morayshire was trying to do its best to consolidate the sums it owed and dispose of its floating debt, whose interest was more than swallowing up all the Company's revenue. The Act of Parliament obtained in 1866 authorising the issue of first Preference shares, might have solved the problem, if more than three quarters of the shareholders had given their permission for a share issue. It was the decision of those at the AGM that the Directors should use all the means at their disposal to obtain the consent of the remaining shareholders to issue the Preference shares.

Encouragement for the Directors came in a letter on December 17th from Mr Inglis, who was acting on behalf of the Preston family, noted receipt of £1000 as part payment in settlement of the claim against the Morayshire. This did not of course stop other bills and Debentures from coming in, but it appeared that the Company was starting at last to move in the right direction.

December 20th saw a Bond to the value of £2250 issued to the Preston family trustees by Grant and Jamieson on behalf of the Morayshire. This would fall due for payment on the last day of February 1869. On New Years Eve 1867 the Morayshire sent its contribution to the Great North of Scotland servant's festival the grand sum of £2!

Mother Nature came calling on February 1st 1868. Reports from the meteorologists state that the severity of the wind and drop in pressure were very unusual for the north of Scotland, resembling a West Indies Hurricane. In Elgin, the heavy rain that accompanied the wind raised the level of the River Lossie to a considerable height. Fortunately for the inhabitants of the City and districts along its banks, damage was minimal. The area up-country did not escape as lightly. Heavy rain brought down with it melted snow from the mountains, changing the appearance of the level ground from Boat of Garten to Balintomb to that of a great lake. Between Grantown and Aberlour, the Spey for the most part of its course runs in a deep channel with few farms on her banks, so little damage was done. At Craigellachie the flooded river almost reached the levels of the Great Flood of 1829, causing substantial damage to the railway bridge. The second pier from the north bank had all but completely disappeared and partial destruction of the north land side pier had taken place. Thirty feet of embankment on that side had almost washed away, leaving the rails and sleepers hanging in mid-air. The level of the bridge itself was fortunately still intact, but it was obvious even to the most casual observer that the cost of putting all the damage right was considerable. The pier that had fallen and the other that had sustained severe damage were both founded on concrete that the river was able to undermine. Metal cylinders sunk into the embankment formed the basis of the south pier and this proved far more resilient and escaped the torrent undamaged.

Concern for the safety of the bridge had been expressed before the collapse, on the Saturday men had been posted to watch for any sign of weakness. These watchers saw nothing so there was no interruption of services on the line. Fifteen to twenty minutes after a train from Elgin traversed that section, the catastrophe occurred.

Repairs at the bridge site were pushed on with speed. The missing portion of embankment had been repaired by the Wednesday. Likewise, where the piers had given way, the bridge sections were now supported with large beams of wood. Considering the River Spey was still in flood, this was most impressive. A start had been made on permanent repairs with piles being driven in at the damaged north end. The workmen however were encountering the same resistance as the original contractor, finding the ground unyielding.

The press seemed encouraged by the progress of repairs, reporting that the GNSR hoped to restart services shortly. Limited working started on February 14th 1868, with goods traffic only permitted to use the bridge. Work on replacement stone piers was not going to take place until in the words of the *Elgin Courant, "The season be so far advanced as will admit the recent damage to be thoroughly repaired."*

Late spring repair work began in earnest. A short while later, Wednesday, May 3rd, a stone of around 1½ tons in weight fell, crushing a workman. The unfortunate labourer named Keil lived at Glenburne, Bunchromb, Parish of Mortlach. He had been working on the repair of the arch between the two north piers when the stone fell. Initially he survived the accident and was taken to Dr Gray's Hospital in Elgin, but such was the seriousness of his injuries he only lived for a few hours. He left a wife and young family.

The prognosis for the Morayshire Company at this time was not bright either. Demands for interest on loans, etc, still kept rolling in. All attempts to find banks or money lenders to meet these calls were at an end. James Grant was practically keeping the Company going by his own pocket.

An unexpected source of danger to some of the users of the Lossiemouth branch came from that town's local volunteer force, as this letter to the *Elgin Courant* on July 3rd illustrates.

> *Elgin*
> *July 2nd 1868*

> *Sir,*

> *Permit me, for the safety of the numerous visitors to Lossiemouth at the present season, to warn those who may indulge in the luxury of sea bathing that the Volunteers engaged in carbine practice have an unpleasant habit of extending their range right into the sea among the bathers.*

> *Last Tuesday, while bathing with a friend, we were considerably alarmed by finding ourselves the centre of continued splashing in the water caused by hissing bullets.*

> *By inserting this you will no doubt be the means of saving some valuable lives -*

> *I am, sir, yours etc.,*

> *A season ticket holder to Lossiemouth*

There was better news for anyone employed as a drover who wished to use the Morayshire for moving his herd. On July 17th, the Great North of Scotland Railway was going to follow the same procedure as its Highland neighbour by allowing free travel to any drover accompanying cattle. At the same time, both Companies had agreed to return livestock being exhibited at the Morayshire Farmers Club show free of charge. Human participants did not fair as well, being subject to excursion fares for that day.

The death of the Elgin Station Agent Mr McConnachie prompted the promotion of Mr Kessock, former clerk to Mr Morrison, Traffic Superintendent Northern Section GNSR. This appointment was confirmed on September 18th and it seemed a popular choice with the local population. *"Mr Kessock well deserves this appointment. Attentive at all times in his work, obliging disposition, and pleasing manners renders him a favourite with the public."*

On October 7th, Mr Watt travelled to Rothes for a meeting of the Parochial Board where he exercised the Railway Company's right to vote on Parish matters. A Mr Gray wished to appoint a Medical Officer for Rothes. Mr Watt, as Secretary for the Morayshire Company, deemed that this was a good thing and voted in favour of the appointment

The following day saw the Great North of Scotland Railway Company meet in Aberdeen for its AGM. The dividends for this Company were not what the shareholders had been expecting. The Morayshire Railway was held to blame for some of the Great North's losses. One of the main costs incurred for 1868 was payment for repair work to the Craigellachie viaduct. Doubtless this damage had been an Act of God, and was not really the responsibility of the Morayshire Board. However, the Morayshire Directors had not made any interest payments to the GNSR for money it had borrowed from the Aberdeen Company, so therefore were culpable for some of the lack of money in GNSR shareholder's pockets. It is perhaps a reflection on the working relationship between the two companies that the GNSR did not at this juncture pursue the matter. Not that by this I suggest relations between the two parties were so good that the GNSR were prepared to let this matter lie. The Aberdeen Company had tried all methods at its disposal to retrieve the cash due to it, before realising they would have more success squeezing blood from a stone.

A little twist occurred on November 13th when the Morayshire attempted to recover the sum of £175 from Mr Preston. It had come to the notice of the Board that the fencing on the Direct line to Rothes was defective and it was the Directors contention that Mr Preston was to blame for this failure.

On Friday, November 27th 1868 James Grant and eleven other shareholders gathered at the Station Hotel in Elgin for the Morayshire AGM. In previous years there had always been complaints about the haphazard manner in which the accounts for the Company had been laid out. A recent Act of Parliament set out a standard manner in which they had to be prepared. The *Elgin Courant* was generally pleased by this arrangement, but still felt there was some room for improvement. Performance for the year up to September 30th 1868 showed a slight decrease in goods traffic handled by the Company. This may have been due in some part to the repairs at Craigellachie. Passenger traffic, in particular between Elgin and Lossiemouth during the bathing season, showed a marked increase. The activities of the Lossiemouth Volunteers were not having an adverse effect. Some 116,568 passengers, not including excursion and season ticket holders, had travelled on the Morayshire, compared to the figure for last year of 114,512. The result of this was that the Company had sufficient funds to meet all expenses, which included interest on debentures and guaranteed share holders, leaving a surplus of £214-16s-9½d. The only exception to this statement was money owed to the GNSR, which the Morayshire claimed they could not pay, due to problems with the Act of Parliament that the Morayshire had obtained in 1866. In consideration of this and furthermore that the surplus was too little to give ordinary shareholders a dividend, it was proposed to hand over the full sum of the surplus to the GNSR. On that happy note the meeting was closed.

On December 2nd 1868 James Grant had £2000 returned to him by the Morayshire. With this payment he had received back most of the money that he had lent to the Morayshire to keep the Company going.

At around 11am on Wednesday, December 23rd, the sea at Lossiemouth was running high. Cast ashore a short distance from the Morayshire station building was a shark. It was twisting like an eel on the railway track, when our old friend James "Rossi" Ross happened upon it. He went on to attack the "sea tiger" with a small crowbar, stunning it slightly. The creature seemed to have the nine lives of a cat, and it took the assistance of Ross's fireman, Archibald Leslie, and his shovel to finally subdue the fish. When killed, the mouth of the of the creature was opened to reveal three rows of teeth in each jaw. The length of the body was within a fraction of five feet.

Stormy, wet weather at Lossiemouth made for unpleasant working conditions on January 29th for a labourer working at the harbour. William McKenzie had just started to discharge a cargo of railway sleepers from a wagon, when due to the wet surface he lost his footing and fell from the wagon onto the pier, causing injury and bruising to his body.

The fate of the shark was revealed in a report in the *Elgin Courant* of February 19th 1869. It appears that the fish was a specimen of Squalus Galeus Linneaus, more commonly known as Tope, a species not common to the upper reaches of the Moray Firth. Transported to Craigellachie, it had been handed over to a local taxidermist for preservation. On completion of this work the creature was then put on display at the goods office of the Great North of Scotland Railway station at Elgin. The reporter for the *Elgin Courant* noted that the fish had been well preserved, and would form a valuable addition to the local collection in Elgin Museum.

The Scotsman newspaper at the start of April suggested that the amalgamation between the Morayshire and Highland Railway companies was back on course. The report suggested that proceedings were so far advanced that a start on working the Morayshire by the Highland was imminent. On being contacted by the local paper, the Secretary of the Morayshire stated *"Any such arrangement is entirely unknown to the Morayshire Railway Company; and could not be accomplished without its sanction."* He further informed the *Courant* that he was sending a letter to *The Scotsman* contradicting their report and asking them on whose authority they made the statement.

The true picture of the state of affairs between the Morayshire and its neighbours in Aberdeen and Inverness was revealed at a Board meeting of April 17th 1869. The possibility of an agreement with the Great North of Scotland Railway had over the past few months become distant. Mr Watt had been in contact with Mr Dougall of the Highland Railway to try to put into place some form of co-operation in the running of services. This scheme fell short of the Morayshire being taken over by the Highland and was referred to as an *"open purse agreement."* This was similar to the arrangement the Morayshire had at the moment with the GNSR. The Directors of the Morayshire were enthusiastic about this prospect of a working arrangement with the Highland and gave sanction to Mr Watt to continue talks with Mr Dougall on this matter.

When the Debenture given to Mr Preston fell due at the end of February, the Morayshire Board was unable to pay the £2500. Messrs Gibson, Craig, Diazel and Brodie, acting for the Preston family on March 26th served a Summons on the Company. The Directors could only offer to settle this amount *"as soon as they could"*. Mr Preston dismissed the claim the Morayshire had made for the fence, on the Direct Line. He informed the Board that Mr Powell his works manager, had personally been involved in the fencing operation.

James Grant gave the Morayshire a loan of £1000 on June 5th.

Confusion surrounded the forthcoming Elgin holiday. With no prior agreement on the date cessation of business was not expected to be universal. The railway companies were offering ample travel facilities for the Elgin folk lucky enough to have the day off. A trip to Foyers and Fort Augustus, organised by the Highland Railway, became a casualty of the uncertainty of the holiday dates with its cancellation because of few passenger numbers.

James Grant arranged to give the Company another loan on Monday, June 14th, to the value of £2000. The other Directors of the Company, Mr Urquhart, Mr Hay and Mr Wainwright, also contributed funds to the value of £1200.

The rest of the population of Elgin, with the exception of one Grocer, decided after all to take this Monday as a holiday. Travellers totalled 1260 on the Highland and 1650 on the GNSR. Lossiemouth or more particularly Covesea proved to be the popular choice. The weather initially was acceptable, but things took a turn for the worse with snow falling in the Laich of Moray and extending down the east coast through Edinburgh to London.

Two new businesses connected with railway services appeared towards the end of June. Hansom cabs took to the streets of Elgin for the first time on June 25th 1869. There were two operators, plying for the trade. Mr Bruce, of the Gordon Arms Hotel, was adding to the omnibus service he already ran from the station to the middle of the town. The other operator was a Mr William Forbes, whose offices were at 51 South Street Elgin. His cabs were based at either end of St Giles church.

The other enterprise was provision of refreshment rooms, at Craigellachie, which, from the glowing terms of this report, in the *Elgin Courant* of July 2nd were much needed.

> When a weary wait occurs at Craigellachie Junction, as it will occasionally due by one mischance or another, the unfailing complaint among passengers, has been there is no refreshment rooms. This has now been supplied, not within the station, but directly across the Fiddich from it close by the end of the bridge. It is not many yards from the platform, and the accommodation is admirable. The place is newly fitted up, and is clean as a Dutch milk pail. Beside a large room downstairs for supplying refreshment over the counter, there are two comfortable furnished parlours upstairs and two bedrooms. Such a place was much wanted and will be of great convenience It will also be seen that a hiring establishment has been commenced close by the junction. This will be another convenience to travelling.

To prevent a repeat of the uncertainty as which day was going to be a holiday in Elgin, a committee was formed on July 9th, that fixed the date for one month hence on August 9th. As a further incentive to the population of Elgin, this group was also proposing to run an excursion, courtesy of the GNSR, to Deeside. The fares at this stage had not been fixed, but the local press added to the encouragement to travel by suggesting that they *"Would be very moderate."* If this proved to be correct, the prospective travellers would be receiving good value for their money, as it was proposed to spend some seven hours enjoying the pure mountain air and fine views around the Highland Home of Her Majesty Queen Victoria.

By the following week, requests were coming in from other parts of Moray and Banffshire to be allowed to travel on the outing. The bargain was therefore extended to the folk of Rothes, Dufftown and Keith. Not prepared to see a large number of Elgin holiday makers desert their network, the Highland Railway offered an alternative excursion. It was controlled locally by Mr Anderson, Jeweller of Commerce Street Elgin, with the chosen destination of Dunrobin Castle, home to the Duke of Sutherland. Again at this stage no figure was given for the ticket price, apart only from the reassurance that it also would be offered at a very moderate price.

An interesting and very profitable sideline to railway companies was the topic of discussion in *Aberdeen Free Press* of July 13th 1869. Under a recent act of Parliament, the Telegraph operation of small private companies was taken over by the Post Office. This proved to be very advantageous to railway companies, in the case of the Great North of Scotland Railway Company a payment amounting to £26,000, plus a further amount in perpetuity for wayleave of £525 for all the GNSR and Deeside lines, but not the Morayshire. Besides these sums, the Government also paid the rate of £1 per mile for maintenance of the wire. The GNSR had free use of the system for sending any of its messages throughout the United Kingdom, whilst receiving a 15% payment on all Post Office messages; all in all, this was a very good deal for the Great North of Scotland Railway.

Competition for the discerning excursionist was hotting up, with reports in the local press of July 23rd, stating that the trips to Deeside and Dunrobin were selling well. Considering that a price for either trip had not been made public, this was good-going. Both companies finally relented on the July 30th. To travel on the Deeside excursion would require the payment of 7/6 for a first class seat, or 5/- for third class. The Highland offered the trip to Dunrobin for the same rates. A large number of people were taking up the opportunity offered by the GNSR excursion to visit the home of their Sovereign. The Highland seemed to be struggling a little, with only a hundred tickets sold. In an attempt to raise numbers, it had been decided to send a coach out to Lhanbryde on the day, to bring people in to join the trip north, then to pick up from stations on the line from Elgin to Inverness.

Monday dawned cloudy, with heavy showers falling later in the day. The special train for Ballater left Elgin station at 5.30am with 560 passengers on board. This number was added to as excursionists joined the train at Rothes, Craigellachie, Dufftown, Keith, and Huntly. On arrival at Ballater, those who wished were conveyed to Balmoral Castle, parts of which were open to the public. The statue of the late Prince Consort was a considerable attraction; the coach houses and stables were also inspected. The Elgin Flute and Drum Band and the Brass Band of the Rothes Volunteers entertained the crowds prior to them setting out on their homeward journey. This, like the outward trip, was accomplished without a hitch. Despite the poor weather, a total of 2260 people used the GNSR on their day off. Lossiemouth attracted just over 1000 people, whilst Strathspey and Aberdeen attracted 200 each and Huntly and Banff 300.

The trip on the Highland Railway to Dunrobin, was slightly less successful than its counterpart, with only 300 passengers travelling, including the Elgin City Band. The castle grounds and gardens were open to the party, with an appearance by the Duke of Sutherland at 2pm. He received a hearty welcome from the excursionists. Total tickets issued by the Highland Railway amounted to 1602, with Forres and Burghead being the other popular choices. A programme of sports events held on the Market Green at

Elgin affected the number of travellers on both railway companies. Some 2000 people went to the meeting, which had a range of events from foot races, putting the stone, hammer throwing and dancing.

With the Company's account empty, one of the loans given by James Grant could not be repaid on September 7th and was extended for three months. The following week, on the 16th, the loan given by the other Directors was also due to be settlement. It too was extended for three months.

Despite its difficulties in paying off its loans, the service provided by the Morayshire was of great benefit to the population that it served. The small community at Birchfield, in the Rothes Glen, wanted better access to the rail network. They had written to the Directors of the Morayshire on September 30th 1869, asking to be provided with a platform similar to the one at Coleburn. The Morayshire Board agreed to approach the GNSR for a costing for this facility.

Four days after another £1000 loan from James Grant was extended for four months (October 11th) the Company books were closed in preparation for the AGM.

The Morayshire's accounts for the year 1869 were published on November 19th, a week before the AGM. That the amount left in the Company coffers, after all the payments had been made, came to only £13-18s-1$\frac{1}{2}$d did not escape the notice of the *Elgin Courant*. *"The revenue and expenditure of the railway from year to year keeps wonderfully near the same sums. Neither in the one or the other has there been more than £200 up or down in the last three years. The line seems to be holding ground, but not making headway as could be wished in clearing off the liabilities of the Company."*

On the day of the AGM, Friday, November 26th, a band of twelve gentlemen assembled in the Station Hotel at Elgin. The only unusual thing about this particular meeting was that James Grant Chairman of the Morayshire was not present. His place in the chair was taken by Alexander Urquhart. An observer from the Great North of Scotland Railway, Mr Morrison, manager of the Northern Section, viewed the proceedings. There were no startling revelations; the Directors believed that the Company was now in a more favourable position and with this statement the meeting was closed.

James Grant had been holding talks with a Mr Chelwynd of the Post Office about the possibility of renting the ground next to the track, to them, for telegraph wires. By December 12th, this source of income looked a good possibility. The Morayshire Directors however would have to make certain that they protected any rental money from the Great North of Scotland Railway, who were doing all that they could to reclaim their loans. James Grant himself had £700 of his £2000 returned on December 12th. The remaining amount of £1300 was continued as a loan to the Morayshire for another four months.

In Britain at the close of 1869, conditions were not too good for the railway industry. Timetable adjustments by the GNSR gave evidence of this. From the start of the New Year there would be fewer trains on the Elgin-Keith services. Most serious, was the cancellation of the 6.20pm service. This now meant that last train to the Granite City left Elgin at 2pm, which was very inconvenient to any businessman and ordinary traveller. Editors for the local papers were very unhappy about this change. They were confident that when journeying between Elgin and Keith, the travelling public would desert the GNSR in favour of the Highland Railway. This hope was dashed on the closing day of the year when the Highland also announced cuts to their service. Elgin was effectively isolated from the rest of the rail and postal network at 4.18pm, not the best end to a decade that had seen such massive advances in communication.

16 NEW DECADE NEW BEGINNING!

James Grant had been successful in his negotiations with the Post Office, and gained for himself another first by placing the City of Elgin on the telegraph system. Soon after word of his latest triumph became well known, the Board of the Great North of Scotland Railway demanded that the Post Office windfall, that they felt was rightfully theirs, should be sent forthwith to Aberdeen. The Morayshire Board declined to reply to the GNSR demand.

Just to make life more interesting for the Morayshire Railway, the Company found itself back in dispute with its northern neighbour the Highland Railway. The Inverness Company had appointed an arbiter to resolve the matter of Orton station hopefully to obtain some money for its use in years past by the Morayshire Railway. Feeling that there was no need for this action, the Morayshire did all that it could to hinder a resolution and delayed accepting the notice of arbitration.

A bad accident on the GNSR system at Huntly had resulted in several people losing their lives. As a consequence of this, the Annual festival held for the servants of that Company was cancelled, an action that saved the Morayshire a few pounds. The accident did not alter the determination of the GNSR to obtain the telegraph money. A summons was served on the Morayshire for its recovery on January 17th. This action was to be defended by James Grant's legal partner Mr Jamieson.

The Morayshire Board met on January 20th to try and formulate some responses to the claims being made by its two neighbours. Mr Urquhart and the Secretary were to travel to Aberdeen to meet with the GNSR and try to come to a settlement without resort to the law. A letter was sent to the Highland Railway in Inverness, agreeing to take part in the arbitration process over Orton station.

For the rest of January, all of February and most of March, the Morayshire defended itself against its two bigger neighbours, neither of who were prepared to leave the Morayshire alone, until substantial sums of money were forthcoming. Legal action by the Great North of Scotland blocked the Morayshire's access to the payment from the Post Office. Mr Watt wrote on March 23rd to Mr Walker Secretary of the North British Railway for his counsel on the best way to obtain a settlement with the GNSR.

The GNSR and Highland Railway seemed less inclined to compete; rather they appeared to be co-operating with each other. Not only were they trying to squeeze some money out of the Morayshire, they had decided not to have a repeat of the events of 1869 when they both ran excursions on the Elgin Holiday. On the first holiday of 1870, the Highland would run an excursion, whilst the GNS would provide this service on the second. Choice of destination for the Highland was Perth, with the fares being the same as they charged for last year's trip to Dunrobin Castle.

June 1st saw the commencement of summer services on the system. The *Elgin Courant* was hoping that if the Highland Railway's excursion to Perth was a success, an offer would be made to the citizens of Perth to travel to Elgin on the occasion of their holiday. According to the report it was the custom of the Highland Railway Company to only offer trips as far north as Blair Athol to the folk of Perth.

Mr Wyness, the Superintendent of the Elgin City Police, on July 8th took a long distant railway trip to the City of Bath. The reason for this extensive journey was to return a young man, named MacDonald, to Elgin to stand trial. He (MacDonald) had previously been employed as goods clerk for the GNSR at Elgin, before disappearing south at the same time as £100 went missing from the Elgin goods depot.

The Board of the Morayshire at last met with Mr Walker of the NBR on July 9th 1870, but it transpired that he was having little luck in resolving the problems with the GNSR.

At least the weather was fine. The *Elgin Courant* of July 15th enthused about the railway service to

Lossiemouth. *"Every morning in the fine weather scores of Elgin people go down to Lossiemouth to have a dip in the sea. The facilities that the railway offer is a great boon to the town. The hours are very suitable, and fares exceedingly moderate, especially to the apprentices."* The paper also carried reports of the trip to be held on the second Elgin Holiday of the year. The Great North of Scotland Railway were intending to run an excursion to Aberdeen. The tickets were on offer at a *"Very moderate price of 5/6 1st class and 3/6 2nd class from both the GNSR and Highland railway stations."*

On August 8th, Mr Watt gave the Board of the Morayshire a report of a meeting he had had with Mr Walker of the NBR at Perth. There had been little progress so advice was also sought from Mr Wainwright. Mr Watt had tried a direct appeal to the GNSR to release the money, but this had met with a threat of further legal action. The Great North of Scotland Railway was holding the revenue against the Morayshire's outstanding debt. Written opinion on this matter from Mr Walker and Mr Wainwright had as yet not arrived with Morayshire Board. The Secretary was therefore instructed to write to the GNSR asking them not to continue with further action until the letters had arrived from Mr Wainwright and Walker.

Things went downhill on August 31st. The Board meeting on that day discussed a letter from the Highland Railway outlining the charges they were making for the use of Orton station. In the opinion of the Deputy Chairman of the Morayshire the sums asked for were *"Preposterous, if not wholly illegal."* He instructed that the letter be returned to the Board of the Highland Railway with a note to the effect that if they wished to go to law over this matter, so be it! This was a dangerous stance to take, particularly as this Board meeting was not legal, as there was not a quorum present. Only the Deputy Chairman Alexander Urquhart and George Hay had bothered to turn up.

Robert MacDonald stood trial at Inverness on September 14th for his alleged theft of £100 from the Great North of Scotland Railway.

By September 23rd the Great North of Scotland Railway was out of favour with the *Elgin Courant*. The railway company was to return to the same winter timetable arrangements as they had had for last year. This meant that the latest departure time from Aberdeen for anyone wanting to reach Elgin was 1pm (arrive Elgin 4.45pm). Salt was rubbed into the wounds by the fact that a later train left Aberdeen but terminated at Craigellachie. The Highland Railway had also made cuts, but in general these were to the morning services.

On September 28th there were enough Board members present for there to be a legal meeting of the Morayshire Railway Company. Mr Stuart, corn merchant of Rothes, had his request for a 99-year lease for land at Rothes station turned down. There had been no correspondence from the GNSR in connection with the telegraph moneys. The Directors hoped that it would not be too long before the GNSR were in a position to give a favourable reply on this matter.

Cash was required on September 30th to pay a promissory note to the Commercial Bank. The £1200 needed for this was paid by directors of the Company, James Grant, Alexander Urquhart and George Hay, with a further contribution coming from a Mr William White. A week later another promissory note fell due. This was for £1500, but as the lender was James Grant the loan was continued on until January 1st 1871. Another repayment due to James Grant for £1000 fell due for payment on October 17th. It was also held over until January 1st 1871.

Just a few weeks after being upset by the GNSR's behaviour, the *Elgin Courant* swung around praising the railway companies. *"We are glad to see from the weekly returns that all our local railways are doing better than the corresponding period for last year."* This feeling was helped by the fact that the Highland Railway had just announced a 4% dividend to its shareholders. Without question, the thought on the Morayshire shareholders minds, would it also be in a position to pay a dividend?

The Morayshire Railway finally conceded to the demands of the Great North of Scotland Railway in respect of the telegraph money on October 27th 1870. They were prepared to release the £2240 but only if the £12,620 that the GNSR held in Morayshire Preference stock was reduced by the same amount, thereby having the effect of substantially cutting its yearly interest payments. The Morayshire Board must have been feeling magnanimous that day because they also paid £8-16/- expenses due in the Preston action.

Catastrophe struck on November 3rd. Grant and Jamieson, solicitors, received a notice of *"Multiple Poinding"* from the Postmaster General. The Post Office wanted this matter resolved once and for all. By serving the notice, one of the parties would have to give up their claim to the telegraph money, or go to court and obtain a judgement as to who should be the rightful recipient. The only snag about going to court to obtain a judgement was that all the assets of any party contesting the judgement would be frozen until the court case was concluded. James Grant had no option other than relinquish, with immediate effect, any claim to the money.

With the loss of the hoped for windfall, the Board of the Morayshire started to make preparations for the Company AGM. Notices for the calling of the meeting had appeared twice in the *Scotsman*, *Elgin Courier* and *Elgin Courant*. The funds of the Company dictated that in the future, AGM calling notices would only appear in the press once.

The Directors felt that the apparent co-operation between the Highland Railway and the Great North of Scotland Railway was a direct threat to the existence of their Company. Advice was to be sought from the shareholders on any action they wanted taken to protect the activities of the Morayshire.

At 11am on November 25th 1870 the shareholders assembled at the Station Hotel in Elgin for the AGM. The Morayshire Railway was doing good business. Passenger numbers had gone up from last year, with some 111,941 people being conveyed. Similarly there was also an increase in goods carried, with a total tonnage of 44,756 using the network. The revenue of the Company was as a consequence also increased, but the crippling interest payments meant a surplus of only £93-5s-8d was left. Yet again the Morayshire Railway Company was unable to pay any dividend to its long-suffering Ordinary Shareholders. No excuse for this was given. The best the shareholders were offered was the promise that all that could be done to reduce the floating debt of the Company, was being done. In the matter of the Great North of Scotland Railway, the Directors assured the shareholders that any threat from that company to the Morayshire Railway Company would be defended against vigorously. No changes were made to the Directorship of the Morayshire Railway or its Auditor and on a vote of thanks from a George Cowie Esq, seconded by Alex Urquhart the proceedings were closed.

In December the Great North of Scotland Railway attempted to stimulate weekend travel by offering return tickets at ordinary daily return rates for all Friday journeys, available to return until the last train on Monday.

Activities of the Board of the Morayshire for the early part of this month were restricted to the rescheduling of various promissory notes and attempts to find lower cost ways of attracting Capital into the Company. To this end they took out advertisements in the local press promising returns of between 4½% to 5% on any loan of £100 and above.

The Board were advised on December 16th of the resolution concerning the payment of the rental money from Post Office for their telegraph wires. By adding the wording *"preserving all Companies rights and powers,"* the ownership of the money paid by the Post Offices could not be disputed by the Great North of Scotland Railway in future years. This excellent news was tempered by the loss of the case with the Highland Railway over the Orton station dispute. With no funds in the Morayshire bank account, Alex Watt, Company Secretary, wrote to the Highland Board advising them that the claim could not be paid at present. They would pay the interest on the amount until sufficient capital became available to settle the Highland's claim.

A ghost from the Morayshire's past resurfaced when the running of a steamer service from Lossiemouth to Wick appeared to be a possibility. Mr Adam Sharp of Rothes and a Mr Birness of Wick gave notice to James Grant that they intended to start a service in the very near future. For his part, James Grant offered to give favourable through rates to any goods using the steamer service.

It does seem a little odd that someone would show interest in a Company that staggers from one financial crisis to another. The Board wrote to a Mr Dickson of Lauder on December 29th and thanked him for his request for information. Inviting him to the area to inspect the railway at first hand, they hoped this visit would assist him in the construction of his proposed railway at Lauder. Mr Dickson had also been persuaded to part with the sum of £3000 as a mortgage to the Morayshire, cash most welcome by the Board, who used it to pay off most of the debts owed to the National Bank. James Grant and his vice Chairman Mr Urquhart provided a further £500 to pay off the rest of the amount owed to this creditor. Other large sums due for repayment were £2500 to James Grant on January 1st and £1200 to the Commercial Bank. Both were extended, the one to James Grant for six months and the bank for three months.

A deal to move timber at 1/6 per ton from Craigellachie to Elgin and 2/6 per ton from Craigellachie to Lossiemouth was agreed with Mr Sime of Arndilly Timber. The note in the Minute Book made it clear that these rates apply would only to Mr Sime.

The last entry in the Minute Book for 1870 shows that, despite all the problems that beset the Morayshire Railway Company, it still had a heart. On the motion of all the Directors it was unanimously agreed to give the Secretary a gratuity of £10 as a New Year's gift for all his diligence in the affairs of the Company. The Directors also wished it noted that they regretted the funds of the Morayshire Railway Company did not permit any increase in his salary in the meantime.

A number of Elgin folk left the City on the afternoon of December 31st to see the New Year in with friends and family residing in Aberdeen. The weather was fine in Elgin, as it was in the rest of the County of Moray. Matters were different in Aberdeenshire. Due to a severe snowstorm the Elgin party began 1871 in a railway carriage embedded in an 18 foot snow drift at Pitcaple and there they stayed for a few days.

For more than the first quarter of 1871, the Morayshire Railway struggled on attempting to pay or reschedule promissory notes. James Grant for the most part, either supplied the hard cash to pay off lenders who had lost patience with the Company, or extended loan periods for money he had lent in the past.

By May local press reports gave a glimmer of hope to increasing the Morayshire's income. There was a possibility of a return of part of the Post Office contract for delivering mail from the south. It had been confirmed that the Highland Railway would continue to take mail north from Perth at 9.30am, arriving in Elgin at 2.45pm. Discussion with the Great North of Scotland Railway centred around on what terms they would run a train north from Aberdeen, leaving at 3am. The mail would then travel on from Craigellachie by the Morayshire.

On May 12th a minor mishap befell Alexander Anderson, porter at Rothes railway station. He had been assisting in the loading of timber into railway wagons, when he broke his arm after trapping it between two logs.

There was disappointment also for the excursionists of Elgin. The Great North of Scotland Railway had intended to run an outing to Edinburgh on the first Elgin holiday of the year, July 3rd. Notices however appeared cutting the trip back to Aberdeen. The GNSR blaming the high costs charged by the southern rail companies for access to Scotland's capital.

James Grant was due to have a £2000 loan returned to him on July 7th. With still no funds in the

Company account, repayment was held over for another six months. The Commercial Bank was not so understanding and on July 16th demanded repayment of a £1500 loan. Step forward once again James Grant who settled this demand from his own pocket.

Around the same time, a new tenant took over the running of the Station Hotel in Elgin. This establishment was still owned by James Grant. Mr W Williams, the new tenant, was having the Station Hotel completely repainted and papered and a "First Class" billiard room erected. He intended that by these efforts he would be running the most elegant and capacious family and commercial hotel in the North.

Whilst the Morayshire Railway and the Great North of Scotland Railway had disputed who collected the rental money for the Post Office telegraph wires running out from Elgin, the business community of the town embraced this new technology. July 14th 1871 saw record business done, with no less than 238 communication messages leaving the Elgin Post Office that day. The local press could give no reason for this large amount of traffic, other than perhaps the commencement of the herring season.

On July 21st the Lossie Free School travelled the complete length of the Morayshire network. The *Elgin Courant* recorded part of their epic journey. *"Accompanied by their teachers and friends the children marched from Craigellachie Junction station to Dandaleith. Thus getting a good view of both fine bridges over the River Spey. Afterwards they proceeded to Easter Elchies where they were given a plentiful supply of milk and strawberries by the landowner Colonel Campbell. Before quitting his grounds the party drew up at his front door to give the Colonel and his Lady three hearty cheers. They then proceeded onto Dandaleith where they picnicked by the station. After a fine day out all arrived safely home at Lossiemouth at 7pm."*

Excursions of a more ambitious nature were the concern of the *Elgin Courant*, on August 11th. Sadly the proposed trip by the Highland Railway to Strome Ferry on the second Elgin Holiday of 1871 did not appear to be attracting passengers. To try and increase numbers, the Highland was thinking about sending an engine and coaches out to Lhanbryde to give more people the opportunity to travel to the West Coast.

Lack of numbers, in the form of fish, meant a downturn in Lossiemouth's business offset a little by an increase in commercial traffic, but even this was not without difficulties, as this report in the *Courant* records. *"The barque Catherine of Aberdeen, carrying timber for Mr Watson of Morayshire Sawmills just made it into the harbour thanks to good weather. Ex Provost Grant is right, if we are to have foreign trade the harbour must be made deeper, because at present it can only admit vessels drawing 12 feet of water."* Certainly a change in position by the *Elgin Courant*, who were in the forefront of those who condemned his plans to expand Lossiemouth harbour a few years earlier.

Things did not go well for the Highland Railway trip to Strome Ferry. The weather on Monday, August 21st was unfavourable with heavy rain. Only 170 brave souls took the trip west. The citizens of Elgin seemed to be in a general malaise. Even the sports event held each year on that date was poorly attended. The Press complained the only attractions were *"Endless shooting galleries and continuous velocipede races."* Perhaps things might have livened up if some of the town's budding marksmen had used the cycles as moving targets!

The Obituary of George Leslie Sheriff Clerk for Elgin was noted in the Courant of September 1st 1871. Mr Leslie had been the partner of James Grant in his Elgin law firm before he took up the post of Sheriff Clerk.

The 12 feet of water in Lossiemouth harbour was put to good use on September 8th. A workman was unloading a goods wagon at the quayside, when he lost his footing and fell from the vehicle. Mr Anderson missed the quayside and plunged into the harbour. The local press claimed this resulted in his life being saved.

Rumour within the railway industry suggested that the Great North of Scotland Railway was about to be taken over by one of its southern neighbours, the North British Railway. Indeed, there had been a story published in the *Glasgow Star* to this effect. The *Elgin Courant* did not believe this article, and after a little investigation reported on September 15th, that *"this story is quite unfounded."* Indulging in a little rumour making of its own, the *Courant* suggested that James Grant's current law partner Mr Jamieson was expected to be appointed as Elgin's new Sheriff Clerk.

On September 29th a promissory note for £1500 due to James Grant fell for payment. Two new notes were issued, one for £1000 and the other for £500.

As fate would have it, on that day the GNSR announced its dividend payments. They were also struggling, but (A) class Preference share holders were paid the rate of $4^1/_2$%. The Ordinary shareholders, like those of the Morayshire, received nothing. When the Highland Railway, on October 6th, declared a dividend for 1871 of 5%, which unlike the dividend declared by the GNSR was for Ordinary shareholders a little jealousy must have been felt by the Morayshire shareholders

The need for economies meant the people of Elgin lost out with the announcement on October 13th of the winter timetable. Anyone having to travel to north from Aberdeen would as in 1869 find his last train home to Elgin leaving the Granite City at 1pm. The *Elgin Courant* launched a plea for an improvement: *"We have frequently opposed the withdrawal of trains that make it impossible to go from Elgin to Aberdeen, a distance of seventy miles on the same day. If the Great North find it would not pay them to run on to Elgin every night, it would be a great convenience if they would say twice a week on Mondays and Saturdays."* Sadly this request met with no response.

The *Courant's* forecast on the choice of a new Sheriff Clerk proved correct, with Mr Jamieson being confirmed in the post on November 3rd. This would appear to make our Mr James Grant a good teacher of law, with two senior court officials coming from his firm.

Telegraph money amounting to £2240 had been paid to the Company and was protected from any legal action from the Great North of Scotland Railway. It was, as indicated earlier, the Morayshire's intention to pay this over to the GNSR, for an equal reduction in Preference Shares By this action the Morayshire would lessen its interest burden by £112. There would this year be some good news to tell the Company shareholders at the AGM on November 24th.

The AGM was held at the Station Hotel in Elgin. Despite a slight decrease in the number of passengers carried, down from 111,941 in 1870 to 110,045 for this year, business was good for the Morayshire. The railway had been carrying a better class of passenger, as receipts had shown an increase of £49-15s-5d. Goods tonnage continued to increase with 47,566 tons travelling over the line, an increase of 3000 tons on last year's figure. This added £212-5s-1d to the Morayshire coffers. Revenue for 1871 was more than enough to meet all the expenses which included payment to the Highland Railway for the Orton station's arbitration award. The Morayshire was left with a surplus of £269-12s-1d, which was enough to give the shareholders a small dividend. Refraining from the excitement of being able to pay something, the Directors decided to carry over the surplus to next year. This decision was wholeheartedly supported by those present at the meeting and by the local press.

The final act before closing the meeting was to elect the Directors of the Company. In previous years this had been a formality, with no real change in the make-up of the Board. However, time and old age were both starting to make their mark on the Directors. Mr George Smith Minmore had been in ill health for sometime. Unable to attend meetings, he no longer wished to seek re-election. This was accepted, but the family connection was not severed. John Gordon Smith, his son who was by now also a large share holder in the Company, took his place. Mr W H Mills had gone to Mexico, and liked that country so much he decided to stay. His place was taken by Mr Topp of Ashgrove who had supported the Morayshire since its early days. With the new Board installed, the meeting was concluded.

The *Elgin Courant* of December 1st carried the obituary of Mr George Smith of Minmore.

On December 5th the Morayshire received a letter from the GNSR who were, put out that the Morayshire Railway account for 1871 showed a cash surplus. They felt that this money should be used to pay off the outstanding debts owed by the Morayshire. It appears that the GNSR were not only feeling the *"bite of winter,"* but also that of financial hardship. Contained within the correspondence asking for further payments, was notice of a proposal to increase the rate for carrying coal from Aberdeen to Elgin to 4/- per ton. This last item concerned the Morayshire Board, who wrote back requesting the reason for the increase and that the new charges were held until an explanation was given. Another year may have passed, but the relationship between the Morayshire and its Aberdeen neighbour had not improved.

The New Year of 1872 was only four days old, when a fatal railway accident occurred on the Highland Railway line at Orbliston. The events of January 4th are unusual because the accident was caused by an explosion of a locomotive boiler. The train was a mile past Orbliston station, known then as Fochabers, on its way to Keith. The time was 10.30am. There were three men on the engine, William Ross, engine driver; David Bruce, fireman; and John Gerrie also a fireman. Being a goods train, there was only one other crew member, the guard William MacKenzie who was in the brake van at the rear of the train. William Ross was thrown by the explosion to one side of the lineside embankment and David Bruce to the other. It appears that John Gerrie was blown backwards by the force of the blast because his body was found under the tender. He lived for twenty minutes, dying whilst being carried from the scene to the shelter of Orbliston farm. Mr Gerrie had until recently been the porter at Burghead station and was well liked within that community. He left a widow and a large family. The other two members of the footplate crew were attended to by Dr Ross and Dr Gordon of Gray's hospital.

The fragments of the boiler were thrown over a 500 yard radius from the railway line. Damage to property was minimal. Only one outhouse at Orbliston farm lost some of its slates as a result of being struck by a piece of iron. The railway track had been torn away by the force of the explosion, causing a large number of the wagons to be derailed. A number of them were carrying a consignment of vitriol in bottles. Some of these were smashed by the blast, spilling burning liquid around the site, adding to the mayhem. The explosion, which is reported to have sounded like a cannon, smashed the couplings of the engine and tender, propelling the frame of the locomotive 600 yards along the track.

Little time was lost in repairing the damage. By the afternoon a team of fifty surfacemen were busy replacing track and re-railing wagons. The incident was placed under legal investigation by Mr Grigor Allan, Procurator Fiscal. News of this accident caused a sensation, mixed with a feeling of regret for the loss of Mr Gerrie.

The Morayshire Board had their first meeting of 1872 on January 10th. Little had changed in the Morayshire's method of operation. The first item for discussion was yet another letter from the Great North of Scotland Railway demanding that the Morayshire's cash surplus be used to pay off the debts owed to it. The Directors of the Morayshire decided that they would not answer this request from the GNSR. They were however distressed to find out that the Aberdeen Company still intended to increase the cost of carrying coal from Aberdeen to Elgin. Another letter of appeal was felt justified, with a further request that no increase be put in place until the full facts behind its imposition were given to the Morayshire. Repayment of the promissory note for £2000 due to James Grant came round on this date and once more arrangements were put in place for the loan period to be extended.

More money issues were discussed on the 9th of February, when Mr Topp wanted a £1000 bond due to him repaid. It was left to James Grant and Mr Smith to "persuade" him to settle for a renewal. Other small bills were shuffled around.

A little gritting of teeth must have gone on when the Morayshire Directors, read the *Elgin Courant* of March 19th. In a piece on local railway companies, it stated the following: *"We are glad to see the*

GNSR, will be able to pay a full dividend on their shares, with a handsome profit to carry forward to the next half year. The Highland Railway is expected to pay 6% and their shares have gone up to £121."

The best that the Morayshire could do was to take another loan from James Grant to the value of £600 for a period of 12 months. This was to part-pay a demand for £1200 from the Commercial Bank that was due for payment on April 8th. This date has a significance in the history of the Morayshire Railway Company, which will become evident shortly. The formal paperwork for the extension to the promissory note for £2000 spoken about on January 10th was finally sorted out on May 10th. Opportunity was also taken to reschedule other Morayshire Company loans.

It was now the turn of the Morayshire and its partner the Great North of Scotland Railway to suffer a fatal railway accident. The incident occurred on the 17th of May 1872 at Rothes. The victim was a seven-year old boy, the son of Mr Sharpe, mason at Rothes. A crowd of boys, including the deceased were watching some wagons being shunted at the Rothes sidings. They were interested in a horsebox that was being removed from an arriving train. Eager to see the animals being taken out, the boys stepped on to an adjacent siding. In their excitement they did not notice that shunting had continued. Consequently, a stationary wagon was struck by a moving one, and was driven upon the group. The lads scattered at the last moment except for young Mr Sharpe, who was struck on the side of the head by the wagon, then run over.

17 The Late Ex-Provost Grant

April 8th 1872 was the date of the last Morayshire Board meeting that James Grant attended. He died at his home Dalehaple House, on the night of Wednesday, May 22nd 1872, after a short illness.

The once square-built powerful man, by slow gradation, came to move about with a shaking frame and slow short step. In the closing year of his life he was seen rarely walking on the streets of Elgin, preferring instead to taking an airing in his carriage, often accompanied by members of his family. Aged 71 years at his death, the infirmities of age had prevented him from taking an active part in business, except for the Morayshire Railway, which he considered his duty to the citizens of Elgin to put back on an even keel.

The local press were fulsome in their praise of James Grant, as this extract from an extensive obituary in the *Elgin Courant* of May 24th demonstrates:

> Where among our most laborious and enterprising citizens shall we find his equal? Where is there the same natural grasp of intellect for business, and the same cool demeanour and resolute resolve in the midst of losses and crosses under which ordinary minds would have sunk? The Provost's countenance was unruffled whatever might happen. He was never down hearted, never cast down, never lost his frank manner and winning affability. He made many friends and like every public man engaged in many undertakings with some perhaps, he was not a favourite, but personally, it may be truly asserted, he was highly esteemed by all. He was generous in his disposition, hospitable, and of so happy a constitution that the smile was ever ready to beam on his countenance. But his suavity of manners was combined with firmness and great decision of character, and the resolve once formed, what obstacle could make him swerve from his purpose? It may be said he was born to command men, and make circumstances bow to his will, and such a character can scarcely fail to be highly respected, as he forms a contrast to the easily persuaded the easily led, who seem to have no mind of their own. In some of his southern journeys he was, we believe called *"The Provost of Scotland,"* and certainly the North had no occasion to be ashamed of sending such a man to London, for he was among our greatest public men, both strong inborn sound sense and happy disposition with great public enterprise in the business of life.

> We have only to add that Provost Grant was married about the year 1838, and has left a widow and family bereaved of a kind husband and indulgent father to lament their irreparable loss.

The funeral of James Grant took place on Tuesday, of May 28th 1872. His family had initially made arrangements for a private funeral. This was to be changed as the people of Elgin wanted to show their respects to the passing of a man who had been such a champion, not only to the City of Elgin, but the whole of Moray. Following a special meeting of the Elgin Town Council on Saturday, May 25th, it was expressed that the Council was *"desirous to show a last mark of respect for one who had so long held high civic honour."* An offer was made to the Grant family for the Council to attend the funeral in their corporate capacity. Formal recommendation was also made that the funeral should be a public affair. This was willingly accepted and notice accordingly given, respectfully inviting all to attend. The Society of Solicitors, of which Mr Grant had been Vice Chairman, also held a meeting on the Monday morning. They, like the Town Council, resolved to do honour to their friend by attending the funeral as a corporate body.

On the Tuesday at 12.45pm a solemn peal from the city knells gave warning that the hour for paying the last tribute of respect to James Grant was approaching. Numerous and influential people assembled in front of Dalehaple House. Accordingly at 1pm, the Reverend Mr Trail, of the Free South Church offered up a prayer, which was followed by a scripture reading by the Reverend Mr McWatt of Rothes. The hearse containing the remains of the deceased then left from the east gate of the house. The funeral cortege was formed up in the following order:

Citizens of Elgin
Society of Solicitors
Directors of the Morayshire Railway
The Town Council of Elgin
HEARSE
Empty carriage of the deceased
Chief Mourners in three carriages
Carriages of The Earl of Fife
Captain Dunbar Brander, Pitgaveny
Mr Maclean, Westfield
Mr Maxwell, Blackhills

Around 500 other gentlemen of position and influence from Elgin and surrounding district followed on in their carriages and on foot. Clergymen of all denominations were in attendance, as were the medical men of the Elgin area.

The solemn procession moved slowly off towards the New Cemetery, which was situated a little to the east of the then village of New Elgin. The roadside along the route was lined with the ordinary people of the town, some of who were visibly affected by the occasion. It was appropriate that, as a person who was first to bring so many varied enterprises to Elgin, his should be the honour of the first funeral procession to use the new road to the cemetery. The order of procession was preserved all the way along the route, despite the very large turnout, no jostling, confusion, or anything out of order.

On arriving at the burying ground, all those in conveyances alighted and walked on foot to the graveside. The coffin was then removed from the hearse and carried on the shoulders of four men to the place of interment, near the north-east corner of the cemetery. It was lowered into the grave by five sorrowing sons. This simple service was accompanied by the mournful sound of the death bell.

During the funeral ceremony the principal shops in the town were closed and business generally suspended. The weather was genial for the mourners and spectators who together made this one of the largest funerals ever held in Elgin. The arrangements were under the superintendence of Mr Hay cabinet maker Elgin.

Such a prominent citizen of course required a substantial monument to his memory. Let us temporarily jump ahead to February 1874. On the 25th of that month, what was described as a *"very handsome monument"* was completed at Elgin cemetery. The design, Italian in style, was carried out by Mr Alex Reid architect and like many of the buildings he crafted in Elgin it does him credit. Construction work was carried out by a Mr Goodwillie, sculptor, whose proficiency in stone work was well known over the whole of the north of Scotland. Still in place today, it can be seen against the north wall of what is now the "old part" of the new cemetery of Elgin. Only the inscription on the centre panel seems to have borne the brunt of the years. If you wish to visit former Provost Grant in his resting place, you should find that the inscription on the centre panel reads as follows:

In memory of James Grant born at Shenval, Inveravon, Banffshire, 25 July 1801; died at Dalehaple House, Elgin 23rd May 1872, in his 71st year. For upwards of 40 years a distinguished solicitor in Elgin as well as an extensive farmer and distiller in the county - he was famed for his public spirit and enterprise in originating and carrying out local improvements and public works, especially the devising and establishing of the Morayshire

Railway. He was 15 years Provost of the city of Elgin, and in that capacity was connected with almost every public institution in it; and used all his talents and energy to advance the Liberal political views which have conferred so great benefit on the country. His merits and exertions were recognised and appreciated, not only by his fellows but by the inhabitants of this and his native county. This monument is erected by the loving widow and children of a fond husband and indulgent father.

How did the death of their Chairman affect the Morayshire Railway Company Board? Well, they seemed to be at a loss as to how they should go on. It was not until June 14th that the remaining Board members met. Even then it was to satisfy the Terms of a Parliamentary Act governing the workings of the Company, rather than the need to press on with the business.

Alexander Urquhart moved up from Deputy Chairman to take the place of James Grant, whilst John Gordon Smith became the vice Chairman. The gap in the Board membership was filled by James Grant's business partner Mr Jamieson. He attending the meeting initially in his capacity of looking after the interests of the Grant family, but it was decided that he should join the Board until the Company AGM in November.

Before continuing with the day's business the Directors resolved to record their deep regret at *"the severe loss,"* which they and the Morayshire Company had sustained by the death of James Grant. The following extract was written up from the Minute Book and sent to the late Provost's family.

> The Directors consider it due to his memory to testify to the zealous and able manner in which James Grant discharged his duties of Chairman, and the high appreciation of his long and valuable services since they became associated with him. They also desire to record their sense of the efforts made at all times by him, both pecuniary and otherwise for the prosperity of the Company from its origin until the very day of his death. The Directors also join in sympathy for his widow in her bereavement, and the large young family which he has left to mourn his loss.

The people of Elgin and District, who had stuck with James Grant and the Morayshire Railway through the good and the bad patches, (the bad being the more numerous), seemed to have lost all confidence in the Morayshire Railway Company since James Grant's hand slipped from the Company's tiller. Now the new Chairman Alexander Urquhart was facing numerous demands for immediate repayment of various bonds and loans totalling some £1400. The only course of action open to him was to instruct the Secretary to endeavour to have said parties extend their demands for repayment for another 12 months.

What was to be the future of the Morayshire Railway Company? After discussion it was decided that the Chairman and the Secretary, or either of them, were to ascertain from the Chairman and Secretary of the Great North of Scotland Railway the terms for an amalgamation between them and the Morayshire Railway. Having done this, the outcome of any discussion was to be made known at a future meeting of the Morayshire Railway Board. The independence that James Grant had so long fought to keep for the Morayshire Railway was readily being given away by his successors. The only question remaining is; would the Great North of Scotland Railway take up the offer placed before them by the Morayshire Board?

18 TIME AND TIDE

Time and tide wait for no man. Although the Grant family, Morayshire Railway and the population of Elgin had suffered a great loss, business opportunities were still available; money could be made. To this end, with an Elgin holiday fast approaching on July 1st 1872, an enterprising committee had been formed to offer the folk of Elgin new adventures and make the organisers a few extra shillings. In the *Elgin Courant* of May 31st a proposal appeared, to run a trip to the Falls of Foyers using the services of the Highland Railway and a steamship. Temptations on offer were moderate prices and the services of the Elgin Brass Band.

On June 4th the Great North of Scotland Railway made alterations to its services. Elgin citizens could now leave for Aberdeen and intermediate stations as late as 7.20pm, more importantly they could return from the Granite City as late as 9.20pm. This improvement met with the wholehearted endorsement of the local press. The Highland Railway who, on the other hand, had made no adjustments to its services was criticised because anyone wishing to travel west from Elgin had to do so before 4.35pm.

A blow to the adventurers of Elgin fell on June 11th when the trip to Foyers was cancelled due to the high cost imposed by the steamship company. Instead, there was to be another chance to visit Strome Ferry. In previous years, this choice of destination had not been a very successful one. The organising committee felt that this was because so few of the people Elgin were aware of the magnificent scenery to be seen west of Dingwall. Now that a few had been and could testify to the beauty of the west coast, it was believed that the trip would attract large numbers.

For the very adventurous, rail travel from the Capital of the Empire to the City of Elgin had also improved. It was now possible to complete this journey in just under 18 hours. Our traveller could leave London at 8.30pm and arrive in Edinburgh at 6am, in time for the north train with an arrival in Elgin of 2.25pm. The *Elgin Courant*, was much impressed. *"These are travelling facilities which the public should feel greatly obliged towards."*

The high quality behaviour, of the folk of Lossiemouth came in for comment from the *Elgin Courant*, of June 25th. *"Thursday last was observed as a holiday in Lossiemouth. A special train was started at 6.40am in order that the holiday seeker arrived in Elgin in time for the 7.10am. A very large number went with this train to Aberdeen, and indeed all the trains on the GNSR were literally "crammed" all day. The Highland Railway had a share conveying travellers to Forres. The holiday was a most successful one, no doubt due to the results of templarism."*

The prospect of the beautiful scenery west of Dingwall, was failing to draw the population of Elgin. To entice travellers the price of the first class fare was reduced from 15/- to 10/-, and an additional pick-up point at Lhanbryde was added to the tour.

The weather on July 1st was bad with rain falling, which did not help the Highland Railway. Only 1600 travellers used their system to reach various destinations on their network, including Strome Ferry, which again failed to be a draw. Ticket sales on GNSR totalled 2305, of which the bulk (1500) were for Lossiemouth.

The holiday season was now in full swing. On July 8th a large number of people from Aberlour plus brass band arrived at the Lossiemouth. They were followed on July 12th by an excursion from Aberdeen made up of GNSR locomotive men, their wives and families. Travelling away from the coast on the 14th, the Lossiemouth Sabbath and Weekday Scholars used the railway to reach Arndilly, the choice for their annual picnic. A few days later the New Elgin Sunday School, whom this year did not favour Lossiemouth, though they still used the Morayshire Railway, went to Aberlour. The loss in business to the shopkeepers of Lossiemouth by the defection of the New Elgin Sunday school was amply made up the people of Knockando who went to the seaside for their holiday on July 18th.

The Great North of Scotland Railway Company was making certain that it was doing all it could to exploit this hubbub of holiday fever, reminding the population of Elgin that their second holiday of the year was almost upon them. No longer competing for the Elgin holiday traffic, August saw the GNSR take its turn to provide the excursion by offering the delights of Aberdeen, with the option of a trip to Dunotter Castle, for only *"A few shillings more."*

The GNSR certainly appeared to be favoured by the *Elgin Courant*, if this report on the second Elgin holiday of the year is anything to go by. *"The success of the recent holiday excursion arranged by the Great North of Scotland Railway Company is due in part to the nominal fares charged, but not least the attention of the GNSR staff and officials and the comfort and punctuality of trains coming and going."*

In previous years the Great North of Scotland Railway had exploited its connection to Royalty by running a holiday excursion from Elgin to Ballater. Friday, September 6th saw the Highland Railway take advantage of a trip north by the Sovereign. Their station at Elgin was decorated along its complete 400 yard length. At each end Gothic arches spanned across the railway track appearing like the gateway to some royal castle. The tops of these were decorated with floral crowns. Under each was the figure of St Giles the patron saint of Elgin, and either side of him were the letters *"V"* and *"R."*

To accommodate spectators, two grandstands capable of holding 900 people were erected each side of the station building. Access to these was by ticket only, numbers 1 to 200 pink on the east grandstand, and 250 to 400 pink on the west grandstand. Blue unnumbered tickets gave access to the rest of the spaces. Spectators were also allowed on the south platform of the station and again access was by ticket only, this time white in colour.

A platform for the Lord Provost, Council officials and assorted local noblemen was built over the railway track on the north side of the station. It was intended that the Royal party would stop at Elgin for ten minutes on their journey north to Dunrobin Castle. A member of the Morayshire Railway Board did manage to squeeze himself onto the official welcoming party platform. Mr James Jamieson, former partner of James Grant, acting in his capacity as Sheriff-Clerk, carried the honour for the Morayshire Company.

A prodigious keeper of journals, the Queens recollection of the visit was that the weather was *"broiling hot."* She seemed to appreciate the arches adorned with flowers and heather and the nosegay presented by the Provost's daughter. The Provost himself, Alexander Cameron, gave the address.

 The Queen's visit to Elgin that day gave the opportunity for enterprise and profit to some of its citizens, in particular two of its photographers. Mr John Anderson of Academy Street Elgin could supply photographs showing the station in all its splendour, just before the arrival of the Royal Train. It was claimed that a great number of the people seated in the grandstands were recognisable with the naked eye. Fellow photographer Mr Gordon, could provide excellent views of the Royal train standing in the station. At the time the picture was taken, the Queen had been moving, so sadly she does not appear clearly. *"Do not be disappointed though, because the carriage door is seen open; and John Brown standing at the back comes out splendidly,"* claims the sales pitch for this product. If a view of John Brown was not enough, it was stated that a number of the people standing around are also recognisable. These photographs were also available as stereoscopic views. In all the excitement of the Royal visit to Elgin, it appears the gentlemen of the local press had credited all the hard work and beauty of the floral displays to the wrong person. A correction on this matter appeared in the *Elgin Courant* of September 13th. *"It should be noted that the floral displays for the Queens visit were done by Mr Alex Gow, gardener Grant Lodge, and reflect the utmost credit to all concerned."*

September 23rd saw the end of the year's holiday business, with Lossiemouth's second holiday of 1872. The weather on that date was far from agreeable for it rained incessantly all day. The Standing Rock lodge of free Templars were not going to allow the inclement weather to dampen their holiday and they set off for a day in Rothes. This sadly was a mistake, for the downpour made it difficult for much of their number to adhere to the principles of their creed. With no band to raise their spirits, many of the Standing Rock free Templars indulged in sprits of a different kind. By the time of the return trip to Lossiemouth, many had converted to "Tipplers." Despite the hearty consumption of alcohol, all the Tipplers and remaining Templars, completed their journey home safely.

Improvements to services in this corner of Moray continued in October of 1872. Both the Highland Railway and Great North of Scotland were working together, re-timing trains to better mail communication from the North to the rest of the country.

The Morayshire Board, throughout this time, had not really met on any regular basis, though the Secretary Alex Watt had been doing all that he could to keep creditors off his Company's back. On November 8th he reported to the Board that he had been partly successful in stemming the demands for repayment made in June. He had managed to retain the sum of £900, by persuading a Mr Cameron of Bilbohall to maintain his bond with the Company. For the rest of the creditors who were not so like-minded, he had managed to find the £500 in funds to repay them. Concerning the matter of the Great North of Scotland Railway taking over the complete business of the Morayshire, the Chairman appeared to have had a little success. It is noted that a letter had been received from Mr Ferguson of the GNSR, which the Board read and approved its contents. Sadly for us the actual statements made in the letter are not recorded in the Minute Book.

The statutory meeting of the Morayshire Railway for 1872, was held on November 29th the venue was the Station Hotel and business began at 11am. Before his report the Chairman, Alexander Urquhart gave an appreciation of the late James Grant. He also used this opportunity to attack those whom he felt, through jealousy of the late Chairman, were responsible in a large measure for the financial position in which the Morayshire Company found itself, opposing at every opportunity the plans by the late Provost Grant to put the Morayshire Railway Company back on a secure footing. He then went on to state that the family of James Grant, the shareholders of the Company and himself had the consolation of knowing that these opponents were wrong. The Morayshire Railway Company was now in a far better state than it had been in 1864, with an increase in revenue from £6486 to £8961. Generally, the working expenses of the line had been covered for the year, leaving a balance of £511. It was the Chairman's intention to use this surplus to liquidate some of the outstanding debts of the Morayshire Company. Again the poor old shareholder of the Morayshire was to miss out on a dividend payout.

The only other business conducted before the close of the meeting was confirmation of Mr Jamieson's position on the Company Board of Directors. No mention was made of the prospect of the Company being taken over by the GNSR, or the fact that tentative steps in this direction had been taken in June. With the departure of the shareholders from the Station Hotel, no further meetings of the Board of Directors of the Morayshire Railway Company took place in 1872.

Craigellachie Junction was the scene of an accident, on January 23rd 1873, that claimed the life of the Stationmaster. The gentleman, named Robertson, had accompanied some wagons that were to be left between Craigellachie and Dufftown in order to be loaded with timber. When the wagons were detached from the train, they started to roll back along the line towards the station. Mr Robertson jumped on to the brake of the wagon he was travelling on, and this eventually brought them to a standstill. Not realising how far he had travelled, because this operation had taken place in the hours of darkness, he stepped down from the wagon expecting to find himself on the embankment. Unfortunately, he had gone further towards Craigellachie station than he though, with the result that the wagons had been brought to a standstill on the bridge over the River Fiddich. His leap from the parked wagon took him over the side of the bridge where he fell sixteen feet into the shallow bed of the river, fracturing his skull. A surface man who was working nearby came to the Stationmaster's aid. Robertson was conveyed first to the station and then to his home. Despite speedy medical attention, the poor chap died at 4.30am the next morning, without ever regaining consciousness.

The Morayshire Board met the following day January 24th. The tragic incident at Craigellachie did not merit a mention as the Company grappled with its finances. A collection of various accounts were all requiring attention, but the one that was causing most concern was a demand from Mr Jamieson claiming the sum of £914-14-11½d. This apparently was for legal work carried out by Grant & Jamieson. To investigate this charge it was decided that a subcommittee should be formed. Compared to the previous year, when there had been few meetings of the Morayshire Board, this staggering demand galvanised the Directors into action. A preliminary report on Mr Jamieson's claim was ready on January 28th.

Finding a replacement for the energetic and amiable Mr Robertson at Craigellachie took a little longer. It was not until February 4th 1873 that Mr Chalmers, station agent at Advie was promoted to Craigellachie Junction Stationmaster. In turn his vacancy at Advie was filled by Mr Taylor, goods clerk at Lossiemouth. He seemed to have been a well-liked individual, with the folk of Lossiemouth holding a presentation for him on February 7th.

The Chairman and Secretary of the Morayshire Railway told the rest of the Board, on 10th March, their intention to pay Mr Jamieson the sum of £138-12s-11½d in full and final settlement of the claim he had made on January 24th. This amount included payments to Messrs Inglis & Co Edinburgh for legal work carried out for the Morayshire.

Lesser complaints were also discussed, viz a letter from Mr MacBean concerning the poor state of the Elgin coal sheds. The Directors resolved that steps should be taken to put these buildings into a proper state of repair. Correspondence had also been received from the GNSR over a request from Captain Dunbar to reopen the platform at Birchfield. The Morayshire Board agreed to this move. Approval was also given for a donation of £3-3/- to the widow of Mr Robertson. This money was to be paid to the Treasurer in charge of the relief fund.

Reports in the *Elgin Courant*, of March 28th 1873, suggested the possibility of another commodity that could end up being carried by the Morayshire Railway. Local landowner Sir Archibald Dunbar was to hold a meeting with other landowners in the area to see what steps should be taken to ascertain if deposits of coal worth mining exist in Moray. Entry to this meeting was by invitation only, but nevertheless was well attended. The local press were glad to learn that test drilling would be permitted on the property of all those present at the meeting. Costs and terms to have this work carried out was to be sought.

Continuing to exploit its tourist potential, a committee had been put together in Lossiemouth to build public baths. The plans that had been prepared showed a building containing eight hot and cold baths, salt and fresh water baths, and a large swimming pool. Estimated cost of this project was £850 without the swimming pool, and with £1350. This enterprise really caught the imagination of the reporter from the *Elgin Courant*. *"Public baths are now an absolute necessity at Lossiemouth, which has won its popularity as a watering place. Many hundreds of visitors would gladly avail themselves and induce others to visit. Shares in this enterprise are to be offered at a £1 each and we trust that the public of Elgin, and many other places will come forward liberally and take shares."*

The Morayshire Board were informed on April 4th, that Mr MacBean had given up the coal business, as of March 31st of 1873. A letter was sent, asking him to reconsider. In the interim, to protect railway business, the stores were to be advertised for let. Various promissory notes to the late James Grant also fell due for payment on this date. The young James Grant of Glengrant was now looking after this part of his late uncle's affairs.

On April 28th, the Morayshire Board received word from Mr MacBean that he had decided to continue in the coal trade, so they agreed to employ a qualified fitter to examine and repair the weighing machine that he used.

Mr Jamieson was very unhappy with the settlement on offer from the Morayshire. He claimed that both the late James Grant and he had done a great deal of background work on behalf of the Morayshire. In reply the Board stated that they would only pay for official requests that came from the Company. Settlement on the terms suggested by the Morayshire to the firm of Grant & Jamieson would only be available for the next ten days. After that period the Directors of the Morayshire Railway would disclaim all liability to Mr Jamieson and refuse to settle.

A request for payment of £160 was made by the Highland Railway Company for construction of a bridge at Elgin station. With this payment the Inverness Company said they would drop all other claims it had made against the Morayshire provided the full sum was in the hands of the Highland Railway within four months.

The first Elgin holiday of 1873 was held on July 7th. It is noteworthy that the excursion fares of 6d to Lossiemouth were, for ordinary travellers, still at the same prices as on the opening day of the Morayshire way back in 1852. The real bargain, for those who could afford it, was a trip to Aberdeen for 5/- first class and 3/- for third. This train left Elgin station in the morning and consisted of 29 carriages in total, the train to Lossiemouth being a "tiddler" in comparison, of only 18 carriages in length. The total number of excursionists who used these trains to reach their holiday destination was 3811. Numbers travelling by the Highland Railway, to Keith in the east or west to Inverness, numbered some 1762. For a city the size of Elgin, which at this time had a population of just under 8000 people, these figures well demonstrate the impact of the railway and the desire of the population to travel. All this fresh air and exercise was not without dangers, as one Elgin lassie found to her cost. Mary Ann Caulder, factory worker, Newmill, had a narrow escape as a result of staying in the water too long whilst bathing. She was observed lying in a state of insensibility upon some rocks and so was conveyed by others to higher ground. Here, "restoratives" were applied and she was attended to by Drs Mackay and Work, who pronounced her case to be a serious one. Besides an attack of cramp, she had also sustained congestion of the lungs. Far from being recovered, she was conveyed home on the evening train. This appears to have been the only misfortune of the day; the rest of the holiday makers returned home in high spirits. All the trains were reported as running punctually.

From reports in the *Elgin Courant* of July 18th, it would appear that Mary Ann Caulder would soon have a safer place to swim. The idea of building public baths at Lossiemouth had been well received by the people of the area, with nearly £600 in shares bought a limited liability company formed and a site for the building chosen. The prospect of increased business to the Morayshire Railway looked assured. It was still doing well out of the Lossiemouth line, with 445 excursionists from Rothes taking advantage of their end of July local holiday to go to the seaside. This gave the Morayshire and its partner the Great North £35 in income £12 up on last year's total.

Holiday fever was dying down in the final days of August. The *Elgin Courant*, in an article of August 26th, was now promoting itself as a supporter of hard work, being far from impressed that folk of Elgin should have a day off at so late in the summer, *"A farmer could not obtain the services of a blacksmith to repair a reaping machine. This resulted in a large quantity of men standing idle a good day, plus money lost. Scholars are also losing a day at school the holiday should be on the 1st Monday in August."* Certainly, the number of passengers carried by the railway was lower than the earlier part of the year, but a good portion of the city had set out to enjoy themselves. The GNSR issued 2020 excursion tickets, earning it and the Morayshire £110-12/-, whilst the Highland carried 2010, bringing in an income of £335-6/-. Lossiemouth had been the popular choice and this was the reason for the relatively low income earned by the GNSR, compared to the number of tickets issued. The holiday season ended on September 29th when the people of Lossiemouth took the day off. No mischief was reported this year by the local press. Perhaps the citizens from the coast had invested their spare money in the proposed public baths. The contract for construction had been agreed on October 16th 1873 at a cost of £950.

The Highland Railway improved its services from Elgin on October 28th by introducing a train leaving for the west at 7pm. It would however take the traveller one hour and five minutes to reach Forres 12 miles distant from Elgin. This was because the new service was provided by a mixed train, one that has both passenger coaches and goods wagons in its formation. Therefore, a substantial amount of time was required to allow for the shunting of wagons at the intermediate stations between Elgin and Forres. Still the Courant was grateful that the business men of Elgin could transact commercial enterprises to the west of the city, after 3pm.

On November 7th, preparations were being made for the AGM, which was held at the end of the month. Just over a dozen shareholders assembled at the Station Hotel on November 28th to hear how the Company had performed in the intervening twelve months. The Morayshire was still able to pay all its working expense. It had, through the payment of £160, settled all the claims against it by the Highland Railway Company and passenger traffic was up by almost 3000 on last year. The only disappointment was that the surplus remaining was a miserly £53. The almost total collapse of the movement of agricultural produce rising from the near failure of the potato and grain crop explained this poor performance. Chairman Alexander Urquhart was confident that the troubles hitting the farming community would not extend into 1874 and that the construction of the baths at Lossiemouth, or more correctly in Branderburgh, which at that time was separate from the fishing village of Lossiemouth, would continue to add to the rising passenger numbers.

To meet this expected increase, the passenger platform at Lossiemouth would have to be extended in length by 100 to 150 feet. Even without the added attraction of the baths, passenger traffic numbers using Lossiemouth had grown to such an extent that improvements were required. Mr Urquhart praised the staff at Lossiemouth, who through their hard work and dedication *"prevented accidents occurring."* He went on to say that he had inspected the site and felt the extension work could be carried out for only a small outlay. To save impeding traffic, he added that this improvement should be completed before the start of the 1874 season. This meant that the prospects of the Morayshire paying its shareholders a dividend was as distant as ever. At the conclusion of Mr Urquhart's report, various vacancies that had fallen due in Board membership were filled. James Jamieson retained his seat on the Board of Directors, although he was still in dispute with the Company over money he claimed was due to his legal firm. Perhaps he hoped he could use his position on the Board to influence a settlement more in his favour.

For the Morayshire Board, the year of 1873 finished like many previous, as they shuffled around assorted promissory notes to keep the Company afloat.

With Christmas, and more importantly for this northern part of the British Isle, Hogmanay gone for another year, the appetite for merrymaking should have been well satisfied. Not for the staff of the Morayshire Railway,

"No sleep till morn when youth and pleasure meet.
To chase the glowing hours with flying feet."

Fifty couples gathered at the Assembly Rooms in Elgin on the first Friday of 1874 for the Great North of Scotland Railway Company (Northern Section) Employees Ball. Mr Cruickshank, the Stationmaster in Elgin, was the master of ceremonies for the gathering of the railway employees and their partners. Proceedings started at 9pm to ensure that everyone connected with the railway was able to enjoy the party. A maze of various dances was whirled through until 11pm, when an adjournment was called so all could partake in a supper prepared by Mr Rowley. After this delightful interlude, there was a return to the "heel and toe" philosophy, under the direction of Mr Cumming of Aberlour, with the whole company thoroughly enjoying themselves. When the party finally broke up, in the small hours of the morning, all who had attended left for home with the hope that the event would become an annual fixture. For the seasoned dancers, or just those with a sturdy constitution, the official GNSR employee ball was held on January 20th at the Institute in Keith.

The past desire of the late Provost James Grant for good sea communication from Lossiemouth was once more dusted off on January 30th. The Aberdeen, Hull and Newcastle Steamship Company made it known that they intended to start a service from Lossiemouth on March 1st 1874. This Company had a steamship especially constructed to ply this route. The vessel named "Northern City" had a light draft that would allow her to enter Lossiemouth and other ports on the Moray Firth, like Buckie. The *Elgin Courant* was enthusiastic in its praise of this enterprise and the person it thought responsible for attracting this trade to Lossiemouth. *"Steam communication cannot fail to be a boon to traders in the north and credit for this service must be given to Mr Fraser Lossiemouth's energetic harbourmaster."*

A note of mystery surrounds a misdemeanour reported in the *Elgin Courant*, of March 3rd. *"Yesterday one of our railway companies was fined £5 for putting an ox into a cattle truck without its being previously disinfected."*

Good news on the March 10th for Great North of Scotland Company shareholders, as it was reported in the *Railway News*. *"After a lapse of several years the GNSR has commenced payment of a dividend on its ordinary stock, viz ½%. This is an improvement on the corresponding period of last year. The proprietors of the GNSR may be congratulated not merely on the fact of a resumption of a dividend, but also on the fact of its being one of the few railways that have any increase in profit during the last year."*

An update for the readers of the *Elgin Courant*, as on May 22nd it reported that the Directors of the Branderburgh Baths had appointed a keeper to the facility. The gentleman in question was a Mr James Stephen, late of the 79th Regiment. Expectation was that the baths would be opened in early July.

One more of the original promoters of the Morayshire Railway, passed away on May 25th 1874. Mr James Samuel the line's builder and first engineer died of paralysis, after an illness of three months. In the intervening years, following the construction of the Morayshire, Mr Samuel had a varied and successful career building railways in Austria, France, Germany, Russia, Mexico and Cape Bretton. Indeed, at the time of his death, he was Consulting Engineer to the Mexican Railway network, which must be as far away from the Rothes Glen as you can get. His passion for inventing had not deserted him. Since 1852 he had taken out a large number of patents, most of which were concerned with reducing the weight and cost of railway rolling stock. The obituary in the Proceedings of the Institution of Civil Engineers, sums him up as thus, *"He was a man of good commercial acumen and sound judgement; but his temperament was very sanguine, and he was easily led."* Our tribute would be to remember him as the person who brought Provost James Grant's dream to reality, by building the first railway in the north of Scotland.

On May 26th the summer timetable was put into operation on the Morayshire Railway and the Company set itself ready for the forthcoming holiday season. The first people of the district to go on an excursion were the folk of Lossiemouth who set out for Aberdeen on June 16th. These outings were now more common than in previous years, attracting little attention from the local press, apart that is from a few lines in the *Elgin Courant* that commented: *"There was not much sign of intoxication in the Lossiemouth holiday makers."*

19 BATHING AND THE BRANDERBURGH PUBLIC BATHS

Whilst the good folk of Lossiemouth and the new town of Branderburgh had gone off to Aberdeen on a day's excursion, the gentlemen of the press travelled to the coast for a preview of the facilities that would soon be on offer. The following is a short extract from the *Elgin Courant*.

The Branderburgh Public Baths

During the spring the works have progressed rapidly, and in the course of ten days or so the baths will be ready for use.

The whole building is 100 feet long, and the breadth is 30 feet inside. The height of the walls is 20 feet. From the bottom of the swimming pool to the roof is 27 feet and the dimensions of the bath are 50 feet by 25 feet. The bath itself was first built of rubble work then faced with Portland cement, and has been finished off with a petrifying silicate wash. The whole is as smooth as a table top, and everything connected with the bath construction on the most approved plan. At the south end of the bath the water will be $2\frac{1}{2}$ feet deep, and at the north or sea end 5 feet deep. The bathers will descend and ascend by convenient ladders, of which there will be six, and there is a rope round the whole bath for bathers to take hold of at pleasure. There is a platform from 2 feet to 5 feet wide between the wall and the edge of the bath for bathers to walk around. At the south end of the bath the water enters by a fountain resembling a dolphin's head. Behind the fountain there are six dressing boxes fitted up with curtains and every convenience. The room is lighted by eighteen skylights, moveable for ventilation, besides a window at the end and the walls being painted white, there will be a flood of light in the swimming bath-room.

Between the front door and swimming bath-room the private bath rooms are situated. They are six in number, three on each side, one for the ladies the other for gentlemen. The floor of each of these rooms is carpeted, and has a chair, toilet table, wash hand basin, mirror and brush. Cold, hot or tepid baths may be had at pleasure, and simply by lifting his hand a bather can give himself a shower bath after enjoying a hot one. There is a bell for calling the attendant if anything be required.

The engine-house is situated underneath the private bath-rooms. The machine for operating the baths is known as a special steam pump, patented by Tangye Brothers, Birmingham, and has been fitted up by Messrs Johnstons of Newmill, Elgin. Five or six horse power in size it pumps water from the sea, through a pipe 140 yds in length and 3 ins in diameter, raising the water 14 feet to the fountain in the bath-room, and another 10 feet higher to two vats, one hot the other cold. The water is warmed by steam sent up from the engine. The pump can take from the sea 3250 gallons of water per hour, when full the swimming bath holds 27,343 cubic feet of water, and the reader may calculate how many hours it takes to fill it.

A serious difficulty occurred from consideration of the scarcity of water at the Links of Stotfield. How was the engine to be supplied? Salt water would soon fill the boiler with salt, or something of the kind. Plumber's Messrs McKenzie have overcome this difficulty by collecting the rain water that falls on to the roof of the bath building and conveying it down to a tank that holds 5000 gallons. The machinery for this purpose on the roof takes the water before it is mixed with any impurities, and an excellent supply is provided for the boiler.

The Branderburgh Baths are well situated, with the broad links behind them on which one can sit for hours looking at the dark blue sea, beyond which rise the lofty hills of Ross and Sutherland. In the foreground the links are studded with villas, the summer residences of gentlemen belonging to Elgin, and on the left hand is the well-built town of Branderburgh - a new town laid out in regular streets.

Bathers whilst enjoying an expansive view of sea and land, will be within fifteen minutes travel of Elgin by the railway train. The baths themselves are not more than half a mile from the station and thus the whole journey from or to Elgin can be accomplished in about twenty minutes.

The bathing ground to the west although well enough adapted for men, is from the rocky nature of the ground, often less pleasant to the gentler sex, but now the baths can accommodate the ladies in any number, where they will be perfectly secure.

The proprietors of the baths deserve to be successful in their undertaking, for they have shown spirit and enterprise, and have supplied what was much wanted. All the world knows a clean skin is essential to good health. So from a sanitary point of view the working classes now have a means of preserving their health.

It may be stated that the contractors, all from Elgin, were - Alexander Robertson, mason; James MacBeth, carpenter; George Ogilvie, slater; David Simpson, plasterer; Peter MacKenzie plumber; and James Johnston & Co. Newmill engineers.

The Highland Railway were not going to let this new attraction take business away from them. To this end on June 19th they announced Saturday excursions to Burghead and back during the "Bathing Season." The train left Elgin at 3pm in the afternoon, returning at 7pm. In an even-handed way the *Elgin Courant* encouraged its readership to make use of this new enterprise. *"This is a step in the right direction by the Highland Railway, and we trust these arrangements will be largely taken advantage of."*

Taking up the bathing metaphor, the Morayshire Railway Company throughout this period was struggling to keep its head above water. They had spent the first six months of 1874 either paying off or rescheduling promissory notes as they had fallen due. So much of the Board's time had been taken up doing this that they had done nothing to carry out the promised extension of the passenger platform at Lossiemouth.

With the first annual Elgin holiday on its way, the excursion committee too was having difficulties in encouraging people to take up what they had on offer. The proposed Highland Railway trips to Perth and Loch Ness were abandoned on June 26th, bringing this comment from the *Elgin Courant, "These cancellations are very much regretted."* Bad luck continued for the Highland Railway, with a derailment of one of their services between Orton station and the bridge over the River Spey on June 30th.

Unknown to all at this time, the country as a whole was entering what we would now describe as a period of recession. This may have explained why the family of the late James Grant required some cash urgently. With a large amount of the family capital still tied up in the Morayshire Railway, and that Company in no position to return any of this investment, what was to be done? Eyes were cast across the street from the Grant family home to the Station Hotel. It was decided by them to dispose of this business, which despite being one of the most modern and best fitted out hotels in the city of Elgin at this time, had never been the success that it should really have been. A buyer for this fine property was soon found and ownership transferred to the "Elgin Educational Institute," for the sum of £2400, that included all the fixtures and fittings. Since the hotel had cost James Grant the sum of £2020 in 1856, no great profit was won by his family in its disposal.

Recession did not stop the population of the area enjoying themselves. Despite people not coming forward to go on a trip to Perth or Loch Ness, the first Elgin Holiday held on July 6th 1874 was a great success. The Highland Railway issued 2000 tickets, an insignificant amount when measured against the 5650 sold by the Great North of Scotland Railway. Destinations on their system were diverse. The first away was an early morning excursion to Aberdeen, followed by another taking revellers plus the Elgin Brass Band to Banff. The greater proportion of holiday-makers, only travelled the short distance to Lossiemouth, though 50 of them continued on by sea from Lossiemouth to Aberdeen and Edinburgh. In an extensive article the *Elgin Courant* gave its readership an insight into the growth of Lossiemouth as a tourist resort. Since the Morayshire Railway features, I make no apology for giving an abridged version of this article. It appeared on July 17th 1874.

Lossiemouth and its Bathing Facilities

During the past few years no watering-place in the North has been advancing so steadily in every way as that of Lossiemouth, in which we include Branderburgh and Stotfield. The railway arrangements have evidently been made with a view to the convenience of all parties. Every morning just now a train leaves the Morayshire Station at Elgin at seven o'clock conveying a large number of bathers, who on their arrival at Lossiemouth station, may be seen sauntering through the streets with their bathing towels hanging over their shoulders on their way to either have a dip in the sea or in the swimming baths opened the other day. Most of the people who come down at this early time are those who are too busily employed during the day to leave their duties. The train stays at Lossiemouth about an hour and ten minutes, starting again for Elgin at 8.30am. The other trains of the day convey either those who through age or infirmity cannot rise early, or whose business occupation do not prevent them from going later.

Saturday afternoon is the time at which the services of the Railway Company are called most into requisition. The cheap fares enable the multitudes to avail themselves to the attraction of the Branderburgh Baths Company. Last Saturday the number of people from Elgin who visited it for the purpose of bathing was something enormous and Mr Stephen the keeper required to summon all his tact to attend to everybody. Not only, however has the baths attracted local people. Tourist and invalids in large numbers have also been visiting it and the seashore here. Lossiemouth may now we think fairly compete for the honour of being termed the "Brighton of the North."

It is now some five years, or thereby since the "pole" was established at Stotfield. This pole is placed on the rock furthest west of the range that runs out to sea some distance, and its intention, we believe, was to give the fair ones of creation an opportunity of monopolising, for four hours of the day, the ground for 300 yards east of it. Mindful of the ladies the authorities gave them undisputed sway of the bay of Stotfield from 10am until 2pm, the favourite of the ladies. We remember being awfully frightened by the awe-inspiring dignitary of the policeman, who used to parade the ground, for the purpose of seeing that the rules were strictly adhere to, and no "bad little boys," should disturb the serenity of the female bathers. His services are no longer required as the male sex seem well to know the rules of decency.

A practical result of the benefit of the baths and the fine bathing grounds of Lossiemouth is the building of villas for summer residence at Branderburgh and Stotfield. In the village of Stotfield we have those of Mrs Cameron, Elgin; Major Culbard, Elgin; and Mr Stables, Cawdor. Close to Branderburgh there are the beautiful marine residences of Captain Stewart, Elgin, and Wm. MacDonald, Esq., banker Elgin.

We are glad that such prosperity is exhibited at present, and we trust that matters may go on improving, and that we shall soon see Stotfield and Branderburgh as a large town of seaside villas.

The above article notes the arrival of the "well to do" of Elgin at Lossiemouth by their building of seaside dwellings for use in the summer season. They were not the only ones to benefit, as a number of the fishing families from Lossiemouth and Stotfield moved from their traditional thatched cottages to new stone-built and slate-roofed houses in Branderburgh. These fishermen's houses conversely at the time of the Elgin gentry's arrival for the summer season, would have been closed up and deserted, the fisher folk having travelled south tracking the annual herring migration round the coast of Britain. The Morayshire Railway Company paid dividend in kind by making the movement of the fishing fleets followers much easier than it had been pre-railway. The late Provost James Grant and his fellow Morayshire Railway shareholders had much to be proud of even though it did not reflect by a bit of extra monetary weight in their pockets.

Having learned the mistakes of the previous year, the second Elgin annual holiday was moved to nearer the beginning of August. Citizens who were not awake at five o'clock in the morning on Monday, August 10th soon were, with the passing of the Elgin Brass Band. They, having been asked to accompany the excursionist on their visit to Aberdeen, appeared to have quite literally "drummed up business," a task at which they were very successful, as 1000 people left for the Granite City on a 22 carriage train. Lossiemouth continued to attract the biggest share of visitors, as some 2747 headed for the seaside. This was despite the weather as it started to rain at 11am. It must have been standing room only in the Branderburgh Baths that day. The Elgin Brass Band did not allow the rain to dampen its musical output, arriving back with the drenched excursionists from Aberdeen at 11pm. On leaving the train they serenaded the passengers with "Auld Lang Syne" outside the gates of the Morayshire station. Still the crowd had not had enough and around 750 of the passengers marched with the band through the streets of Elgin to the local Drill Hall, the band playing a variety of appropriate marching tunes. Finally they closed their impromptu concert by playing "God save the Queen;" responded to by three hearty cheers from the crowd.

The autumn season passed, making no real impact on the day to day running of the Morayshire Railway Company.

The Board met on November 6th to prepare for the statutory ordinary meeting of the Company to be held on the 27th of the month. With its normal gathering place, the Elgin Station Hotel sold off this year's AGM took place in the Morayshire Company office. This office was the original station building of the Morayshire, which had been replaced by the new station built just before the GNSR took over the running of services. Changes in the track layout, following the opening of services to Aberdeen, meant that the position of the Elgin station had moved in a southern direction, leaving the Morayshire office situated in front of the new station building.

A small band of shareholders gathered to receive a report on the company's performance in the past year. Things did not get off to a good start. It appears that despite a "final" payment being made to the Highland Railway Company in the previous year, the Highlanders were not content to relinquish claims that they had against the Morayshire. The surplus of £2507 left after paying all expenses was lost after the Highland Railway Company made a demand and received payment from the Morayshire of £2051 for interest and various instalment payments linked with the Orton station claim. Things were getting worse for shareholders, apart for Mr Jamieson. The reason he had to feel cheerful was that the sum of £441 was paid over for legal and parliamentary expenses. I suspect that this would have been for the official requests made by the Morayshire to his firm of Grant and Jamieson. By adding what remained to last year's surplus the magnificent sum of £68 was carried forward to 1875.

Mr Urquhart, as Chairman, had obviously been a good apprentice and learned well his skills of optimism from James Grant. Notwithstanding a slight decrease in the amount of stones, lime, timber and general merchandise carried, the number of passengers had grown by a substantial 10,485, taking the total number of passengers carried in 1874 to a very healthy 129,693. He made much of this point in his report, along with settlement of the sums to the Highland Railway and legal expenses, seeing these as savings in interest payments over the coming years. The shareholders at the meeting seemed happy at this explanation and unanimously adopted his report. There was however one major thing that had been overlooked: the increase in platform length at Lossiemouth station promised at last year's meeting. This station was already working well past its capacity and many of the additional passengers using the system were travelling to the Branderburgh Baths. Money would have to be found to carry out the required improvement work before the Morayshire Company found itself with another fatal accident on its hands.

The year ended with some bad news and some good news. A young lad named James Dean from Rothes plead guilty to a charge of maliciously breaking telegraph insulators at Rothes on the 15th of December. He was sentenced to a fine of 15/- with the alternative of six days in prison. The good news was that Mr Peter Anderson platform, porter at Craigellachie, was presented with gifts by the people of the district on his promotion to railway guard on the Strathspey section. This ceremony was presided over by Mr Chambers, Stationmaster, and took place rather fittingly for gift-giving, on December 25th.

Severe frost with the occasional light snow flurries saw out most of the rest of 1874, before the New Year was greeted with one of the most terrific storms seen. The intense frost had powdered the lying snow into fine particles, which a hurricane wind swirled up into large drifts. On the evening of New Year's Day scarcely anyone could venture out into the streets. Many a celebration dinner had guests missing because of the harshness of the weather. Things became progressively worse as the day wore on with heavy snowfalls adding to the whiteout. The railway lines in all directions out of Elgin were soon choked with gigantic drifts which engines and ploughs were unable to clear. Elgin and many of its neighbouring towns found themselves isolated and cut off from the outside world.

By order of officials from the railway companies, the town crier was sent through the streets to collect men to help clear the lines. The Highland Railway already had one engine and plough derailed just east of Elgin at a place known as Barmuckity. Instead of following the line of the railway track, the engine had followed the route of the drift, finding itself twenty yards off the track. Fortunately for the crew it had come to a rest embedded in a bank, for had it travelled a few yards further on, it would have plunged over an embankment.

On the Lossiemouth Branch of the Morayshire Railway, things were battling along. The first service of the day to Lossiemouth reached its destination safely, but on its return it was required to stop at Greens of Draine to pick up passengers. The engine had difficulty in starting off and required the assistance of some surface men, who were travelling with the service, to dig parts of the line clear. The midday train completed the round trip with no problem. However, the service timed to depart Elgin at 3.30pm was kept waiting in the station for the late running Craigellachie train. This should have arrived in Elgin at 3.15pm, but was well over an hour late. During the delay large volumes of snow had gathered at the front of the Lossie engine, preventing it from moving off. Eventually through the hard work of men with the shovels, the train was able to set off for the coast. No doubt it would have reached there if it had continued to move at speed, but unfortunately, a halt had to be called at Linksfield to pick up a passenger. The wheels of the engine continually slipped on the snow and no progress was made, despite the heroic efforts of the surface men. Passengers on board had the choice of continuing their journey on foot or trying to find somewhere to shelter. Walking was difficult and dangerous, yet with the wind in their backs some of the Lossiemouth passengers accomplished the journey home. The prospect for those attempting to return to Elgin was not so good. Several tried, but facing the tempest full on made the trip impossible even for the strongest. One young lady nearly succumbed, but fortunately shelter was found for her in a nearby house. Comment was made in the press concerning the *"Christian attitude"* of the Linksfield blacksmith, who accommodated as many of the train's passengers as his house would hold. On the following day (Saturday 2nd) an engine was dispatched from Elgin to rescue the stranded train, and from that time onward this line remained clear.

The rest of the Morayshire network now remained free from snow drifts. The same could not be said for the Great North of Scotland network which was blocked in several places, with the 9.30am train from Elgin stuck in a tremendous drift between Drummuir and Auchindachy, where it remained until Sunday. The rest of the way to Aberdeen was obstructed at several places, in particular at Huntly and Insch, where the snow was nine feet in depth. In the other direction, the Strathspey fared no better and all attempts to clear their line were fruitless, until a strong thaw set in on the Sunday night.

The eventful start to 1875 was summed up by the *Elgin Courant*.

> The state of the weather prevents all out door amusements like curling and skating. Consequently, the great majority of people kept indoors to enjoy themselves as best they could, though some anticipated unions were rendered impossible. The only people who profited by the ill weather were the labourers in the town, for who there was a great demand to help the railway people in getting the lines clear. These men who are not commonly well off in the wintry season could in one sense be thankful for the ill wind which blew them if no other person some good.

The same paper was less than complimentary on January 8th about the Highland Railway. This company had made some changes in its timetables, but forgot to inform the general public, therefore passengers had turned up at Elgin station to find that the trains had already departed!

An important case in law for all railway companies concerning the way that they looked after goods in transit was heard at Elgin Sheriff Court on March 17th 1875. Maconnachie versus The Great North of Scotland Railway Company was brought about in consequence of barrels of fish being delivered late to market in Glasgow, with the result that they arrived spoiled. It was bad enough that it had happened once, but when other consignments were delayed, Mr Maconnachie decided to act. The first failure of service occurred on September 23rd 1873, when 18½ barrels of fresh fish were loaded onto the 8.40am service from Lossiemouth. They should have arrived in Glasgow by 7am the following day. It was noted and ticketed by the GNSR that that the consignment was perishable goods. Despite this branding, the cargo did not reach its destination until September 26th. I don't know who the lucky porter was that had the job of unloading the fish, but I reckon that a large percentage of the Glasgow cat population must have followed him home after he finished work.

Why the delay? Normal practice for the GNSR was to send goods for Glasgow via Aberdeen for transfer to the Caledonian Railway. Due to a blockage at Bridge of Dun, it was decided to send the fish along the Speyside line and thence onto the Highland network. The distance to Glasgow by this line was somewhat less than by Aberdeen. Difficulties occurred at Boat of Garten, where the wagon containing the fish was detained for some time, due according to the Highland Railway to a large volume of traffic using that route. It could not however explain why more recently dispatched goods, coming from its own system were sent south before the consignment of fish. Therefore, it would seem that the GNSR could shift blame to the Highland for the loss. In an unusual display of solidarity with its northern neighbour, both railway companies blamed Mr Maconnachie. He apparently committed an act of folly by sending his fish by "special risk forwarding notes." This meant that the goods were sent at a lower cost, because the carrier absolved himself of all liability for loss or damage. Both companies contended that to have any claim, the consignment should have been sent at passenger rates which gave protection, but at a higher cost of carriage. A similar set of circumstances occurred on December 29th 1873 that resulted in the loss of 29 barrels of fresh fish. After long hours of debate, Sheriff Substitute Smith found in favour of Mr Maconnachie, for the following reasons. The defenders failed to show that the delays incurred were reasonable or necessary and that although the problems at Boat of Garten were known about, Mr Maconnachie was not advised of this before handing over the fish. The sum of £78-9/- was awarded, along with costs to Mr Maconnachie.

As this judgement would have disastrous effects for any items sent by the railway outwith passenger rates, both railway companies contested the judgement and lodged an appeal.

More mundane matters occupied the Board of the Morayshire Railway, as it did its best to find sufficient funds to pay for the platform extension at Lossiemouth. They turned to the Great North for financial assistance, only to find the request refused on March 19th. Even so the Board felt that they could not put off this much-needed work and would go ahead with the changes.

Along with this refusal the GNSR informed the Morayshire that they wanted to increase the price of carrying coal from Aberdeen to Elgin to 4/- per ton. The rate charge for coal to be taken from Aberdeen to Lossiemouth was to be increased to 4/3 per ton. Understandably the Morayshire was very unhappy about this proposed rate change. A letter of protest was sent to the GNSR management that also contained the Morayshire's concerns about differences over the carrying of mails. I suspect the Board were unhappy with their percentage of the deal that they were getting. The Secretary of the Morayshire also sent a letter to Mr Mills asking for the provision of a suitable crane for Rothes.

John Charles, 7th Earl of Seafield, a major landowner in the area and Director of the Highland Railway, had by the end of March bought up £400 worth of promissory notes in the Morayshire Railway. This certainly was not out of any philanthropic feeling towards the Morayshire, but more out of the opportunity to cause difficulty to the Highland Railway's main rival, the Great North of Scotland Railway.

Friday, April 9th 1875 a slight accident occurred to the 4.35pm Keith service. As the train approached Craigellachie station, five wagons ran off the line, causing a five hour delay to the traffic on the system. The explanation given for the accident was the "too firm loading" of three wagons with heavy logs of wood. This derailment fortunately did not cause any damage to the permanent way.

May 25th saw some minor changes in the GNSR timetable, though it was Saturday, June 5th that the Elgin community were waiting for as this report from the *Elgin Courant* shows. *"As in former years the Morayshire Railway have arranged to run early trains to Lossiemouth for those who like to have an early dip in the briny before commencing a day's business. We feel sure that many this summer will take advantage of this very convenient arrangement. Particularly that there is now the additional inducement at the Branderburgh Baths which also deserve to be well patronised."*

Certainly, Saturday the 12th of June 1875 saw a large crowd of visitors from Elgin arrive in Lossiemouth. The weather looked dark and heavy, so a large number of the pleasure seekers took up the *Courant's* advice by having a refreshing plunge in the Branderburgh Baths. Invigorated by the swim, a number of the bath's patrons concluded the day by a sail from the harbour. A cargo of slender shabby-looking Shetland cattle attracted attention as they were unloaded. The animals appeared jaded and lame after their long sea journey, and concern for them was felt when it was believed that one of the beasts had fallen into the harbour. On closer inspection by the crowd, it turned out to be one of Lossiemouth's fishers who had fallen into the water. Confusion was caused because the crowd mistook his heavy wool jumper for the coat of an animal. No one attempted to rescue the son of the sea, and after he had floundered around for some time he managed to pull himself up onto the stern of his boat, where he sat to dry off.

Monday the 14th saw the railway traffic travel in the opposite direction, as the population of Lossiemouth had its first holiday of the year. A special train left the coast at 6.45am to allow the holiday-makers to catch the first train to Aberdeen. The service was well patronised, leaving only a few women, children and elderly to look after Lossiemouth. The *Elgin Courant*, ever watchful of the inhabitants of the coastal town, were pleased to report that there were few cases of intoxication in the returning evening crowd.

The June 18th Board meeting of the Morayshire brought good news to the Company. The Great North of Scotland Railway paid over an extra £40 per annum from the Royal Mail contract. This increase was to be back-dated to July 1st. A two ton crane was also to be provided by the GNSR for Rothes station at a cost of £24, which the Morayshire Board accepted. In view of the success at obtaining a crane at a reasonable cost, the Board decided to write to the Secretary of the GNSR concerning the construction of a gatekeeper's cottage at Linksfield. Meanwhile, Miss Isabella Cumming gatekeeper at Linkwood asked for a reduction in the rent for her garden, from £4 per year, to £1. The meeting agreed on a new rental sum of £2. Lastly the turntable at Dandaleith was to be disposed of, with the payment from the sale going to the Great North of Scotland Railway.

A special train consisting of 32 coaches left Elgin for Aberdeen at 5.30am on Monday, July 5th 1875, the first Elgin holiday of the year. The day was very warm, so many of the pleasure-seekers on this trip ended up at Aberdeen beach. The vast majority of the 5483 passengers carried by the GNSR that day went to Lossiemouth for their dip, taking advantage of both the sea and the baths.

The Highland Railway throughout the months of June and July seemed to be doing its best to upset its passengers in the Elgin and district area. The good people of Burghead were first to take umbrage. To try and compete for the Morayshire's bathing traffic, the Highland Railway had introduced a Saturday service from Elgin to Burghead at 6d per return trip from Elgin. If, though, you lived in Burghead and wished to come into Elgin on a Saturday, the Highland would charge you the sum of 1/2d for the privilege. This matter had been put before the Provost of Burghead, and his associated Bailies, who had protested to the Highland Railway. The Inverness company ignored the request for fair play, so the Provost of Burghead decided to form a company to run a bus between Burghead and Elgin during the summer season. The *Elgin Courant* added to the attack on the Highland Railway. *"To be fair with passengers and make money the Highland Railway Company should make the Elgin, Burghead, and Forres fare all one on a Saturday, thereby securing a great deal more passengers at no more expense to the railway."*

This paper went on in its attack of the Highland Railway, who were also failing to provide a decent service west from Elgin, compounding matters with late trains. *"At least twice within the last month, people attending Elgin market have left their business, in some cases unfinished and gone down to the station to return home by the 2.25pm service on the Highland Railway. They have been kept waiting for an hour on the platform, and the most aggravating part of the matter is that no reliable information is given by the company of when a train is expected. It would be easy to wire from Inverness on the progress of the train and when it would reach Elgin. People could then with confidence go about their business."*

September 3rd brought news of an additional source of traffic from Lossiemouth, with news that an English firm had leased the lead mines, with a view to putting them back into production.

A hint of a prospect of a dividend to the Morayshire Ordinary shareholders was suggested on September 10th. The Great North of Scotland Railway was paying 3% on its half year profits, which was up $1\frac{1}{2}\%$ on the corresponding period for the last year. On the same date, Mr Chalmers the Stationmaster at Craigellachie Junction was appointed Superintendent of the New Market in Aberdeen. Whilst all congratulated him on his advancement, both the Company and the people of the District were sorry to see him go. His replacement was Mr John Lyon, formerly head platform porter at Aberdeen.

The GNSR seemed keen to reinvest some of its profits in the business. September 14th 1875 saw them take delivery from the Metropolitan Railway Works of Birmingham of 13 new coaches. The vehicles consisted of four first, three composite, three third, and three brake thirds. They were expected to be used on the Aberdeen-Elgin service. The *Elgin Courant*, relished the prospect of their introduction and was lavish in its praise of the new vehicles. *"They are without exception, most substantial and elegantly built, and are somewhat higher on the springs than those presently used. At some $30\frac{1}{2}$ feet long, they are more commodious and much more airy and light than the stock in use at present. An improvement has also been made upon the brake power, which is fixed in the centre of the brake carriages."*

20 Amalgamation!

By the middle of September, it looked as if the long promised amalgamation between the Morayshire Railway and the Great North of Scotland Railway would soon take place. At a Director's meeting on September 17th 1875, it was noted that the accounts of the Company were with the GNSR's auditors, William Fletcher of London. This date also saw a member of the Grant family return to the Board of Directors of the Morayshire, with the appointment of Mr James Grant Glengrant. In addition, the Board also welcomed the completion of the much awaited platform extension at Lossiemouth and the approval for the provision of cattle pens at Rothes by Mr Milne of the GNSR. Sadly for the crossing keeper at Linksfield, there was no word of a cottage being built for him at this location.

The fame of the Morayshire Railway had spread to the land of George Stephenson. Alexander Urquhart, Chairman, intimated that he had received and accepted an invitation sent by the North Eastern Railway to attend the Railway Jubilee at Darlington on September the 27th and 28th. His colleagues on the Board were delighted to learn that the Morayshire Company was to be represented at this prestigious occasion and they wished the Chairman much joy on the trip.

On September 21st two calves tethered in a field next to the Rothes line broke loose and wandered through an open gate into the path of the 7.40am mixed train from Elgin to Craigellachie. Both animals belonging to Mr P Drumbreck of Rothes were killed, derailing two wagons in the process. The passengers were transferred to a van and went with the engine to Craigellachie. The train then returned with passengers for Elgin, and after the two wagons were replaced on the line, continued on to its destination, arriving some two hours late.

Mr Alexander Watt found himself, through no fault of his own, involved in an argument that would drag on for a number of years, over the provision of an organ for the Elgin Parish Church. It seems a lady, who described herself as a member of the established church, sent Mr Watt £11-14s-11d as a contribution towards the purchase of this instrument. He in turn passed the cash to Mr Gail of the British Linen Bank. The *Courant* reported on the transaction and decided that this donation warranted a full fund-raising campaign. *"This is a beginning which we hope will soon be followed by others. The sooner an organ is got the better, the harmonium good as it is, being merely a piping apology for the organ."* The same edition, of October 1st reported on an incident at Elgin station that resulted in a member of the public being injured. *"A rather serious accident occurred on Wednesday, September 29th to a man named John Smith, servant of Mr Sharp bank agent. He was driving coals from the Morayshire station when a lump of "Scotch" coal weighing fully 1 cwt, fell from the cart and struck him on the ankle fracturing the bone and dislocating the joint."*

The Highland Railway Company may, in the eyes of the people of the City of Elgin and surrounding area, have been giving a poor service, but it provided its shareholders with a good half-year dividend of $5\frac{1}{2}\%$.

Traffic increases on the Morayshire system had affected other stations as well as Lossiemouth. November 5th saw the start of substantial alterations at Rothes. The loading bank was to be moved to the site of the coal store, new cattle pens constructed and a gatekeeper's cottage built. The sum of £65 was to be supplied by the GNSR towards this project, with the Morayshire giving a further £100. The crossing keeper at Linksfield was also to have a house built for him. Both these cottages were to be of the same pattern as the one at Linkwood.

The rate for transportation of coal from Elgin to Aberdeen was to be increased to 5/6. On this occasion there was no protest from the Morayshire Board, as this price change brought the Morayshire and the GNSR into line with the amount charged by the Highland. Some of the money laid out on the improvements at Rothes could possibly be offset by the disposal of property at Lossiemouth. A Mr Thom was interested in doing a deal with the Morayshire.

Notes used by the Morayshire in its preparations for the 1875 shareholder's meeting reveal the amount due by the Company to the Executors of the late James Grant was a staggering £7922-15s-3d. The total track mileage of the Morayshire was also noted and given as 21 miles, 24 chains of which (18 miles 4 chains) were daily worked. The difference is accounted for by the Orton branch, which though no longer used, was still considered an asset by the Morayshire Directors.

The shareholders met together at the Morayshire offices at the end of November. They were eager I am sure to hear what their Company had been up to in the past year. Much was made by Chairman Urquhart of the continued growth in the Morayshire's business in particular the increase won from the GNSR in the share of the postal traffic. However he was still convinced that the Morayshire was not receiving all that it should for transporting the mail. Going on he informed the meeting that he intended to enter into separate negotiations with the Post Office at the end of the current contract period.

The next item discussed was the extension of Lossiemouth platform, which now allowed the largest trains to be handled in complete safety. A new ticket office had been built there, but as yet was not ready for use. When it was, the current building would be converted into a ladies waiting room. The poor condition of Elgin station was noted and described as *"dirty and dilapidated."* As this was fully the responsibility of the Great North of Scotland Railway Company, all Mr Urquhart could do was to continue to ask the Aberdeen people to put the Elgin buildings into proper order. In closing he made mention of the building work at Rothes and the construction of the gatekeeper's cottages. The cost of these last items had swallowed up all the Morayshire's surplus so no dividend was paid. Curiously, although the Company books had been in the hands of the GNSR auditors, no mention was made of the amalgamation of the two companies.

The Morayshire was not the only company to find trading difficult. At the meeting of the Directors of the Branderburgh Baths, the lack of money required explanation. Their Directors, claimed that their shortfall was because the establishment had not been well patronised in 1875. This fact seems to be contradicted in every other independent report. Anyway to solve this problem, the Directors intended, subject to shareholder's approval, to erect refreshment rooms in time for next season.

On Saturday, December 10th, a woman named Janet Sharp or Bowman was injured on the Morayshire Railway. This lady had been on her way to the Pansport area of Elgin, and to avoid water that had collected on the road under the railway bridge, took to the line for her journey. Being a little deaf, she did not hear the train coming up behind her, or the warning whistles being sounded by the driver. As there was insufficient distance to allow the train to come to a halt, part of the front end of the engine struck the woman's side, knocking her down the embankment. Fortunately, she had been walking at the edge of the track, otherwise she would have been killed. With a little assistance she was able to return to her home. Her condition worsened and she was later admitted to hospital. Thanks to medical attention, she did eventually fully recover.

The New Year of 1876 got off to an ignominious start with two rather gruesome and wholly preventable railway accidents. The first occurred on the evening of New Years Day. William Morrison, an unmarried man aged 40, employed by the Highland Railway as a surface man, decided to return home to Alves by walking along the railway line from Elgin. He left Elgin at 6.30pm, and nothing more was heard of him until the following day, when railway officials were contacted at Elgin and advised that a man's body was lying on the line, and could it please be moved before the 10.20am mail train ran over it. What was left of Morrison was located between the bridges at Bilbohall and Palmercross. The poor man had been decapitated and as the remains of his body had lain out on the line overnight, his corpse had been savaged by dogs from the neighbouring farms. It was surmised that he left Elgin station a little later than first thought and the 7.00pm train that leaves at that hour ran him down. Confirmation of this was made by the finding of the poor man's watch with its hands frozen at 7.20pm.

The second accident occurred on the Monday night, this time on the Morayshire Railway. Mr William Lawson, a clothier from Rothes was returning home from visiting friends in Lossiemouth on the 4.50pm train. When the service arrived at Birchfield, Mr Lawson thought it was Rothes and left the carriage. As the train departed, he perceived his mistake, and it is assumed that he intended to walk home, as he was seen at the crossing by a woman who put him on the road leading to Rothes. For some reason, he instead returned to the railway compounding his error by wandering along the line in the direction of Elgin. He walked for about three miles from Birchfield, where, opposite Whitewreath, the Elgin train due in at 6.30pm ran him down. The deceased had been accompanied by his son who, when changing trains at Elgin, went into a separate carriage from his father, and never missed him until Rothes. A search was at once instituted, and the body found. The late Mr Lawson was about sixty-five years of age.

Happier times were had at the Railway Employees Festival and Ball, held on January 18th at the Longmore Hall in Keith. This gathering saw railway staff from both the Great North of Scotland Railway and the Highland Railway come together, making the attendance at the 1876 event considerably larger than on previous years. The festival began at 8pm, by which time upwards of 400 people of all ages had assembled. Speeches, music, and an excellent tea were enjoyed by all. The Chairman of the event, J Geddes Brown Esq, gave an interesting portrayal of the coming of the railway on the town of Keith. We shall not go into it here as it is outside the scope of this book. The only item of interest to us is that mention is made of the intention to build a railway from Keith to Buckie. In connection to this proposed development, the harbour at Buckie was being very extensively increased in size. This combination would have an effect on the shipping using Lossiemouth.

On January 28th a promotion was given to Mr John Moir the guard on the Elgin to Lossiemouth line to the Elgin - Keith section of the GNSR main line. His place on the Lossiemouth service was taken by Mr William Ewan, platform porter at GNSR station.

Mr Maconnachie versus the GNSR and HR appeal case reached a conclusion on February 4th. Sheriff Bell had upheld the decision made by Sheriff Smith, that the railway companies were at fault. The Great North of Scotland Railway Company, being the receivers of the goods, were in the first instance found liable. They thereupon claimed relief against the Highland Railway Company, who were reluctant to settle. The matter was referred to the Railway Clearing House in London for a definitive judgement. They concluded that the Highland Railway was the more responsible for the delay and they had to pay three-fourths of the claim and expenses, with the Great North contributing the remaining quarter. Mr Maconnachie had won more than his money and costs back, with his action forcing the railway to take far better care of goods in transit.

As part of the main line to Aberdeen, the Rothes section of the Morayshire was creating business along its length. This was very welcome, as it gave more prospects of revenue to the Morayshire. On March 17th 1876, Mr John Duff Innkeeper at Lhanbryde, had entered into negotiations with Lord Seafield for a piece of land at Birnie to construct a distillery. He was the same Lord Seafield who had done so much to prevent the construction of the line back in 1860. So perhaps it may have been appropriate for him to thank the Morayshire Railway for the increase to his fortune by the extra rental he was now collecting, though I doubt that he did.

Back at Elgin in the Police Court on Saturday, March 18th, a farm servant from Croy was brought before Bailie Black on a charge of assault. This offence took place on the loading bank at Elgin's Morayshire Railway station. The defendant plead guilty to the charge of assaulting a young lad.

Neglectful of its care of Elgin station, the Great North of Scotland Railway was nonetheless spending heavily on its rolling stock. The *Aberdeen Free Press*, on March 28th gave details of a new accident van, which had just been fitted out by Mr William Cowan locomotive superintendent with a multiplicity of materials and tools for clearing the line of wreckage. An order for half a dozen new locomotives, designed by Mr Cowan and built by Neilson and Company Glasgow, was to arrive at the same time.

Each of these new machines weighed 65 tons, had a six wheel tender, a boiler pressure of 150 lbs, and had taken a leaf from the Morayshire's book by having covered cabs for the crew. Giving a positive comment on this last item the *Aberdeen Free Press* said: *"On wet and stormy days, when the men have to be exposed to the inclement weather, this protection will be found to be of greatest possible advantage."*

In early summer the "Committee for Annual Holiday Excursions" had an interview with the Highland Railway, and had arranged a special fast excursion on July 3rd, going to Inverness and Strathpeffer. The local press reported that the cost of the fares would be, *"Very moderate."*

Catering for prospective summer bathers, the refreshment rooms at the Branderburgh Baths had been completed and were ready for the forthcoming season.

Minor improvements were made to the facilities at Elgin station with the construction of a new departure platform.

The Highland Railway on the other hand still seemed to be able to irritate the people of Elgin, as this letter to the Editor of the *Courant* illustrates.

> Sir,
>
> I trust you will allow me through your paper to call attention of the people of Elgin to the way we are being used by the Highland Railway. It is surely a matter of some importance to the City that there should be an evening train from Forres. A traveller from the West Coast cannot reach Elgin in a day, but must stay at Forres. A tourist by the Caledonian canal is in the same fix as there is no train leaving Inverness after 5.30pm by which Elgin can be reached.
>
> This is not to the credit of Elgin, nor is it to the advantage of the town that a railway drawing from it a revenue of perhaps £20,000 a year should not have a room in which a gentleman can wait, and hardly a seat he can sit upon.
>
> I am yours etc.,

August 8th 1876 saw the second Elgin holiday of the year, and a mass of 6000 people left Elgin by train. The majority went to Lossiemouth, but 1500 "early risers" left at 5.30am for Aberdeen. Despite offering no reduced fares, a number of holiday-makers went by the Highland Railway to Nairn and Inverness.

Through September and October the prospects of increased business from the Lossiemouth lead mines continued to improve with on the 15th of September, a nugget of ore 1 cwt in weight being recovered. The new operators were confident that they had struck the right vein and were now tunnelling in a landward direction, opposite to the previous operators who had been mining in a seaward direction. The gentleman leaseholders arrived in Lossiemouth from London on October 20th, to oversee the sinking of a new shaft, and make arrangements for miners arriving from the south.

The Morayshire Directors had had a very relaxing year. They did not hold a meeting until November 3rd, leaving poor old Alex Watt the Secretary to look after the day-to-day requirements of the Company. Matters attended to at this first meeting of the year were to make arrangements for the forthcoming AGM. It appears that there had been no contact from the GNSR regarding amalgamation with the Morayshire. No record exists concerning the conclusions of William Fletcher, following his investigation of the Morayshire's Account Books. I assume they must have been returned to the Morayshire, with a "not interested" letter at sometime in the period between the 1875 AGM and September 30th 1876.

Other matters now seemed to be engaging the minds of the Morayshire Directors, with the possible return to full use of the Orton Branch. Several of the leading citizens in the towns of Buckie and Keith had been looking to the possibility of connecting these two places by rail. Mr Urquhart, Chairman of the Morayshire, considered it in the best interest of the Buckie people to first take their proposed line eastward through Cullen to connect with the railway at Portsoy. The benefit to the Morayshire would come from the westward course of the railway from Buckie. This line was to avoid Keith, travelling instead to Fochabers to connect with the rest of the rail network at Orton Junction. Chairman Urquhart considered, and was quite correct in the fact, that this route would give the town of Buckie the shortest way to Perth at 139³/₄ miles. The alternative distances using the other railways were, by Aberdeen 155¹/₄ miles, through Forres at 161¹/₂, along the coast through Portsoy 161³/₄ miles, and via Keith and Speyside 148¹/₂. As a good Victorian businessman, he reckoned time was as good as money. The prospect of saving 8³/₄ miles on a journey south would make his proposal of a connection at Orton too good to turn down. Therefore he intended to make this proposition one of the main items for comment at the 1876 AGM.

The Annual Meeting took place at the Company offices on Friday, November 24th. Again the Chairman could report on a healthy increase in business for the Company. Passenger revenue was up by £71-10/-, general goods by £200, minerals by £299 and the mail service contract was returning £414 per year. Enthused by the good news, he closed this section of his report with these words. *"By and by the way for payment of a much longed for dividend is being opened."* Mr Urquhart then moved on to the prospect of a return to service of the Orton branch, thereby not allowing anyone the opportunity to ask the embarrassing question as to when they would have a return from their long held investment in the Morayshire. Provost James Grant's spirit must have been with him that day, for the assembled crowd was whipped up into a frenzy of cheers and applause by the thought of a railway from Buckie using the Morayshire to reach the markets of the South. Mr Urquhart's report was unanimously agreed to. The only dissenting voice heard that day was from a Reverend Mackie, who wished to draw attention to the fact that in the summer months the early morning bathing train rarely if ever left Elgin at the advertised time. In reply Chairman Urquhart assured him that the Directors would see that this matter of complaint was remedied.

The run-up to Christmas began with a great storm starting on Thursday, December 21st, which continued without a break over the next four days. At Linkwood the deep cutting on the Morayshire line to Rothes soon filled with snow, and despite much effort was not cleared until the afternoon of Friday 22nd. The first train to use the line after clearance was the 1.50pm to Keith which reached its destination more or less at its advertised time. The service coming in the opposite direction was not so fortunate; large drifts of snow at Drummuir much delayed its progress. Upon reaching Craigellachie Junction, it was decided that an attempt to take the train through the Glen of Rothes would meet with failure so the service was terminated. No further trains reached Elgin until late on Saturday.

The conditions on the railway however were slight in comparison to those at sea. Terrible losses of both life and vessels were reported between Montrose and Wick, with some 50 ships being wrecked. The boats involved for the most part seemed to have come from the Baltic ports. At Lossiemouth there was an investigation under way into the reason for the failure of the lifeboat to be launched when a ship from the port of Danzig was in trouble just off the west beach. The lifeboat crew had made ready to take to the waves, but were stopped from going to sea by the womenfolk of the town. For days afterwards the tide brought in the bodies of the poor foreign sailors.

By Boxing Day, Tuesday 26th, all traces of snow had disappeared from the lower reaches of Moray. Winter though had not fully loosened its grip as the line beyond Craigellachie started to become covered with drifts, the section between Elgin and Craigellachie succumbing later in the day, requiring attention from railway staff to allow the 3.15pm service to pass. Traffic along Speyside was suspended by a blockage and did not recommence until later in the week.

Their new relaxed style of management seemed to suit the Directors of the Morayshire, and they wished it to continue in 1877. On January 4th and 5th when the combined sum of £1500 fell due for payment to the family of James Grant. The Directors left the work of rescheduling this payment to Alex Watt. He also sorted out a request from Captain Dunbar to heighten the platform at Birchfield, and arranged repainting of Dandaleith station. The latter would cost the Morayshire the sum of £20-6s-7d.

The Railway Servant's Ball at Keith, had now become a permanent and much anticipated social event. On January 12th some 500 Ladies and Gentleman of the Morayshire, Highland and Great North railway companies came together for a meal and a dance, prefaced by speeches from assorted local, Big Wigs.

Glenlossie distillery started production in the middle of February and although some distance from the Morayshire railway station of Longmorn, this enterprise by John Duff of Lhanbryde looked set to add to the business of the railway company. At the same time demands to improve the service offered to travellers between Elgin and Boat of Garten were also being made. The Morayshire felt that it was losing out when passengers and goods went south, as most of this traffic preferred to use the Highland Railway to reach Perth. The Great North remained to be convinced of this argument even though they would benefit from mileage charges between Craigellachie and Boat of Garten.

Mrs Julia Matilda Grant, James Grant's widow, again found herself without any repayment when another promissory note for £1500 fell due on April 2nd 1877. Mr Watt rescheduled the payment date for one year hence.

The death of another of the original Directors of the Morayshire Railway also occurred on April 2nd. Mr William Topp of Ashgrove who been in a rather delicate state of health for some time died aged 70 at home. He had spend 17 years as first Secretary to then Governor of the Gold Coast in Africa. Engaged in trade sending products back to London, Mr Topp had a strong abhorrence of the slave trade being carried out by Arab and Portuguese merchants. At a local level he kept his distance from the strife of Parliamentary and local elections, but did take a lively interest in all matters pertaining to the City, hence his involvement with the Morayshire Railway. Besides this he was also a Justice of the Peace and held Directorships of Gray's Hospital and the Elgin Literary and Scientific Association.

On the afternoon of Tuesday, April 3rd, the 4.30pm train from Lossiemouth ploughed into the gates at the Pinefield level crossing. *"The ironwork was much bent, and the gates otherwise considerably damaged."* (*Elgin Courant*) The gatekeeper, who was sitting in his home when the train approached, claimed that he did not hear it or the sound of the whistle, because his front door had closed.

Still remaining to be convinced about benefiting the Morayshire Railway by improving services on the Speyside line, the Great North of Scotland Railway did decide that an evening train from Elgin would be a good thing with this service leaving Elgin at 7.00pm and Keith at 7.35pm. In the other direction, a train left the Granite City at 5.15pm travelling through to Elgin, giving the city's business community a better communication. This adjustment was very much appreciated according to reports in the *Elgin Courant*. The paper also used the announcement of this change to criticise the poor service provided by the Highland Railway. *"It is however very awkward that the last train from Inverness which reaches any place in the east leaves the Highland capital so early as 3.30pm."*

Upcountry, the Morayshire was involved in yet another fatal accident. This happened on Wednesday, June 27th, when the 5pm train was heading from Elgin towards Rothes. James Anderson, age 72, of Fevar Rothes had been feeding a calf inside the railway fence. The animal wandered off as the train approached and Mr Anderson ran after it in an attempt to drive it off the track. The beast was saved, but the buffer beam of the engine caught Mr Anderson, knocking him down the embankment. Some people working in a nearby field ran to render assistance - too late however, as the impact had instantaneously killed him, leaving a widow and a grown-up family to mourn his passing.

Fine weather greeted the Elgin Holiday on July 2nd 1877. Arrangements for the day followed much the same pattern of past years. A special excursion to Aberdeen saw 1500 people travel to the Granite City.

Traffic on the line to Lossiemouth was also heavy, with a 20 coach train taking almost 2000 people to the seaside. The Highland Railway did not miss out; some 2289 travellers headed west to Inverness and on by steamer to the Falls of Foyer. All trains on both systems ran to time and all excursionists returned home safely.

Summer travel did not just see people depart Elgin. The city was the chosen destination of the Great North of Scotland Locomotive Employees. Some 900 workers, accompanied by their wives and sweethearts, came to Elgin the following Saturday. On arrival, the visitors formed up into a procession headed by the Bon Accord Brass Band for the walk to the High Street where a general break-up took place as visitors set off to discover the delights of Elgin, including a cricket match to be played in the afternoon between the clubs of Elgin and Aberdeen. Disappointingly the match was abandoned when rain stopped play. The conduct of the visitors impressed the *Elgin Courant* who thought, *"The whole company was well behaved and orderly."*

An unusual display of compassion was witnessed at Elgin Sheriff Court on July 31st. In the dock was a boy named Andrew Forsyth on a charge of breaking telegraph insulators on the Lossiemouth railway line, a charge to which he plead guilty. The Procurator Fiscal stated that it had become known to him that the boy's home circumstances were most unfortunate, being debarred from the family home by his father. The Fiscal went on to state that today was the harvest market day and if the boy were to receive an admonishment, he might obtain a situation *"and get in the way of doing well."* Sheriff Smith concurred with this view and duly admonished the lad.

By August 17th the preparations for the second Elgin holiday of the year were well-advanced. The *Courant* advised that the Highland Railway intended to run an excursion to Strathpeffer at the cost of 3/- first class and 2/- second class, and possibly even lower rates than that. The Great North gave notice that it was to start its excursion early on the day to enable visitors to be in Aberdeen for 9am. The article went on to hope for fine weather.

On the actual day, Monday the 20th it rained heavily and continued to do so until midday. This affected the number of people travelling to Aberdeen, but the opportunity to travel to Strathpeffer still attracted large numbers. In the afternoon the sun came out, so business to Lossiemouth picked up considerably, which benefited the Morayshire.

September brought the rich and famous to Elgin when Her Majesty Queen Victoria passed through on her way to the west coast on Wednesday 12th September 1877. The local press reported that the Queen's journey was by *"secret arrangement,"* so no cheering crowds or waiting dignitaries impeded her progress. A similar circumstance occurred on her return journey, on the Tuesday, September 18th. On this occasion the Royal train only made two stops, one at Keith, for the exchange of engines from the Highland Railway to the Great North Scotland Railway, the other at Dyce to take on water which allowed this section of the journey to run non-stop all the way back to Ballater.

Alexander Graham Bell did linger a while in Elgin, returning on September 28th to the school at which he used to teach, Weston House College. The establishment had by this time amalgamated with the Elgin Education Institute and relocated, as stated earlier, to the former Morayshire Station Hotel at the bottom of Moss Street. It is not recorded what this eminent gentleman thought of these new premises.

Sea communication between Lossiemouth and Newcastle was bettered on October 9th 1877 when a handsome new cargo vessel the "Mignonette" began operations. This was a bit of a double-edged sword to the Morayshire, as it was specifically designed to carry coal. Drawing only 8 to 9 feet of water, it could enter Lossie harbour at all states of the tide. Double holds allowed rapid discharge of its cargo which, with two teams of men at work, could unload its 200 tons of coal in 24 hours. The first consignment was destined for James Johnston, Newmill, Elgin. Business was put the Morayshire's way by transporting the shipment, but it undercut the price being charged by the railway companies for bringing coal north. Another order had already been placed by a different Elgin business for a full load of 200 tons of coal. The *Courant,* was very sympathetic towards the service provided by the vessel's owners *"There will be plenty more trade to make this enterprise pay."*

Business was also looking up for Glengrant distillery, with major improvements having just taken production up to 4000 barrels per week. Shipment of this finished product would without doubt add to the profits of the Morayshire Railway.

Discussion for the agenda of the forthcoming shareholder's meeting took place on November 9th. Due to the easy style of management now being operated by the Morayshire Directors, this was the first time in 1877 that they had all met together. Alex Watt, the Secretary again throughout all this time had been looking after the day to day affairs of the Company. As the poor gatekeepers at Linksfield and Green Street Rothes continued to wait, plans for their houses were brought before this meeting. The Directors agreed that building should begin, with the stipulation that the cottages be ready for occupation by Whitsunday 1878. Alex Watt then went on to detail the items sorted out by him in the previous few months. A new tenant Mrs Knight took up a three year lease on the Station Hotel in Lossiemouth on Whitsunday 1877. Other applications for railway property had come from Mr Sime, who wished a coal shed at Lossiemouth, and from Mr Petrie acting on behalf of a Mr Muir coal merchant Stirling who also required premises to begin trading in the Lossiemouth area. The whisky trade must have been enjoying an increase in demand for its product, as following on from the note of increase in capacity at Glengrant, the new distillery at Glenlossie was making such extensive demands on the Morayshire Railway that facilities at Longmorn station had and were continuing to be extended and improved.

The 25th Annual General Meeting of the Morayshire Railway Company was held on November 27th. While delighted that the Morayshire had reached its quarter century, the Chairman was saddened that none of the gentlemen who had set up the enterprise had survived to be present at the 1877 meeting. Mention was made by Mr Urquhart of the part played by the late Mr Topp in the growth of the Morayshire.

On to business proper, to which the Chairman was happy to report that all departments of the railway were seeing increases and after meeting all expenses the Company had a surplus of £116-10s-10¾d. This sum was to be carried over to next year. Only the passenger traffic, though £90 more than 1876, was not quite what had been expected, and this disappointment was put down to cold and wet weather through the summer bathing season. Improvement in the supply of water at Lossiemouth was expected to encourage more of Elgin's nouveau riche to build summer houses in the coastal town, which they hoped would negate the effect of future poor summer weather. More important perhaps than the increase in business was the hard work undertaken in the most part by Alex Watt to pay off outstanding debts owed by the Company. This was anticipated to have a significant effect in the next few years at reducing ongoing interest payments that continued to cripple the Morayshire. It was expected that by November 1878 the Morayshire would be free of all debt to the Highland Railway Company. The meeting of shareholders concluded on this happy note. It may have been their "silver anniversary" but with the cash surplus carried over there was no silver to jingle in the shareholder's pockets.

The Directors then had a meeting at which financial matters figured largely. An offer had been made from a Mr Cruickshank of Coleburn to discharge all future rent from the Morayshire to him for a payment of £80. This claim came as a shock to the Directors, as they were not aware that they were paying rent to him. Before discussion went any further with this party, the Directors wanted to see the lease and agreement that this gentleman claimed he held with the Company. Use of the Morayshire's reserve fund was sanctioned for two payments. The first was for £633-15s-5d to pay off a claim from Lord Seafield which dated back to September 30th 1868. The second, £1000, paid to reduce the principal sum of debit owed to the estate of the late James Grant, which must have come as welcome relief to the former Provost's widow. The final item discussed was a request for a store at Elgin station for a Mr Ogilvie, which was left in the hands of the Chairman and Secretary to sort out.

Various locations were about to be used to test the new telephone invention of Elgin's recent visitor Alexander Graham Bell. The first was on December 7th when a set apparatus was demonstrated at the Elgin High Church. A more practical application took place on the 11th, when a telephone was connected between the signal boxes on the Highland Railway at Inverness and Elgin. *"Despite unfavourable weather, the sound of speaking and singing could be heard with remarkable clarity,"* commented the *Elgin Courant*. In amongst this use of new technology, the Morayshire played a very small and possibly tenuous part. The location was the Station Hotel at Lossiemouth, owned by the Company and leased to Mrs Knight. On the same day as the Highland had its trial, two telephones were set up between the bar and one of the rooms. Several songs were transmitted by various ladies and gentlemen. After this there was what is possibly the first use in the area of the telephone for commercial purposes as the *Courant* illustrates. *"Several orders for liquor were also transmitted and executed with Mrs Knights well known promptitude."* The paper then goes on to report that later that evening a telephone was connected between the Hotel and the Post Office, and a number of successful experiments were carried out. The only thing that the press fails to disclose is whether liquor was ordered and supplied to the Post Office!

Unlike previous winters, the months of December 1877 and January 1878 caused no problems to the services on Morayshire Railway.

Prosperity and employment were looked forward to in Lossiemouth at the beginning of February. Captain Dunbar transferred the lease of the lead mines for a period of 20 years to a new company based in London. By the end of April it was expected that between 150 and 200 people would be employed at this enterprise. The quality of the ore being extracted was very high with the deposits extending for some distance. The local press were encouraged by this development. *"Mineral resources are the very thing we need to move the trade of this district to prosperity."* In the interim until transportation of ore became a reality, the Morayshire Railway went about its business in a workmanlike way.

The Highland Railway let it be known on May 24th 1878 that it intended to run an excursion to Dunrobin Castle on this year's Elgin holiday. The excursion committee expected a large turnout, as this was the first time in nine years that this destination had been offered.

The herring season was in full swing throughout May and the landings at Lossiemouth were good, if somewhat handicapped by the inability of the Morayshire and Great North of Scotland Railway to cope with the demand. If you were in the fish business at Lossiemouth at this time, life could become very "exciting," as this witness describes what he calls a, *"raid on the Lossiemouth Railway."*

> Having had occasion to be at the Railway station, Lossiemouth, on Friday the 24th inst., I was very much struck to see the quantity of fish lying to go away to the Southern markets, and nothing to send them in - not one wagon at the station. There was about five hundred barrels and boxes of fresh herrings driven up to the bank in the expectation of wagons arriving with the twelve train, and you may consider the anxiety of every curer at the station when the approach of the train was heard. I am sure there were about one hundred men and women collected on the platform to put the fish into the wagons should any come. As I understand it, the regulations were that every man had a chance alike, and the strongest would get the most into the wagons. One large curer had all his employees waiting, men and women, for the train, and they were not a few; and he was at the same time in Elgin himself making inquiry for wagons. Accordingly the train arrived, and the cry was, There are three wagons, very good. Then the stir commenced, every man doing his best, and the women keeping up their side, for they don't like to be beaten. But then came a great obstacle in the way. The large curer mentioned claimed two of the wagons, and said he bought them for himself, and he would not allow anyone to put fish into them but himself. What was to be done? Just one wagon left to seven curers, and our large friend had the best chance of it.

While his men were loading the two wagons that he bought, others in his employment were putting fish into the one wagon that was common property as busily as they could. Soon it was loaded, and all it could take of the fish was never missed from the loading bank. What was to be done now? Another wagon was extemporised, and before five minutes it was full also. Then the wagons were booked, some for Liverpool, and some for Manchester, and off went the train leaving the senders to wait the results, which I have heard since that time were very bad. Some of the wagons went wrong, and the fish were lost. I don't know whom the loss will fall on - whether on the railway company or the sender; but I think there should be more order at this station, and give every man fair play, not to let one curer get away all his fish, and plenty time to do everything right, while others did not know what to do. The Stationmaster had no control.

Obviously the lessons of the Maconnachie case had been forgotten and the ability of the Morayshire to look after its customers was woefully lacking.

Other forms of transport were becoming envious of the business going to the railway companies and had decided to try and take a share of the market. Therefore on June 7th the Moray Firth Steamship Company decided to enter the passenger excursion market. They let it be known that they too would be offering a day trip to Dunrobin Castle in competition with the Highland Railway's trip of July 1st. To encourage passengers they claimed that their outing would only take three hours, which was quicker than by rail.

The Morayshire Railway Company entered the fray by actively canvassing for the excursionist's pennies. This broke the long-standing gentleman's agreement between the Highland and the GNSR, and for its part the *Elgin Courant*, relished this plethora of choices. *"The terms being offered by the [Highland] Railway Company should make the trip to Dunrobin a successful one. The Elgin Brass Band will accompany the excursionists. In addition, there will also be a trip by steamer from Lossiemouth to Golspie, onward to Dunrobin and the pleasure of a short sea trip has its attractions. The Morayshire Railway also offers good attractions to pleasure seekers. A finer place for a splendid holiday could not be found than Speyside, which at this season of the year is at its best."*

Events on July 1st disrupted all the careful planning of the Moray Firth Steamship Company. The weather though it threatened rain in the morning turned out fine, with a cooling breeze. At Lossiemouth the "breeze" whipped the sea up to such an extent that it was impossible for the steamship to enter the harbour, leaving 200 disappointed passengers at Lossiemouth. Had they not been tempted away, they could have travelled with the mere 200 patrons carried to the North by the Highland. The outright winner on the day was the Morayshire. Not only had they benefited by taking the majority of prospective passengers for the sea trip to Lossiemouth, they carried just under 3000 passengers to various destinations on its system.

In a possible attempt to win passengers for the Elgin cattle show on July 17th, the Highland Railway announced cheap excursion fares into the City that day, but this was quickly followed by a similar offer from the Great North of Scotland Railway.

Disappointment was expressed on July 19th at the abandonment of a new destination for the second Elgin holiday of the year in August. It had been hoped to visit Dundee to allow the people of Elgin and District to marvel at the latest engineering triumph, the Tay Bridge. The North British Railway, perhaps to raise revenue to pay for this new link in their network, demanded a large payment to take a train south from Aberdeen and a minimum number of passengers to travel on it. Fares would have had to be set at 13/6 for first class and 7/- for second class, a price that the excursion committee felt would detract rather than attract the 3000 passengers that the NBR were demanding travel on the outing. Under these circumstances, it was decided that Aberdeen would once again suffice as a destination for Elgin folk.

The Highland Railway offered not only a chance to travel to Inverness at excursion rates, but extended the offer allowing passengers to travel on by steamer to admire the falls of Foyers. This combined piece of marketing attracted 1800 passengers on August 5th, but did not affect the Morayshire and Great North, who managed to attract 4500 passengers. Twenty-six carriages were required on the long distant trip to Aberdeen to carry 1500 patrons. The remainder of the excursionists stayed within the Morayshire network, with Lossiemouth being the firm favourite.

On August 20th 1878 the service between Keith and Elgin was interrupted for a short period following a derailment at Craigellachie. A locomotive was running round its train in preparation for a journey up Speyside, when the timbers under a set of points gave way, dropping the engine onto the ballast.

September saw the minds of the citizens of Elgin return to the matter of the Tay Bridge. The business community were pressing the Great North of Scotland Railway to use this bridge to speed up and improve its southern connections. Chief among these was one of Elgin's former Provosts Alex Cameron. He wasted no time in informing the Chairman of the GNSR of his displeasure in the lack of good connections with Edinburgh, or for that matter Aberdeen.

My Dear Sir,

There are at present five trains daily between Aberdeen and Elgin, which stop at every roadside station, thus consuming upwards of four hours for the journey. The irritation caused to through travellers by these constant stoppages has to a great extent killed through traffic between Aberdeen and Elgin. People living here, avoid going to Aberdeen, except upon very urgent business, and no person intending to go to Edinburgh ever avails himself of the Aberdeen route.

If your board would run one train per day each way in connection with the fast Tay bridge trains, I am satisfied you would not only confer a great boon to the travelling public between Aberdeen and Elgin, but also benefit the company you represent.

Mr Leslie replied on September 19th, that as the faster south trains had only come into operation two months previously, the GNSR considered it too early to change its service. Mr Milne the manager of the company was to investigate the matter, and if appropriate would sanction any change required.

Far from impressed with the reply Mr Cameron sent another letter in an attempt to persuade the GNSR into giving the people of Elgin good connections with the south.

Dear Sir,

I am quite aware that it is only recently, since the opening of the Tay Bridge, that trains have been accelerated, but the sooner that advantage is taken of this improvement, the better it will be for the people in the north, as well as the GNSR.

Considerable traffic from Speyside, all of which goes by Boat of Garten, would if you put on a proper service attract traffic to Aberdeen. I trust you will urge the General Manager to take this matter up with as little delay as possible.

For a company that held its first meeting of 1878 on October 4th, the Morayshire hardly seemed placed to be a champion of improving services, anyway they decided to enter this affray on Mr Cameron's side and wrote to the Great North of Scotland Railway asking for one express train per day to make a connection with the NBR's Tay bridge services. It was also decision time for the Morayshire and one of its prominent shareholders concerning outstanding debts. Another repayment of £1052-15s-3d was given to Mrs Grant, taking the amount owing to the estate of James Grant down to £6922-15s-3d. Though long overdue, this repayment was rather remarkable when considered against the business climate of that time. Many firms were finding it a struggle to operate or even continue to trade, for instance, the City of Glasgow Bank, an organisation which in the past had lent money to the Morayshire, and after forcing repayment refused to lend any more sums to the railway company because it considered it a bad risk. The tables had now turned, and as the Morayshire found itself in a stronger trading position better able to pay its creditors, the City of Glasgow Bank found itself facing liquidation. This turn of events was to have some interesting outcomes to the Morayshire and the people and businesses the railway company served.

On the evening of Wednesday, November 20th, pointsman John Webster had been assisting in shunting operations following the arrival of a train at 6.30pm; for some reason he climbed onto a wagon which the shunting engine met heavily. This caused Webster to fall between the wagon and the engine, where two of the locomotive's wheels passed over his left leg, mutilating it frightfully. The unfortunate man was dragged seventeen yards along the line before he was seen by his fellow workmen. Medical aid was promptly in attendance and he was conveyed to Dr Gray's Hospital where the smashed limb was amputated. Sadly he only survived for a few hours, the combined effect of shock and blood loss causing his death. A waste of life, made more so because the individual was only 21 years old.

The Annual General Meeting of the Morayshire took place on November 29th 1878, at the Company offices. Despite difficult trading conditions, revenue had continued to increase, and this had enabled the Morayshire to undertake alterations and extensions at various stations where extra traffic had required improved facilities. In addition some of these costs were recouped from higher rental charges for the improved facilities. The only noticeable decrease in traffic on the Morayshire was in the carriage of building materials, but Mr Urquhart the Chairman did not expect this to last. He was confident that the increase in the price of granite would see a demand from Aberdeen for lower cost freestone that the Elgin quarry industry could supply and the Morayshire would transport. Playing to the demand of the moment, Mr Urquhart then went on to criticise the Great North of Scotland's reluctance to speed up connections with south trains using the Tay Bridge. *"It is our opinion that it would greatly benefit both them and us, as well as give great satisfaction to the general public by running one express train a day in connection with the North British through Dundee to Edinburgh via the Tay Bridge."* These remarks brought forth a burst of applause. Despite this all round improvement, after paying all its interest charges the Company was left with a balance of £1976-1/-. No payment was to be made to ordinary shareholders as Chairman Urquhart and his Board were determined to rid the company of its floating debt. The meeting supported the Chairman and Board in these aims.

Mr Jamieson, one of the Board members then gave notice of the intention of the Morayshire Railway Company to follow the example of the GNSR and reduce the composition of the Board of Directors, to seven. The GNSR had reduced the number of their Directors in October by two. This matter concluded the public meeting, but the Directors had other business to discuss.

There was to be a determined effort to put the Morayshire Board back on a more professional footing; it was agreed that from the commencement of 1879 the Directors would meet on the 1st Friday of each month. Attempts were also to be made to improve relations between the GNSR and the Morayshire, not just to improve traffic management, but also to clear the way for the two companies becoming one. To this end, two places on the Morayshire Board were offered to the Great North Board. This proposal was turned down by the Aberdeen Company. Increase in workload caused by their cutback in Director numbers was cited by the GNSR, claiming that it would be inconvenient for any of their Directors to travel to Elgin to attend meetings

Thoughts also turned to the Highland Capital with the news that the final instalment of the Orton station claim was paid on November 30th 1878. Dealings with the Highland Railway had in the past been fraught with difficulty. To verify that the Morayshire was free of its Highland burden, the Chairman had travelled to Inverness to confirm complete settlement of the claim. The Highland Railway as usual was not forthcoming with confirmation of a settlement. As we know, the interchange point of Orton station caused much trouble. Now that the line between Orton and Rothes was to all effect abandoned, it was not a complete financial loss to the Morayshire, as it did generate a payment of £200 each year from the GNSR.

Reports in the *Elgin Courant* of December 3rd gave notice that the Great North of Scotland Railway was having difficulty in paying its way in the economic climate of 1878. With the number of Directors trimmed back, it was the turn of the workforce to make a sacrifice for the good of their railway company. From December 16th 1878 wages of surfacemen, porters and guards were to be reduced by between 1/- and 6d per week.

Heavy snow began to fall in mid December with 10 to 12 inches lying in the lowland parts of Moray and twice that amount on Speyside. Road traffic was stopped and the folk of Elgin and other towns found it difficult to go about their business. The rail network, with no wind causing drifting, handled this difficult situation well with trains running to time.

The day before Christmas, news was given of a former friend, turned adversary of the Morayshire Railway. Mr Hendry Inglis W S of Edinburgh found himself in Duke Street Prison Glasgow. This gentleman, who had been one of the first directors of the Morayshire before becoming involved with the I&AJR, had gone on to become a Director of the City of Glasgow Bank. The resulting failure of this institution had been the catalyst that caused Mr Inglis' present predicament.

On this Tuesday morning, a marked deterioration in the weather conditions began, with the snow now accompanied by gales. A team of men left by railway engine to set about clearing the line between Elgin and Craigellachie. They had not travelled far before they met a series of big drifts on the line at a place called Whitewreath. Cutting of the snow was started and slow progress was made up the Glen of Rothes, where as darkness fell the day's operations had to be concluded. Work was recommenced at first light on Christmas Day, but there had been considerable drifting throughout the night, and the line that had been cleared on the Tuesday was again covered over. During the day a slight thaw set in, aiding the workmen in their task allowing Craigellachie to be reached before darkness fell and, as a crew had also been working from Keith to Craigellachie, services were able to recommence. The following day trains were running the whole distance between Aberdeen and Elgin, bringing delayed mails and Aberdeen newspapers to the town. Temperatures again began to fall with severe frost occurring. The newspapers asked their readership if anyone could remember a previous period of such prolonged bad weather. The *Courant* rather uncharacteristically praised the Highland Railway, whose services had continued to run. This in the opinion of the paper was because the Inverness company had equipped itself with *"magnificent snowploughs,"* which when coupled up with three locomotives kept their lines operating in the most difficult conditions.

The year ended on a disconsolate note for the Branderburgh Baths Company, who on December 31st let it be known that they would cease to trade on January 6th 1879. This company was another casualty of the City of Glasgow Bank collapse. Would the loss of this facility cause a reduction in the number of travellers on the Morayshire Railway?

21 A SUCCESSFUL CONCLUSION

A combination of bad weather and the proximity of the festive season saw the Morayshire Board's intention to meet on the first Friday of each month founder at the first attempt. Convening in February, confirmation was noted in the Company Minute Book that on December 10th 1878, full and final settlement on the Orton claim had been made to the Highland Railway. It was not all good news though. On the 7th, a demand arrived for the sum of £3500 from the executors of the Grant family. A law firm called Forsyth and Stewart were now acting for Mrs Grant. They however were no more successful than Mr Jamieson had been in obtaining payment from the Morayshire. The Board decided to defer their request until the Company had the funds to make the payment. A decision was made at the meeting that a deputation from the Company was to travel to Aberdeen to meet with the Great North of Scotland Railway to improve matters of traffic management at Elgin. The last item of business on this day concerned the approval for construction of a store at Elgin station by one John Reid.

Sunday, February 16th saw the return of winter storms, with an easterly gale that continued through the night, bringing heavy falls of snow on the Monday. The Morayshire and Great North networks continued to operate, as did the Highland Railway around the Elgin area, but elsewhere the Inverness company was badly affected and Elgin did not receive any mail from the south until Wednesday 19th.

On February 21st, the death of Mr William Leslie the Chairman of the GNSR was announced in the *Elgin Courant*. The same edition of this newspaper brought news of Mr Inglis. He had been moved from Duke Street prison in Glasgow to Ayr prison on Tuesday 18th. The stress and strain surrounding the collapse of the City of Glasgow Bank was obviously affecting Mr Inglis, as the report states that he had been admitted to the prison hospital. Attempts to sell off the City of Glasgow Bank buildings in Elgin had met with failure. Offers for their premises closed on Friday 21st, but no one was prepared to meet the asking price of £4600, or in fact make any offer at all.

The fall of Mr Inglis was one of the more spectacular outcomes of harsh trading conditions. Others were attempting to make the best of a bad situation, amongst them the Highland Railway. In a bold move they tried to stimulate traffic by reducing the cost of travel on their system by 1d per mile for third class passengers and 2d per mile for first class. Even more remarkable than its price cut, the Highland Company was listening and reacting to criticism from the Elgin Town Council about both its early morning and late train services. From March 1st it would be possible for a traveller to leave Elgin at 8.05am, go to Keith by the Highland change on to the GNSR system and be in Aberdeen at 11.50am. Return at night was possible on the 4.45pm service, changing at Keith for the connecting Highland service and home in Elgin for 9.25pm. This improvement, though welcome by the business community of the town, would without doubt have a detrimental affect on the services of the Morayshire.

The Board meeting of March 3rd failed to attract enough members to form a quorum. Only the Chairman and John Grant turned up at the appointed time; the meeting was abandoned.

Perhaps Mr Jamieson had his mind on other things, as he too became entangled in the affairs of the City of Glasgow Bank. The liquidators expected each of the shareholders to pay the sum of £500 for every £100 of shares held in the failed company. The first call of £250 per share was due for payment on March 18th. Listed amongst the defaulters was Mr James Jamieson. He held stock to the value of £2000 in the City of Glasgow Bank so was facing a substantial loss, now compounded by the serving of a warrant to force payment.

There was some satisfaction for the Morayshire Board meeting of April 4th 1879 in addition to the fact that enough Directors turned up to allow it to take place. Mr McAndrew of the Highland Railway agreed that the matters relating to Orton station were now settled with the Morayshire. For the time being matters relating to traffic improvements with the GNSR were to go unresolved because of the death of their Chairman.

Less satisfactory, an additional claim for money was lodged. The Drainie Parish Ecclesiastical Building fund were demanding a payment of £31-8s-11d from the Railway Company. The Board could see no reason for this demand, though admittedly the railway passed through the parish on its way to the Lossiemouth terminus. Until more information became available the Chairman refused to pay. As the Harbour Company were also facing a similar claim, it was the intention of Mr Urquhart to meet with them and mount a joint defence.

At Rothes the Morayshire was facing complaints from a Mr William Grant of Glenrothes Distillery over lack of loading accommodation at the station. The Directors wrote to inform Mr Grant that remedying this situation was the responsibility of the GNSR, but the Morayshire would pursue this matter with the Aberdeen Company. A site visit was proposed with the Chairman (Mr Urquhart) and James Grant Glengrant, meeting with Mr William Grant, to enable an accurate report on this problem to be compiled for the Great North.

Though struggling to find funds to pay off its creditors, it appears the Morayshire was still intent on entering into other financial dealings. A piece of land at Milnefield * had become available for purchase. The Board, thinking that this property would be most suitable for *"railway interests,"* ordered an investigation into its purchase.

Announcements of the GNSR's intended summer service in the *Elgin Courant* of April 22nd, brought forth very favourable responses from the Elgin paper. It is doubtful if the Morayshire had any hand in the improvements, the changes being more likely a response to the new services introduced by the Highland Railway. Travel to Rothes and Craigellachie was now possible in the evening, with a train departing Elgin at 7.40pm and Keith at 7.35pm. The speeding up of services from the Granite City was also to happen. The former 1pm service had its departure changed to 1.15pm, and by missing out several smaller stations, Elgin was reached at the normal afternoon time, taking $3\frac{1}{4}$ hours to travel from Aberdeen to Elgin instead of the normal $3\frac{1}{2}$ hours. On this matter the *Courant* said *"It is a small instalment of gain but it is gladly welcomed, especially as it seems an earnest attempt of better things to come."* The "better things" being of course a connection with the fast Tay Bridge services, which had still not been taken up.

It was noted at the Board meeting of May 2nd 1879 that Mr Jamieson had been asked for a legal opinion on the claim made by the Parish of Drainie.

The Company seemed to be in the mood to spend some money. The land at Milnefield had been bought, along with the store recently erected by Mr Reid at Elgin station. This profligate spending had its consequences, as two EGMs had to be arranged on May 14th and 22nd of to sort out various money matters.

A bright bit of news was received by the Directors at their June 6th meeting. The Branderburgh Baths, bought by a Mr Hugh J McKenzie of Elgin for the bargain price of £500, had reopened for business. Concerning the Railway Company itself, the Directors tackled the demand for repayment of £1500 to the trustees of the late Provost James Grant with an extension for repayment for twelve months hence. An application by the station agent at Longmorn had come in for a house to be built at that station to accommodate his family and himself. In a blatant attempt to stall for time, the Morayshire Directors advised the agent to make the request for a house to the Great North of Scotland Railway.

The competition for holiday traffic seemed to have quietened down in 1879, with all sides returning to a gentleman's agreement not to compete. The holiday in Elgin was set for July 7th, with the Great North of Scotland Railway to be the provider of the cheap excursion. They proposed a trip to Aberdeen, with

* Milnefield is opposite the southern boundary of the Morayshire station.

onward connections to Deeside, Stonehaven and Dundee to view the Tay Bridge. (The connections to Stonehaven and Dundee were made in collaboration with the Caledonian Railway.) The *Elgin Courant* conceded that times were hard, but gave encouragement to the local population to travel on the holiday. *"There is less money to spend than in some former years when times were better, but a holiday has become a necessity of existence, and ways and means of enjoying it will be found. Those who wish to go as far as Dundee may accomplish it on very moderate terms."*

On the day of the 7th despite heavy rain, some 1259 passengers boarded the 25 coach train for the south. How much of this group travelled on to Dundee is not recorded. A further 2635 inhabitants of Elgin used the Great North's services for their holiday, with the weather improving as the day progressed. The Highland had some 2037 passengers travelling west on their system, with quite a number going on by steamer to view the falls of Foyers. It was a long day, with the last of the merrymakers returning from Aberdeen at 11pm, on a train of such a length that it required two locomotives to power it. Thanks were given by the *Elgin Courant* to Mr Young and Mr Cruickshank, the Stationmasters of the Highland and GNSR for all their hard work. Praise as well for the people of Elgin on their good behaviour with the paper confirming that *"Intoxication was not very much observed among the thousands who travelled."*

Despite the number of people travelling at the holiday period, business on the railway was still in a slump. To try and encourage traffic further, the Highland Railway announced on July 15th, its intention to reduce rates for the carriage of consignments of goods under 3 cwt.

A proposed trip to Fort Augustus was cancelled because the Highland Railway and Steamer Company could not come to an agreement. Alternative destinations suggested for the second Elgin holiday were either Dingwall or Strathpeffer.

The Highland Railway's intention to replace a wooden bridge on the Forres - Elgin line at Palmerscross with a metal bridge fell foul of the Elgin Clergy because this work was to be conducted from Saturday night through Sunday to early Monday morning. The Church was very unhappy at the prospect of a large number of *"mechanics and engineers"* working on the Sabbath.

There was better luck for the executors of the late James Grant in August. On the 5th of that month the Board agreed to pay over the sum of £500 plus interest in part payment of money owed to the Grant family. The station agent at Longmorn was less lucky with a decision on the provision of a house for him being deferred to a later date.

Amid excellent weather the second Elgin holiday of the year took place on August 11th. Some 550 passengers travelled on the Highland Railway excursion to Strathpeffer. Others also travelled to Inverness and onward to Loch Ness for a sail on the steamship "Fingal." Despite not being the favoured railway company for this holiday, the GNSR did very well. No less than 3472 tickets were sold by them, with most travellers using the Morayshire line to Lossiemouth for their day out.

September 2nd found the Morayshire Directors under attack from various quarters. A petition, signed by 49 farmers and residents of the district of Longmorn, demanded that the Morayshire Railway Company build a house for their station agent at Longmorn. Reluctantly the Board agreed to the demands of the petitioners, with a few stipulations. The dwelling house was to be constructed on land owned by the Company and costs for the construction of the house must not exceed £120. Instructions were sent by the Secretary Alex Watt to the Great North of Scotland's engineers to build the house, on this basis. An application had also been received from Mr James Grant Glengrant for another £1500 to be paid to the executors of the late James Grant. He was offered £1000 now, with rest coming when the Company had sufficient funds.

At Banff Sheriff Court ten days later, James Stewart of no fixed abode appeared on a charge of breaking into Craigellachie Junction station and stealing 4/8d, a pocket book and some books on fishing. The offence had taken place on August 28th.

With the end of the summer season, the Great North of Scotland Railway confirmed in the *Elgin Courant* of September 26th that the late evening services to and from Elgin would be discontinued on October 1st.

The October 3rd Board meeting brought mixed fortunes to the Longmorn Stationmaster and the Grant family. Things were not looking good at Longmorn. The report from the GNSR engineers stated that there was insufficient railway-owned land at Longmorn for the house to be built. The Morayshire would have to seek permission from Mr Lawson, factor for Earl of Fife to obtain a site near the station. However there was better news for the Grant family, as the Company was able after all to pay in full the claim of September 2nd.

Despite the reports of good behaviour of the travelling public and diligence of the railway staff, during the holiday excursion, accusations of wrongdoing were made. A local councillor was convinced that both the holiday committee and the railway companies were up to no good. Councillor Mitchell contended that the Committee members received a bribe in the form of free tickets to send the folk of Elgin to the destinations of the railway companies' choice. Most damning of all, according to Councillor Mitchell, was that they sent their poorest quality third class stock to make up the excursion trains and when a gentleman who had sampled the *"pleasure"* of third class travel reached his destination, he would rebook into a first class compartment, thereby making the railway company additional profits. The letters pages of the local press were alive with scathing attacks on the hapless councillor. Yes, the Committee members did receive free travel passes for the day of the holiday, but this was just recompense for a lot of unpaid hard work done by the members of the Excursion Committee. In respect of the rebooking charge, following extensive investigation at various stations, no instance of rebooking could be found. It appeared that the local population had far more affection for its railway companies than it had for its councillors.

At 10.45am on October 7th there was a slight mishap at Craigellachie Junction during a shunting operation. The last wagon of the train being marshalled came off at a set of points and an attempt to rectify the situation made it worse. A rope was attached to the wagon, but just as it was coming back onto the track, the rope snapped and the wheel of the offending wagon now became wedged in the point work. A number of willing hands were recruited, supplied with pinch bars and levers to free the trapped wagon. This objective was achieved and the detained train was able to go on to Elgin only 30 minutes late.

Confirmation from Mr Lawson that he was considering the request for a plot of land at Longmorn to build a house on was given to the Board meeting of November 7th. The rest of this meeting was taken up with the preparations for the forthcoming AGM.

Friday, November 28th 1879 saw one of the largest turnouts of shareholders at a Morayshire AGM for many years, with eleven people crowding into the Company offices. Despite the numbers present, there was limited good news and still no dividend. The Morayshire, like its two larger neighbours, had experienced a slowing up in the growth of its business. Fortunately, unlike the Highland and Great North, it had not had a serious decrease in business. Only the movement of agricultural produce showed a major downturn, but this had been offset by an increase in the transport of coal and stone. The repayments to the Grant family reduced the debts owed by the Company and this, the Chairman felt, would go a long way to improving the circumstance of the Morayshire's surplus for the coming years, paving the way for the payment of a dividend *"In the course of a few years."* The assembled shareholders unbelievably seemed pleased by this, marking their appreciation of the Chairman's efforts by a round of applause. A vote of thanks then followed and the proceedings of the main meeting closed.

The Directors stayed on to discuss other Company business. Mr Ferguson of the GNSR had written a strongly worded letter on November 26th demanding resolution of traffic handling at Elgin and payment for same. The Morayshire for its part replied reminding Mr Ferguson that it had arranged a meeting with the GNSR in February, which he had cancelled on the 18th of that month. Also in his cancellation letter he had advised the Morayshire that he would write giving a new date for a meeting, but they had received no communication from either the GNSR or Mr Ferguson until now. Any delay in resolving matters between the two Companies was therefore not of the Morayshire's making. They closed on a conciliatory note stating that they looked forward to meeting with Mr Ferguson. No record is on file of Mr Ferguson's reply, so I will leave it to you, dear reader, to fill in the blanks.

The weather through December caused no operational difficulties to the Morayshire or its railway neighbours. The situation a little to the south was much different. A fierce gale on Sunday, December 28th 1879 had disastrous effects for the North British Railway Company and the people of Dundee. On the evening of that day, at just past 7pm NBR locomotive number 224 and its six coach train entered the high span of the Tay Bridge. The storm pitched the centre section of the bridge, the locomotive, the coaches, the crew and all 75 passengers into the swirling waters of the River Tay. There were no survivors. News of this disaster was quickly transmitted to Elgin by means of the telegraph system installed at the behest of the former Chairman of the Morayshire Railway James Grant. (No one within the immediate Elgin area was involved in this calamity.) Speeding up of communication brought about by the telegraph helped tell of the events at Dundee, including graphic eyewitness accounts, only a few hours after the fall of the bridge.

The horror of the collapse of the Tay Bridge affected the whole of the United Kingdom. In Elgin for the first two months of 1880, the local newspapers carried extensive reports on the investigation of the disaster at Dundee. The will to carry on railway affairs seemed to be lost and the Morayshire Board did not meet until the beginning of March, with the dispute between it and the Great North forgotten about. The general gloom that was hanging over the Country had been added to at a local level with the failure of another enterprise. The Elgin Educational Institute had gone up for sale on February 27th.

Set to follow in his father's footsteps, Mr Alexander Grant, the son of the late James Grant, passed as an advocate at Edinburgh University on March 3rd 1880.

The Board of the Morayshire Railway also met on this date, with various financial matters requiring prioritising. In amongst the discussion of figures, the subject of the house for the Stationmaster at Longmorn came to the fore. The Earl of Fife was prepared to sell some land to the Morayshire at a premium price. The Directors were not impressed by this, and Alex Watt sent this reply to his Lordship: *"A site ought to be granted at a reduced rate, considering that the station was erected at Longmorn principally to accommodate the Fife tenantry."*

The rest of the railway industry seemed to be putting the events of December 28th behind it. The Highland Railway was taking steps to increase its size, with its amalgamation with the Skye Railway on March 5th. Encouraging news too from the South West of Scotland with the Glasgow and South Western Railway publishing good trading accounts. That company paid its ordinary shareholders a dividend of 4%, and was still able to carry forward a sum of £6000 to the credit of next year's stock. Mr Wainwright, one of its Directors, was also a Director of the Morayshire Board, which must have given encouragement to the shareholders of the Morayshire to hope that some of his money-making expertise would be put to their benefit.

Notice appeared in the *Elgin Courant* of April 6th of a new business enterprise in Elgin. Mr James Allan an Elgin solicitor had purchased the building previously occupied by the Elgin Education Institute, for a sum just under £3000. Following repainting and some restoration work, to be carried out by Elgin cabinetmaker Mr Hay, this building would reopen as a hotel. William Christie, formerly of the Stag Hotel Elgin, was to become tenant to run the establishment.

The Morayshire Railway was also starting to attract the attention of speculators, as the often rumoured amalgamation with the Great North of Scotland Railway again surfaced in the public domain. Business seemed to be brisk in both shares and preference shares at the beginning of May.

Under the auspices of its new manager, William Moffat, the Great North of Scotland Railway was at long last speeding up its services, so that now, "express trains" really did live up to that title. The whole of the GNSR system benefited from this improvement, with one exception. Services between Aberdeen and Elgin were still painfully slow. The reason for this lack of improvement was, according to the *Courant,* due to the reluctance of the Highland Railway to re-time its services to connect with improved Great North timings. The Highland for their part claimed that they were *"Willing to listen to any reasoned representation and give effect to it as far as they can."*

There was a hastily convened EGM of the Morayshire Company, on June 11th 1880, to report on the outcome of two meetings between the Managing Directors and Secretaries of the Morayshire and GNSR. Amalgamation of the two companies was beginning to look like a distinct possibility. Terms that the Great North expected the Morayshire Directors to agree to were discussed. The Aberdeen company wanted an answer by June 17th. The Morayshire Board members did not feel they had enough day-to-day knowledge of railway matters to understand the intricacies of the Great North's proposals. An urgent request was therefore sent by Alex Watt to Mr Wainwright, vice Chairman of the Morayshire, asking him to come to Aberdeen on the 17th for the meeting with the Great North. His expertise as a Director of the Glasgow and South Western Railway was just what the Morayshire Board required at this stage of the negotiations.

Notification came from Mr Wainwright on June 15th that he would be unable to travel to Aberdeen for the meeting with the Great North Board. He did however send a detailed list of conditions that the Morayshire Directors should insist on from the GNSR for the amalgamation of the two companies to take place.

1) GNSR to take over and pay all obligations and debts of the Morayshire of whatever kind from the 30th of September 1880.

2) GNSR to pay all interest due on Debentures of the Morayshire after 30th September.

3) Ordinary stock to be paid at the rate of 2%, rising each year by 1% until it reaches 5% and hereafter in perpetuity at the same rate as the GNSR.

The Morayshire Board liked what Mr Wainwright was saying. In fact they were so impressed that they cancelled the forthcoming meeting with the Great North with a new date to be arranged to allow Mr Wainwright to be present at all future negotiations. Mr Wainwright conversely was kept well-occupied by the Glasgow and South Western Railway Company and could spare very little time for his friends in the North. Mr Watt was thus dispatched to Glasgow to take further advice. He duly returned home with a prepared minute that was to be given to the Great North of Scotland Railway Directors at a meeting in Aberdeen on July 1st.

Not too unexpectedly, Mr Wainwright's proposals were received "unfavourably," by the Great North Board. The meeting broke up with no decision being made, but the prize of the Morayshire was still too great a one for the GNSR to walk away from the negotiation table, hence after the main meeting Mr Watt and Mr Moffat had a discussion. It was agreed that the Morayshire Chairman along with Mr Watt would meet with Mr Moffat on July 2nd for more talks. A private memo was given to the Morayshire pair by Mr Moffat at this get-together. This laid out in detail the terms that the GNSR were expecting the Morayshire to accede to for the amalgamation to take place. No decision was made by the Morayshire duo and the memo was sent south for Mr Wainwright's comment.

It was now Mr Wainwright who was unfavourable in his response. He believed that the GNSR were offering a very poor deal. His response caused the Morayshire Board to suspend talks on this matter until Mr Wainwright could travel to Aberdeen.

In the interim the ongoing saga of the Longmorn Stationmaster's house was still unresolved. The price being asked for land by Mr Lawson, factor for Lord Fife, was still too high. The Board decided to offer to pay rental of 10/- per year to the Fife estate instead. Disheartened with endless conflict the Morayshire Board proclaimed the meeting over, which must have come as a blow to a Mr Clark, who wished permission from the Morayshire to open refreshment rooms at Elgin, and his proposal was to have been tabled next.

On July 23rd a quick meeting was held to discuss further amendments to the amalgamation. Fresh statements had come from both the GNSR board and Mr Wainwright. This resulted in a meeting in Glasgow on August 3rd attended by Mr Moffat and Mr Ferguson of the Great North, and Mr Watt and Mr Wainwright for the Morayshire. Mr Watt reported back to the Morayshire Board on August 7th in Elgin. On hearing the details, Mr Urquhart, Chairman of the Morayshire declared that the verbal offer from the Great North should receive the *"Very best of consideration."* An agreement that another meeting should take place at Perth, on the Saturday, August 21st 1880, was made.

August 8th saw the Great North of Scotland Railway publish its trading results for 1879. In one way they were getting closer to the Morayshire's way of doing business There would not be any interest payment for ordinary shareholders. Instead the GNSR carried forward the slender sum of £2880 to its following year account.

A report to the full Morayshire Board on August 23rd was given of the meeting at Perth that had been held on the preceding Saturday. Various small adjustments had been made by both sides, which seemed to clear the way for the coming together. The 30th of September had been agreed by both parties to be the actual day of amalgamation.

This consensus did not last long and Mr Watt and a few other of the Morayshire Directors were invited to Keith on September 6th to meet with Mr Moffat and Mr Ferguson. The two Aberdeen gentlemen wished to alter "slightly" the arrangements agreed to at Perth. No great discussion took place between the two parties. The Morayshire Directors were disappointed by their fellow Great North Directors' change of heart. The only thing that both sides could now agree to was that any discussion on amalgamation should be suspended until after the Morayshire's annual accounts were made up, on September 30th. The suggestion from the Great North side was that the Morayshire's bookkeeping was flawed, whilst of course the Elgin people were confident in their figures.

Away from this boardroom intrigue, in the real world, details of the coming together of the two companies became common knowledge. In the *Elgin Courant* of September 21st, there was a very accurate picture of the now stalled Perth agreement. The paper saw gains to both parties from this union and favoured the merger. Amongst the helpful suggestions given by the press was the starting up of a steamer service from Lossiemouth to ports on the opposite side of the Moray Firth. The late Provost James Grant would have, I am sure, been proud that someone was still trying to promote one of his long-held beliefs!

The fifty-sixth ordinary general meeting of the GNSR was held at the Douglas Hotel on September 23rd. The main topic of discussion was the proposed amalgamation with the Morayshire. The Chairman of the Great North, Mr Ferguson of Kinmundy, underlined his unease in respect of a deal with the Morayshire, convinced that the Morayshire Directors had talked up the value of their Company. *"We must not buy them too dear, and the utmost I can say to you today is that the present proposals from the Morayshire Directors are not such as I consider I would be justified in asking your consent to proceed."*

Even if the Great North no longer wished to take control of the Morayshire, it did not stop them from interfering in the running of the Company. The GNSR's pronouncement was discussed by the Morayshire Board on September 24th. Draft accounts were now available and appeared to confirm the claims that Mr Watt and his Directors had made. The Directors resolved that Mr Watt should take the accounts to Aberdeen and meet with Mr Ferguson and Mr Moffat with the aim of persuading the GNSR to return in full to the Perth agreement of August 21st. Business then moved on to the matter of the provision of refreshment rooms at Elgin, about which Mr Moffat laid out his demand that, at all costs, such a facility should be *"Strongly discouraged!"*

James Grant, Glengrant and Mr Watt travelled to Aberdeen on October 18th to meet with Mr Ferguson and Mr Moffat. In the run-up to this meeting, various letters had been exchanged between the GNSR and Mr Wainwright, and the draft accounts of the Morayshire had been examined in detail by the GNSR board. Accountants from the Aberdeen company had also visited Elgin and checked all the Morayshire's books and accounts. The accuracy of the Morayshire's book-keeping passed all the Great North's tests. Despite this the GNSR Directors still felt the need for further discussion. A three way meeting between the Boards of the Morayshire and the Great North and Mr Wainwright were to be arranged as soon as possible. For its part the Morayshire was confident of its case and decided to press on with items pertaining to amalgamation, including seeking Counsel on the legal matters surrounding the coming together of the two companies. In the interim, at the request of the GNSR, the public release of the Morayshire accounts and the fixing of an AGM were to be delayed.

Lighter matters were attended to on the evening of the 28th of October 1880, with a public dinner to celebrate formally the opening of the "new" sumptuously refurbished Station Hotel.

While the Elgin folk enjoyed a party, the Great North of Scotland Railway prepared to do some serious work. No longer content just to add the Morayshire Railway to its portfolio, reports in the *Elgin Courant* and *Aberdeen Free Press* told of more ambitious plans. It was the intention of the Great North to increase its presence on the Banffshire coast by constructing a line from Portsoy through Cullen and Buckie, before turning inland to Fochabers. Things did not stop there though, as they continued on by crossing the River Spey, then following its course and connecting with the old Morayshire route to Rothes at Orton station. The press reporters concluded that by connecting with the Morayshire system at Orton, the Great North and Morayshire had agreed terms for amalgamation. This was not the case.

For the moment, the Great North was locked into a battle with the Highland Railway, both of whom were vying for the custom of excursionists wishing to view the Prince of Wales Presents that were on display at the municipal buildings in Aberdeen. Despite this event being held on the Great North's own territory, the Highland Railway was managing to convey far larger numbers of the public to the exhibition. On November 5th the Great North finally hit back by offering a special train service to carry the folk of Elgin to Aberdeen. The price matched that of the Highland Railway's at 5/6 for first class and 3/6 for third.

The amalgamation slowly moved forward. A meeting had taken place in Aberdeen on November 7th between all the parties concerned and a report given to the Morayshire Board on November 12th concluded that everything looked settled. Mr Jamieson completed the organisation of legal counsel for the Morayshire and suggested that a revised statement should be prepared for the shareholders advising them of a possible amalgamation.

There was a minor panic in the Morayshire camp on November 17th. Mr Moffat had intentionally misinterpreted part of the proposals surrounding the amalgamation, displeasing the Morayshire Directors who immediately dispatched a letter to said gentleman. A copy of this was sent to Mr Wainwright in Glasgow with a covering letter that also asked for his advice concerning the most suitable way to recompense Mr Watt. The hard working, underpaid and practical Mr Watt, when informed of the Board's intention to present him with either 100 sovereigns or a piece of inscribed plate to the value of 100 sovereigns, plumped for the 100 sovereigns.

To stop Mr Moffat making further "misinterpretations," Mr Wainwright suggested that the Morayshire should be as independent as possible from the Great North in legal matters concerned with the amalgamation. To this end the Morayshire arranged for its own Bill. This would allow it to accumulate dividends, and raise additional capital. Money raised by this method would not amount to very much, but would protect the interest of the Morayshire shareholders, confirming to the Great North that the Morayshire Railway was professional in its business matters.

This professional competence was put thoroughly to the test on Tuesday the 30th of November 1880, the day of its annual meeting. The gathering was extremely well attended by shareholders and a large number of proxy votes were also registered by the people who could not come in person. The clamour by shareholders to have their voice heard was so great that a number of the proxy votes arrived too late to be officially used.

The Chairman, Bailie Urquhart, opened the proceedings by giving some background into the proposed amalgamation. He referred to a report he had made in 1878 in which he had stated that the Directors of the Morayshire wished to make a dividend payment to shareholders who had Preference Shares in the Morayshire. To raise the necessary finance to do this, would he claimed require the coming together with the GNSR.

The appointment of Mr Moffat at the GNSR had changed the style of operation of the Aberdeen company. This enterprise now wished to speed up its train services. Meeting this improvement would not only necessitate extensive alterations to the Morayshire's network, but would also require better goods handling facilities, a combination amounting to £10,000. All of this under the working agreement between the two companies would be the responsibility of the Morayshire Railway to finance. This was a very serious matter for the Company, as the traffic for the year 1878 - 79 had not made any material progress. Things for the year just past had improved slightly, but were not at a level sufficient to bear the cost required to pay for the improvements.

The Chairman then went on to say that as an act of courtesy he had held talks with Elgin Town because of the £1000 the Council had invested in the Morayshire to help fund the building of the line to Lossiemouth. He reported that the Council were sympathetic to the coming together of the two companies.

In closing his address Bailie Urquhart said that at this stage of negotiations certain details were, *"Private and confidential."* He could however assure all the Morayshire's shareholders that they would obtain the best possible deal from the amalgamation with the Great North. To make certain that was the case, the Morayshire Board had arranged an Act of Parliament in connection with the amalgamation. This (as I have outlined) he informed the meeting would not only protect the Morayshire's interests, but put it on to its best footing for dealing with the Great North. At the close of this address the adoption of the Chairman's report was seconded by Major Smith of Minmore.

Things were however were not to the liking of everyone, in particular a gentleman named Mr Scott. He was not only a shareholder in the Morayshire, but was also a supervisor of the Inland Revenue. What interested him in particular was the issue of Preference shares in 1856. It appears that this stock, to the value of some £10,000, had never appeared in any of the Company's balance sheets! Obviously the Morayshire had substantially more creditors to be paid than had previously been thought. The Chairman did his best to avoid answering this question by claiming that to discuss this would be a breach of confidence and only when the proposed amalgamation had been agreed to, would it then be the time to go into details. Mr Scott was not satisfied with this rather weak reply. He was further concerned that the 1856 Preference stock, unlike any other of the Morayshire's share issues, had a cumulative dividend attached to it. This was not common knowledge; until this point the only thing that a shareholder in the Morayshire Railway had been certain of was that his investment had continued to go down in value. Any share in the Morayshire Railway bought for £10, was in 1880 worth around £1 to £2. However, according to Mr Scott, shareholders who held any of the 1856 Preference stock could expect a return of around £20 per share. Unaware of this, a number of shareholders had recently sold some of this stock to a *"gentleman from London"*, who had been offering to buy Morayshire 1856 Preference stock at £3 per share. Mr Scott also said that he had heard rumours in Elgin that some of the Morayshire Directors had also been buying the 1856 issue. This last claim was too much for the Directors to take. Mr Jamieson came to the defence of his Chairman by saying that the claims made by Mr Scott were not true. A long and generally good-humoured debate continued. Through persistence, some of the details surrounding these shares were revealed. According to the Secretary Alex Watt, the total issue of 1856 stock amounted to £11,500. There was a payment of £10,000 due against these shares. As for the Morayshire Board, the first the Directors knew about this matter was in June of 1880. Concerning the payment of outstanding sums, these would be due for settlement on the amalgamation with the Great North of Scotland Railway. Under the terms of the agreement, the Great North would be responsible for payment, not the Morayshire Railway. This should therefore prevent any major shortfall in remuneration to the Morayshire's shareholders. Mr Scott was still not satisfied and it took a vote, which Mr Scott lost, to enable the meeting to move on.

Re-election of directors then followed. By this stage in proceedings, things had become acrimonious. An attempt was made by Mr Scott to have the Chairman deposed, and replaced by the Elgin Provost Mr Culbard. Fortunately for Bailie Urquhart, Provost Culbard felt that he had more than enough to do in looking after the affairs of Elgin, so declined Mr Scott's offer. Despite this it still took the intervention of James Grant Glengrant, to retain Bailie Urquhart to the position of Chairman of the Morayshire Railway. The suitability of each Director was then checked into, with particular attention being paid to Colonel Forteath, the Earl of Caithness, and most surprisingly Mr Wainwright. They appeared to be singled out because of their lack of regular attendance at the Morayshire's meetings. On being given details of the volume of work Mr Wainwright had carried out on behalf of the Company, he was unanimously voted back on to the Board. After extensive discussion, the other two Directors survived to retake their seats.

Civility returned as a Mr Forsyth declared the following motion: *"In the event of the amalgamation being carried out, the services of Mr Watt be substantially recognised by the Company."* There was applause all round the meeting room as the shareholders recognised that without Mr Watt's hard work, the Morayshire would not be in its present promising position. Mr Urquhart told the meeting that one of the stipulations in the amalgamation agreement was that Mr Watt would have employment with the Great North. On this gratifying note the main meeting concluded.

The Directors stayed on after the close of the annual meeting. They agreed that the 1856 stockholders should receive a guaranteed 3% or equivalent shares in the GNSR. As the terms for amalgamation with the Great North were practically settled, Mr Watt, Mr Jamieson and Mr Wainwright were to travel to London to meet with the Great North's legal representatives and their Parliamentary agent. It was hoped that following this meeting, the terms for the Amalgamation Bill to be set before Parliament would be agreed.

To the east of Elgin, other parties hoped to join with the Great North of Scotland Railway. A deputation of gentlemen from Keith interested in building a railway from Buckie to Keith and thence on to Fochabers met with Mr Ferguson on December 7th. The estimate for this scheme showed a figure of £80,000. The GNSR Director told the Keith party that he was sympathetic to their cause, but did not intend to abandon the scheme that his company had proposed to serve that area.

On December 13th, Mr Wainwright advised the Morayshire Board to continue working towards amalgamation with the Great North, despite Mr Moffat making minor adjustments to the agreement's details. One of these was that the Morayshire must abandon its own Parliamentary Bill. This last item was only agreed to after a flurry of telegrams between the various parties. Mr Watt was missing from these negotiations as at this time he was confined to his bed with a bad cold.

Operational difficulties occurred on December 14th when the 9.40am train from Keith was brought to a standstill half way between Dandaleith and Rothes as a result of a tyre failure on one of the tender wheels. The requirement for assistance was telegraphed to Elgin and the Lossiemouth branch engine was sent to the rescue. It removed the failed locomotive to a siding at Rothes before taking the train to Elgin, arriving some two hours late.

Notices of the amalgamation appeared in the local press on December 21st. Parliamentary time had, however, run out for the Bill to sanction construction of the Great North of Scotland Railway's proposed coastal line linking up with the Morayshire branch at Orton. The GNSR said that this was a temporary delay and with the commencement of the new Parliamentary session, a slightly amended bill for construction of a line from Portsoy to Portgordon would be presented.

Friday, December 24th saw another engine failure on the Morayshire. The 4.10pm departure from Lossiemouth was delayed due to the failure of a piston. A one hour delay ensued as an engine had to be dispatched from Elgin to rescue the failed service. As the year ended, snow also caused some delays, but all lines remained opened.

On the final day of 1880, the Press were speculating about a rail service to the village of Hopeman. *"If the line extended to Hopeman summer residences would rise like mushrooms. The site and facilities for pleasure houses are so great that it is likely Lossiemouth and Stotfield as places for the summer would be forgotten. Quarry business is also a draw."* The benefactor of this increase in business would be the GNSR's rival, the Highland Railway.

The death of the much respected George Morrison was reported on January 11th 1881. Since 1863 he had been the Great North of Scotland Railway's superintendent of the northern section, setting up his headquarters in Elgin when the GNSR took over the running of the Morayshire's train services. He had been in frail health for sometime, but with the support of GNSR, who wished to retain his services, he managed to continue in his post with the active part of his job being carried out by his assistant Mr John Ross.

Mr Wainwright returned from London to Glasgow on January 18th after finalising the details of the Amalgamation Bill with the London Firm of Dyson & Co. That day the rest of the Morayshire Directors approved of the details worked out by Mr Wainwright and decided to call a meeting of all the shareholders for February 4th.

January 21st saw the area around Elgin badly affected by snow. A substantial snowdrift some 10 to 11 feet in depth filled the cutting just south of Longmorn station, preventing the 7.10am train to Keith reaching its destination. It returned to Elgin, and another with a van load of men was dispatched to dig through the snow. By this time the Keith train coming to Elgin had become stuck fast in this drift and it took until 5pm to restore running. On the Lossiemouth section an equally severe drift near the Loch of Spynie also caused problems to the morning service. At this location the engine and train became trapped and it took a team of workmen and another engine to effect a rescue. Services to the coast were abandoned until noon. Poor weather continued for several days, but despite this services on the now cleared main line through Rothes and Craigellachie continued to run, though well behind advertised times.

Public notices announcing the Bill for the amalgamation of the GNSR and the Morayshire appeared in the press on January 28th. Mr Wainwright met with his fellow Morayshire Directors that day to arrange payment of £600 for Mr Watt, to make up *"for poor salary and lack of rise brought about through the hard financial pressure that the Morayshire had found itself under."*

A few days later on February 1st, the *Elgin Courant* reported that the Bill had passed the standing orders of the House of Commons, with Mr Frere being named as examiner.

Friday, February 4th 1881, saw the Station Hotel at Elgin become a hive of activity. More shareholders appeared for the Amalgamation Meeting than had turned up for the annual meeting in November of the previous year. The signs were not good; it looked as though the Morayshire Directors were in for a rough ride.

The Chairman opened the proceedings by paying tribute to his predecessor Provost James Grant and his family who had done so much to benefit the Morayshire Railway. He swiftly moved on to propose the transfer and amalgamation of the Morayshire to the Great North of Scotland Railway. Major Smith of Minmore seconded the motion. Almost before the Chairman had resumed his seat, a gentleman called Mr Dunlop rose to his feet, and whilst not opposing the amalgamation, he had a number of questions regarding the 1856 Preference Shares. Mr Dunlop asserted that as an ordinary shareholder he had been severely disadvantaged because of the extra payments made to the holders of the 1856 stock. What aggrieved him even more was that the Directors had taken advantage of their positions by buying bundles of this stock at low prices. He was aware that the Morayshire Chairman had recently bought a large parcel of these shares.

In reply Mr Urquhart indicated that he had held £220 of 1856 shares for over twenty years, before buying a further £1000 of stock from his brother in 1878. This attempt to pacify Mr Dunlop resulted in the Chairman walking into a trap of Mr Dunlop's making. What, according to Mr Dunlop, the Morayshire Chairman had not said was that he had bought the £1000 worth of shares from his brother for £300. Mr Dunlop deduced that anyone who would profit to such an extent from their own brother would not have any consideration for other shareholders. Provost Culbard had to intervene, because things were starting to get a little out of hand. The Provost accepted the statement made by the Chairman and stated that the purchase arrangements made by Bailie Urquhart was a family matter. In his public role however, the Provost was concerned about the rumours sweeping Elgin of profiteering by Morayshire Directors. To clear up this hearsay he asked that the Secretary give notice of all recent purchases of 1856 shares. Mr Watt said that without his ledgers, which were in the Morayshire Company offices, he could not give such an answer. Several people at the meeting demanded that Mr Watt fetch the ledger. Whilst he was doing so, more details surrounding the 1856 shares and the premium they attracted were revealed. Under the terms agreed by the GNSR, the accumulated dividend only came in to play on years that the Morayshire declared a profit. A long and bitter argument ensued as to when if at all, in the years since 1856 the Morayshire had made a profit. Mr Watt returned with the Company ledger, which showed that Chairman Bailie Urquhart owned some £4200 worth of 1856 stock. The last purchase that he had made was actually on October 9th 1880 when he bought £1000 worth of shares. All in all the price that Mr Urquhart had paid for his holding was £1132, which meant he stood to gain a tidy profit.

Adding fuel to the fire, the Chairman gave the following ruling in respect of the accumulated dividend clause; it would come into effect whenever the Morayshire declared a profit. The trading conditions had substantially improved and profits would be in the hands of the shareholders shortly, so it was correct to pay the full amount on the 1856 stock. This did not go down well. The shareholders wanted full details of when and by whom 1856 shares were bought. As some very prominent local names were on the list, one shareholder, Mr Forsyth, tried to have the meeting adjourned so that a proper investigation could be carried out into the circumstances surrounding the shares. A warning came from Mr Jamieson that if the amalgamation meeting was stopped, the agreement with the Great North would be cancelled. Signed and sealed the contract had to be in London on Monday morning.

The amalgamation meeting was scheduled to have finished at 1pm, for at this hour the meeting to discuss the Bill for the construction of the line from Portsoy to Portgordon was due to start. It was now 1.30pm and things were becoming more confused, because participants for the construction meeting were joining in with the amalgamation meeting. Again Mr Jamieson gave a warning that any delay would end the amalgamation with the Great North. Worse still he said that it would also prevent the construction of the coast line from taking place, as these two matters were bound together. Mr Forsyth persisted that the meeting be adjourned. A vote was called and on a show of hands, the decision to adjourn proceedings until Saturday morning was agreed. The Chairman ruled that this vote was out of order and must be taken again because he feared that some of the participants for the later meeting had joined in with the show of hands. This time each shareholder's name was called and his decision to adjourn or continue was noted. Fifty-five shareholders voted for a delay with only thirty-seven wishing to continue. The Chairman now took a bundle of proxy votes from his pocket and declared that the motion to proceed had won the day!

Not a favourable decision: a question was immediately asked about the number of proxy votes. Mr Jamieson said they amounted to £60,000 worth of shares and it would take the Secretary Mr Watt three hours to count them accurately. After some consultation, Provost Culbard, speaking for those who wished a delay, agreed that Mr Watt was a man of honour and the meeting would accept his word that the proxy votes were valid and that the decision to continue with the meeting had won the day. On hearing this the motion for the adoption of the agreement of amalgamation with the Great North of Scotland Railway was put before the meeting and approved.

The presentation to Mr Watt for his services to the Company was the final matter to be decided. This honour was left to Mr Forsyth to propose. Instead of the previously suggested £600 payment Mr Watt received a larger payment of two years' worth of salary.

Before the Morayshire shareholders departed the Station Hotel, a very short meeting was held to approve the construction of a new section of the Great North of Scotland Railway. The decision to build the line from Portsoy to Portgordon was enthusiastically confirmed. With this agreement the official story of the Morayshire Railway ends.

James Grant Glengrant, also a man of honour, distanced himself from the profiteering of his fellow Directors with this letter to the *Elgin Courant*.

> *Sir,*
>
> *In a report of the Morayshire Railway meeting held at Elgin yesterday, I have seen it stated that the Secretary said, I along with some others were purchasers of 1856 stock. The Secretary did no such thing - The Grant he mentioned being Mr William Grant distiller, Glen Rothes and Mr William Grant, accountant Elgin, who are one in the same person. Earlier in the meeting I distinctly disavowed having anything to do either directly or indirectly, with 1856 stock.*
>
>
>
> *I am sir yours*
>
> *James Grant Glengrant*
>
> *February 5th 1881.*
>
>

On the coast the folk of Lossiemouth and Branderburgh were saddened at the passing of, "Miss Morayshire." The following notice appeared in the local press.

> The people are deeply grieved for the demise of Miss Morayshire at a premature age. Her loss will be deeply felt as she was so agreeable in her manners, so obliging in her disposition, so helpful to the old and infirm, so punctual in her mode of doing business. She carries to her grave the respect of the community which can appreciate her real worth. We can remember her birthday when the music charmed the young, and the old leaped for joy, because of her nifty and reasonable appearance. But alas she is gone, as Cowper has said -

> *She has come, she is gone; we have met*
> *and meet perhaps, never again;*
> *the sun of that moment is set,*
> *and seems to have risen in vain.*

22 SOME OF THE LOOSE ENDS

Though the Morayshire ceased to exist following the meeting of February 4th 1881, the railway that it built continued to serve the towns of Lossiemouth, Elgin, Rothes and Craigellachie for many years. The Great North of Scotland Railway never did build its line through Fochabers to link up with the Morayshire at Orton. Instead they continued along the coast to Spey Bay, Garmouth, etc, to connect with the Morayshire at Bareflathills on the outskirts of Elgin, the point where the railway revolution began in the north of Scotland. Unused, the Orton Branch and its connections to the Highland and Great North systems were cut, though the track itself remained in place until 1907 before it was finally lifted and sold for scrap.

The arrival of a second Great North route into Elgin by the coast, which was viewed by the Aberdeen Company as a stepping stone to its ultimate prize of Inverness, was welcomed by the people of Elgin and all the villages that were now connected to the national railway system.

Less enamoured was the Highland Railway, turning the relationship between it and the Great North hostile. The Inverness company threatened to compete by building a coastal line to Lossiemouth. Construction of part of this resulted in the extension of the railway to Hopeman in October 1892.

By 1894, traffic on the original Morayshire line to Lossiemouth had grown to such an extent that the station and surrounding sidings had become too cramped to cope with all the demands made of it. A new sea wall was built and additional sidings laid. This quickly proved to be insufficient and in 1896 the station site was moved further back with another part of the seashore reclaimed by the building of a *"large sea wall."* An acre of additional space had thus become available, on which a loading bank of *"gigantic proportions,"* capable of handling 40 to 50 wagons at a time was built. Also constructed was a new goods shed, signal box, and station. The whole undertaking took a team of 55 masons four months to complete and the new facilities could store 70 to 80 wagons. Improvements to the harbour rails to aid loading of ships complemented the improvements made by the railway company.

Trade also grew on the Rothes line, with practically every station gaining a distillery. Longmorn gained two, both of which were connected to the Great North system by their own rail network with its own locomotive. This system in turn eventually extended out to Glenlossie distillery at Birnie.

The Great North of Scotland Railway and the Highland Railway realised that the damage they were inflicting on each other was doing harm to no one but themselves. In 1897 relations between the two improved to such an extent that talks were held with a view to amalgamation. This scheme did not find favour with the Highland shareholders and the two companies remained as separate entities, but on much more favourable terms.

The extra traffic generated by the combination of all the above factors overwhelmed the facilities at Elgin station. Conditions were not improved as the roof that offered protection to the platforms and the passengers waiting for trains became unsafe and had to be removed. Despite protests from the Elgin Town Council, the Great North was reluctant to provide a replacement. After a great deal of arm twisting, the GNSR did the honourable thing and in 1902 Elgin at last had a station that its population considered worthy of the city.

In 1905 the Great North took a leaf out of the Morayshire's book and introduced a passenger locomotive of unusual design on the Lossiemouth service. This was a rail motor, which combined locomotive and passenger coach in one unit. Like the "coffepots," this experiment was also a failure.

The Great War brought more traffic to the line, as the route via Aberdeen was used to take the pressure off the Highland main line and its effort to supply the navy at Invergordon and Scapa Flow. A regular service was the "tattie train", code for the working of a munitions train from Keith to Dingwall by GNSR engines and crews, conveying mines part way to their ultimate destination, Kyle of Lochalsh.

Cessation of hostilities in 1918 saw the start of the downturn of the railway industry. On January 1st 1923 both the Great North of Scotland Railway and the Highland Railway ceased to exist. The former became part of the London and North Eastern Railway, the latter part of the London Midland and Scottish Railway. The LNER introduced a sleeper service from Lossiemouth to London Kings Cross station. Larger engines arrived in the area, but the contraction in the railway business continued, as services started to lose out to lorries and buses. This situation was not helped by the LNER who sold off its bus service to Walter Alexander & Sons Falkirk in 1930.

The Second World War was generally good to the railways in Moray, slowing the decline in traffic.

Nationalisation in 1948 brought all four private railway companies together as British Railways. As little changed in the service given by the railway, the reduction in the number of people travelling by train continued. By the mid 1950's the unofficially named "Pram Special" that ran every Thursday afternoon (half day closing in Lossiemouth) lost its passengers when Alexander's introduced double-decker buses. No longer did the young mums require the space of the railway guard's van to carry their prams. A double-decker bus could cope and offered transport into the centre of both Elgin and Lossiemouth.

Reduced passenger and freight business on the former Morayshire Railway attracted the attention of Doctor Beeching. On April 6th 1964 the last passenger service left the station at Lossiemouth with the local press and various amateur cameramen recording the passing of the line. Mr Ian Lloyd the last Stationmaster at Lossiemouth also left the area to take up a new post as Stationmaster at Lenzie.

In true Morayshire Railway tradition, the loss of the service could not happen without incident. Someone attempted to derail the first goods train of that day by placing sleepers on the line at the section nearby Spynie Palace; no damage occurred and the press reported that the police at Lossiemouth were looking for the *irresponsible persons.*

Complete closure of the Lossiemouth line came on March 28th 1966.

The remainder of the former Morayshire empire stayed in business a little longer. Passenger traffic ceased on the inland portion on May 6th 1968. The goods service continued on until November 4th 1968, when it ceased to exist bringing to a close a proud 116 years of service. By 1968 the loss of railway lines had become common place, so sadly the passing went unrecorded.

As for **"The Travellers Joy"**: this was a large stone similar in shape to a roadside milestone. It sat unmolested next to the railway line to Lossiemouth, between the bridge on the Pitgaveny Road and the level crossing on Linksfield Road, marking the spot of a well, which I believe had originally supplied water to the Linksfield crossing keeper's house. The date 1852 was inscribed on it and I suspect it may have been a mason's test piece, chiselled out by an apprentice at the time of the line's construction, as the inscription was done in various letter styles. With the closure of the railway, the old track bed became popular with walkers and the stone became a curiosity. In 1977 the Moray Society thought that this artefact might be worthy of a place in the Elgin Museum and prepared to record and possibly preserve it. However, before any proper research could be carried out, the stone was removed by persons unknown.

To anyone interested in viewing the remains of the Morayshire Railway a number of portions exist to this day. Most of the track bed of the Lossiemouth branch is intact with two bridges at Calcots Road and over the River Lossie still in place. Large portions of the track bed of the Direct line to Craigellachie also remain. The bridge over the River Spey is long gone, though the stone piers are still in place. On the main Aberdeen to Inverness line the embankment of the much disputed connection just passed Orton station is still visible and was recently used by Railtrack to gain access to repair subsidence on the main line. In Elgin, the second engine shed still stands, though now fulfilling a function as a garage. And still guarding the foot of Moss Street remain two buildings crucial to our story, the present-day Laichmoray Hotel and the Royal Hotel; respectively, they were the Elgin Station Hotel and the home of the Morayshire's champion, James Grant.